Welcome to Agenda

Welcome to Lotus Agenda® 2.0. Your package now includes the following enhancements and extra features.

- **Support for the HP LaserJet® III printer.** Just select this printer during installation so you can use it to print your Agenda files.

- **An Agenda icon and program information file (PIF) for Microsoft® Windows™ users.** It's easy to set up Agenda to run under Windows. See *Adding Agenda to a Windows Program Group* below.

- **A utility to check the integrity of your Agenda files.** If you think you have a damaged file, use Checker to analyze the file. See *A New Agenda Utility: Checker* on page 2.

- **A 60-day money-back guarantee.** If, for any reason, you are not satisfied with Agenda®, we'll refund your full purchase price.

Adding Agenda to a Windows Program Group

To use the Agenda program and icon in Windows:

1. Install Agenda and note the drive and directory where you installed it (for example, c:\agenda).

2. Start Windows and highlight the program group where you want to add Agenda.

3. From the menu, choose **File**, then **New**, and select **Program Item**.

4. Type a description for the program in the **Description** text box (for example, Agenda 2.0).

5. Type the path of the Agenda program directory followed by the PIF file name (agenda.pif) in the **Command Line** text box. For example:

```
c:\agenda\agenda.pif
```

6. Select **Change Icon** and type the path of the Agenda program directory followed by the icon filename (agenda.ico) in the **File Name** box. For example:

```
c:\agenda\agenda.ico
```

7. Choose **OK** twice to return to the Program Manager.

The Agenda icon and description appear in the program group. To start Agenda, double click on the Agenda icon.

A New Agenda Utility: Checker

The Checker utility lets you test the integrity of any of your Agenda application files. If you suspect that a file may be damaged, use Checker to analyze the file before doing any more work on it.

To use the Checker utility:

1. Go to DOS and change to the drive and directory where your Agenda program files are stored. For example:

```
c:    (Enter)
cd \agenda    (Enter)
```

2. Type the **AG_CHK** command along with the name and path of the Agenda application file you want to check. For example:

```
ag_chk apps\planner.ag    (Enter)
```

To check more than one file at a time, list each one (separated by a space) after the AG_CHK command. For example, to check the files *Q1* and *Q2* that are stored in the APPS subdirectory:

```
ag_chk apps\q1.ag apps\q2.ag    (Enter)
```

Another way to check more than one file, is to use the standard DOS wildcards (* and ?). For example, to check every Agenda file in the APPS subdirectory that begins with *NEW*:

```
ag_chk apps\new*.ag    (Enter)
```

To check all the files in a directory, just type the name and path of that directory after the AG_CHK command. For example, to check every Agenda file in the *SALES* directory:

```
ag_chk c:\sales  [Enter]
```

For each file you specify, the Checker utility tells you whether that file is damaged or not.

To Fix Minor File Damage

In addition to testing a file, Checker can also fix some common types of minor damage. If you want to make these fixes to a file, include the /f parameter when typing the AG_CHK command.

For example, to test the PLANNER file and make fixes to it:

```
ag_chk /f apps\planner.ag  [Enter]
```

To Recover a Damaged File

If the Checker utility tells you that one of your Agenda files is damaged, don't use that file anymore. Instead, run the Agenda DB2STF utility to recover the contents of the damaged file.

To learn about using DB2STF, see Appendix I in the Agenda *User's Guide*.

Part No. 37343

Agenda®2.0
Made Easy

Agenda®2.0
Made Easy

Mary Campbell

Osborne McGraw-Hill

Berkeley New York St. Louis San Francisco
Auckland Bogotá Hamburg London Madrid
Mexico City Milan Montreal New Delhi Panama City
Paris São Paulo Singapore Sydney
Tokyo Toronto

Osborne **McGraw-Hill**
2600 Tenth Street
Berkeley, California 94710
U.S.A.

Osborne/McGraw-Hill offers software for sale. For information on software, translations, or book distributors outside of the U.S.A., please write to Osborne **McGraw-Hill** at the above address.

This book is printed on recycled paper.
This book was produced using Ventura Publisher Version 2.0.

Agenda 2.0™ Made Easy

1234567890 DOC 99876543210

ISBN 0-07-881675-0

Acquisitions Editor: Liz Fisher
Copy Editor: Jeff Green
Proofreader: Barbara Conway
Word Processor: Lynda Higham
Composition: Bonnie Bozorg
Cover Design: Bay Graphics Design, Inc.
Production Supervisor: Kevin Shafer

CONTENTS
AT A GLANCE

TABLE OF CONTENTS

ACKNOWLEDGMENTS

I would like to thank the following individuals for the many contributions to this book:

Martha Studnicka, for her help with all aspects of this revision. The many hours that Martha spent on this product were invaluable not only to completing this book but in being able to finish the revisions on other current book projects. Steve Ormsby, for all of his help in checking the accuracy of the manuscript. After using the original release for so long it was important to have a double check that all information was for the most recent release of the product. Steve's knowledge of the current product was invaluable. Chris Raffo, for checking the keystrokes in each chapter to ensure error free exercises for readers. Alexander Trevelyan, Mary Beth Butler, Steve Ormsby, Andrew Hammond, and the many others at Lotus who were there to supply software and to answer questions.

INTRODUCTION

Agenda is an exciting software program that can help you organize all types of information. Agenda 2.0 builds on the basic features offered in the first release but offers a streamlined user interface and many new features. The new version of Agenda still offers the basic building blocks of items, notes, categories, and views for information storage and access. In addition, the new release provides sample applications, expanded date features, and math capabilities that extend the usefulness of the package. Regardless of your area of expertise you will find the features in Agenda 2.0 can make you more productive. Not only can you put together an easy to use to-do list but you can store and work with all types of information without the rigidity of a regular data management package.

ABOUT THIS BOOK

Agenda 2.0 Made Easy is designed to meet the needs of the new Agenda 2 user. It covers both the new features of Agenda 2 and the basics of the older release. You will find everything you need, from coverage of the basic building blocks of Agenda files to more advanced features and application ideas.

If you have not yet installed Agenda you will want to begin with Appendix A. You will find simple instructions for installing Agenda in this appendix.

If you have already installed Agenda, you will want to begin with Chapter 1, the overview of the package features. After completing the overview you will want to complete chapters 2, 3, and 4 since they cover the basic building blocks needed for all Agenda applications. From there you can look at additional chapters that discuss Agenda's features at your leisure or skip to the application chapters 12 and 13 for some ideas as to how you might put the package to work for you.

If you have already mastered the basics of Agenda you can still use this book. You can begin with the overview and then skip to the application chapters or specific topics such as math or dates that you have not used in your applications. You should feel free to proceed sequentially through the chapters or to use the table of contents to locate the specific topics you want to learn more about immediately.

ORGANIZATION OF THE BOOK

Agenda 2.0 Made Easy is organized into 13 chapters and 3 appendices. Each chapter can easily be completed in a single session. As you finish each chapter you will have added a new set of Agenda skills. Because the chapters are self-contained, you can complete the later chapters without having to complete the early chapters.

Chapter 1 provides an overview of Agenda. It introduces some of the sample applications that come with Agenda when you purchase it. These applications get you up and running with real applications with only a minimum of invested time.

Chapter 2 introduces items and notes. These two building blocks of Agenda databases are the primary vehicles for entering important pieces of information. You can try a few of the exercises in this chapter and then start a new file of your own to immediately begin building a database of important information.

Chapter 3 discusses categories in Agenda. Categories allow you to organize the information that you enter in items to make it more meaningful and accessible.

Chapter 4 introduces the last important building block, views. Views let you customize your perspective of the data in your file at any time. With views you can look at a narrow subset of your items or a wider variety of information. You can define many different views of your data to provide just the access you need for any situation.

Chapter 5 teaches you about file management tasks and printing. You will learn how to work directly with your files in this chapter. You will also learn how you can control the print features to obtain the reports that you need to share your Agenda information with others.

Chapter 6 covers date and time features. You will learn about different dates that are already part of the Agenda package such as Done and When dates. You will also learn how to establish dates and times for your items as well as options for formatting them.

Chapter 7 covers the new math features that were added with Agenda 2. You will learn how to add the numbers in a column or compute simple statistics.

Chapter 8 covers conditions. With conditions you can have Agenda do some work for you. Rather than explicitly assigning all of your items to categories you can teach Agenda how to conditionally assign them.

Chapter 9 discusses actions that you can define. Actions are similar to conditions but are more versatile. You can use actions to assign items to many different categories. You can also perform other activities with items based on the actions that you define.

Chapter 10 covers another important productivity feature, macros. Macros allow you to define tasks to Agenda. When you need to perform the task again, rather than reentering all the keystrokes you simply ask Agenda to execute the macro for you.

Chapter 11 covers import and export features. These options allow you to write out Agenda data for use with other applications. They also allow you to bring data from other applications into Agenda.

Chapter 12 provides a look at a variety of business applications for Agenda. Although these do not require you to duplicate exercises, they do provide an overview of some sample applications for the package.

Chapter 13 provides a look at a few more Agenda applications. These applications are more specialized and cover medical, legal, and writing applications.

Appendix A covers installation of Agenda 2. Appendix B provides a glossary of terms. Appendix C is a command reference that you can use as a quick reference for all Agenda commands.

CONVENTIONS USED IN THIS BOOK

Several conventions are used throughout this book to offer consistency and speed your mastery of Agenda.

Entries that you must make to duplicate examples are shown in boldface in numbered steps.

The word "type" is used to indicate information that you must type from the keyboard.

The word "select" is used to indicate a choice that you must make from Agenda's menus.

The word "press" is used to indicate keys that should be pressed to invoke a feature.

Uppercase letters are used for filenames, although you may use either upper- or lowercase.

AGENDA'S
BUILDING BLOCKS

1

A QUICK LOOK
AT SOME OF
AGENDA'S FEATURES

Starting Agenda
Using PLANNER To Manage Your Activities
Using ACCOUNT for Client Tasks
Working with the People Manager Application

Agenda is such a versatile package that you will find it useful regardless of your job or responsibilities. It is designed to help you develop your own base of personal information. It is more flexible than database packages because it does not have the rigid definitional requirements that databases require. You can immediately start entering bits and pieces of information and Agenda will start organizing them for you.

To speed the path to productive use of Agenda, Lotus has bundled four starter applications with the package. These applications allow you to keep track of activities you need to perform, people you manage, client account information, and articles you have read. When you use any of these four applications, you will have a structure to help organize your data from the first time that you use the application because some of the work of setting up the application structure has already been done for you. Some of these predefined Agenda files already have macros to help you use the files more efficiently.

This chapter is designed to start you thinking about the things Agenda can do for you. It is not designed to provide you all the information on a particular component of Agenda. In this chapter you will use three of the Lotus starter applications, since they will save you a significant amount of typing time and will help you to get a general overview of many of Agenda's features. You will have an opportunity to create your own Agenda files and to look at the various Agenda features in more detail later.

If you have already been working with these starter application files, you can create another copy of them by copying the PLANNER, ACCOUNT, and PEOPLE files from the Utilities and Application (3 1/2") disk or Applications (5 1/4") disk. You can call your new copies PLANNER2, ACCOUNT2, and PEOPLE2 and use these filenames rather than the ones shown in this chapter to leave your earlier work intact. Type the following entry at the DOS prompt to copy the PLANNER file:

COPY A:PLANNER.AG C:\AGENDA\APPS\PLANNER2.AG

This makes a copy of the original starter application PLANNER in the default Agenda application directory and allows you to access it with the name PLANNER2. Repeat this procedure for the ACCOUNT and PEOPLE files.

STARTING AGENDA

If Agenda is already installed on your system, all you need to do to start the program is activate the directory where your Agenda files are stored and type **AGENDA**. If you followed the installation instructions that came with your package or the ones provided in Appendix A, Agenda is stored on drive C in the subdirectory AGENDA. To switch to this directory you type **CD \AGENDA** at the DOS prompt.

When you begin each new Agenda session, the name of the Agenda file that you used in the last session is suggested as the file to use this time. When Agenda is first installed you will not have yet worked with a file, but Agenda still suggests using a file. Agenda places a File Retrieve box on the screen like the one shown in Figure 1-1. This box shows PLANNER as the suggested file. Notice from the path designation that this file is located in the APPS directory beneath the AGENDA directory. This is the default location that Agenda uses for applications files when you complete the installation procedure described in Appendix A. If you have already been using Agenda and are working in a different directory, you will need to type the path and filename, as in **C:\AGENDA\APPS\PLANNER**. You can also highlight ..\ Parent Directory in the Select File box and after pressing (ENTER) choose APPS\ <DIR> and continue as described. If you have been working in the APPS directory, you can press (F3) (Choices) and select PLANNER from the list of filenames on the current directory.

```
Type the name of the file you want to open or create.
Press F3 for a list of files.
```

```
┌──────────────── File Retrieve ────────────────┐
│ File name: C:\AGENDA\APPS\PLANNER               │
│          ──────── Press ENTER when done ──────  │
└────────────────────────────────────────────────┘
```

FIGURE 1-1.   File Retrieve box

USING PLANNER TO MANAGE YOUR ACTIVITIES

Most of us have a list of tasks that need to be accomplished that we call our "to-do list." Sometimes this list is not really a list but is just scattered scraps of paper or ideas in our head that we never remember to write down. Even if your list is more formalized, you need to keep rewriting it if you want to keep it orderly. You probably also find that it is difficult to organize all the related activities together. Agenda's PLANNER file is set up and ready to accept your tasks and activities and help you organize them. Figure 1-2 shows the initial screen where you begin your entries. Agenda can immediately begin to categorize some of your entries by the type of activity they represent and is able to group together activities for this week, month, or other time periods. Agenda can also categorize activities as calls you need to make, follow-up activities, and any other categorization that you teach it to make. Highlight Activities and press (F3) (Choices) to see the types of activities PLANNER is already set up for. Use the (ARROW) keys to browse through the options, ignoring for now the abbreviations, which will be discussed later. When you are finished looking, press (ESC) to remove the list of activity choices from the screen.

```
File: C:\AGENDA\APPS\PEOPLE                        09/13/90  11:12am
View: Employee Summary                                  ←  *
      ──People───────────Hire Date─Level──────Salary─Last Rev─Next Rev──
   •   ·Coyle, Stephen   ·06/01/88 ·GS-8    $42500 ·06/15/90 ·12/15/90
   •   ·Jones, Peter     ·02/28/90 ·GS-7    $21500 ·08/30/90 ·02/28/91
   »   ·Larson, Mary     ·01/12/86 ·GS-8    $42500 ·04/02/90 ·10/02/90
   •   ·Smith, Paul      ·04/15/87 ·GS-7    $35000 ·03/30/90 ·09/30/90
```

FIGURE 1-2.   Initial PLANNER screen

The function key map at the bottom of the screen is there to remind you of what the function keys will do for you. If you press the (ALT), (SHIFT), or (CTRL) key, the function key map changes to display what the combination of the function keys and that special key will do.

Entering Tasks

Entering activity items in your Agenda file is easy. All you need to do is remain in the Tasks column as you type each new item and press (ENTER) after typing each one. The task entries you make in this column are called *items*. If the item text that you type is longer than the item column width, Agenda wraps the text to the next line. Follow these steps to add a few activities to the file:

1. With the highlight on Tasks, type **Call Steve about spreadsheet tips** and press (ENTER).

   You must press (ENTER) to finalize the item entry before you can start making the next item entry.

   Agenda records your entry and then places the entry **Calls** in the Activity column since it recognizes from the text you entered that this activity requires you to make a call. Lotus set up the PLANNER file to recognize some commonly used activity categories. Later you will learn how to teach it to recognize Steve as an entry for the People column, and you will also assign a when date to the activity.

2. Type **Finish writeup on print features** and press (ENTER).
   Agenda does not categorize this entry because it does not recognize this activity. You will teach it to recognize it later.

3. Type **Meet with Larry on enrollments**.
   Agenda categories this entry as a meeting activity by entering **Mtg** in the Activity column.

4. Type **Read latest survey data** and press (ENTER).

5. Type **Check with Tim on article** and press (ENTER).

6. Type **Call Sally about lunch on 9/15** and press (ENTER).
   This is the first task that has a date in the entry. After the WRKG message disappears from the upper-right corner of the screen, you will notice that Agenda has entered 9/15/90 in the When column since it assumes the date is in the current

year. The WRKG message indicates that Agenda is working at categorizing your entries or handling some other task for you.

7. Type **Read Fortune Article on computers** and press (ENTER).

8. Type **Meet with Cindy on staff salary increases** and press (ENTER).

9. Type **Schedule follow up with Paul on office furniture next Tues** and press (ENTER).

   The When categorization for this item will depend on your system date at the time of your entry. Since the entries in this book were made on 9/13/90, the When date entry is 9/18/90, the Tuesday following the entry. Your date in the when column will be different since you will be making the entry on a different date.

Figure 1-3 shows all the to-do items that you have entered and the categorizations that Agenda was able to make on its own.

Agenda has been working hard to make assignments based on your entries. Although the specifics of all this may not been clear at this time, you will learn exactly how this occurs as you progress through the chapters in this book.

```
File: C:\AGENDA\APPS\PLANNER                         09/13/90  12:07pm
View: Tasks
Tasks                          Activity People  Project  When
  • Call Steve about            ·Calls
    spreadsheet tips
  • Finish writeup on print
    features
  • Meet with Larry on          ·Mtg
    enrollments
  • Read latest survey data     ·Reading
  • Check with Tim on article
  • Call Sally about lunch on    ·Calls                    ·09/15/90
    9/15
  • Read Fortune Article on      ·Reading
    computers
  • Meet with Cindy on staff     ·Mtg
    salary increases
  • Schedule follow up with      ▸Follow                   ·09/18/90
    Paul on office furniture
    next Tues

  F1       F2       F3      F4     F5     F6     F7     F8      F9      F10
 Help     Edit   Choices  Done   Note  Props  Mark  Vw Mgr Cat Mgr  Menu
```

FIGURE 1-3.   Tasks entered into PLANNER

Categorizing Tasks

You can categorize a task by placing an entry in any of the categories shown at the top of your screen. Once you have made an entry to categorize a task, Agenda remembers it and supplies this entry the next time it thinks you want the same type of categorization. You will learn more about these categories in Chapter 3.

Since it can be convenient to compile a list of all the items that you have for an individual, it is worth taking the time to complete the People column. You can even use this column if you delegate tasks to different individuals, although the column is not used in this way within this example. As mentioned before, Agenda will remember the names you enter and automatically assign them in the future when your task includes these name entries. Agenda has an *automatic-completion* feature that can save you time when you type entries in the People column. If you start an entry that begins with the same letters as one of the existing entries, Agenda attempts to complete it for you by using the existing entry again, but you can always change this category assignment if this is not the one you want.

Follow these steps to categorize tasks by the people they involve:

1. Press the (HOME) key to move to Tasks at the top of the screen and then move to the first item entry in this column. Press (RIGHT ARROW) twice to move to the People column.

2. Type **Steve** and press (DOWN ARROW) to move to the People entry for the next item.
   Do not be alarmed if Agenda beeps and displays Sample Person when you type the first letter of Steve. This is an example of Agenda's auto-completion feature. Agenda thinks you may want to use the entry Sample Person and is attempting to save you typing time. Just continue typing **Steve** and press (ENTER). The next time you type **St**, Agenda will auto-complete the entry **Steve**.

3. Press (DOWN ARROW) again to skip the current entry, type **Larry**, and press (DOWN ARROW) twice.
   The second item is a personal activity that does not require an entry in this column.

4. Type **Tim** and press (DOWN ARROW).

5. Type **Sally** and press (DOWN ARROW) twice.

6. Type **Cindy** and press (DOWN ARROW).

7. Type **Paul** and press (ENTER).

You can also add other categories to the Activity column. Notice that Agenda was not able to tell from the text entered what it should place in the Activity column for the second item. Follow these steps to make some additional assignments:

1. Move to the second item and place the highlight in the Activity column.

2. Type **Writing** and press (ENTER).

3. Move to the Task column and press (END).

4. Type **Call Steve about writing a database article** and press (ENTER).

Agenda assigns your entry to both Calls and Writing in the Activity column and assigns it to Steve in the People column. Your screen should look like Figure 1-4.

```
File: C:\AGENDA\APPS\PLANNER                        09/13/90  12:11pm
View: Tasks
Tasks                          Activity People  Project  When
   • Call Steve about           ·Calls   ·Steve
     spreadsheet tips
   • Finish writeup on print    ·Writing
     features
   • Meet with Larry on         ·Mtg     ·Larry
     enrollments
   • Read latest survey data    ·Reading
   • Check with Tim on article           ·Tim
   • Call Sally about lunch on  ·Calls   ·Sally            ·09/15/90
     9/15
   • Read Fortune Article on    ·Reading
     computers
   • Meet with Cindy on staff   ·Mtg     ·Cindy
     salary increases
   • Schedule follow up with    ·Follow  ·Paul             ·09/18/90
     Paul on office furniture
     next Tues
   • Call Steve about writing a »Calls   ·Steve
     database article           »Writing

  F1     F2     F3     F4    F5    F6     F7     F8     F9     F10
 Help   Edit  Choices Done  Note Props  Mark  Vw Mgr Cat Mgr Menu
```

FIGURE 1-4. People assignments and additional Activity assignments

Customizing Category Assignments

You use categories to classify the items you enter in Agenda. Although it is fine to use the PLANNER file with its established categories, you may need to add or delete categories to make the file more closely match your needs.

The Project column in the PLANNER file allows you to assign each item to a project. If your activities are not project-oriented, you might want to remove this column. You may also feel that you need new categories to better classify your information.

REMOVING THE PROJECT CATEGORY   Removing the Project column is easy. Although it will disappear from the current view, you can always add it back at a later time. To delete the Project column, follow these steps:

1. Move to the Project column and then use (UP ARROW) or press (HOME) to move to the column head.

2. Press (DEL) to indicate that you wish to delete this column.

    Agenda displays the message "Remove this column from the view?" with a default response of Yes.

3. Press (ENTER) to complete the deletion.

ADDING A PRIORITY CATEGORY   You can add a new column to the display. You can show an existing category for your entries in this column or you can display a new category and place entries beneath the main category entry. Both the column head and the entries beneath it are categories. The column head is called the *parent* category, and the categories placed under the column head are called the *children*. You can think of the entire group, consisting of the column head and the entries beneath it, as a *family*.

Follow these steps to add a new category named Priority to the right of the People category:

1. Move the highlight to the People heading at the top of the display.

2. Press (F10) (Menu) and select View Column Add.

3. Type **Pri** and notice Agenda's auto-completion.

    Agenda indicates that there is one matching category entry and displays Priority.

4. Press (ENTER) to accept this category and then press (ENTER) again to complete the addition of the new category column.

Now you can assign each task a priority of high, medium, or low.

5. Position the highlight in the Priority column for the first task, type **h** and press (ENTER), and then press (DOWN ARROW). Agenda auto-completes **High**.

6. Type **m**, press (ENTER), and then press (DOWN ARROW).

7. Type **l**, press (ENTER), and then press (DOWN ARROW).

Since each of your Priority categories start with a unique letter, you type the first letter and press (ENTER) or (DOWN ARROW) to accept Agenda's suggestion of a category name.

8. Type **h, and press** (DOWN ARROW).

9. Type **m** and press (DOWN ARROW).

10. Type **m** and press (DOWN ARROW).

11. Type **l** and press (DOWN ARROW).

12. Type **h** and press (DOWN ARROW).

13. Type **h** and press (DOWN ARROW).

14. Type **m** and press (ENTER).

Note that you do not need to press (ENTER) after each entry since pressing the (DOWN ARROW) key accepts Agenda's suggestion and moves to the next entry.

Assigning Completion Dates

Now that you have added a Priority column and categorized each of your tasks as high, medium, or low priority, you should be ready to assess when you will complete each of the tasks. You will make many of the entries with relative date entries such as **today** or **Saturday**. Agenda will assign the proper dates to these items based on your computer's system date. Once assigned they will not change. Remember that the dates on your screen will not agree with those in the example here since the example was completed on 9/13/90. Follow these steps to complete the date entries:

1. Press the (HOME) key to move to the Priority column heading, press (RIGHT ARROW) until the highlight is in the When column, and then press (DOWN ARROW) and type **today**.

2. Press (DOWN ARROW) and type **tomorrow**.

3. Press (DOWN ARROW) and type **next Fri**.
   In this example a date of 9/21/90 was assigned because the system date at the time of entry was Thursday 9/13/90. Remember that your date will be different.

4. Press (DOWN ARROW) and type **today**.

5. Press (DOWN ARROW) three times and type **Sat** to add an entry for the task "Read Fortune article on computers."

6. Press (DOWN ARROW) and type **today**.

7. Press (DOWN ARROW) twice to skip the next item, which already has an entry assigned under When. Type **today**.

You have been using relative dates in your entries, so Agenda has had to calculate actual dates based on the current date when you made the entries. You can enter actual dates with an entry such as **09/22/90**. Actual date entries are useful for scheduling tasks for which you have more lead time.

Your screen should now look like Figure 1-5. The date entries will be different, but the other parts of the entries should be identical.

There are many other date features that you will learn about in later chapters. If you press (ALT-C) or (F3) (Choices) in the When column, you can select a date graphically from Agenda's calendar. The ability to change when dates depends on how they were entered. When dates that are based on dates in the text of item entries can be changed by editing the item. When dates that are entered explicitly in the When column cannot be changed by editing the item text. To change this type of when date entry you must edit the entry in the When column.

Looking at the Data From a Different Perspective

One advantage Agenda offers over other information products is its ability to allow you to view the same data in many different ways. You do this by using categories established in the file and assigning individual items to one or more categories. Agenda allows you to define views and specify exactly which categories of information to show and in what order to present the items in these categories. The PLANNER file you have been working with has many different views defined. You can choose to

```
File: C:\AGENDA\APPS\PLANNER                           09/13/90  12:15pm
View: Tasks                                                       *
Tasks                          Activity People  Priority When
   • Call Steve about           ·Calls   ·Steve  ·High    ·09/13/90
     spreadsheet tips
   • Finish writeup on print    ·Writing         ·Medium  ·09/14/90
     features
   • Meet with Larry on         ·Mtg     ·Larry  ·Low     ·09/21/90
     enrollments
   • Read latest survey data    ·Reading         ·High    ·09/13/90
   • Check with Tim on article           ·Tim    ·Medium
   • Call Sally about lunch on  ·Calls   ·Sally  ·Medium  ·09/15/90
     9/15
   • Read Fortune Article on    ·Reading         ·Low     ·09/15/90
     computers
   • Meet with Cindy on staff   ·Mtg     ·Cindy  ·High    ·09/13/90
     salary increases
   • Schedule follow up with    ·Follow  ·Paul   ·High    ·09/18/90
     Paul on office furniture
     next Tues
   » Call Steve about writing a ·Calls   ·Steve  ·Medium  ·09/13/90
     database article           Writing

  F1      F2       F3     F4     F5     F6     F7     F8      F9     F10
 Help    Edit   Choices  Done   Note  Props  Mark  Vw Mgr Cat Mgr Menu
```

FIGURE 1-5.   When dates and Priorities completed

look at a view that displays items by activity. You can also look at calls, tasks for next week, people, and items completed this week.

Changing the view that you are looking at does not alter the data in your Agenda files. You can always return to a prior view and your screen will again display the items in that view. Changes that you make to the data items in any view will affect the appearance of the item in any view. Editing an item in one view will change the same item in all other views.

LOOKING AT THE CALLS VIEW   To change the view of your file to another existing view, press (F8) to activate the View Manager. A box like the one in Figure 1-6 appears on the screen for the PLANNER file. To activate any of these views, use the (ARROW) keys to highlight the view name and press (ENTER). Follow these steps to activate and use the Calls view:

1. Press (F8) (Vw Mgr), press (UP ARROW) until Calls is highlighted, and then press (ENTER).

   Only the items that were categorized as Calls in the Activity column are displayed in the new view. A new column is displayed for phone numbers.

```
┌══════════════════ View Manager ══════════════════┐
│                                                   │
│     Activities                                    │
│     Calls                                         │
│     Completed This Week                           │
│     Expense Analysis - Type                       │
│     Expense Entry                                 │
│     Expense Reports                               │
│   * Next Week                                     │
│     Overdue                                       │
│     People                                        │
│     Priorities                                    │
│     Projects                                      │
│     ▐Tasks▌                                        │
│ ↓ * This Month                                    │
└═══════════ Press ENTER when done, ESC to cancel ══┘
```

FIGURE 1-6. Views available in the PLANNER file

2. Move the highlight to the Phone # column for the first item and then type **(217)423-0978** and press **(ENTER)**.

   The telephone number is automatically added in both of the calls to Steve.

3. Press **(DOWN ARROW)** twice and then type **765-8976** and press **(ENTER)**.

Although your entries do not seem any different than other entries that you have made, the phone numbers are being stored in a note attached to the category entry. This makes it easy for you to enter additional numbers or contact information if you need it.

4. With the highlight still on Sally's telephone number in the last item, press **(F5)** (Note). You can also position the highlight on the item text for Sally before pressing **(F5)** (Note). A note screen with the telephone number is displayed. You can enter a number of text pages here, but only one additional sentence is needed in this example.

5. Move to the end of the telephone number entry and press **(ENTER)** to place the cursor on a new line.

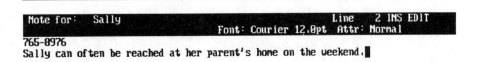

F1	F2	F3	F4	F5	F6	F7	F8	F9	F10
Help	Paste	Copy	Cut	Return	Marker	Mark			Menu

FIGURE 1-7.   Note containing Sally's phone number and other information

8. Type **Sally can often be reached at her parent's home on the weekend.** The note matches the one in Figure 1-7.

9. Press (F5) (Return) to return to the Calls view.

Your screen should look like Figure 1-8. You can toggle back to the previous view, Tasks, by pressing (ALT-F8).

LOOKING AT THE ACTIVITIES VIEW   In the Task and Calls views, all the items are displayed in one section. The Activities view is structured a little differently, since there is a section of the view for each activity defined, even if no items are assigned to the activity. Follow these steps to display the Activity view and add a few items to unused activities:

1. Press (F8) (Vw Mgr) to display the list of Agenda views for the current file.

2. Highlight Activities and press (ENTER).
   You will see the view divided into the following sections: Calls, Follow up, Ideas, Issues, Mail, Meetings, Miscellaneous Activity, and Reading. Three of these

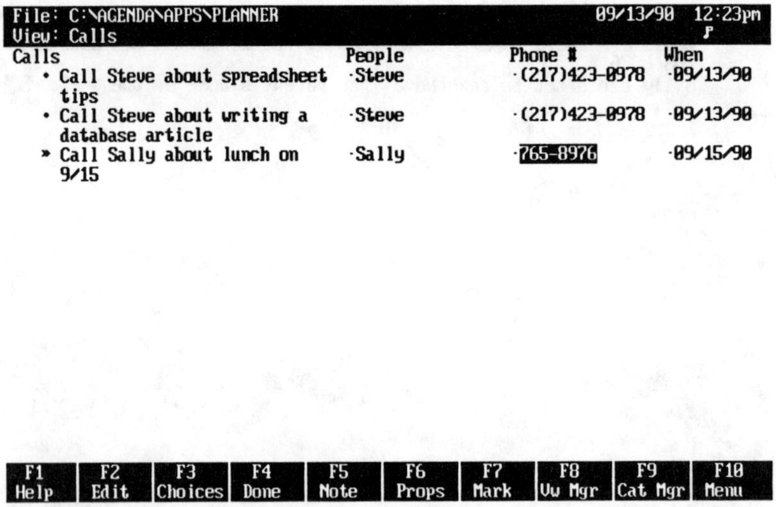

```
File: C:\AGENDA\APPS\PLANNER                          09/13/90   12:23pm
View: Calls                                                      P
Calls                          People         Phone #        When
   • Call Steve about spreadsheet  ·Steve       ·(217)423-0978  ·09/13/90
     tips
   • Call Steve about writing a    ·Steve       ·(217)423-0978  ·09/13/90
     database article
   » Call Sally about lunch on     ·Sally       ·765-8976       ·09/15/90
     9/15
```

```
 F1     F2      F3     F4     F5     F6     F7     F8     F9    F10
Help    Edit  Choices  Done   Note  Props  Mark  Vw Mgr Cat Mgr Menu
```

FIGURE 1-8.   The Calls view

sections are empty since no items have been assigned to these activities. You can hide empty sections through a change to View Properties. This change is described in Chapter 6.

3. Press (DOWN ARROW) until Ideas is highlighted.

4. Type **Sponsor contest for area softball teams** and press (ENTER).

5. Press (DOWN ARROW) to highlight Issues, type **Lack of parking during October festival events**, and press (ENTER).
   Your screen should look like Figure 1-9.

6. Press (F8) (Vw Mgr), type **t** to highlight Tasks, and press (ENTER).

7. Move the highlight to view the two new items at the end of the task list.

You can add other items to any view and the items will appear in any view in which a category they are assigned to is displayed. For example, you can add an item and assign it to the Reading category and it will appear in the Tasks and Activity views but not the Calls view, if the item is not assigned to that view.

```
File: C:\AGENDA\APPS\PLANNER                              09/13/90  12:32pm
View: Activities                                                    ↓
Calls                              People       Phone #           When
   • Call Steve about spreadsheet   ·Steve       ·(217)423-8978   ·09/13/90
     tips
   • Call Steve about writing a     ·Steve       ·(217)423-8978   ·09/13/90
     database article
   • Call Sally about lunch on 9/15 ·Sally       ·765-8976        ·09/15/90

Follow up                                                         When
   • Schedule follow up with Paul on office furniture next Tues   ·09/18/90

Ideas                                                             When
   • Sponsor contest for area softball teams

Issues                                                            When
   • Lack of parking during October festival events               »

Mail                                                              When

Meetings                                                          When
   • Meet with Cindy on staff salary increases                   ·09/13/90
   • Meet with Larry on enrollments                              ·09/21/90
┌──────┬──────┬───────┬──────┬──────┬──────┬──────┬──────┬──────┬──────┐
│ F1   │ F2   │ F3    │ F4   │ F5   │ F6   │ F7   │ F8   │ F9   │ F10  │
│ Help │ Edit │Choices│ Done │ Note │Props │ Mark │Vw Mgr│Cat Mgr│ Menu │
└──────┴──────┴───────┴──────┴──────┴──────┴──────┴──────┴──────┴──────┘
```

FIGURE 1-9.   The Activities view

Printing the Current View

You will want to print different views of your Agenda file to share with others or to use when you are not sitting in front of your computer. With Agenda's preview features you can even look at your print output on your screen before sending it to your printer. To print a copy of the Tasks view, follow these steps:

1. With the Tasks view on your screen, press (F10) (Menu). Select Print Preview and press (ENTER).
     You will need to wait while Agenda formats the print output for your screen.

2. Press (F10) (Menu) and select Content to enlarge the print display to full screen.

3. Press (ESC) to cancel the preview and return to the Tasks view, and then press (F10) (Menu).

4. Select Print Layout and press (DOWN ARROW) until the left margin selection is highlighted.

5. Type **1.5** and press (ENTER) twice.

6. Press (F10) (Menu), select Print Final after turning your printer on, and press (ENTER). Agenda saves your file every time you print.

You can continue to work with the PLANNER file, printing other views or adding as many new items and making as many changes as you wish. The file is yours so you should alter it to reflect your needs.

USING ACCOUNT FOR CLIENT TASKS

The ACCOUNT file that comes with Agenda is an ideal tool for individuals in consulting or sales who work with a number of clients. It is designed to allow you to monitor tasks, track expenses, follow up with prospects, and analyze important customer issues. Although the first view that you will see with this application is designed for task entry, you can also enter expense report information or use the file to look at existing entries from other perspectives. Because many categories and views are already established, you will find that it is easy to begin with the starter application even if you decide to make modifications at a later time.

Adding Tasks To the Client File

As you enter all the tasks that you need to complete on client projects, Agenda automatically categorizes these tasks by activity and date. If you add contact names and accounts to Agenda's category hierarchy, it will automatically make these assignments for you where possible. Follow these steps to open the ACCOUNTS file and have Agenda save the PLANNER file with all the changes you have made:

1. Press (F10) (Menu) and select File Retrieve.

2. Highlight ACCOUNT and press (ENTER).

Agenda displays the empty Tasks view. The top of the screen should look like this:

```
File: C:\AGENDA\APPS\ACCOUNT                        09/14/90  12:14pm
View: Tasks                                                →
Tasks                           Contact  Account  Activity When
```

SETTING UP THE CATEGORY ENTRIES BEFORE USING THEM

You can teach Agenda about your accounts and contacts by modifying the list of category entries that Agenda is aware of. If you use any of these entries within items that you type later, Agenda will know enough to complete the entries in the Contact and Account columns. (You will learn more about categories in Chapter 3.)

1. Press (F9) (Cat Mgr) to display a list of all the categories that Agenda uses.

2. Use the (ARROW) keys to highlight Contact;People (People is a synonym for Contact), press (DOWN ARROW) to move to Sample Person, and press (INS).

3. Type **CGW** and press (ENTER).

4. Press (INS), type **SCF**, and press (ENTER).

5. Press (INS), type **HGS**, and press (ENTER).

6. Move back up the list to Sample Person, press (DEL), and then press (ENTER) to remove this entry.

7. Move the highlight to Sample Account under Account, press (INS), type **Butler**, and then press (ENTER).

8. Press (INS), type **Office**, and press (ENTER).

9. Press (INS), type **Halloway**, and press (ENTER).

10. Press (INS), type **J&S**, and press (ENTER).

11. Highlight Sample Account, press (DEL), and then press (ENTER) to confirm the deletion.

COMPLETING THE DETAIL ENTRIES   With the category hierarchy updated, Agenda will now recognize these entries when you enter items. If an item contains text that matches one of the existing category entries, it will automatically place this entry in the proper column of your display.

1. Press (F9) (To View) to return to the Task view.

2. Type the following task entries, remembering to press (ENTER) or (INS) after
entering each task:

Call Chris tomorrow about page layout
Write memo today about parking for open house on 10/15/90
Meet with Steve Monday on Halloway book
Meet with Jamison & Smith to discuss marketing campaign for 1991 next
Thursday
Schedule production for Butler brochure Monday

Agenda was able to categorize some of your entries based on the initial definitions
set up for this file, including calls, mail, meetings, and dates. Other category entries
were made based on the new facts that you taught Agenda in the previous section,
such as Halloway and Butler in the Account column. There are also some entries that
you will still need to make since the contact initials and some account names were not
referenced in the item text that you entered.

3. Refer to Figure 1-10 to complete the remaining column entries. Remember that
your date categories are based on your system date at entry time and do not need
to be changed to match the figure.

```
File: C:\AGENDA\APPS\ACCOUNT                        09/14/90  12:39pm
View: Tasks                                             →
Tasks                              Contact  Account  Activity When
   • Call Chris tomorrow about      ·CGW     ·Butler  ·Calls   ·09/15/90
     page layout
   • Write memo today about                  ·Office  ·Mail    ·09/14/90
     parking for open house on
     10/15/90
   • Meet with Steve Monday on      ·SCF     ·Hallowa ·Mtg     ·09/17/90
     Halloway book
   • Meet with Jamison & Smith to   ·HGS     ·J&S     ·Mtg     ·09/20/90
     discuss marketing campaign
     for 1991 next Thursday
   » Schedule production for        ·CGW     ·Butler   Calls   ·09/17/90
     Butler brochure Monday
```

```
┌─────┬─────┬───────┬─────┬─────┬─────┬─────┬───────┬───────┬─────┐
│ F1  │ F2  │  F3   │ F4  │ F5  │ F6  │ F7  │  F8   │  F9   │ F10 │
│Help │Edit │Choices│Done │Note │Props│Mark │Vw Mgr │Cat Mgr│Menu │
└─────┴─────┴───────┴─────┴─────┴─────┴─────┴───────┴───────┴─────┘
```

FIGURE 1-10.   The ACCOUNTS file after task entries

Looking at a Calendar Perspective

The calendar perspective views that are defined for this file allow you to look at all the activities that you need to perform today, tomorrow, or this month. Although there are only a few tasks defined at this point you should take a look at how this view shows your data in a different perspective. Follow these steps to look at the activities planned for this month:

1. Press (F8) (Vw Mgr).

2. Highlight This Month and press (ENTER).

Agenda displays a view of the activities, as shown in Figure 1-11. The month that appears on your display will be different. Whether or not the same list of activities appears will depend on how close to the end of the month it was when you made your entries. If you entered the items on the last day of the month, only the item entered for

```
File: C:\AGENDA\APPS\ACCOUNT                              09/14/90   12:41pm
View: This Month                         Datebook For: Tasks            *
─When┐                 ┌─Sun 08/26/90•Sat 09/01/90 ─────────────────────────
─────────────────────────Sun 09/02/90•Sat 09/08/90 ─────────────────────────
─────────────────────────Sun 09/09/90•Sat 09/15/90 ─────────────────────────
·09/14/90              • Write memo today about parking for open house on 10/15/90
·09/15/90              • Call Chris tomorrow about page layout
                       ┌─Sun 09/16/90•Sat 09/22/90 ─────────────────────────
·09/17/90              • Meet with Steve Monday on Halloway book
·09/17/90              • Schedule production for Butler brochure Monday
·09/20/90              • Meet with Jamison & Smith to discuss marketing campaign
                         for 1991 next Thursday
                       ┌─Sun 09/23/90•Sat 09/29/90 ─────────────────────────
```

```
┌────┬──────┬───────┬─────┬──────┬──────┬──────┬───────┬───────┬──────┐
│ F1 │  F2  │  F3   │ F4  │  F5  │  F6  │  F7  │  F8   │  F9   │ F10  │
│Help│ Edit │Choices│Done │ Note │Props │ Mark │Vw Mgr │Cat Mgr│ Menu │
└────┴──────┴───────┴─────┴──────┴──────┴──────┴───────┴───────┴──────┘
```

FIGURE 1-11.   Looking at the tasks for this month

today would appear on your list since the other items would all be slated for next month.

Focusing on Important Issues

You may want to bring out important points in discussions with clients. These might be based on concerns the client has raised for the current project or your observance of critical issues on prior projects. The Tasks view has columns for Product and Issues that you did not use when making the initial entries. Since the Products column is not needed, you can delete it and move the Issues column to the left for easier access. Follow these steps to make the changes:

1. Press (F8) (Vw Mgr), highlight Tasks, and press (ENTER).

2. Press (HOME) and then press (RIGHT ARROW) until the Product and Issues columns are visible.

   Since these columns are to the right of the When column, they may not be visible until you move the highlight beyond When.

3. Highlight Product, press (DEL), and press (ENTER).

4. Highlight Issues, press (F10) (Menu), select View Column Move, and then press (LEFT ARROW) until the Issues column is next to the Contact column, and press (ENTER) to confirm.

5. Complete the entries in this column as shown in Figure 1-12.

   Notice that some items have more than one issue. Type each issue and press (ENTER) before typing the next issue for the item. Or, you can use the (INS) key and type the category name to add categories to the same item.

Entering and Monitoring Expenses

When you work with a number of different clients, you will want to keep expenses for each project that you work on separate. You can use the ACCOUNT file to enter

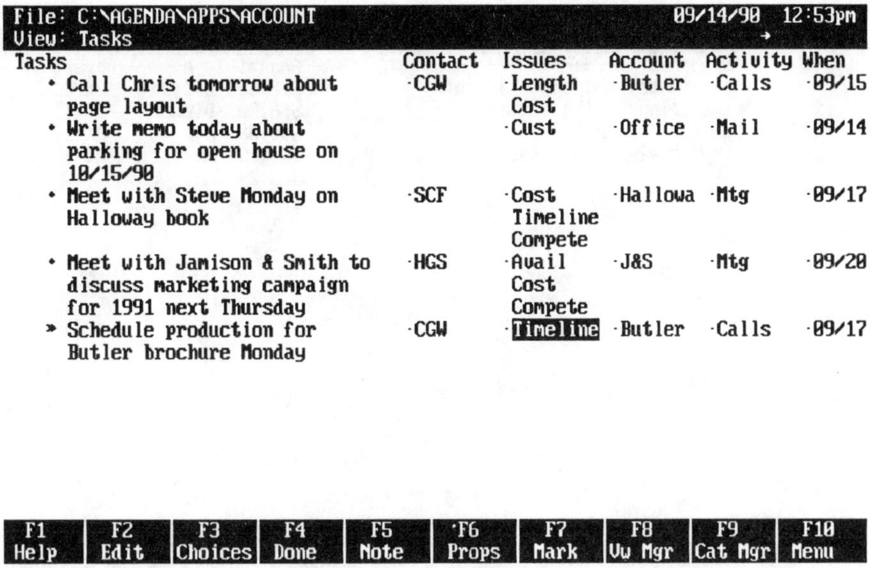

```
File: C:\AGENDA\APPS\ACCOUNT                          09/14/90  12:53pm
View: Tasks                                                   →
Tasks                          Contact  Issues    Account  Activity When
   • Call Chris tomorrow about    ·CGW    ·Length   ·Butler  ·Calls   ·09/15
     page layout                          Cost
   • Write memo today about               ·Cust     ·Office  ·Mail    ·09/14
     parking for open house on
     10/15/90
   • Meet with Steve Monday on    ·SCF    ·Cost     ·Hallowa ·Mtg     ·09/17
     Halloway book                         Timeline
                                           Compete
   • Meet with Jamison & Smith to ·HGS    ·Avail    ·J&S     ·Mtg     ·09/20
     discuss marketing campaign            Cost
     for 1991 next Thursday                Compete
   ⇒ Schedule production for      ·CGW    ·Timeline ·Butler  ·Calls   ·09/17
     Butler brochure Monday
```

```
 F1      F2      F3     F4     F5    ·F6     F7      F8      F9     F10
Help   Edit  Choices  Done   Note  Props  Mark  Vw Mgr Cat Mgr  Menu
```

FIGURE 1-12.   The Issues column relocated

your expenses and to display these expenses by expense report or type. Follow these steps to enter a few expenses:

1. Press (F8) (Vw Mgr), highlight Expense Entry, and press (ENTER).

2. Type **Hotel Lodging - Toronto**, press (TAB), type **312**, press (TAB) twice, type **AX-15**, press (TAB), type **09/01/90**, and press (ENTER).

3. Complete the three remaining expense entries shown in Figure 1-13.

As you complete the entries in the Type column, Agenda will recognize some, such as Dinner, and will auto-complete them for you. Others such as Meals are not known to Agenda, but your entry here will teach Agenda to recognize them for later use.

4. Press (F8) (Vw Mgr), highlight Expense Reports, and press (ENTER).

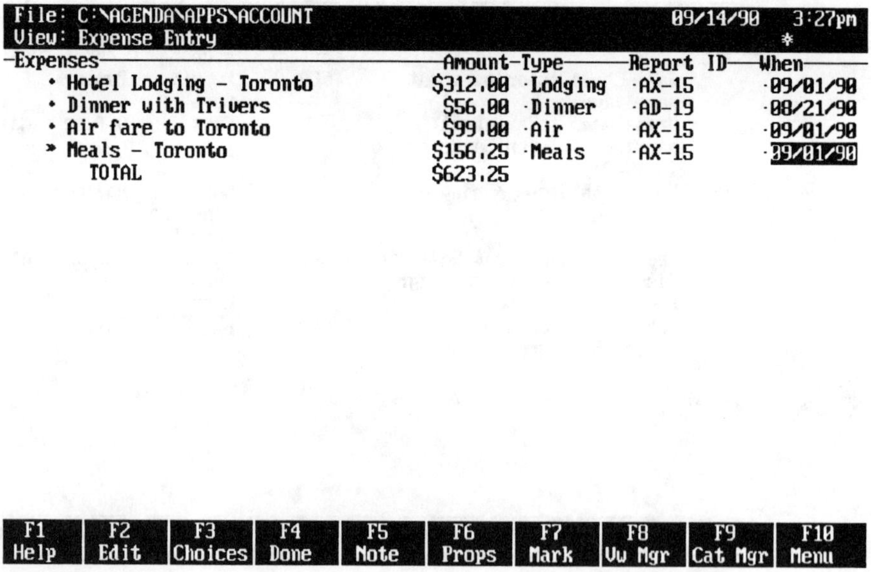

```
File: C:\AGENDA\APPS\ACCOUNT                         09/14/90    3:27pm
View: Expense Entry                                              *
-Expenses-                          -Amount-Type-      -Report ID-When-
   • Hotel Lodging – Toronto        $312.00 ·Lodging   ·AX-15    ·09/01/90
   • Dinner with Trivers             $56.00 ·Dinner    ·AD-19    ·08/21/90
   • Air fare to Toronto             $99.00 ·Air       ·AX-15    ·09/01/90
   » Meals – Toronto                $156.25 ·Meals     ·AX-15    ·09/01/90
        TOTAL                       $623.25
```

```
┌─────┬─────┬───────┬─────┬─────┬─────┬─────┬──────┬───────┬──────┐
│ F1  │ F2  │  F3   │ F4  │ F5  │ F6  │ F7  │ F8   │  F9   │ F10  │
│Help │Edit │Choices│Done │Note │Props│Mark │Vu Mgr│Cat Mgr│Menu  │
└─────┴─────┴───────┴─────┴─────┴─────┴─────┴──────┴───────┴──────┘
```

FIGURE 1-13.   An Expense Entry view after entering expenses

Agenda displays the expense detail organized by expense report, as shown in Figure 1-14. Sections for No Purpose and Sample Trip also appear on the display since they have not been deleted.

WORKING WITH THE PEOPLE MANAGER APPLICATION

If you have individuals reporting to you, you can use Agenda's PEOPLE file to help you track their assignments and performance. You can work with a summary view of all your employees or you can focus on the data for one specific employee. In addition to predefined items and views, PEOPLE contains an auto-execute macro that is invoked when you retrieve the file. A macro is an advanced technique that allows you to define a precise procedure for accomplishing a task.

```
File: C:\AGENDA\APPS\ACCOUNT                    09/14/90   3:31pm
View: Expense Reports [Expenses]
-AD-19--------------------------------Amount-Type--------When----
   • Dinner with Trivers              $56.00 ·Entertainmen ·08/21/90
        TOTAL                         $56.00
-AX-15--------------------------------Amount-Type--------When----
   • Meals - Toronto                  $156.25 ·Meals       ·09/01/90
   • Air fare to Toronto              $99.00 ·Air          ·09/01/90
   • Hotel Lodging - Toronto          $312.00 ·Lodging     ·09/01/90
        TOTAL                         $567.25
-No Purpose---------------------------Amount-Type--------When----
        TOTAL                         $0.00
-Sample Trip--------------------------Amount-Type--------When----
        TOTAL                         $0.00
```

FIGURE 1-14.   Entries in the Expense Reports view

Entering Data For Your Employees

When you first open the PEOPLE file, Agenda runs a macro that asks you to enter a first name for an employee entry, and then a last name. It then combines the names into one entry for the People column. This approach is useful since it ensures consistency, as all names are displayed by last name, a comma, and then first name. Follow these steps to enter the data for your four employees:

1. Type **Stephen** and press (ENTER), and then type **Coyle** and press (ENTER). After a short delay, Agenda enters **Coyle, Stephen** in the People column and creates an individual view for Stephen that you can access later.

2. Press (ENTER) to accept the highlighted Yes to enter another name. Type **Peter** and press (ENTER), and then type **Jones** and press (ENTER).

3. Press (ENTER) to accept the highlighted Yes, type **Mary** and press (ENTER), and then type **Larson** and press (ENTER).

4. Press (ENTER) to accept Yes, type **Paul** and press (ENTER), and then type **Smith** and press (ENTER).

5. Highlight No and press (ENTER) without supplying an entry to end the entry of names.

```
File: C:\AGENDA\APPS\PEOPLE                        09/13/90  11:12am
View: Employee Summary                                    ← *
     ┌People──────────────Hire Date─Level──────Salary─Last Rev──Next Rev─
  •    ·Coyle, Stephen     ·06/01/88 ·GS-8   $42500 ·06/15/90 ·12/15/90
  •    ·Jones, Peter       ·02/28/90 ·GS-7   $21500 ·08/30/90 ·02/28/91
  »    ·Larson, Mary       ·01/12/86 ·GS-8   $42500 ·04/02/90 ·10/02/90
  •    ·Smith, Paul        ·04/15/87 ·GS-7   $35000 ·03/30/90 ·09/30/90
```

FIGURE 1-15.   The Employee Summary view in the PEOPLE file

6. Enter the remaining data as shown in Figure 1-15. Note the salaries can be entered without dollar signs and Agenda will supply them for you.

Entering Objectives and Tasks

The PEOPLE file has a view for each employee that you add. Agenda creates these views after you complete the entry for each new person. You can use these views to monitor the objectives of each individual, to monitor whether the tasks that make up each objective are completed on time, and to measure the quality of the performance. Follow these steps to add some data to the view for Mary Larson:

1. Press (F8) (Vw Mgr).

2. Highlight Mary Larson Review and press (ENTER).
   The default view available for each employee that you added is shown in Figure 1-16.

3. Move the highlight to Objective 1 and press (F2) (Edit).

4. Press (CTRL-ENTER) to remove the existing description, type **Prepare Trivers Advertising Campaign**, and press (ENTER).

5. Type **Develop new slogans** and press (ENTER).

6. Press (TAB), type **o** to have Agenda suggest Outstanding, and press (ENTER).
   Agenda's automatic-completion feature saves a significant amount of time on this entry since there is only one category that begins with the letter o.

7. Press (TAB), type **e**, and press (ENTER) to accept the suggestion Early.

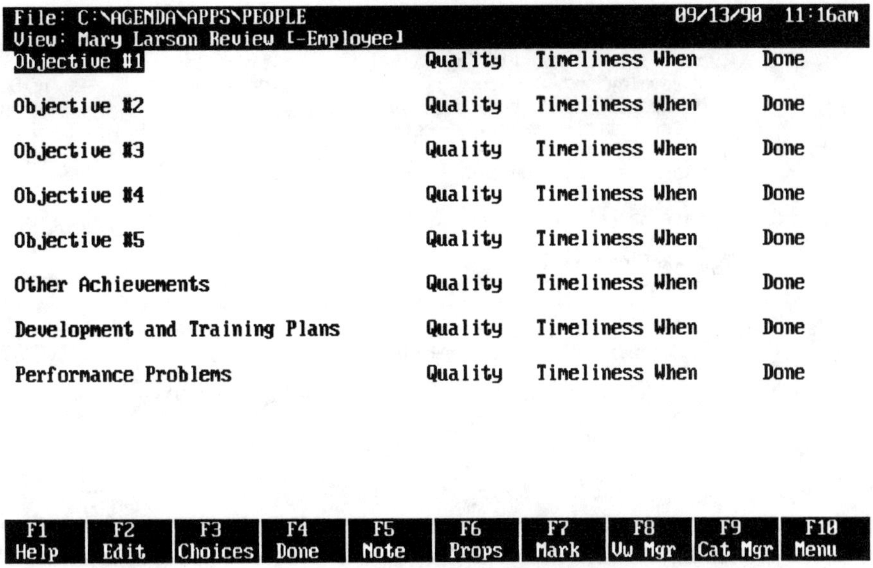

```
File: C:\AGENDA\APPS\PEOPLE                              09/13/90  11:16am
View: Mary Larson Review [-Employee]
Objective #1                      Quality   Timeliness When      Done

Objective #2                      Quality   Timeliness When      Done

Objective #3                      Quality   Timeliness When      Done

Objective #4                      Quality   Timeliness When      Done

Objective #5                      Quality   Timeliness When      Done

Other Achievements                Quality   Timeliness When      Done

Development and Training Plans     Quality   Timeliness When      Done

Performance Problems              Quality   Timeliness When      Done
```

F1	F2	F3	F4	F5	F6	F7	F8	F9	F10
Help	Edit	Choices	Done	Note	Props	Mark	Vw Mgr	Cat Mgr	Menu

FIGURE 1-16.   The default view for an individual employee

Note that when you enter text in item columns or standard category columns, you can accept the text and move one column to the right by pressing (TAB). You cannot do this for date and numeric entries. (RIGHT ARROW) only works for standard item columns.

8. Press (TAB), type **08/15/90**, and press (ENTER).

9. Press (TAB), type **08/01/90**, and press (ENTER).
     Agenda marks the task beneath the objective as done since a Done date is supplied.

10. Move the highlight back to "Develop new slogans", type **Conduct focus group sessions,** and press (ENTER). Press (TAB) until the highlight moves to the When date column and type **09/30/90**.

11. Move the highlight to "Conduct focus group sessions", type **Conduct client review meeting,** and press (ENTER). Press (TAB) to move to the When column and type **10/15/90**.

```
File: C:\AGENDA\APPS\PEOPLE                            09/13/90  11:51am
View: Mary Larson Review [-Employee]                            *
Prepare Trivers Advertising Campaig   Quality  Timeliness When      Done
  !! Develop new slogans              ·Outstan ·Early     ·08/15/90 ·08/01/90
   • Conduct focus group sessions                         ·09/30/90
   • Conduct client review meeting                        ·10/15/90

Develop training programs for new s   Quality  Timeliness When      Done

Prepare marketing brochure            Quality  Timeliness When      Done

Other Achievements                    Quality  Timeliness When      Done
   • United Way chairperson

Development and Training Plans         Quality  Timeliness When      Done
   » Supervisory leadership class                         11/10/90

Performance Problems                  Quality  Timeliness When      Done
```

F1	F2	F3	F4	F5	F6	F7	F8	F9	F10
Help	Edit	Choices	Done	Note	Props	Mark	Vw Mgr	Cat Mgr	Menu

FIGURE 1-17.   Mary Larson's view after customizing it with her objectives and tasks

12. Move to Objective 2, press (**F2**) (Edit), press (**CTRL-ENTER**) to delete the current entry, and type **Develop training program for new staff** and press (**ENTER**).

13. Replace Objective 3 with the text shown in Figure 1-17, and add the tasks shown under Other Achievements and Development and Training Plans. You should also delete Objectives 4 and 5.

You can use the same procedure to add objectives and tasks for other employees, but first you should take a look at the math features covered in the next section.

Using the Math Features

You can perform mathematical computations on numeric type columns that contain numeric entries. The Salary column in the Employee Summary view is a good location to try this feature since it is a numeric column and you can total and average salaries. Follow these steps to display the computations for total and average salaries:

1. Press (F8) (Vw Mgr).

2. Highlight Employee Summary and press (ENTER). Since this starter application has special settings, you must disable protection for this view before you can add the new computations. Protection is a special setting that prevents changes to the columns and sections in a view.

3. Press (F10) (Menu) and select View Properties.

4. Press (END) to move to View protection, press (F3) (Choices), highlight Global (No protection), and press (ENTER) twice.

5. Press (HOME), move to the Salary column, press (F10) (Menu), and then select View Column Properties.

6. Move to Total and Average and change both entries to Yes.

7. Press (ENTER) to display the Employee Summary view again, with the total and average for the Salary column displayed below the detail entries.

The TOTAL and AVERAGE headings appear vertically since this column is only five characters wide. Widening this column would allow these words to display horizontally. Widening columns is covered in Chapter 6.

2

ITEMS AND NOTES

Working with Items
Working with Notes
Adding Data to an Existing File
Marking Items
Deleting Item Data
Using Search-and-Replace Features

Items are the basic units for storing information in an Agenda file. Items in an Agenda file are not structured like items in a database package. There are no rules to follow for the types of information or ideas that you can place in an item. Whatever you think is important can be recorded in an item, even if it is totally unlike the information in any other item.

Most of your Agenda activity will center on the creation of items that will become integral parts of your Agenda reports. In this chapter you will learn how to create a new Agenda file that will be used to illustrate the creation and use of Agenda items. You will also learn how to attach notes to Agenda items. Notes allow for longer entries that more fully describe items or provide supporting detail. The combination of items and notes is the heart of Agenda and makes the package a powerful addition to your business or personal software library.

WORKING WITH ITEMS

Items are used to store information in Agenda regardless of the type of entry you wish to make. Agenda's only rule for adding information is that an item cannot exceed 350 characters. Outside of the length restriction, any type of text entry consisting of numbers, symbols, and letters is acceptable. You can enter a number, a word, a name, a phrase, or several sentences into an Agenda item. In short, you can enter any important piece of information into your Agenda files.

Free-Form Entries

You do not need to specify how long your Agenda item entries will be or the type of data that you plan to store in them. Each item entry can be a different length and contain a unique type of information. Items that you have already entered do not affect subsequent items. The following are all examples of acceptable item entries:

- **4/15/87 regional sales meeting**

- **Call Bill Jones today**

- **Last Robinson Company shipment was not sent air express as requested. Delayed receipt of critical items by 4 days.**

- **$1.03 price increase for widgets effective May 1**

- **987-5670**

The topics that you cover with your items will depend on the type of information that you work with. As the previous examples indicate, item entries do not require any specific structure. You can use free-form text entry and allow Agenda to handle the word wrap necessary to place the item information on the screen. With word wrap, Agenda will move text to the next line when the current line is filled.

Limitless Entry

You can enter as many items in Agenda as your disk space allows. You will not find the many limitations that you might with a database package. There are no field names, field types, or other limiting factors. All you need to do is focus on what is important to you.

Creating a New File
And Entering the First Item

Before entering an item in Agenda, you must start the program and have a file active. You are not restricted to a single file with Agenda; you can create as many separate files as you wish. Multiple files can help organize your information, but only one file can be open at a time.

The following steps illustrate how you create a new Agenda file and enter an item:

1. Start Agenda and press (F3) when the File Retrieve screen appears.
   The Select File screen appears, and the highlight will be on the file you used in your last Agenda session, as shown in Figure 2-1.

2. Press (INS) to create a new file.
   Agenda prompts you to enter the new filename or directory.

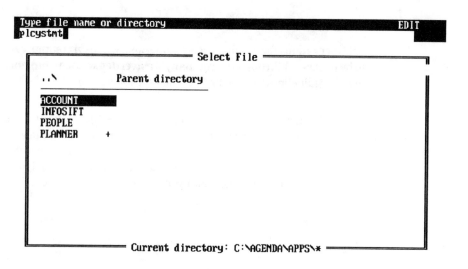

FIGURE 2-1.   Selecting a file to open

If you had wanted to use the highlighted file, you would press (ENTER) instead of (INS). To use another existing file, you would use the (UP ARRIW) and (DOWN ARROW) keys to move the highlight to the file that you wanted and then press (ENTER).

3. Type **plcystmt**. Your screen should look like the one shown in Figure 2-1.

The filename is limited to eight characters, numbers, and/or some special symbols. You should not use spaces in the filename. You should attempt to use a name for the file that has some relationship to its contents. This approach will help you to remember what the file contains at a later date.

4. Press (ENTER). the New File screen appears.

5. Type **Company Policy** and press (ENTER) twice. Your screen should look like this:

```
File: C:\AGENDA\APPS\PLCYSTMT                          09/07/91   1:50pm
View: Initial View
Initial Section
```

At this point you can begin to type any item you wish in this Agenda file by just starting to type or by pressing the (INS) key. You will need to press the (INS) key when the section head is highlighted.

6. Type the following:

   All reservations for lodging accommodations while on company business are to be processed through the company's travel department and must conform to price guidelines established for the location visited.

Figure 2-2 shows several item entries in your new file. Notice that each item is marked with a dot (.) to indicate the start of a new item. Also notice that the highlight changes to a cursor when an item is being created. In order to accept an item for inclusion in your file, you must press (ENTER) at the conclusion of each item. The item you just completed is highlighted until you begin to enter a new item.

7. Press (ENTER).

8. Type the remaining items shown in Figure 2-2.

```
File: C:\AGENDA\APPS\PLCYSTMT                          09/07/91  12:36pm
View: Initial View
Initial Section
    • All reservations for lodging accommodations while on company business
      are to be processed through the company's travel department and must
      conform to price guidelines established for the location visited.
    • Certain grade requirements must be met for tuition reimbursement.
    • Expenses for job related courses must receive the prior approval of an
      employee's supervisor.
```

FIGURE 2-2.   Item text

Adding Items

If you wish to add an item, all you need to do is begin typing, and Agenda automatically creates the new item when you press (ENTER). If you accidentally press (ENTER) before finishing, or if you need to fix a typing error after finalizing an item entry, you will need to use the editing techniques described in the next section. A new item is always added beneath the currently highlighted item. If you enter items in sequence without moving the highlight, they are added one beneath the other down the screen. If you wish to place an item in a different location, move the highlight to the item that you want to be above the new item and begin typing.

In Figure 2-2 the highlight is on the third item entered. To add an item after this item, press (INS) to add a blank item or simply begin typing. As you type, new text is placed in this blank line. Additional lines are added to accommodate your entry up to the maximum of 350 characters. When you are finished with your entry, press (ENTER) to finalize it.

Editing an Existing Item

The data that you enter in an item can be changed even after the entry is finalized. To add a word or otherwise alter the data in an item, you need to enter Edit mode by pressing (F2).

Edit mode changes the display. The highlight changes to a cursor just as when you are entering an item, and this cursor marks the current location in the item. The cursor is always at the beginning of the item, but you can use the (ARROW) keys to move it to a new location. There are also a few special keys to help you move around more quickly. The keys that you can use to move the cursor in Edit mode are listed in Table 2-1. The (CTRL) key options require you to hold down (CTRL) while pressing the other key shown. For example, to move to the beginning of an item, you hold down (CTRL) while you press (HOME) and then release both keys. When you have finished your changes, press (ENTER) to finalize them. To add text to the end of an existing item you

Key	Function
(UP ARROW)	Moves cursor up one line.
(DOWN ARROW)	Moves cursor down one line.
(RIGHT ARROW)	Moves cursor right one character.
(LEFT ARROW)	Moves cursor left one character.
(CTRL-RIGHT ARROW)	Moves to next word.
(CTRL-LEFT ARROW)	Moves to previous word or beginning of the current word.
(HOME)	Moves to beginning of line.
(END)	Moves to end of line.
(CTRL-HOME)	Moves to beginning of note or item.
(CTRL-END)	Moves to end of note or item.
(DEL)	Deletes character at cursor.
(BACKSPACE)	Deletes character to left of cursor.
(CTRL-BACKSPACE)	Deletes word to left of cursor.
(CTRL-ENTER)	Deletes from cursor to end of line.
(INS)	Toggles between Insert mode (new characters push existing characters to the right) and Overstrike mode (new characters replace existing characters). This works only in a note attached to an item, not in the item itself. In an item, (INS) completes the edit and adds a new item.
(TAB)	Inserts spaces in a note to move cursor to next tab stop.

TABLE 2-1.   Cursor Movement Keys for Edit Mode

need to enter Edit mode with (F2) (Edit) and then press (END) to reach the end of a single-line item (or (CTRL-END) for a multiple-line item) before you start typing.

FUNCTION KEYS TO ASSIST WITH EDITING TASKS   Agenda provides several function key features to assist you during the edit process. As an example, you might want to remove part of an item. This requires several steps:

1. Move the highlight to the item and press (F2) to edit the item.

2. Move the cursor to the beginning of the text you want to remove and press (F7) (Mark).

3. Move the highlight until it covers the area to be removed and press (F4) (Cut) or (ALT-F4) (Delete).
    Agenda removes the highlighted area from the item immediately.

    If you press (F4) (Cut) without highlighting the area to be removed, Agenda displays a selection box to ask whether to delete the current word, the current line, or all text. Use the (UP ARROW) or (DOWN ARROW) key to cycle between the options and press (ENTER). Agenda will remove either the word, the line, or the entire item.

4. After cutting text with (F4) (Cut) you can use (F2) (Paste) to paste the cut text back into the item at the cursor location. Text cut with (ALT-F4) (Delete) cannot be pasted back after deletion.

SPLITTING AN ITEM   Occasionally you may want to split an item into two separate items. For example, you might decide to split the first item you entered in your company policy statement. This would be accomplished with the following steps:

1. Highlight the item that you want to split.
    You can use the (UP ARROW) or (DOWN ARROW) keys to move between items.

2. Press (F2) (Edit) to activate the Edit mode.

3. Move the cursor to where you want to split the item and press (ALT-F7) (Split).

4. Press (ENTER).

TRYING A SPLIT-AND-EDIT EXAMPLE   Try now to split the first item entry into two different items. To have each item read as a full sentence, you will need to edit after the split. Follow these instructions to complete the edit-and-split operation:

1. Move the highlight to the first item.

2. Press (F2) (Edit) to enter Edit mode.

3. Move the cursor within the item text to the position between the words "department" and "and".

4. Press (ALT-F7) to split the item into two items.
   You are in the second of the two items and are still in Edit mode.

5. Press (CTRL-HOME) or (HOME) to move to the beginning of the second line in the item, press (UP ARROW) once, and then press (DEL) four times to remove the space and the word "and."

6. Type **Travel reservations** and press (ENTER).

7. Press (UP ARROW) and then press (F2) (Edit).

8. Press (END) followed by (DOWN ARROW) and type . (period)

9. Press (ENTER) to finalize the item entry.

You now have four items in your file, as shown in Figure 2-3.

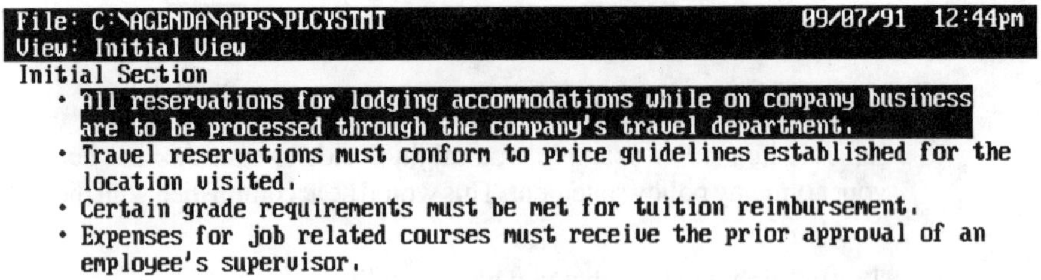

```
File: C:\AGENDA\APPS\PLCYSTMT                      09/07/91   12:44pm
View: Initial View
Initial Section
   • All reservations for lodging accommodations while on company business
     are to be processed through the company's travel department.
   • Travel reservations must conform to price guidelines established for the
     location visited.
   • Certain grade requirements must be met for tuition reimbursement.
   • Expenses for job related courses must receive the prior approval of an
     employee's supervisor.
```

FIGURE 2-3.   Items after split-and-edit operation

WORKING WITH NOTES

Agenda's note feature allows you to expand the information associated with any item. Your notes can be as large as 10K (about 10,000 characters) or approximately five printed pages of information. You can add a note to an item any time you want additional detail or clarification for an item. For example, you can use the note feature to attach additional information that explains a company policy in your file in more depth. Or, if you are using Agenda to assist in planning your day-to-day activities, you could add a listing of the specific points you want to cover in an item like "Call Bill Jones today."

Creating a Note for an Item

You can create a note for the last item in your PLCYSTMT file in the following manner:

1. Highlight the last item.

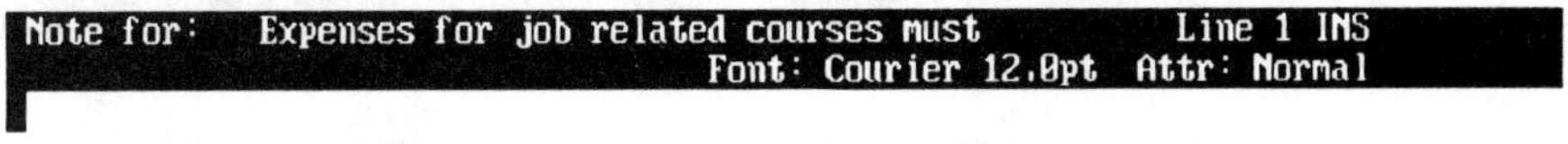

```
Note for:   Expenses for job related courses must        Line 1 INS
                        Font: Courier 12.0pt  Attr: Normal
```

FIGURE 2-4.   Blank note screen

2. Press (F5).

    Agenda provides a blank note screen like the one in Figure 2-4 or displays any existing note attached to the item already.

3. Type the following:

    To be reimbursed for courses taken, an employee must meet the following qualifications:

    Agenda adds this information to your screen and word wraps the text for you.

4. Type the additional text shown in Figure 2-5 to complete the note.

    To move around within a note, use the same keystrokes that you use when editing an item, as described in Table 2-1. Since notes can contain up to 10 pages of text, these keys are even more important in order to review the contents of longer notes quickly.

5. Press (F5) to finalize the note.

    This takes you back to the item and the view where you requested the note entry. Instead of a dot, a musical note now appears to the left of the item to which

---

```
Note for:    Expenses for job related courses must         Line 8 INS
                              Font: Courier 12.0pt   Attr: Normal
To be reimbursed for courses taken, an employee must meet the following
qualifications:

1. The course must be a college level course with an accredited institution.
2. The employee must inform his supervisor before enrolling in the course.
3. The course must pertain to his profession. An exception will be made for
courses taken to fulfill the degree requirements for a degree that pertains to
his profession.█
```

FIGURE 2-5.   Note text

you added the note. This musical note remains at the left margin and also appears in the right corner of the control panel whenever the highlight is on an item that has a note attached.

The Note Menu

When a note is active on your Agenda screen, you can activate a special note menu that allows you to perform various tasks with the text in the current note. You can print the note, import or export data to the note, clear the note from the file, or quit and leave the Agenda program. Printing from the note will be discussed in Chapter 5. The example that follows shows you how to clear a note from your screen. First you must create a new note.

1. Highlight the third item in your PLCYSTMT file.

    This item states that "Certain grade requirements must be met for tuition reimbursement."

2. Press (F5). A blank note screen appears.

3. Type **The employee must receive a grade of "C" or better.**

    You can now try to clear this note from the file.

1. Press (F10).

2. Use the (RIGHT ARROW) key to highlight the Clear command and press (ENTER) or type **c** to select it.

    Agenda asks if you want to "Clear all text from the note? Yes". If you use the (DOWN ARROW) key to respond "no" and move to the next step you are returned to the note screen and the Clear command is canceled.

3. Press (ENTER).

    Agenda erases the note from the file and returns you to a blank note screen. You can then enter new information for a note or return to the main file by pressing (F10). Remember that selecting Clear will erase the entire note, and it cannot be brought back with (F2) (Paste).

ADDING DATA TO AN EXISTING FILE

You can add notes and items to an existing file after you open the file. Use the same procedures that you used earlier when creating a new file to enter information into an existing Agenda file. The only difference is that the file you have been working with in this chapter has only one section where you enter all the items. Other files may have multiple sections. When adding items to multi-section files, you will have to choose which section you want the item to appear in and place the item in that section. You can press (ALT-F5) to list and select a section to go to in the view. You will learn more about views in Chapter 4.

MARKING ITEMS

While using Agenda there will be times when you will want to mark certain Agenda items in order to perform specific activities on them. For example, you may want to print an Agenda file and include only certain items in the hard copy you are planning to distribute within the organization. As you are introduced to additional Agenda features in later chapters, you will see more occasions where the mark feature will help you get the most from your Agenda files.

Figure 2-6 shows how your Agenda screen appears when you have marked certain items in your file. The first and fourth items in the file have been marked in this figure. Notice the large diamond that appears before each of the marked items. Also notice in the upper-right corner of the screen that Agenda tells you that the currently highlighted item, the fourth item, has a note attached, and that at least one item in the file has been marked. The symbol indicating that an item is marked will remain as long as any item is marked, no matter which item in the file is current. This will serve as a reminder that you marked items even if you navigated far away from the marked item.

The following steps demonstrate how to mark items in your PLCYSTMT file that you have created in this chapter:

1. Highlight the first item in your file.

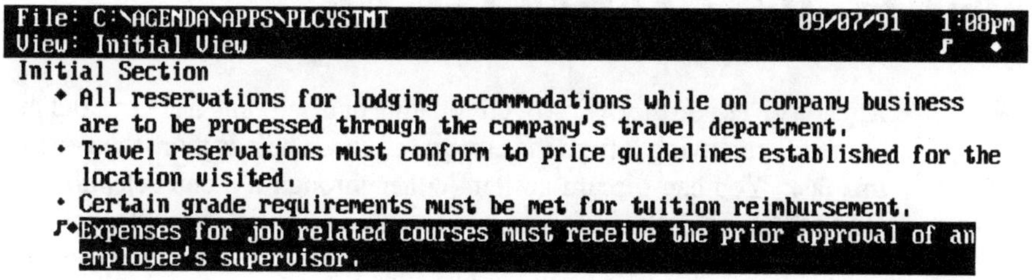

```
File: C:\AGENDA\APPS\PLCYSTMT                           09/07/91   1:00pm
View: Initial View                                              ♪    ◆
Initial Section
    ◆ All reservations for lodging accommodations while on company business
      are to be processed through the company's travel department.
    · Travel reservations must conform to price guidelines established for the
      location visited.
    · Certain grade requirements must be met for tuition reimbursement.
   ♪◆Expenses for job related courses must receive the prior approval of an
      employee's supervisor.
```

FIGURE 2-6.   Marked items with diamonds

2. Press (F7) (Mark).

    Agenda places a large diamond next to the item. Also notice that a diamond is shown in the upper-right corner of the screen.

3. Use (DOWN ARROW) to move the highlight to the last item in your file.

4. Press (F7) (Mark).

    Once again Agenda marks the item with a diamond and shows both a diamond and a note symbol in the upper-right portion of the screen.

5. Press the (ALT-J) key combination. You must hold down the (ALT) key while pressing the (J) key.

    This feature moves the highlighted area between only the marked items in your file. This is particularly useful when you have marked items that do not appear on the screen at the same time and you want to edit, add, or modify a note, or perform some other activity on one of the marked items.

6. Press (ALT-F7) (UnmkAll).

    Agenda has now unmarked all the items in your file. Your screen now appears the same as it did when you began this section.

DELETING ITEM DATA

Agenda gives you the option of eliminating or discarding an item from the file entirely or merely removing it from the current section. There is more than one way to handle this task. You can discard an item either through a menu selection or by pressing (ALT-F4) (Discard). To discard an item with a menu selection, follow these steps:

1. Position the highlight on the item that you wish to remove and press (F10) (Menu).

2. Type **I** to select Item.

3. Type **D** to select Discard.
   Agenda displays the confirmation box shown here:

```
┌─────────────────────────────────────────────┐
│                                             │
│ Discard this item?  Yes                     │
│   ─── Press ENTER to accept, ESC to cancel ─── │
└─────────────────────────────────────────────┘
```

4. Press (ENTER) to remove the item from the file permanently, or press (ESC) to cancel the request.

If you have used the item in multiple categories (covered in Chapter 3), pressing (ALT-F4) (Discard) causes Agenda to remove the item across the entire file.

You can use the (DEL) key as a shortcut that is less permanent than Discard. Pressing (DEL) removes the current item. If an item marked to be deleted appears in multiple sections, it is deleted only from the section that is highlighted when you make the request. If any item in the file is marked, pressing the (DEL) key produces a confirmation box that reads "Remove :Marked Items". You can press (SPACEBAR) to delete the current item instead if desired. Pressing (ALT-F4) (Discard) with items marked presents a similar confirmation box.

USING THE SEARCH-AND-REPLACE FEATURES

Agenda permits you to search items and notes for a text string of up to 24 characters. From a note you also have the option of specifying Replace Text String, which will replace the original character string in the note with a string you specify. The display and options of the Search screen differ depending on whether you are in an item or note when the feature is invoked.

Searching Text Strings in Items

You can ask Agenda to search for the first occurrence of a text string in items from the View mode. Perform the following steps to search for a string in your PLCYSTMT file:

1. Highlight the first item in the file and press (**ALT-F6**) (Search).
   Agenda presents a dialog box like the one in Figure 2-7.

2. Type **Expenses for job related** and press (**ENTER**).

3. Use (**DOWN ARROW**) to move to the Match On selection.
   The default setting is Item Text.

4. Press (**F3**) to see the other options.
   You can select Item Text, Note Text, or Both Item & Note. If you wanted to change the default option you would highlight the desired option and press (**ENTER**).

5. Press (**ESC**) to return to the Search screen.

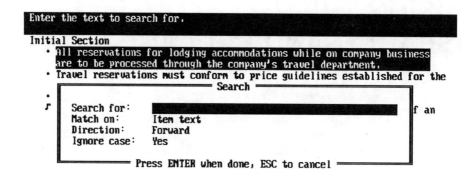

Enter the text to search for.

Initial Section
• All reservations for lodging accommodations while on company business
  are to be processed through the company's travel department.
• Travel reservations must conform to price guidelines established for the
  •   Search
  ♪   Search for: f an
         Match on: Item text
         Direction: Forward
         Ignore case: Yes
              Press ENTER when done, ESC to cancel

FIGURE 2-7.   Dialog box for searching item text

6. Use (**DOWN ARROW**) to move to the Direction option.

7. Press (**F3**) to see the other options.
    Forward moves from the current cursor location toward the bottom of the
    document as it searches. Backward moves from the current location of the cursor
    toward the beginning of the text. The Search from the beginning option starts from
    the beginning of the file and works down to the first match.

8. Press (**ESC**) to return to the Search screen.

9. Move with the (**DOWN ARROW**) key to the current setting for Ignore Case.

10. Press (**F3**) to see the other option.
    The Yes option tells Agenda to ignore the upper- and lowercase of the letters
    you typed in your search string. The No option tells Agenda that you want an exact
    match of upper- and lowercase letters.

11. Press (**ESC**) to return to the Search screen.

12. Press (**ENTER**) to start the search.
    When Agenda finds an item with matching text, it highlights the item and
    presents the dialog box shown in Figure 2-8. You can search for the next matching

```
File: C:\AGENDA\APPS\PLCYSTMT                          09/07/91
View: Initial View
Initial Section
        • All reservations for lodging accommodations while on company business
          are to be processed through the company's travel department.
        • Travel reservations must conform to price guidelines established for the
          location visited.
        • Certain grade requirements must be met for tuition reimbursement.
      ♪ Expenses for job related courses must receive the prior approval of an
        employee's supervisor.

              ┌──────────────Continue Search─────────────┐
              │                                          │
              │ Searching for: Expenses for job related  │
              │ Press ALT-N for next match, ALT-P for previous, F7 to mark. │
              │                                          │
              └────────Press ENTER when done, ESC to cancel────────┘
```

FIGURE 2-8.   Message box with information for continuing the search

entry by simply pressing (ALT-N). If Agenda cannot find any more matches, you will get a message stating "Agenda couldn't find any matches for the text you entered". If you are on the last line, Agenda only beeps. At this point you can press any key and Agenda returns you to the last highlighted item.

13. Press (ENTER) to complete the search.

Searching and Replacing Text in Notes

With a note in view on the screen, you can have Agenda search quickly for a text string in up to 10 pages of the note. You can search from the cursor location toward the end or the beginning of the current note. This allows you to invoke a search without having to reposition the cursor before beginning. You can also choose to use or ignore case in entries. With the replacement feature, you can choose whether to replace every occurrence of the text string or just the first occurrence. You can also confirm the replacement before Agenda makes the change.

You can also search for entries in note text when you do not have a note open. You can set Match On to "Note Text" or "Both item and note". When a match is found, the item to which the note is attached is highlighted. If you wish to search for the exact location of the text within the note, open the note and press (ALT-F6) (Search) again.

SEARCHING FOR TEXT WITHIN A NOTE   A completed search operation places the cursor on the first occurrence of the search string if a match is found. To find the next match, you must press (ALT-F6) (Search) again since each search finds only one occurrence. If there are no more matches, you hear a beep.

Follow these steps to locate a text string in a note:

1. Highlight the last item in your PLCYSTMT file that has a note attached and press (F5).

    The note attached to the item now appears on your screen.

2. Press (ALT-F6) (Search).

    A dialog box like the completed sample shown in Figure 2-9 appears on your screen. You can type a string of up to 24 characters that you want to locate in the note.

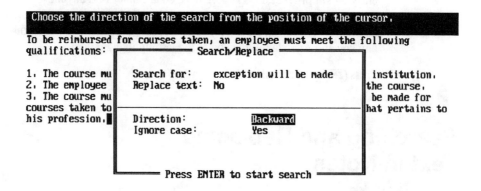

FIGURE 2-9.   Replace dialog box for notes

3. Type **exception will be made** and press (ENTER).

4. Check to ensure that the Replace text option is set to No. If it is not, move to this option and press (F3) to change the setting to No.

5. Move to the Direction setting and press (F3) to change the setting to Backward.

6. Move to the Ignore Case option and make sure it is set to Yes.

7. Press (ENTER) after completing the setting to locate a match for the text string. If you hear a beep, Agenda could not find a match.

8. To look for the next occurrence, press (ALT-F6) and (ENTER). If you hear a beep and see a message, Agenda could not find another match.

9. Press (ESC) to return to the item display.

REPLACING NOTE TEXT   To replace text in notes you follow the same basic process as searching except that you have a few more decisions and entries to make. Follow these steps to replace text in a note in your file:

1. Highlight the last item in your PLCYSTMT file and press (F5).

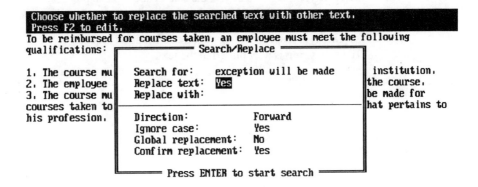

FIGURE 2-10.   Specifying the text to search for

2. Press (**ALT-F6**) (Search).
   The screen shown in Figure 2-9 appears.

3. Type **exception will be made** and press (**ENTER**).

4. Press (**DOWN ARROW**) to highlight Replace text and type **Y** or press the (**SPACEBAR**)
   to change the option to Yes.
      Your screen should look like Figure 2-10.

5. Press (**DOWN ARROW**) to highlight Replace with.

6. Type **exception may be made** and press (**ENTER**).

7. Leave the remaining options in their preset options.

   Agenda assumes that you only want to replace the text the first time the match is
found. If you want the text replacement to occur throughout the document, you must
highlight the Global Replacement option and type **Y** to change the option to Yes.
   The last option you can set is the Confirm Replacement option. The default is Yes.
This means that Agenda will provide you a dialog box asking you to confirm the
replacement. You will see this box when you complete the next steps. If you wish to
turn the confirm feature off, highlight the option with the (**DOWN ARROW**) key and type
N. Agenda will make the changes without asking you for confirmation.

8. Press (**ENTER**) and Agenda begins the search and replace process.
      If an error message displays, try changing the direction of the search.

9. Press (**ENTER**) in response to Agenda's confirmation request.
      The new string is now placed in the text.

3

CATEGORIES

Every day you are exposed to many different pieces of information. Mentally you categorize this information to better remember and understand it. In many instances, information is slotted into a more specific category because it pertains to sales leads, a salary increase, a price reduction on a particular make of cars, or any of hundreds of other types of information.

A category is one of the tools used within Agenda to make items (information) more meaningful. Categories are used in much the same way as you would mentally categorize pieces of information. You might not enter items into your Agenda database in any specific order. You could enter them as you think of them, as they occur during the day, or in any other haphazard fashion. Later, the items would be more useful if they were organized with related information appearing together.

Agenda allows you to assign items of information to one or more categories. Agenda can even make automatic assignments to categories for you. Once items are assigned to categories, the items can be displayed in views by one or more categories.

Thus categories can organize data by grouping related pieces of information. They can improve recall of an individual item because the categorization often enhances the meaning of the data. Also, categories often provide a clearer overview of a specific knowledge area because all the related information pertaining to the family of items appears within the same classification.

This chapter covers the specifics of Agenda's category features. You will learn how to create categories that provide a relationship between items and how to assign items to one or more categories. You will learn how to add columns to the display to show additional category assignments. As the category structure for your files evolves, you will learn to create families of related categories. Most important, you will learn to adapt the category hierarchies you create to your ever-changing data management needs.

THE CONCEPT
OF CATEGORIES

Categories in Agenda can be words, names, phrases, or numbers. Each category that you create can consist of as many as 69 characters, and you can create as many categories as you need to organize your data.

You can create categories that are all on the same level. All these categories would be grouped under the default level of Main, which is included in any Agenda file or database that you create. If all the categories you put in the database are on the same level, they might look something like this:

```
Main
       Initial Section
       Contacts
       Promotions
       Volume
```

You can retain the initial categories of Main and Initial Section, or you can use other names for them. You can also create different levels in your category structure. These different levels allow you to create a hierarchy similar to an outline with main headings and more detailed topic headings beneath them. As you add new levels, you might revise the previous category hierarchy to look something like this:

Sales Data
    Background Information
        Company
        Personnel
            Sales managers
            Sales staff
    Contacts
    Promotions
        Regional
        Branch
    Volume
        Current year
        Historical data

In this hierarchy there are four major categories under Sales Data, and most of these categories now have levels beneath them. Categories with levels beneath them are called *parent* categories, and the categories below them are called *children*. In the sample hierarchy Company and Personnel are children of the category Background Information.

Just as in real families, children may have their own children. For example, in the hierarchy shown, Personnel is a child of Background Information; it is also a parent category since it has two children beneath it. The child categories under the same parent category are considered *siblings* of each other. This allows a hierarchy to have many different levels. The hierarchy that you use for your database is determined by the data and your preferences. As the database and your needs change, you can change the structure of the hierarchy to meet those needs.

CREATING A NEW CATEGORY

Agenda has two ways of showing categories within a view: using section heads or columns. You can see both of these methods as you take a quick look at some items in a company policy file. When you look at categories as the headings for a section, you see the assigned items listed beneath the section head, as shown here:

```
File: C:\AGENDA\APPS\EX1CH3                               09/09/90   9:49pm
View: Types of Policies
Software
    • Unauthorized copying of company software is not allowed
    • Software is only to be used on the computer for which it is licensed
```

The items under Software are assigned to that category.

When you look at categories as column headings and column entries, the items are assigned to the corresponding column entries. In this example, both items are assigned to the Company Policy category:

```
Software                                        Company Policy
    • Unauthorized copying of company software is not    ·Unauthorized Copying
      allowed
    • Software is only to be used on the computer for    ·Unauthorized Use
      which it is licensed
```

The first item is assigned to the Unauthorized Copying category, which is a child of Company Policy.

As you saw in the first example, a section in an Agenda database consists of a category followed by all the items that belong to it. A column requires a little more work and is a more sophisticated structure since it includes both parent and child categories. To distinguish the two options, think of a column as a series of vertical entries that show additional category assignments for items in a section of the database.

Once you understand that items can be categorized within views using section heads and columns, assigning items to different categories is simple. All you need to do is add section heads and/or columns to views of your Agenda database.

Adding a Section

Adding a category to an Agenda database is as easy as setting up a new section of the database. Initially a section contains only the category name. Later you can add, move, assign, or copy items to this section. Figure 3-1 shows an Agenda database with two sections. The first two items are assigned to the Quick Jobs category, and the last two items are assigned to the Writing category.

```
File: C:\AGENDA\APPS\TODOLIST                        09/07/90  11:08am
View: Initial View
Quick Jobs
    • Schedule meeting for the Planning Committee
    • Call Jim S. to plan the scheduled Miller presentation

Writing
    • Develop proposal for Whytt Corporation
    • First draft of word processing chapter for network user manual
```

FIGURE 3-1.   Agenda database using two categories as section heads

Try now to create the database shown in Figure 3-1. Start by creating an Agenda database named TODOLIST. Review Chapter 2 if you have forgotten how to do this. Initially, the first section head is named Initial Section. Change the name of this section head (which changes the name of the category) as follows:

1. Move the highlight to the section head Initial Section and press (F2) (Edit) to change the category name.

2. Press (CTRL-ENTER) to delete the Initial Section entry. You can accomplish the same task by pressing (DEL) 15 times.

3. Type **Quick Jobs** and press (ENTER) to exit Edit mode.

The section head Quick Jobs should now be displayed at the top of the database. Add the first item assigned to the category Quick Jobs by typing **Schedule meeting for the Planning Committee** and press (ENTER). This creates the first item. Add the second item by typing **Call Jim S. to plan the scheduled Miller presentation** and press (ENTER). When you have finished, your screen should look like the top half of Figure 3-1. Now you are ready to create a second category using section heads for your database.

When you add the Writing category, it will be created as a sibling category of Quick Jobs. You can move the category or change its level in the category hierarchy. When

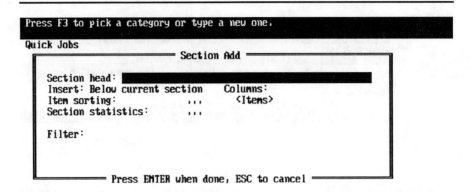

Press F3 to pick a category or type a new one.

Quick Jobs

┌─────────────────────── Section Add ───────────────────────┐
│   │
│ Section head: ████████████████████████████████████   │
│ Insert: Below current section   Columns: │
│ Item sorting: ...   <Items>   │
│ Section statistics: ...   │
│   │
│ Filter: │
│   │
│   │
│   │
│   ════════ Press ENTER when done, ESC to cancel ════════ │
└───┘

F1	F2	F3	F4	F5	F6	F7	F8	F9	F10
Help	Edit	Choices			Props		Default		

FIGURE 3-2.   Adding a section head to a database

you change a category's level you can promote it or demote it. A new category is always added as a sibling of the current category when added from View mode.

To add a category as a new section heading, use the following steps:

1. Press (F10) (Menu).

2. Select View Section Add by using the arrow keys and (ENTER) or by typing the first letter of the words (**VSA**). The Section Add dialog box displayed in Figure 3-2 appears on your screen. If you want to use a shortcut approach, try the accelerator keys (ALT-D) and (ALT-U) depending on whether you want the section below or above the current section, respectively.

3. Type **Writing** and press (ENTER).

If the category Writing had already existed within your database, you could have avoided typing in the category for the section head by pressing (F3) (Choices) to see a listing of all the categories, highlighting the Writing category, and selecting it as the section head name. For this example, however, no Writing category was previously defined. Thus, you create the category as you type in the name of your section head.

4. Accepting the default responses for the other settings, press (ENTER) to indicate you are done with this box.

Now you are ready to add the two items associated with the Writing category. Type **Develop proposal for Whytt Corporation** and press (ENTER). Type **First draft of word processing chapter for network user manual** and press (ENTER). Your screen should now look similar to Figure 3-1.

Adding a Column

Agenda supports several types of column entries. In this chapter you will learn to use column options that affect the display of categories. You add a column to a view by making entries in a dialog box or by using the accelerator keys (ALT-L) or (ALT-R) to add a left or right column, respectively. The variety of options available makes it seem like a more lengthy process than it actually is. To continue creating our TODOLIST database, follow these steps to add a column to your database view:

1. Press (F10) (Menu).

2. Select View Column Add by using the arrow keys and (ENTER) or by typing the first letter of the words (**VCA**). The Column Add dialog box displayed in Figure 3-3 appears on your screen.

3. Type **People** as the category for Column head and press (ENTER).

If the category People had already existed within your database, you could have avoided typing in the category for the column heading by pressing (F3) (Choices) to see a listing of all the categories, highlighting the People category, and selecting it as the column name. For this example, however, no People category has been previously defined. Thus, you create the category as you type in the name of your column head.

If any of the default settings for adding a column were inappropriate, you would highlight the setting and make a selection. The Category Type setting will be discussed in later chapters. The Width setting refers to how many characters will be made available to display the column entries. The default for a standard category is 12. The Position setting refers to the location of the new column relative to the highlight. The Insert In setting allows you the choice of having the new column appear in all sections of the view or just the section where the highlight is located. The Format setting will be discussed later in this chapter.

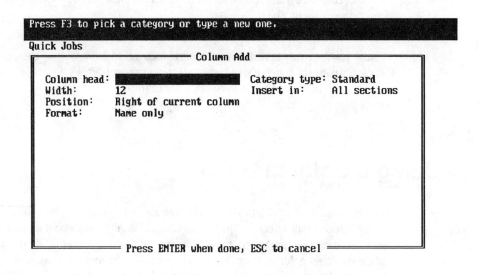

FIGURE 3-3.   The Column Add dialog box

4. Accept the default values for adding a column by pressing (**ENTER**) to indicate you are done with this box. Your screen should appear similar to Figure 3-4.

ASSIGNING ITEMS TO CATEGORIES USING COLUMNS

You can use a column to show existing category assignments or to create additional assignments. Although adding the People column created a new category and provided a means of displaying existing assignments, the items are not assigned to the People category by adding the new column. Entries must be made under the People column that correspond to the items. These entries will be child categories of People.

```
File: C:\AGENDA\APPS\TODOLIST                    09/07/90  11:21am
View: Initial View
Quick Jobs                                       People
   • Schedule meeting for the Planning Committee
   • Call Jim S. to plan the scheduled Miller presentation

Writing                                          People
   • Develop proposal for Whytt Corporation
   ➤ First draft of word processing chapter for network user
     manual
```

FIGURE 3-4.   Adding a People column to the database

Entering Category Names

To assign the first item in the Quick Jobs section to a category named Jim, do the following:

1. Using the cursor keys, highlight the location under the People column and next to the Schedule meeting item.

2. Type **Jim** and press (**ENTER**). Your screen should appear similar to Figure 3-5.

Jim is now a category that has an item assigned to it. Since the People category is a parent of the Jim category, this item is considered assigned to both the Jim and People categories.

Using Agenda's Automatic Completion Features

You will now assign the second item of the database to the Jim category. Because this category was previously defined, Agenda will try to save you keystrokes by evaluating what you are typing and prompting you with a beep when it thinks it might have a

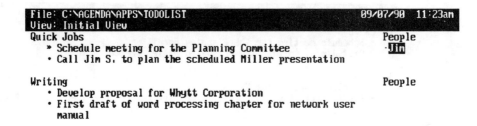

```
File: C:\AGENDA\APPS\TODOLIST                        09/07/90  11:23am
View: Initial View
Quick Jobs                                                     People
  » Schedule meeting for the Planning Committee                -Jim
  • Call Jim S. to plan the scheduled Miller presentation

Writing                                                        People
  • Develop proposal for Whytt Corporation
  • First draft of word processing chapter for network user
    manual
```

FIGURE 3-5.   Assigning items to children of the People category

match. It checks for matches on a letter-by-letter basis. If there is more than one possible match, it prompts you with the one that comes first alphabetically.

Agenda uses the following procedure when you type in a category:

• Using what you have typed in, Agenda prompts you on the first line of the screen with what it thinks the category may be. To choose the category displayed in the prompt, press (ENTER).

• Agenda may make a high-pitched beep. This indicates that Agenda has narrowed the possible matches of category names and typed material to a single choice. To accept this choice, press (ENTER). To reject the choice, ignore the beep and continue typing.

• Agenda may make a low-pitched beep. This indicates that Agenda has determined that what you have already typed in does not match anything in that group of categories. Continue typing in the name of the category unless you expected a match. If you expected a match, check for spelling errors.

Assign the second item in the database to the Jim category using the automatic completion feature as follows:

1. Press the (DOWN ARROW) key to move to the second entry under the People column. This position should be at the same horizontal position as the Call Jim item.

2. Type **J** to start the entry of the category Jim. The computer should beep. Using what you have typed in, Agenda prompts you on the first line of the screen with Jim as a possible category.

3. To accept the Jim category displayed in the prompt, press (ENTER).

The first two items of the database have both been assigned to the Jim category under People.

Showing Multiple Categories For an Item in a Column

Sometimes you will need to have an item assigned to more than one category within a column. For example, the first item in our database refers to scheduling a planning committee meeting. Since it is highly likely that more than one person is a member of the planning committee, you might want to list all members under the People column.

Add other People assignments to the first item now:

1. Move the highlight to the first Jim under the People column using the cursor keys.

2. Type **C**. Agenda beeps because it is using its automatic completion features. Since you are adding a new category to the database, continue typing **arol** and press (ENTER). You have now assigned a second member to the planning committee in the first item.

3. To add a third member, type **Joyce** and press (ENTER).

At this point, your screen should look like Figure 3-6.

Using the Select Category Dialog Box to Assign Categories

You have seen how Agenda uses an automatic completion feature to save keystrokes as you enter categories into your database. Another time-saving feature lists the defined categories and allows you to make selections.

You are going to assign the first item in the Writing section to Joyce. Instead of typing in **Joyce**, follow these steps to have Agenda list the possible choices for you:

1. Using the cursor keys, highlight the empty People entry next to the Whytt Corporation item.

```
File: C:\AGENDA\APPS\TODOLIST                          09/10/90  12:54am
View: Initial View
Quick Jobs                                             People
   • Schedule meeting for the Planning Committee       ·Jim
                                                        Carol
                                                        Joyce
   • Call Jim S. to plan the scheduled Miller presentation  ·Jim

Writing                                                People
   » Develop proposal for Whytt Corporation            ████████████
   • First draft of word processing chapter for network user
     manual
```

FIGURE 3-6.   Assigning multiple categories to one item

2. Press (F3) (Choices). A Select Category dialog box similar to the one in Figure 3-7 should appear on your screen.

3. Use the cursor keys to highlight Joyce, or use Agenda's automatic completion feature by beginning to type the entry. Press the (SPACEBAR) to select the category Joyce.

   An asterisk appears next to the category selection. If you wanted to make additional selections at this time, you would do so by highlighting each selection and pressing the (SPACEBAR). To eliminate a selection, you just highlight the asterisked category and press the (SPACEBAR) since it toggles between select and deselect.

4. Press (ENTER) to accept Joyce as your choice.

Moving Items to Change Their Assignment

If the category you wish to assign items to is a section in the current view, you can move the items to the section to assign them. Moving an item unassigns it from the current section and assigns it to the new section.

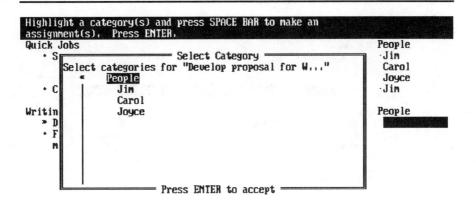

FIGURE 3-7.   Selecting categories from a list of defined categories

For this example, change the second item in the Quick Jobs section to read **Develop the script for the Miller presentation**. To do this, follow these steps:

1. Highlight the item using the cursor keys.

2. Press (F2) (Edit) to edit the item.

3. Using (DEL), delete the first seven words.

4. Type **Develop the script for the** and press (ENTER) to accept the edited item.

When this item was originally entered, it was appropriately categorized as a Quick Job. Now that the scope of the task has been modified, it no longer belongs in the Quick Jobs section of the database although Agenda has not changed its category assignment. Since it requires writing, you will move it to the Writing section. To do this, follow these instructions:

1. Make sure the item is still highlighted. If not, use the cursor keys to highlight the item.

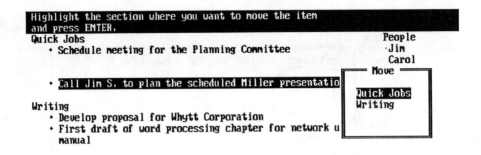

FIGURE 3-8.   Moving an item from one section to another

2. Press (ALT-F10) (Move). A Move dialog box similar to the one in Figure 3-8 appears.

3. Use the (ARROW) keys to highlight the Writing section category.

4. Press (ENTER) to accept the location of the new section. Your screen should now look like Figure 3-9.

Occasionally you will want to move more than one item at a time to the same section. The process is similar to the one just described with a couple of additional steps. You would first individually highlight each item to be moved and press (F7) (Mark) to mark the item. Once all items to be moved are marked, press (ALT-F10) (Move). A dialog box similar to the one in Figure 3-10 would ask if you want to move the marked items. Press (ENTER) to accept. A Move dialog box appears listing the current sections. Highlight the section head where the marked items are to be moved and press (ENTER).

If an item was also previously assigned to another section, that assignment is not affected by the move.

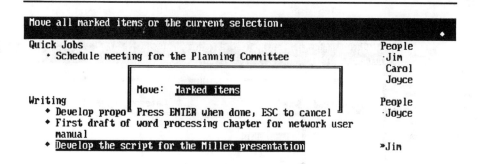

FIGURE 3-9.   Database screen after moving an item from the Quick Jobs section to the Writing section

FIGURE 3-10.   Moving marked items to one section

CHANGING THE FORMAT OF CATEGORY DATA IN COLUMNS

Earlier in this chapter you created a column using the People category. One of the default values you accepted for the column was the Format setting. There are six possible format choices for columns. The default format is the Name Only format that you used with the People column (see Figure 3-3). You are now going to explore another format called Yes/No.

To add another column to the TODOLIST database, do the following:

1. Press (F10) (Menu).

2. Select View Column Add by using the (ARROW) keys and pressing (ENTER) or by typing the first letter of the words (VCA).

3. Type **Done?** as the category for Column head and press (ENTER).

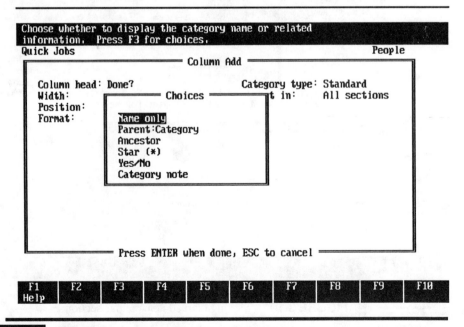

FIGURE 3-11.   Format choices for columns

The ? is an important addition since the entry auto-completes for the first four characters and is only made unique from an existing entry by the ? character. This is because there is already a category called Done without the ?.

4. Press (DOWN ARROW) three times to highlight the Format setting. Press (F3) (Choices) to display a listing of the choices for the Format, as shown in Figure 3-11.

5. Highlight the Yes/No selection by pressing (DOWN ARROW) four times, or allow Agenda to auto-complete your entry by typing a **y**. Press (ENTER) to accept your selection.

6. Highlight the Width setting, type **5**, and press (ENTER) to make the column 5 characters wide. You can also change the column width either up or down with the gray + or - keys.

7. Press (ENTER) to accept your selections from the Column Add dialog box. Your screen should now be similar to Figure 3-12.

The only acceptable entries for a column formatted as Yes/No are **Y** or **N**. Table 3-1 describes all six different format selections.

```
File: C:\AGENDA\APPS\TODOLIST                          09/10/90   2:22am
View: Initial View
Quick Jobs                                            People       Done?
     • Schedule meeting for the Planning Committee     ·Jim          N
                                                        Carol
                                                        Joyce

Writing                                               People       Done?
     • Develop proposal for Whytt Corporation          ·Joyce        N
     • First draft of word processing chapter for network            N
       user manual
     » Call Jim S. to plan the scheduled Miller        ·Jim          N
       presentation
```

F1	F2	F3	F4	F5	F6	F7	F8	F9	F10
Help	Edit	Choices	Done	Note	Props	Mark	Vw Mgr	Cat Mgr	Menu

FIGURE 3-12.   Using a Yes/No Format for a column

Format Setting	Description
Name Only	Displays the actual category name in the column. If there are several descriptors for the column entry and the space is not large enough for the first one but is large enough for the second entry, the shorter word will appear.
Parent:Category	Both the parent category and the actual category appear in the column separated by a colon.
Ancestor	The child category of the column header is displayed for the item if the item belongs to a child category directly or through the property of inheritance.
Star (*)	An asterisk (*) in the column indicates that the item belongs to the category that is the column header or is one of the column header's child categories. Assignment made with (SPACEBAR) with highlight in * column.
Yes/No	A "Y" in the column indicates that the item belongs to the category that is the column header or one of that category's children. An "N" indicates otherwise.
Category note	Displays as much of the specified line number of a category note as can fit in the column width.

TABLE 3-1.   Format Selections for a Category Column

Even after you have added a column, you can change the format used to display data in the column. Changing the format of a column alters the way it looks, of course, but it may also change the method used to enter data in the column. To change the format of a column that already exists, position the highlight on the column to be formatted. Press (F10) (Menu) to activate the menu and select View Column Properties. Agenda displays a Column Properties dialog box that looks similar to the one you used to add a column. You can also place the highlight anywhere in the column, press (HOME), and then press (F6) (Properties).

EDITING CATEGORIES

Editing a category is no different from editing an item. Changes can be made to a category's name whether it is used as a section head, a column heading, or a column entry.

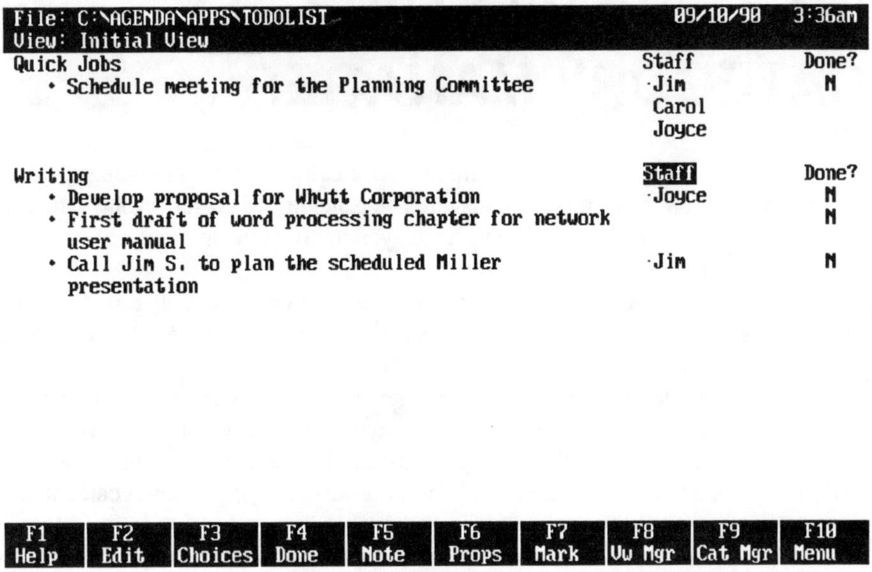

```
File: C:\AGENDA\APPS\TODOLIST                          09/10/90   3:36am
View: Initial View
Quick Jobs                                            Staff       Done?
   • Schedule meeting for the Planning Committee      ·Jim          N
                                                       Carol
                                                       Joyce

Writing                                               Staff       Done?
   • Develop proposal for Whytt Corporation           ·Joyce        N
   • First draft of word processing chapter for network            N
     user manual
   • Call Jim S. to plan the scheduled Miller         ·Jim          N
     presentation
```

```
 F1     F2     F3     F4     F5     F6     F7     F8     F9     F10
Help   Edit  Choices Done   Note  Props  Mark  Vw Mgr Cat Mgr Menu
```

FIGURE 3-13.   Editing the name of a column category in View mode

You can change the current category entry by pressing (F2) (Edit). Change the People column heading to Staff as follows:

1. Use the cursor keys to highlight one of the People column headers.

2. Press (F2) (Edit) to edit the name.

3. Delete the name People, type **Staff**, and press (ENTER). Your results should look like Figure 3-13. Note that all occurrences of the People category have been changed to Staff.

When you edit a category, you change its name. Any changes that you make will appear everywhere the category appears. Changing the category name in a column does not affect assignments unless the assignment is based on an old category name within the item text. If you type in a new category, the new category is added as a child category of the column header. Remember, typing a different category name when you are not in Edit mode assigns the current item to the category that you type.

WORKING WITH THE CATEGORY MANAGER

Agenda provides a direct method of creating and manipulating the data's structure through the Category Manager. The Category Manager displays the categories currently in the database and permits you to affect the hierarchical structure that relates them.

You can add, remove, and copy categories in the Category Manager just as you can in View mode. The Category Manager cannot assign items to categories, but it has some new features that are not available in View mode.

While in the Category Manager, you can rearrange categories into families by grouping them as children to a parent category. Child categories are immediately obvious because they are automatically indented to the right of the parent category. For example, in Figure 3-14, Jim, Carol, and Joyce are child categories to the parent category Staff.

You can change the level of categories within the hierarchy from the Category Manager. The Promote and Demote options handle this task quickly.

FIGURE 3-14.   Example of the Category Manager screen

Activating
The Category Manager

To leave View mode and enter the Category Manager, press (F9) (Cat Mgr). To return to View mode, press (F9) again. While in the Category Manager, (F9) is shown as To View; in the View mode key map, (F9) is shown as Cat Mgr.

Changing the Level
Of a Category

Agenda allows you to change the level of a category from the Category Manager. Raising a category to a higher level is called *promoting* the category, lowering its level is called *demoting* it. When you change the level of a category, it moves to the right if demoted or the left if promoted.

The database structure shown in Figure 3-14 illustrates the different levels of categories before making any changes. When a category within this structure is demoted, the Category Manager shows the change by indenting the demoted category. Demoting a category changes its relationship to surrounding ones by making it a child of the category above it. If the demoted category has children of its own, they become its siblings.

In this example, you are going to demote the Writing category.

1. Press (F9) (Cat Mgr) to go to the Category Manager.

2. Using the cursor keys, highlight the Writing category.

3. Demote the Writing category by pressing (F8) (Dem).

The following dialog box appears:

```
┌─────────────────────────────────────────────┐
│  Demote the category?   Yes                  │
│── Press ENTER to accept, ESC to cancel ──────│
└─────────────────────────────────────────────┘
```

4. Press (ENTER) to confirm that the Writing category is to be demoted. Notice that Writing has been tabbed to the right. It is now indented under the Quick Jobs category. This means Writing is now a child of Quick Jobs.

5. Return to the View mode by pressing (F9) (To View). The screen should now appear as in Figure 3-15.

Notice that all the items that appear in the Writing section also appear in the Quick Jobs section. The Quick Jobs section includes all items assigned to it and also to its children. Since the Writing category is now a child of Quick Jobs, Writing's assigned items are also contained in Quick Jobs.

Promoting a category raises it a level. When you promote a category, you change its relationship to the surrounding ones by making it a sibling of the category that was originally its parent. These changing relationships may cause some unexpected changes in the relationships in your database.

```
File: C:\AGENDA\APPS\TODOLIST                      09/10/90    3:58am
View: Initial View
Quick Jobs                                         Staff        Done?
 • Schedule meeting for the Planning Committee      ·Jim          N
                                                     Carol
                                                     Joyce
 • Develop proposal for Whytt Corporation           ·Joyce        N
 • First draft of word processing chapter for network             N
   user manual
 • Call Jim S. to plan the scheduled Miller         ·Jim          N
   presentation

Writing                                            Staff        Done?
 » Develop proposal for Whytt Corporation           ·Joyce       ▮N▮
 • First draft of word processing chapter for network            N
   user manual
 • Call Jim S. to plan the scheduled Miller         ·Jim          N
   presentation
```

```
 F1     F2      F3      F4     F5     F6      F7     F8      F9     F10
Help   Edit  Choices  Done   Note  Props   Mark  Vw Mgr Cat Mgr Menu
```

FIGURE 3-15.   Reassignment of items after demoting the Writing category

Adding and Deleting A Category Through The Category Manager

The Category Manager is convenient for adding new categories because it allows you to control exactly where in the hierarchy the new category is added. Adding categories from View mode does not offer the same level of flexibility.

Use the following steps to insert two new child categories called William and Bruce to Staff using the Category Manager:

1. Go to the Category Manager by pressing (F9) (Cat Mgr).

2. Place the cursor just above where you want the new category and press (INS). In this case, use the cursor keys to highlight Carol.

3. Press (INS).

4. Type **William** and press (ENTER).

5. Press (INS) again.

6. Type **Bruce** and press (ENTER).

The screen should look like Figure 3-16. Agenda assumes that the inserted category should be at the same level as the highlighted category. You may have noticed a row of dots where Agenda inserted the new category. You can insert a new category and promote or demote it at the same time by pressing (ALT-R) (Demote) or (ALT-L) (Promote).

This process of adding a category does not assign specific items to the new category. It simply makes the new category available as an option for automatic completion when you are typing a category assignment for an item or adding items to the file.

To delete a category from the hierarchy and the database, place the cursor over the category to be removed, press (DEL), and then press (ENTER) to accept the confirmation default of Yes. If items are attached to that category or if the category has children, Agenda warns you of this and asks for confirmation. Delete the Carol category in the database hierarchy as follows:

1. If you are not already in the Category Manager, press (F9) (Cat Mgr).

2. Highlight Carol using the cursor keys.

```
File: C:\AGENDA\APPS\TODOLIST
Category Manager
  MAIN
  * Entry
  * When
  * Done
    Quick Jobs
      Writing
    Staff
      Jim
      Carol
      William
      Bruce
      Joyce
    Done?
```

```
 F1      F2      F3      F4      F5      F6      F7      F8      F9      F10
Help    Edit                    Note   Props  Prm (←) Den (→) To View Menu
```

FIGURE 3-16.   Adding two categories to the hierarchy while in the
Category Manager

3. Press (DEL). The following confirmation dialog box appears on the screen:

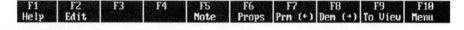

Category has assignments. Discard the category? Yes

Press ENTER to accept, ESC to cancel

4. Press (ENTER) to confirm that the category Carol is to be deleted.

5. Press (F9) (To View) to return to View mode. Notice that Carol is no longer
   assigned to the first item of the Quick Jobs section, as shown in Figure 3-17.

   Deleting a category with attached items deletes the accompanying items unless the
items are also assigned to other categories. If the deleted category has children, both
the category and its children are deleted.

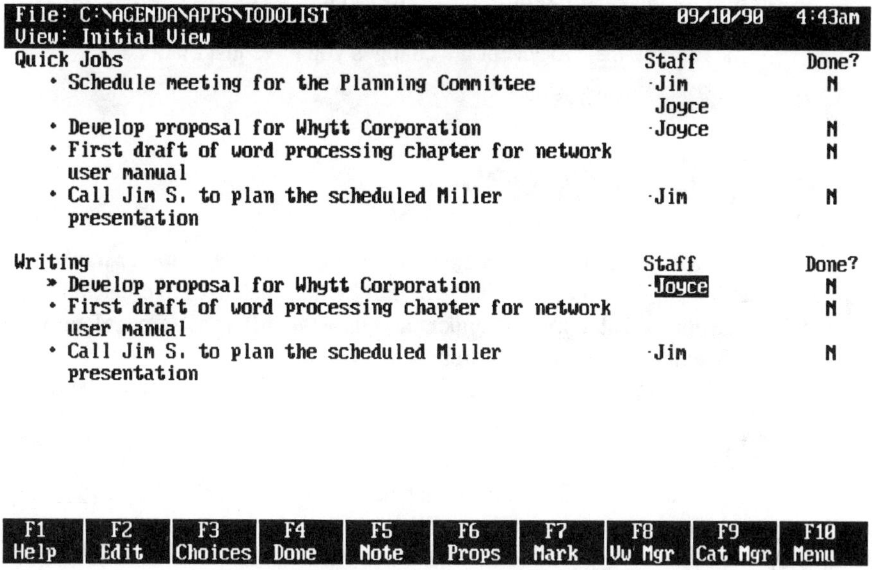

```
File: C:\AGENDA\APPS\TODOLIST                        09/10/90   4:43am
View: Initial View
Quick Jobs                                           Staff      Done?
 • Schedule meeting for the Planning Committee        ·Jim        N
                                                      Joyce
 • Develop proposal for Whytt Corporation             ·Joyce      N
 • First draft of word processing chapter for network            N
   user manual
 • Call Jim S. to plan the scheduled Miller           ·Jim        N
   presentation

Writing                                              Staff      Done?
 ➤ Develop proposal for Whytt Corporation             ·Joyce      N
 • First draft of word processing chapter for network            N
   user manual
 • Call Jim S. to plan the scheduled Miller           ·Jim        N
   presentation
```

F1	F2	F3	F4	F5	F6	F7	F8	F9	F10
Help	Edit	Choices	Done	Note	Props	Mark	Vw Mgr	Cat Mgr	Menu

FIGURE 3-17. Deleting Carol from the Category Manager results in her deletion from the database view

Changing a Category Name Through the Category Manager

Previously, you changed the name of the Initial Section category while you were in View mode. You can also edit a category name while in the Category Manager. As in View mode, editing the name of a category does not change an item's assignment to that category.

Changes made to a category appear anywhere the category does. To change the category name Joyce to Joy in the Category Manager, do the following:

1. If you are not already in the Category Manager, press (F9) (Cat Mgr).

2. Use the cursor keys to highlight the category Joyce or begin typing Joyce until Agenda auto-completes the entry and press (ENTER).

3. Press (F2) (Edit).

4. Use the cursor keys to move over to the "c" in Joyce. Press (DEL) twice.

5. Press (ENTER) to accept the changes you have just made.

Moving Categories

The Move feature in the Category Manager provides another method for promoting and demoting categories in the hierarchy. It is also used to create a logical diagram of categories that helps you understand how the different items relate. When you move a parent category, the children move with it.

You are now going to move the Staff category to the end of the hierarchy. Follow these steps:

1. While in the Category Manager, use the cursor keys to position the highlight on the Staff category.

2. Press (ALT-F10) (Move).

3. Highlight the Done? category, which is just above where you want to place the category.

4. Press (ENTER). Figure 3-18 shows the new position of the Staff family.

If you had wanted to place the category above the highlight instead of beneath it, you would have pressed (CTRL-ENTER) instead of (ENTER) in the last step.

Sorting Categories

Besides moving categories around in the hierarchy, Agenda provides a way to sort sibling categories in alphabetical order. This can make it easier to find particular categories when there is a long list of siblings.

The steps required to sort the siblings within the Staff category are as follows:

1. While you are in the Category Manager, place the highlight over the Staff category, which is a parent category.

```
File: C:\AGENDA\APPS\TODOLIST
Category Manager
  MAIN
  * Entry
  * When
  * Done
    Quick Jobs
      Writing
    Done?
    Staff
    Jim
    William
    Bruce
    Joy
```

F1	F2	F3	F4	F5	F6	F7	F8	F9	F10
Help	Edit			Note	Props	Prm (←)	Dem (→)	To View	Menu

FIGURE 3-18. Moving the Staff family to the end of the category Manager screen

2. Press (**ALT-F5**) (Sort). The following confirmation dialog box appears:

Sort these categories? **Yes**

Press ENTER to accept, ESC to cancel

3. Confirm the sort by pressing (**ENTER**).

The sorted results appear in Figure 3-19. Agenda keeps track of which grandchildren, if any, belong to each of the children being sorted (for example, child categories of Jim). However, these categories are not alphabetized unless you press (**ALT-F5**) with Jim highlighted.

```
File: C:\AGENDA\APPS\TODOLIST
Category Manager
  MAIN
  * Entry
  * When
  * Done
    Quick Jobs
      Writing
    Done?
    Staff
      Bruce
      Jim
      Joy
      William
```

```
  F1  |  F2  |  F3  |  F4  |  F5  |  F6  |  F7  |  F8  |  F9  | F10
 Help | Edit |      |      | Note | Props|Prm (←)|Dem (→)|To View| Menu
```

FIGURE 3-19.   Alphabetical listing of Staff children after sorting

MUTUALLY EXCLUSIVE CATEGORIES

Sometimes an item can belong to only one of several categories within a group. This means that each choice is mutually exclusive of the other choices.

For example, in a project-planning situation, items cannot be planned to be completed today, tomorrow, and next week. To force this mutual exclusion feature into the structure for your database, highlight the parent category whose siblings must be mutually exclusive. While you are in the Category Manager, press (F6) (Props). A Category Properties dialog box appears on the screen, as shown in Figure 3-20.

Turn your attention to the Exclusive children setting. The default setting is No. To change it to Yes, highlight it, choose "yes" by typing y or toggle with the (SPACEBAR) and press (ENTER). A relational bracket connects the mutually exclusive sibling categories within the Category Manager, as shown in Figure 3-21.

Existing category assignments in the database may prevent you from setting up the mutual exclusion feature if you have already assigned one item to multiple categories in a group. If you try to make sibling categories mutually exclusive and this conflict

Press F2 to edit the category name or type a new one.

MAIN

┌──────────────────── Category Properties ────────────────────┐
│   │
│ Category name: Staff   Type: Standard   │
│ Parent is MAIN   Match category name: Yes │
│ Short name: Match short name: Yes │
│ Also match: │
│ Note: ...   │
│ Note file: │
│ Exclusive children: No   Assignment conditions: │
│ Special actions: No action   │
│   │
│   Assignment actions: │
│ Statistics: ...   │
│ Advanced settings: ...   │
└──────────── Press ENTER when done, ESC to cancel ───────────┘

F1	F2	F3	F4	F5	F6	F7	F8	F9	F10
Help	Edit	Choices			Props		Default		

FIGURE 3-20.   Creating mutually exclusive siblings from the Category Properties dialog box

File: C:\AGENDA\APPS\TODOLIST
Category Manager
    MAIN
  * Entry
  * When
  * Done
    Quick Jobs
       Writing
    Done?
    Staff
      ┌Bruce
      ├Jim
      ├Joy
      └William

F1	F2	F3	F4	F5	F6	F7	F8	F9	F10
Help	Edit			Note	Props	Prm (←)	Dem (→)	To View	Menu

FIGURE 3-21.   A bracket marks the Staff children as mutually exclusive

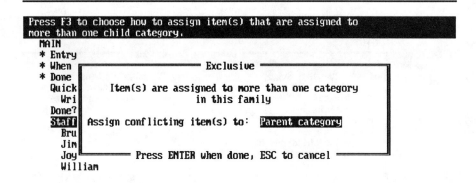

FIGURE 3-22.   The Exclusive message box warns that more than one
sibling has been assigned to at least one item

exists, you get an error message. Figure 3-22 shows the error message that appears if
you try to make the children of the Staff parent category mutually exclusive. The
database has two categories in this family assigned to one item. Agenda gives you a
warning about conflicting assignments and lets you choose whether to assign the items
to Parent Category, Existing Category, or New Category. Press (F3) (Choices) to list
these options. Make your selection and press (ENTER) or press (ESC) to acknowledge
the error and return to the Category Manager without making any changes. For items
entered after the mutual exclusion is established, conflicting assignments are resolved
by assigning the new item to the category physically located last.

UNINDEXED CATEGORIES

Some categories you use will contain information that is unique or close to unique for
every item in the database, such as a salary category in an employee file. Keeping
these items indexed would slow Agenda down, so Agenda lets you unindex them. This
speeds Agenda's processing and makes the category hierarchy less cluttered.

You would not want to unindex a category such as Staff since unindexing will prevent you from assigning additional items to this category. You would want to add another category for a quick number or rating list and then unindex it.

To unindex a category's child categories, move the highlight to the category that you want to unindex and press (F6) (Props). The Category Properties dialog box appears on the screen as shown previously in Figure 3-20. Highlight the setting Category Type and press (F3) (Choices). Highlight the Unindexed setting and press (ENTER). If you look at the category in the Category Manager, Agenda displays the unindexed category with a (△) symbol next to it.

The following confirmation dialog box appears to warn you that once a category has been unindexed, you cannot reindex it:

```
┌─────────────────────────────────────────────────────────────┐
│                                                              │
│  Convert to unindexed category (can't be changed back)?  Yes │
│ ══════════════ Press ENTER to accept, ESC to cancel ════════ │
└─────────────────────────────────────────────────────────────┘
```

Press (ENTER) to confirm that the category is to be unindexed or press (ESC) to cancel the command.

4

VIEWS

Agenda's views allow you to look at the same pool of information in many different ways. In the previous chapters you learned about the basic Agenda components that are used to create views. You learned that items, sections, categories, and columns are all important components when displaying your Agenda data. The examples were restricted to looking at the basics one step at a time to examine each of the components.

Applications for views extend far beyond the basic initial views you have seen. This chapter integrates the material covered in the previous chapters and adds some more advanced features. It focuses on the ways in which views can be used to enhance the utility of the Agenda package. The examples presented in this chapter focus on a simple company database used to track the routing for mail distribution. A variety of views are created with emphasis on presenting skills that you can apply to your own databases.

USING VIEWS

A view of an Agenda database is your definition of the information in the Agenda file that you want to see. When you define a view to Agenda, it is as if you have told Agenda what folders to pull from its large file cabinet of information. Since you can determine exactly what Agenda shows in a view, views give you the capability of treating one Agenda database as if it were many databases. At any time you can configure the exact view you need to meet your information needs.

You can work with any of the information in your database in a view. Although the item column is frequently shown in the first column of a view, you can position it anywhere in the view. You can display any of the categories in your database as sections in a view, and the items assigned to each category will appear beneath it. You can also display categories as column heads and assign children of that category to appear in the column below with items assigned to those children appearing in the item column. A specific line in a note entry for a category can also be shown as a column entry in a view.

The number of columns you can use is limited only by the 200-character display width and the width used by existing columns. This means that many columns may exist in the view but they may be beyond the border of the visible 80-character view. You can scroll laterally with the (RIGHT ARROW) and (LEFT ARROW) keys to bring these columns into the visible 80-character portion of the view.

CREATING THE INITIAL VIEW

For this chapter, you need to start with an Initial View of an Agenda database. You created an Initial View in the previous chapter called TODOLIST. For this chapter you will create a new Agenda database called EMPLMAIL, which is used to coordinate different mailings within a large firm. In creating this database, you will not only review what you have learned in the previous chapters, but learn more advanced features. This database lists all employees who receive mail, the mail route on which they are located, and their office numbers. It also lists job classifications and departments, because some mass mailings are distributed based upon these categories.

Follow these steps to create your database:

1. Load Agenda by typing **AGENDA** and pressing (ENTER) at the DOS prompt.

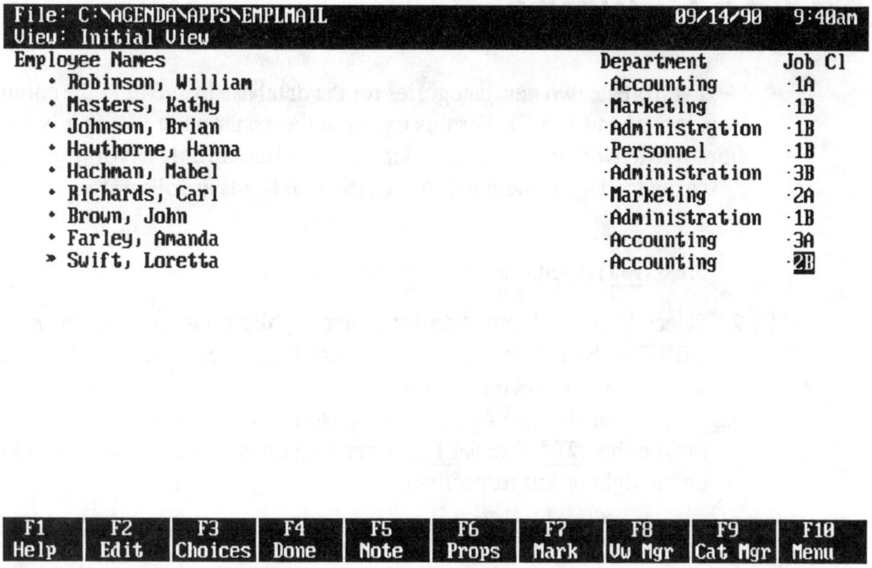

```
File: C:\AGENDA\APPS\EMPLMAIL                        09/14/90    9:40am
View: Initial View
Employee Names                              Department        Job Cl
   • Robinson, William                      ·Accounting       ·1A
   • Masters, Kathy                         ·Marketing        ·1B
   • Johnson, Brian                         ·Administration   ·1B
   • Hawthorne, Hanna                       ·Personnel        ·1B
   • Hachman, Mabel                         ·Administration   ·3B
   • Richards, Carl                         ·Marketing        ·2A
   • Brown, John                            ·Administration   ·1B
   • Farley, Amanda                         ·Accounting       ·3A
   ➤ Swift, Loretta                         ·Accounting       ·2B
```

F1	F2	F3	F4	F5	F6	F7	F8	F9	F10
Help	Edit	Choices	Done	Note	Props	Mark	Vw Mgr	Cat Mgr	Menu

FIGURE 4-1.   Initial View of the EMPLMAIL database

2. Name the database by typing **EMPLMAIL** and pressing (ENTER) twice.

The Initial View of the database you are about to create appears in Figure 4-1. Employee Names is the only section head. Department and Job Cl (short for Job Classification) are the two column heads. To duplicate this view, first change the default section head to Employee Names:

1. Highlight Initial Section (if it is not highlighted already).

2. Press (F2) (Edit).

3. Delete the current entry by pressing (ALT-F4) (Delete). Press (F3) (Choices) and highlight the Line choice. Press (ENTER).

4. Type **Employee Names** and press (ENTER).

The category Employee Names is now the section head of this view.

Adding Columns

Next you create two new categories for the database by creating the column heads for Department and Job Cl. For this example the assumption is that it is possible for an employee to work in one or more departments, but can only have one job classification.

Create the Department and Job Cl column heads as follows:

1. Press (F10) (Menu) to enter the Agenda menu.

2. Select View Column Add by either highlighting each selection and pressing (ENTER) or by typing the initial letters of each selection (**VCA**). A Column Add dialog box appears on the screen.

   You can also use Agenda's time-saving accelerator keys to perform this task. Press either (ALT-R) or (ALT-L) depending on whether you want to add the column on the right or left respectively.

3. Type **Department** and press (ENTER) to name the column head.

4. Make the width of the column 15 characters by pressing (DOWN ARROW) to highlight Width, typing **15**, and pressing (ENTER).

5. Press (ENTER) to add the Job Cl column.

6. Press (F10) (Menu) to enter the Agenda menu.

7. Select View Column Add by either highlighting each selection and pressing (ENTER) or by typing the initial letters of each selection (**VCA**). A Column Add dialog box appears on the screen.

8. Type **Job Cl** and press (ENTER) to name the column head.

9. Make the width of the column 6 characters by pressing (DOWN ARROW) to highlight Width, typing **6**, and pressing (ENTER).

10. Press (ENTER) to add the Job Cl column.

The top of the view now contains the column heads that appear in Figure 4-1.

Entering Items into a View

Enter the items for the database with their category assignments as follows:

1. Highlight Employee Names.

2. Type **Robinson, William**, press (TAB), type **Accounting**, press (TAB), type **1A**, and press (ENTER).

   Notice that you can press (TAB) instead of (ENTER) to end an entry and also move your highlight one column to the right. This can save many keystrokes as you enter data.

   Remember that as you typed in Accounting and 1A, you were adding child categories under the Department and Job Cl categories, respectively. This is important to remember because you will use the automatic-completion capabilities of Agenda to save you further keystrokes.

3. Press (CTRL-LEFT ARROW) to quickly move to the leftmost column. You are now ready to enter the information for the second item. You can also press (ALT-I) to open a new item when you are in one of the other columns.

4. Type **Masters, Kathy**, press (TAB), type **Marketing**, press (TAB), type **1B**, and press (SHIFT-TAB).

5. Press (SHIFT-TAB) again to move to the Employee Names column.

   (SHIFT-TAB) works similar to (TAB) except that it moves the highlight one column to the left.

6. For the third entry, type **Johnson, Brian**, press (TAB), type **Administration**, and press (TAB). This places the highlight under the Job Cl column.

   Notice that 1B already exists as a Job Cl category from the Kathy Masters entry. You can use Agenda's automatic-completion process to save yourself the (SHIFT) keystroke of typing an uppercase **B**.

7. Type **1b**. Notice that the "b" is lowercase. The automatic completion at the top of the screen indicates a match with category 1B. Press (ENTER) to accept the match. 1B appears as the entry instead of 1b.

   The automatic-completion process for entries is not case-sensitive. Once the category is entered as you want it to appear in your database, you can use automatic completion to eliminate using the (SHIFT) key. This can save many keystrokes.

8. Press (CTRL-LEFT ARROW) to move to the first column of the database.

9. Type **Hawthorne, Hanna**, press (TAB), type **Personnel**, press (TAB), type **1b**, and press (ENTER).

10. Press (CTRL-LEFT ARROW) to move to the first column of the database.

11. To enter the next item, type **Hachman, Mabel,** press (TAB), and type **ad.** Since Administration is a previously entered category, typing **ad** flags the wanted entry for you. Press (TAB) to accept the entry selection, type **3B,** and press (ENTER).

12. Continue entering the next four entries as shown in Figure 4-1. Use automatic completion to reduce the number of keystrokes.

Mutually Exclusive Categories

In the description of the database you are creating, it was noted that each employee could have no more than one job classification. You can assure this by telling Agenda that all children of Job Cl are mutually exclusive. Once this is done, you will be unable to enter more than one job classification for a particular item.

Creating mutually exclusive children is done in the Category Manager as follows:

1. Press (F9) (Cat Mgr) to invoke the Category Manager screen.

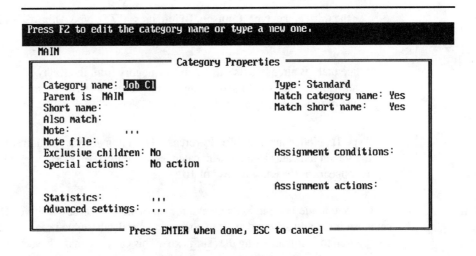

FIGURE 4-2.   The Category Properties box

2. Highlight Job Cl using the (UP ARROW) or (DOWN ARROW) keys.

3. Press (F6) (Props) to go to the Category Properties dialog box. Your screen should be similar to Figure 4-2.

4. Use (DOWN ARROW) to highlight the Exclusive children setting.

5. Type **y** to change the setting to Yes.

   You can also toggle Yes/No settings to the opposite selection by pressing the (SPACEBAR).

6. Press (ENTER) to indicate to Agenda that you are finished with the dialog box. You are returned to the Category Manager screen.

   Notice in Figure 4-3 that the children of Job Cl have square brackets on their left, indicating that they are mutually exclusive categories. This assures that no item can be assigned to more than one job classification.

7. Return to the view by pressing (ESC) or (F9) (To View).

```
File: C:\AGENDA\APPS\EMPLMAIL
Category Manager
   MAIN
 * Entry
 * When
 * Done
   Employee Names
   Department
     Accounting
     Marketing
     Administration
     Personnel
  Job Cl
    ┌1A
    ├1B
    ├3B
    ├2A
    ├3A
    └2B
```

F1	F2	F3	F4	F5	F6	F7	F8	F9	F10
Help	Edit			Note	Props	Prm (←)	Dem (→)	To View	Menu

FIGURE 4-3.   The Category Manager indicates mutually exclusive categories with square brackets to the left of each category

Adding entries to mutually exclusive columns works differently than adding them to non-mutually exclusive columns. With normal columns, you can enter more than one assignment per item. But by definition you can have only one entry assignment per item in a mutually exclusive column. To see how mutually exclusive categories work, modify the current database as follows:

1. Use the (ARROW) keys to move the highlight to the Accounting entry in the first item (Robinson, William).

2. Type **m** to activate the automatic completion feature, and select Marketing by pressing (ENTER). William Robinson is now assigned to both the Accounting and Marketing Departments.

You will now make a similar entry under the Job Cl column, but the results will be different.

1. Move the cursor to the 1B job classification for Brian Johnson (the third item). Assume that Mr. Johnson's job classification has changed to 1A.

2. Type **1a** and press (ENTER).

Notice that Agenda did not insert the entry 1A as a second entry as it did with the previous example, but instead replaced the previous entry with the new one. This is because the children under Job Cl have been defined as being mutually exclusive. Your database should now look similar to Figure 4-4.

CREATING A SECOND VIEW

You have already learned most of what you need to know to create other views of databascs. You know how to add individual components to an existing view, how to add items, and how to make category assignments using section and column heads. Now you will learn how to create new views.

One of the ways you can create a new view in an existing Agenda database is through the menu. Although there are many optional settings that you may address

```
File: C:\AGENDA\APPS\EMPLMAIL                          09/14/90  10:55am
View: Initial View
Employee Names                            Department        Job Cl
  • Robinson, William                     ·Accounting        ·1A
                                           Marketing
  • Masters, Kathy                        ·Marketing         ·1B
  ➤ Johnson, Brian                        ·Administration    ·1A
  • Hawthorne, Hanna                      ·Personnel         ·1B
  • Hachman, Mabel                        ·Administration    ·3B
  • Richards, Carl                        ·Marketing         ·2A
  • Brown, John                           ·Administration    ·1B
  • Farley, Amanda                        ·Accounting        ·3A
  • Swift, Loretta                        ·Accounting        ·2B
```

F1	F2	F3	F4	F5	F6	F7	F8	F9	F10
Help	Edit	Choices	Done	Note	Props	Mark	Vw Mgr	Cat Mgr	Menu

FIGURE 4-4. Changing an item's Job Cl to another category

while creating the new view, only two settings are required: the view name and an initial section. Follow these steps:

1. Press (**F10**) (Menu) to activate the menu.

2. Select View Add by highlighting each option and pressing (**ENTER**) or by typing **va**. The View Add dialog box appears on the screen.

3. With the View name setting highlighted, type **Mailing Route Assignments By Employee** and press (**ENTER**). You can use up to 37 characters to describe the view.

4. Using the (**ARROW**) keys, highlight the Sections setting.

   At this point you need to enter at least one category to use as a section header. You can do this in more than one way. You can type the name of each category; type the first few letters of the category and let Agenda's automatic-completion feature complete the entry for you; or press (**F3**) (Choices) to display all the categories, highlight the choices, and press the (**SPACEBAR**) to mark them.

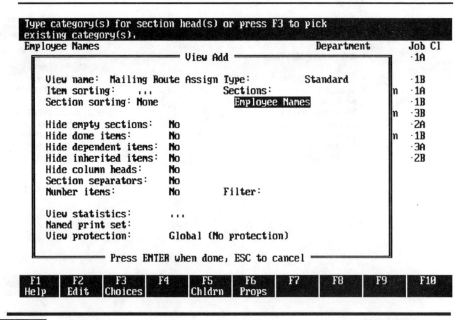

FIGURE 4-5.   Creating a view for mailing route assignments by employee

5. Type **emp** and press (ENTER) to accept the category name Employee Names as the section head. At this point you could define other section heads, but for this example you are done. Your screen should now look like Figure 4-5.

6. Press (ENTER) to accept the view as currently defined. You immediately are placed in the new view, as shown in Figure 4-6.

The Mailing Route Assignments By Employee view contains the section Employee Names, which is the same as in the Initial View. As you will see when you create additional views, the section(s) can be any of the defined categories. This example uses the Employee Names category as the section head.

This view will be used to add other categories of information to the database; specifically, the information pertaining to the mail delivery routes and the office number of each employee. If you were to add another item (employee name) to the database from this view, it would appear in the Initial View as well.

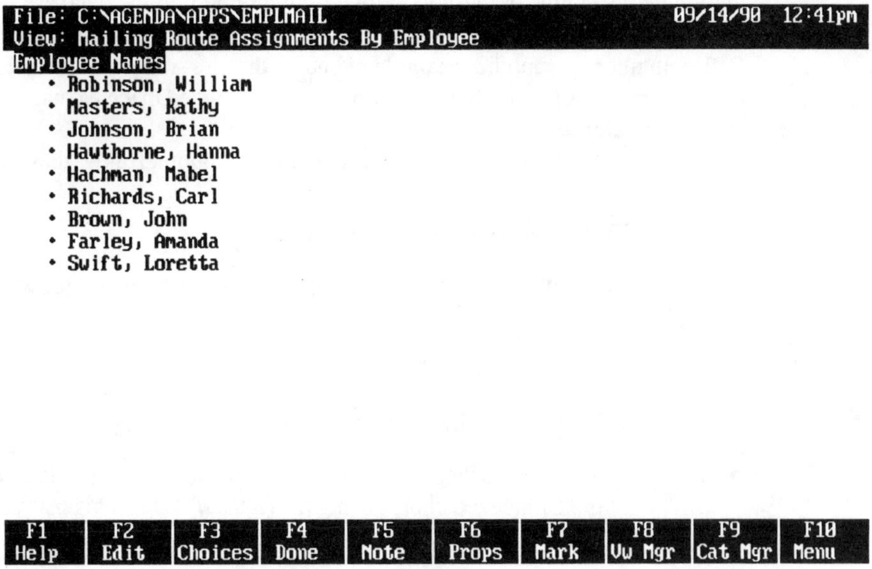

```
File: C:\AGENDA\APPS\EMPLMAIL                          09/14/90  12:41pm
View: Mailing Route Assignments By Employee
Employee Names
   • Robinson, William
   • Masters, Kathy
   • Johnson, Brian
   • Hawthorne, Hanna
   • Hachman, Mabel
   • Richards, Carl
   • Brown, John
   • Farley, Amanda
   • Swift, Loretta
```

F1	F2	F3	F4	F5	F6	F7	F8	F9	F10
Help	Edit	Choices	Done	Note	Props	Mark	Vw Mgr	Cat Mgr	Menu

FIGURE 4-6.   The initial Mailing Route Assignments By Employee view

Because you wish to assign the individual items to mail routes and office numbers, the categories to be added to this view must be columns. Follow these steps to add the mail route column:

1. Press (F10) (Menu) to activate the menu.

2. Select View Column Add by highlighting each selection and pressing (ENTER) or typing **vac**.

3. Type **Mail Rte** for the column head and press (DOWN ARROW) to highlight the Width setting.

4. Type **8** and press (ENTER).

5. Press (ENTER) to return to the view. The Mail Rte column has been added to the view.

Before you continue on to add the office number column, recall unindexed categories described in the previous chapter. Some categories you use contain information that is unique or close to unique for every item in the database. Examples of these include salaries, addresses, social security numbers, and telephone numbers. Office numbers are another example of entries that are somewhat unique. There is no real need to index them. Therefore, when you create the Office No category, you will make it unindexed.

To add the Office No column as an unindexed column, follow these steps:

1. Press (F10) (Menu) to activate the menu.

2. Select View Column Add by highlighting each selection and pressing (ENTER) or typing **VCA**.

3. Type **Office No** and press (ENTER).

4. Press (RIGHT ARROW) to highlight the Category type setting.

5. Press (F3) (Choices) to display the dialog box that lists the possible category types. Highlight the Unindexed choice using the (ARROW) keys. This list will auto-complete.

6. Press (ENTER) to select Unindexed.

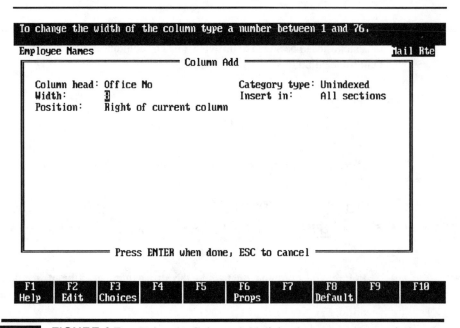

FIGURE 4-7.   Using the Column Add dialog box to create an unindexed category

```
File: C:\AGENDA\APPS\EMPLMAIL                    09/14/90   8:43pm
View: Mailing Route Assignments By Employee                  ◊
Employee Names                                   Mail Rte  Office No
  • Robinson, William                             ·Rte A    ·213
  • Masters, Kathy                                ·Rte C    ·322
  • Johnson, Brian                                ·Rte C    ·233
  • Hawthorne, Hanna                              ·Rte D    ·645
  • Hachman, Mabel                                ·Rte C    ·235
  • Richards, Carl                                ·Rte B    ·123
  • Brown, John                                   ·Rte B    ·654
  • Farley, Amanda                                ·Rte A    ·234
  » Swift, Loretta                                ·Rte D    ░523░
```

F1	F2	F3	F4	F5	F6	F7	F8	F9	F10
Help	Edit	Choices	Done	Note	Props	Mark	Vw Mgr	Cat Mgr	Menu

FIGURE 4-8.   The Mailing Route Assignment By Employee view with data

7. Press (RIGHT ARROW) to move to the Width setting. Type **8** and press (ENTER). Your screen should now look like the one in Figure 4-7.

8. Press (ENTER) to return to the view.

Use Figure 4-8 to make the category assignments under the Mail Rte and Office No columns using the techniques discussed earlier. Notice the special symbol (◊) that appears in the right corner of the control panel whenever you highlight an entry from the Office No column. This symbol indicates that the highlight is currently on an unindexed entry.

CREATING ADDITIONAL VIEWS

Agenda does not restrict the number of new views that you can add to a database. Any time a new information need arises, you can create a new view that contains the information you need to display.

Once you have created a new view, it operates the same as the initial view that you worked with. You can alter the information displayed by using the techniques covered so far, as well as some of the more advanced options covered later in this chapter.

You are now going to create a view that does not require adding any additional categories to the database. You will use the categories and their assignments that were created in the first two views. This view will be used to display the items (Employee Names) organized by the mail routes. The office numbers of each of the employees will also be included. To create the new view:

1. Press (F10) (Menu) to activate the menu.

2. Select View Add by highlighting each option and pressing (ENTER) or by typing **va**. Figure 4-5 displays an example of the View Add dialog box.

3. With the View name setting highlighted, type **Employee Listing By Route** and press (ENTER). You can use up to 37 characters to describe the view.

4. Using the (ARROW) keys, highlight the Sections setting. At this point you must enter at least one category to use as a section header.

5. Press (F3) (Choices) to activate the Section Select box.
   This box shows the category hierarchy so you can select a category to use as a section head.

6. Use (DOWN ARROW) to highlight the Mail Rte category, as shown in Figure 4-9.

For this view, you want the database to be displayed by mail routes. This means that the view should contain each route as a section head. You could highlight each route individually and press (SPACEBAR) to select it as a section head, but Agenda provides a means to mark all the routes at once.

7. Select all the Mail Rte children by pressing (F5) (Chldrn). An asterisk appears to the left of the four routes.

8. Press (ENTER) to accept the section choices.

9. Press (ENTER) to return to the new view. The employee names are now organized by mail route.

10. Add a column to this view to display the employees' office numbers by pressing (F10) (Menu) and selecting View Column Add in order to activate the Column Add dialog box.

11. Type **Office No** until auto-matching selects name and press (ENTER).

12. Press (DOWN ARROW) to highlight the Width setting. Type **8** and press (ENTER).

13. Press (ENTER) to return to the view. Your screen should appear similar to the one shown in Figure 4-10.

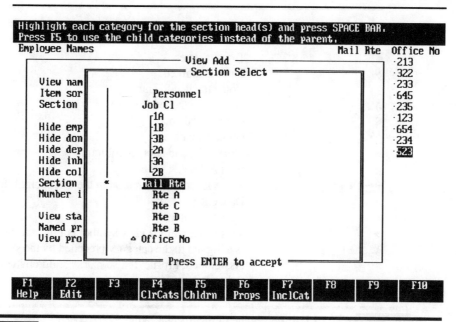

FIGURE 4-9.   The Section Select dialog box used to mark categories to be used as sections

```
File: C:\AGENDA\APPS\EMPLMAIL                          09/14/90   9:04pm
View: Employee Listing By Route
Rte A                                                  Office No
   • Farley, Amanda                                      ·234
   • Robinson, William                                   ·213

Rte C                                                  Office No
   • Hachman, Mabel                                      ·235
   • Johnson, Brian                                      ·233
   • Masters, Kathy                                      ·322

Rte D                                                  Office No
   • Swift, Loretta                                      ·523
   • Hawthorne, Hanna                                    ·645

Rte B                                                  Office No
   • Brown, John                                         ·654
   • Richards, Carl                                      ·123
```

F1	F2	F3	F4	F5	F6	F7	F8	F9	F10
Help	Edit	Choices	Done	Note	Props	Mark	Vw Mgr	Cat Mgr	Menu

FIGURE 4-10.   The Employee Listing By Route view which includes an Office No column

Symbol	Meaning
●	Tag character.
◆	Entry is marked.
♪	Note attached to entry.
♫	Note file attached to entry.
§	Collapsed display.
△	Unindexed category.
»	Marks place in another column.
‼	Item is done.
⇥ ↑ ↓ ↕ ↔	There is more information in the direction of the arrow(s).
✿	Date entry.
#	Numeric entry.
*	This is not really a view symbol but indicates that the item is assigned to the category preceded by the symbol * in Assignment Profile. It also marks children in the Section Select Box.

TABLE 4-1.   Some of the Special Symbols Used in a View

SPECIAL SYMBOLS USED TO MARK A VIEW

Agenda uses a variety of shorthand symbols to mark items and categories in a view. These symbols provide information in a very concise fashion. Although they will seem foreign at first, after a short time you will recall what they represent as soon as you see them. Table 4-1 lists some of the special symbols you might see in a view and explains their meaning.

USING THE VIEW MANAGER

Once you have created a new view, it remains available for your selection at a later time. You can use the View Manager to select a different predefined view for display.

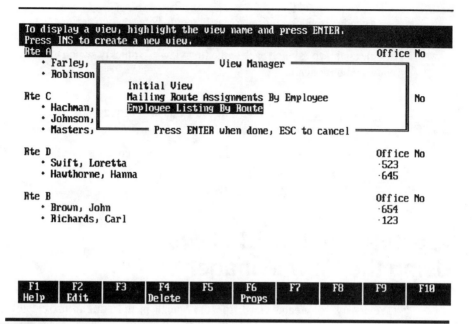

FIGURE 4-11.   The View Manager dialog box lists the available views for selection

You can also use it to create, redefine, reorder, and delete views. Figure 4-11 shows the screen that appears when you press (F8) to invoke the View Manager.

Selecting a Different View

From the View Manager dialog box, you can move the highlight to the view that you want to make current and press (ENTER). You can also toggle back and forth between two views with (ALT-F8) (Last Vw).

To display the view named Initial View, follow these steps:

1. Press (F8) (Vw Mgr) if you have not already done so. The View Manager dialog box displays on the screen as shown in Figure 4-11.

2. Use the (ARROW) keys to highlight the view named Initial View.

   You can use Agenda's auto-complete feature here, provided your views all start with unique letters.

3. Press (ENTER). The Initial View screen displays on the screen.

Agenda provides a means to easily toggle between two defined views. The toggle switches the view currently displayed on your screen to the last view displayed. If you toggle again, you switch back to the first view. To quickly switch to the last displayed view and back again:

1. Press (ALT-F8) (Last Vw). The view that was displayed before the current view now appears on your screen.

2. Press (ALT-F8) (Last Vw) again. The screen now contains the view that it displayed before you executed step 1.

Creating Additional Views Using the View Manager

Previously, you created views from the Agenda menu. You can also create a new view from the View Manager. The same screen that lets you select a view to display can also be used to create a new view.

In the EMPLMAIL database example, assume that mailings are occasionally distributed by department, so you need to create a list of employees by department. To create a view that lists all employees by department from the View Manager:

1. Press (F8) (Vw Mgr) to activate the View Manager.

2. Press (INS) to activate the View Add dialog box.

3. Type **Employee Roster By Department** and press (ENTER) to name the view.

4. Press (RIGHT ARROW) and (DOWN ARROW) to highlight the Sections setting.

5. Press (F3) (Choices) to display a list of choices for the sections to the view.

6. Since you want to divide this view by department, you want to select all the children of the Department category. You could do this by individually highlighting each child of the Department category and pressing the (SPACEBAR) to choose it. A quicker method is to highlight Department and press (F5) (Chldrn). This second method selects all the children of Department at once.

7. Press (ENTER) to accept your choices for the sections of the view. Your screen should now appear similar to Figure 4-12.

8. Press (ENTER) to leave the View Add dialog box and display the new view. Your screen should be similar to Figure 4-13.

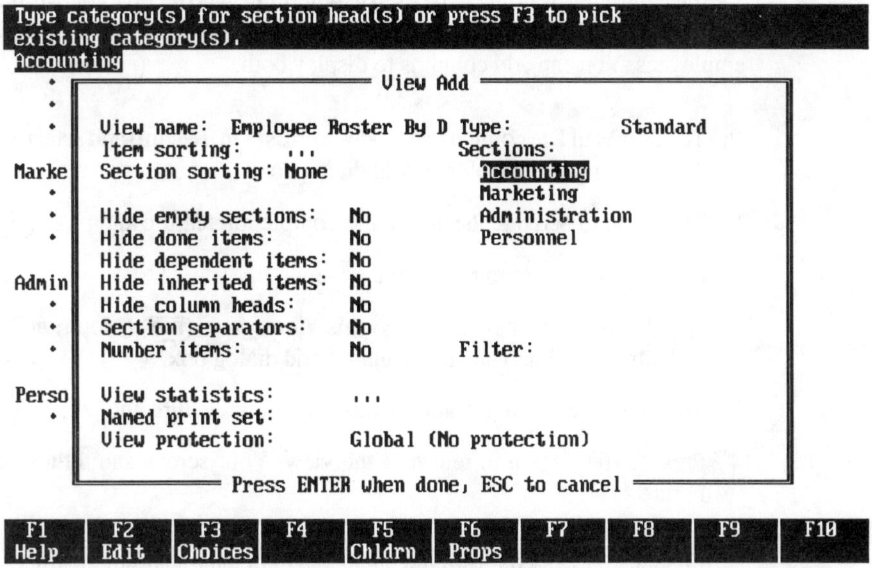

```
Type category(s) for section head(s) or press F3 to pick
existing category(s).
Accounting
    •              ┌──────────────── View Add ───────────────────┐
    •              │                                             │
    •              │ View name:  Employee Roster By D Type:        Standard │
                   │ Item sorting:    ...              Sections:          │
Marke              │ Section sorting: None             Accounting         │
    •              │                                   Marketing          │
    •              │ Hide empty sections:   No         Administration     │
    •              │ Hide done items:       No         Personnel          │
                   │ Hide dependent items:  No                            │
Admin              │ Hide inherited items:  No                            │
    •              │ Hide column heads:     No                            │
    •              │ Section separators:    No                            │
    •              │ Number items:          No         Filter:            │
                   │                                                      │
Perso              │ View statistics:       ...                           │
    •              │ Named print set:                                     │
                   │ View protection:       Global (No protection)        │
                   │                                                      │
                   └──────────── Press ENTER when done, ESC to cancel ────┘

┌──────┬──────┬──────┬──────┬──────┬──────┬──────┬──────┬──────┬──────┐
│ F1   │ F2   │ F3   │ F4   │ F5   │ F6   │ F7   │ F8   │ F9   │ F10  │
│ Help │ Edit │Choices│     │Chldrn│ Props│      │      │      │      │
└──────┴──────┴──────┴──────┴──────┴──────┴──────┴──────┴──────┴──────┘
```

FIGURE 4-12.   The View Add dialog box for Employee Roster By
Department view

```
File: C:\AGENDA\APPS\EMPLMAIL                      09/16/90   4:42pm
View: Employee Roster By Department
Accounting
    • Swift, Loretta
    • Farley, Amanda
    • Robinson, William

Marketing
    • Robinson, William
    • Richards, Carl
    • Masters, Kathy

Administration
    • Brown, John
    • Hachman, Mabel
    • Johnson, Brian

Personnel
    • Hawthorne, Hanna

┌──────┬──────┬──────┬──────┬──────┬──────┬──────┬──────┬──────┬──────┐
│ F1   │ F2   │ F3   │ F4   │ F5   │ F6   │ F7   │ F8   │ F9   │ F10  │
│ Help │ Edit │Choices│ Done │ Note │ Props│ Mark │Vw Mgr│Cat Mgr│ Menu │
└──────┴──────┴──────┴──────┴──────┴──────┴──────┴──────┴──────┴──────┘
```

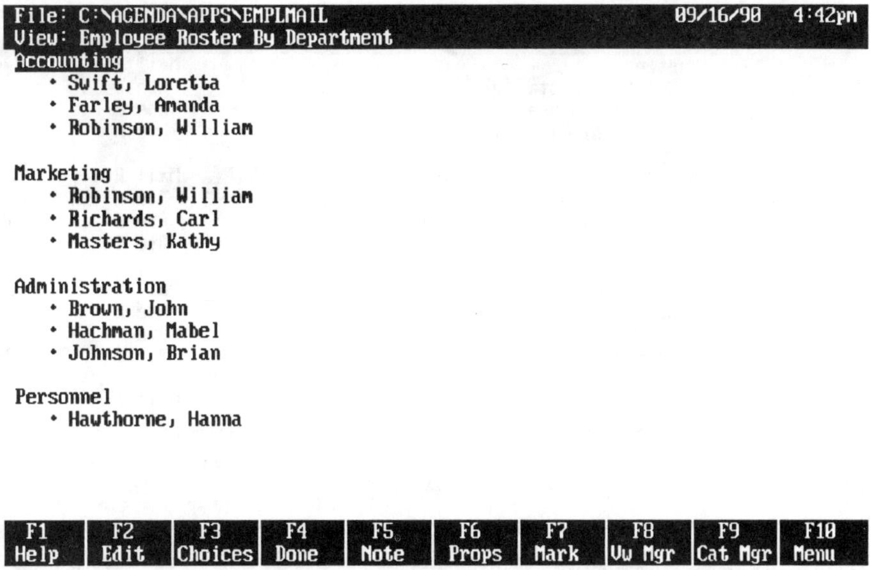

FIGURE 4-13.   The Employee Roster By Department view before
columns are added

Since this view is going to be used to determine who receives department mailings, it would help to also display the mail routes and the office numbers for each of the employees. You can add columns to display both.

9. To add a Mail Rte column to this view, press (F10) (Menu) and select View Column Add to activate the Column Add dialog box.

10. Type **Mai** to activate the automatic-completion feature and press (ENTER).

11. Press (ENTER) again to return to the view.

12. To add an Office No column to this view, press (F10) (Menu) and select View Column Add to activate the Column Add dialog box.

13. Type **Off** to activate the automatic-completion feature and press (ENTER).

14. Press (ENTER) again to return to the view. Your screen should now appear as in Figure 4-14.

If you were to add items to this view, the item would automatically be assigned to the Department category where the item appears. Remember, you can add items to any view and the item is incorporated into the entire database.

```
File: C:\AGENDA\APPS\EMPLMAIL                          09/16/90   4:53pm
View: Employee Roster By Department                              ^
Accounting                               Mail Rte      Office No
  • Swift, Loretta                         ·Rte D       ·523
  • Farley, Amanda                         ·Rte A       ·234
  • Robinson, William                      ·Rte A       ·213

Marketing                                Mail Rte      Office No
  • Robinson, William                      ·Rte A       ·213
  • Richards, Carl                         ·Rte B       ·123
  • Masters, Kathy                         ·Rte C·      ·322

Administration                           Mail Rte      Office No
  • Brown, John                            ·Rte B       ·654
  • Hachman, Mabel                         ·Rte C       ·235
  • Johnson, Brian                         ·Rte C       ·233

Personnel                                Mail Rte      Office No
  • Hawthorne, Hanna                       ·Rte D       ·645
```

```
 F1      F2      F3      F4      F5      F6      F7      F8      F9      F10
Help    Edit  Choices  Done    Note   Props   Mark   Vw Mgr Cat Mgr  Menu
```

FIGURE 4-14.   The completed Employee Roster By Department view

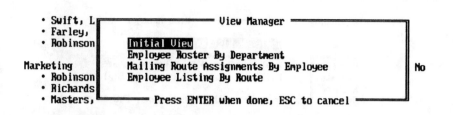

FIGURE 4-15.   Highlighting Initial View in the View Manager

Changing the Name of a View

You will often want to change the name of a view. This is especially true of the first view that you create for a database because Agenda provides the default name of Initial View. You can change the name of a view from the View Manager or View Props.

Change the name Initial View to Employee Roster as follows:

1. Press (F8) (Vw Mgr) to activate the View Manager dialog box.

2. Highlight Initial View using the (ARROW) keys, as in Figure 4-15.

3. Press (F2) (Edit) to edit the name.

4. Press (CTRL-ENTER) to delete the entire entry.

5. Type **Employee Roster** and press (ENTER). The View Manager dialog box appears as in Figure 4-16.

6. Press (ENTER) to activate the view.

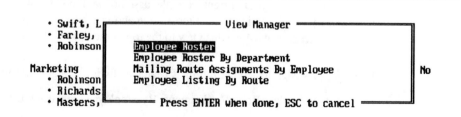

FIGURE 4-16.   Changing Initial View to Employee Roster

```
• Robinson┌─────────────── View Manager ───────────────┐·1A
          │                                            │
• Masters,│  Employee Listing By Route                 │·1B
• Johnson,│  Employee Roster                           │·1A
• Hawthorn│  Employee Roster By Department             │·1B
• Hachman,│  Mailing Route Assignments By Employee     │·3B
• Richards│                                            │·2A
• Brown, J└──────── Press ENTER when done, ESC to cancel ────┘·1B
```

FIGURE 4-17.   The View Manager listing views in sorted order

Changing the Order
Of Views in the View Manager

As you create views, their names appear within the View Manager box in the order they were created. Having a relatively random listing of the views is probably okay in a database where there are not many to choose from. However, if you are working with a database with a large number of views, you need to arrange their listing in an order that makes some kind of sense.

One method would be to arrange them in alphabetical order. Agenda provides a means to quickly sort the views into alphabetical order.

1. Press (F8) (Vw Mgr) to display the View Manager dialog box.

2. Press (ALT-F5) (Sort) to have Agenda sort the views. The views are now arranged in alphabetical order, as shown in Figure 4-17.

Most of the time, having the view names appear in alphabetical order is very convenient. Sometimes other arrangements are better. For example, most of the views could appear in alphabetical order, but the views used most often could appear together at the top of the list. For your current example, assume that the view Mailing Route Assignments By Employee is used the most often and you want it to appear first in the View Manager screen. Move this view to the top of the list as follows:

1. Press (F8) (Vw Mgr) to activate the View Manager if it is no longer on your screen.

2. Highlight the Mailing Route Assignments By Employee view using the (ARROW) keys.

```
 • Robinson┌──────────── View Manager ──────────────┐13
 • Masters,│                                        │22
 • Johnson,│ ≫  Employee Listing By Route           │33
 • Hawthorn│    Employee Roster                     │45
 • Hachman,│    Employee Roster By Department       │35
 • Richards│   ▐Mailing Route Assignments By Employee│23
 • Brown, J│                                        │54
 • Farley, └──────── Press ENTER when done, ESC to cancel ────┘34
```

FIGURE 4-18.   Pointing to the new location of a view within the View
Manager

3. Press (**ALT-F10**) (Move).

4. Use (**UP ARROW**) to move the pointer (the >> to the left of the view names) to the
first view in the list, as shown in Figure 4-18.

Pressing (**ENTER**) at this point would insert the highlighted view in the position *below*
the pointer, thus making the view appear in the second position. You want the view
to be inserted above the pointer.

5. To insert the highlighted view above the current position of the pointer, press
(**CTRL-ENTER**). Your screen should now appear as in Figure 4-19.

The view most often used now appears first in the list, while the rest of the views
are listed in alphabetical order.

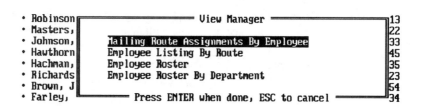

FIGURE 4-19.   The resulting View Manager after moving the view name

Removing a View
From the Database

You can remove a view from an Agenda database through the View Manager. Highlight the view to be deleted and press (F4) (Delete) or (DEL). A confirmation dialog box similar to the one shown here appears:

```
  Delete the view?  Yes
  ── Press ENTER to accept, ESC to cancel ──
```

Press (ENTER) to confirm the deletion.

CHANGING THE
VIEW DISPLAY

You have learned how to create views and add sections and columns to increase the amount of useful information appearing on the screen. You have also learned how to delete previously defined views. Now you will learn additional techniques for using views and changing their appearance.

Positioning Within a View

The database you are currently working with has very few entries. Normally, your databases will be larger. There will be too many items for all items and sections to appear on the screen at once. In a view with many sections, you need alternatives to the (UP ARROW) and (DOWN ARROW) keys to move between sections quickly.

The quickest method for jumping from one section to another is the (ALT-F5) (Go To) option. When you press (ALT-F5), Agenda displays the section names in the current view in a dialog box for your selection. You highlight the section name and press (ENTER) to immediately reposition the highlight to the selected section name. If the list of possibilities is long, you can begin typing and have Agenda auto-complete the section name for you.

To see how this works perform the following steps:

1. Press (**F8**) (Vw Mgr) to display the View Manager.

2. Highlight the view Employee Listing By Route using the (**ARROW**) keys.

3. Press (**ENTER**).

4. To quickly move to the Rte D section, press (**ALT-F5**) (Go To). The following dialog box appears, although the location of the highlight will depend on which section was active when you last exited the view:

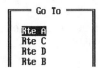

5. Highlight Rte D using the (**ARROW**) keys and press (**ENTER**). The view reappears with the highlight on the Rte D section.

You can also reposition the highlight in View mode by pressing (**PGUP**) and (**PGDN**) to move the highlight up or down a screen, respectively. (**CTRL-PGUP**) moves the highlight to the section head of the previous section, and (**CTRL-PGDN**) moves the highlight to the section head of the next section. The (**HOME**) key moves the highlight to the section head in the current section (or the previous section head if the highlight is on a section head), and the (**END**) key moves to the last item in the current section. The (**RIGHT ARROW**) and (**LEFT ARROW**) keys move the highlight from one column to the next.

Table 4-2 summarizes some of these movement keys and special keys available with Agenda in View mode.

Collapsing and Expanding a View

If a database view can show only one section of the database because of the number of entries in the current section, you can *collapse* the view by pressing (**ALT--**) ((**ALT**)-minus key). When you press (**ALT--**) one time the section currently highlighted is collapsed to display only the section name. If you press (**ALT--**) in a section that is

Key Sequence	Action
(INS)	While editing a category or item, ends edit and inserts a new item or category. When editing a section, ends edit and inserts a new item. When editing categories in the Category Manager or the Section Select box, ends edit and inserts a new category. In the View Manager, inserts a new view by opening the View Add box.
(DEL)	In Edit mode, deletes a character. In the View Manager, deletes the highlighted view. In View mode, removes item's assignment to the section or column category; also removes section from view.
(ENTER)	In View mode, moves highlight to next item or category. In Edit mode, finishes Edit mode. In the View Manager, selects view to be made current.
(ARROW) keys	Move cursor or highlight in direction of arrow. If the cursor or highlight cannot move in that direction, pressing the arrow elicits a beep sound.
(PGUP)(PGDN)	In View mode, moves highlight up or down a screenful at a time, respectively.
(CTRL-PGUP)/(CTRL-PGDN)	In View mode, moves the highlight to the previous or next section head, respectively.
(CTRL-RIGHT ARROW)/ (CTRL-LEFT ARROW)	In View mode, moves the highlight to the far right or left column of the view, respectively. In Edit mode, moves the cursor to the next or previous word, respectively.
(HOME)	In View mode, moves the highlight to the section or column head. In Edit mode, moves the cursor to the beginning of the line.
(END)	In View mode, moves the highlight to the last item or column entry in the section. In Edit mode, moves the cursor to the end of the line.
(CTRL-HOME)/(CTRL-END)	In View mode, moves the highlight to the top or bottom of the database, respectively. In Edit mode, moves to the beginning or end of the text, respectively.
(CTRL-BACKSPACE)	In Edit mode, deletes current word.
(ALT--)	Pressed once, collapses the current section in View mode. Pressed a second time collapses all sections.
(ALT-=)	Pressed once, expands the current section in View mode. Pressed a second time, expands all sections.

TABLE 4-2.   Movement and Special Keys

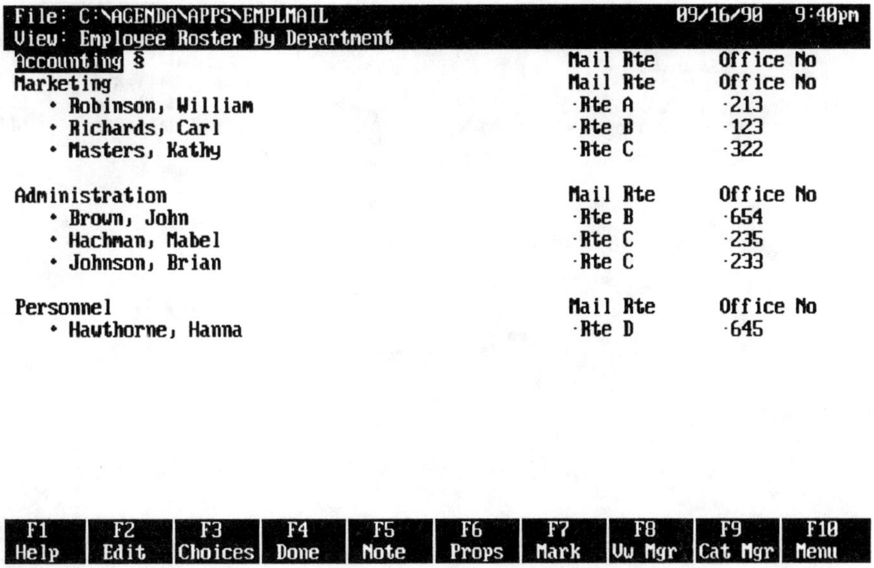

```
File: C:\AGENDA\APPS\EMPLMAIL                        09/16/90    9:40pm
View: Employee Roster By Department
Accounting §                                   Mail Rte    Office No
Marketing                                      Mail Rte    Office No
   • Robinson, William                          ·Rte A      ·213
   • Richards, Carl                             ·Rte B      ·123
   • Masters, Kathy                             ·Rte C      ·322

Administration                                 Mail Rte    Office No
   • Brown, John                                ·Rte B      ·654
   • Hachman, Mabel                             ·Rte C      ·235
   • Johnson, Brian                             ·Rte C      ·233

Personnel                                      Mail Rte    Office No
   • Hawthorne, Hanna                           ·Rte D      ·645
```

F1	F2	F3	F4	F5	F6	F7	F8	F9	F10
Help	Edit	Choices	Done	Note	Props	Mark	Vw Mgr	Cat Mgr	Menu

FIGURE 4-20.   A view with a collapsed Accounting section

already collapsed, then all the sections in the view collapse. Collapsed sections are displayed with a § symbol to their right. To collapse all sections in the Employee Roster By Department view:

1. Press (F8) (Vw Mgr) to activate the View Manager.

2. Highlight Employee Roster By Department using the (ARROW) keys. Press (ENTER) to activate the view.

3. Use the (ARROW) keys to highlight the Accounting section.

4. Press (ALT--) to collapse the section currently highlighted. The screen should look similar to Figure 4-20.

5. Press (ALT--) again to collapse the entire view. The screen should look similar to Figure 4-21.

The effect of the (ALT--) combination is not permanent. You can expand the display of sections by using the (ALT-=) combination. If you are in a section that is currently

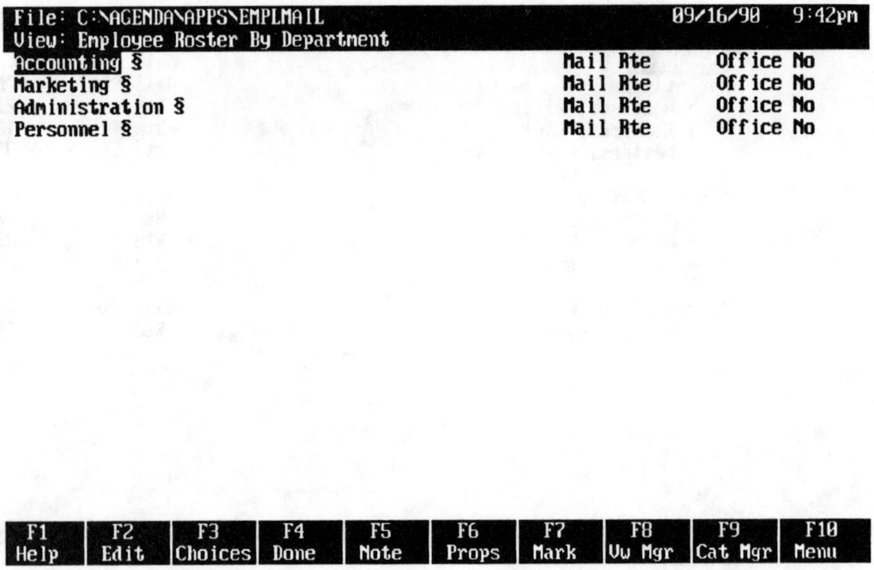

```
File: C:\AGENDA\APPS\EMPLMAIL                        09/16/90   9:42pm
View: Employee Roster By Department
Accounting §                              Mail Rte    Office No
Marketing §                               Mail Rte    Office No
Administration §                          Mail Rte    Office No
Personnel §                               Mail Rte    Office No
```

F1	F2	F3	F4	F5	F6	F7	F8	F9	F10
Help	Edit	Choices	Done	Note	Props	Mark	Vw Mgr	Cat Mgr	Menu

FIGURE 4-21.   A view with all sections collapsed

collapsed, pressing the (ALT-=) combination expands the current section to display the item data again. If the current section is not collapsed or if you press the (ALT-=) combination a second time, all the sections in the current view are expanded. To expand the current view:

1. Press (ALT-=) to expand the current section.

2. Press (ALT-=) again to expand the entire view.

Category collapsing and expanding is useful in many database applications. As sections are added to views and more items are added to sections, it becomes nearly impossible to keep the structure of the particular view in mind. Collapsing and expanding large views helps you develop and use the views.

Moving Elements of a View

Sometimes it becomes necessary to change the order that certain sections, items, or columns appear in a view. Agenda allows you to move any of these elements within a view of a database.

MOVING SECTIONS OF A VIEW   When you add a section, you can choose where it is inserted. Once it is inserted, you can change the order in which it is displayed within the view. The View Section Move command lets you choose the order to be used for displaying sections within a view. To make Marketing the first section to appear in the Employee Roster By Department view, follow these steps:

1. Activate the Employee Roster By Department view by pressing (F8) (Vw Mgr), highlighting the view, and pressing (ENTER).

2. Move the highlight to the Marketing section entry.

3. Press (F10) (Menu) to activate the menu.

4. Choose View Section Move by typing **vsm**. The display changes to look like that in Figure 4-22. Each of the sections is collapsed to show only the section head and category headers for that section.

5. Press (UP ARROW) to move Marketing to the top of the view. Notice that Marketing is immediately moved up one section as you press (UP ARROW). Note that (ALT-F10) (Move) also moves sections in this way.

6. Press (ENTER) to finalize your selection and see the sections expand.

MOVING ITEMS BETWEEN SECTIONS   Sometimes you want to move an item from one section to another. For example, in the Employee Roster By Department view, you could change Loretta Swift from Accounting to the Personnel department section. Note that a move such as this changes the category assignment of an item. After you make the move, Loretta Swift's department entry changes to the Personnel category for *all* views.

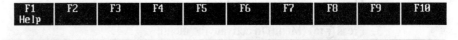

```
Use up & down arrow keys to reposition section,
Press ENTER when done,
Accounting §                                    Mail Rte      Office No
Marketing §                                     Mail Rte      Office No
Administration §                                Mail Rte      Office No
Personnel §                                     Mail Rte      Office No
```

| F1 | F2 | F3 | F4 | F5 | F6 | F7 | F8 | F9 | F10 |
| Help | | | | | | | | | |

FIGURE 4-22.   The view of collapsed sections after selecting View
Selection Move from the menu

Assuming the view displayed is still the Employee Roster By Department view
from the previous example, change Loretta Swift to Personnel as follows:

1. Use the (ARROW) keys to highlight the Loretta Swift item.

2. Press (ALT-F10) (Move). The Move dialog box appears on the screen, as shown in
    Figure 4-23.

3. Highlight Personnel using the (ARROW) keys or auto-complete and press (ENTER).

4. Press (ENTER) to activate the move.

Loretta Swift now appears in the Personnel section and no longer appears in the
Marketing section. Remember that you can also assign Loretta to Personnel in addition
to Accounting by using Item MakeAssign, as long as departments are not mutually
exclusive.

MOVING ITEMS WITHIN A SECTION   The Item Reposition command lets
you move items to another location within a section instead of to a different section.

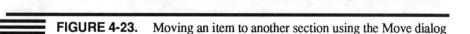

```
Highlight the section where you want to move the item
and press ENTER.
Marketing                                    Mail Rte      Office No
    • Robinson, William                      ·Rte A          ·213
    • Richards, Carl                         ·Rte B          ·123
    • Masters, Kathy                         ·R┌────── Move ──────┐
                                             Ma│ Marketing        │
Accounting                                   Ma│ Accounting       │
    • Swift, Loretta                         ▸R│ Administration   │
    • Farley, Amanda                         ·R│ Personnel        │
    • Robinson, William                      ·R│                  │
                                             Ma│                  │
Administration                               Ma└──────────────────┘
    • Brown, John                            ·R
    • Hachman, Mabel                         ·Rte C          ·235
    • Johnson, Brian                         ·Rte C          ·233

Personnel                                    Mail Rte      Office No
    • Hawthorne, Hanna                       ·Rte D          ·645
```

```
┌─────┬─────┬─────┬─────┬─────┬─────┬─────┬─────┬─────┬─────┐
│ F1  │ F2  │ F3  │ F4  │ F5  │ F6  │ F7  │ F8  │ F9  │ F10 │
│ Help│     │     │     │     │     │     │     │     │     │
└─────┴─────┴─────┴─────┴─────┴─────┴─────┴─────┴─────┴─────┘
```

FIGURE 4-23.   Moving an item to another section using the Move dialog box

To make John Brown appear last in the Administration section of the Employee Roster By Department view, follow these steps:

1. Move the highlight to the John Brown item.

2. Press (F10) (Menu) to activate the menu.

3. Choose Item Reposition by typing **ir**.

4. Press (DOWN ARROW) twice. Each time you press (DOWN ARROW), the John Brown entry moves down within the current section.

5. Press (ENTER) to accept the change.

You cannot reposition an item if the section is sorted automatically or if the section has a child category. If Sort is set to "On leaving a section..." repositioning will work until you leave the section. It will also work if Sort is set to "On Demand" until you perform your sort with (ALT-S).

MOVING COLUMNS IN A VIEW   Like sections, when you add a column you can choose where it is inserted. Once it is inserted, you can change the order in which columns are displayed within the current section. If you have more than one section in a view and you want the same column to be moved in each section, you will need to move the column individually for each section.

The View Column Move command lets you choose the order in which columns are displayed in a section. To switch the order of the Department and Job Cl columns of the Employee Roster view, follow these steps:

1. Use the Activate the Employee Roster view by pressing (F8) (Vw Mgr), highlighting Employee Roster, and pressing (ENTER).

2. Use the (ARROW) keys to move the highlight to the Job Cl section.

3. Press (F10) (Menu) to activate the menu.

4. Choose View Column Move by typing **vcm**.

5. Press (LEFT ARROW) to move the Job Cl column one column to the left.

6. Press (ENTER) to accept the current location of the column. The resulting view should appear similar to Figure 4-24.

Removing Sections and Columns from a View

Occasionally you may need to remove a column or section from a view. The steps for removing a section are as follows:

1. Activate the view containing the section you want to remove by pressing (F8) (Vw Mgr), highlighting the name of the view you want, and pressing (ENTER).

   If you want to remove a section from the current view you can omit this step.

2. Highlight the section to be removed using the (ARROW) keys.

3. Press (F10) (Menu).

4. Choose View Section Remove by typing **vsr**.

```
File: C:\AGENDA\APPS\EMPLMAIL                          09/16/90  10:30pm
View: Employee Roster
Employee Names                                        Job Cl  Department
    • Robinson, William                                ·1A     ·Accounting
                                                               Marketing
    • Masters, Kathy                                   ·1B     ·Marketing
    • Johnson, Brian                                   ·1A     ·Administration
    • Hawthorne, Hanna                                 ·1B     ·Personnel
    • Hachman, Mabel                                   ·3B     ·Administration
    • Richards, Carl                                   ·2A     ·Marketing
    • Brown, John                                      ·1B     ·Administration
    • Farley, Amanda                                   ·3A     ·Accounting
    » Swift, Loretta                                   ·2B     ·Personnel
```

```
  F1       F2       F3     F4     F5     F6     F7     F8     F9     F10
 Help    Edit   Choices  Done   Note  Props   Mark  Vw Mgr Cat Mgr Menu
```

FIGURE 4-24. The Employee Roster view after moving the Job Cl column to the left

You can also press (DEL) with the section head highlighted.
The steps for removing a column are as follows:

1. Highlight the column to be removed using the (ARROW) keys.

2. Press (F10) (Menu).

3. Choose View Column Remove by typing **vcr**. The following dialog box appears:

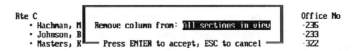

```
Rte C                                                 Office No
    • Hachman, M   Remove column from: All sections in view  ·235
    • Johnson, B                                      ·233
    • Masters, K   Press ENTER to accept, ESC to cancel  ·322
```

4. Answer whether the column should be removed from all sections or just the highlighted one by pressing the (SPACEBAR) to display your response and pressing (ENTER). You could also press (F3) (Choices) to make your selection.

USING FILTERS

Filters create a screen that items must pass through before they are shown in a view. You can create filters to include or exclude items with assignments to certain categories, and you can establish a filter with one category or many in the database.

Normally the categories are joined with an implied "and" as Agenda processes the items against the current filter screen to create a view. In other words, for an item to be displayed when more than one filter category is chosen, the item must possess all the necessary category assignments to be displayed in the view. In a filter, a plus symbol next to the category means the item must be assigned to the category, and a minus symbol means the item must *not* be assigned to the category.

For the first example, you are going to create a view that lists all employees from the Marketing department by mail route. To make the creation of this view easier and less time consuming, you will use the Copy command to copy the Employee Listing By Route view to the new view. After that, you will assign a Marketing filter so that only Marketing employees will be listed in the view.

1. Activate the View Manager by pressing (F8) (Vw Mgr).

2. Highlight the Employee Listing By Route view if it is not already highlighted. Do not press (ENTER) yet.

3. Press (ALT-F9) (Copy). This produces a copy of the view that needs to be named. The Copy View dialog box appears on the screen, as shown in Figure 4-25. This box is very similar to the View Add dialog box you worked with at the beginning of this chapter.

4. Type the View name **Marketing Employees By Route** and press (ENTER).

5. Use the (DOWN ARROW) and (RIGHT ARROW) keys to highlight the Filter setting.

6. Press (F3) (Choices) to display the Filter box shown in Figure 4-26. This box shows the category hierarchy so you can choose a category to filter your data through.

7. Highlight the Marketing category using the (ARROW) keys or by starting to type Marketing and allowing the auto-complete feature to finish it, and then press (ENTER).

8. Mark the category as being assigned to the filter by pressing the (SPACEBAR) once. A plus symbol appears to the left of Marketing. This indicates that an item must be assigned to Marketing to be displayed in this view.

    If you pressed the (SPACEBAR) a second time, a minus symbol would appear to indicate that the item must *not* be assigned to Marketing to be displayed in this view. To turn Marketing off as a filter, you would press the (SPACEBAR) a third time.

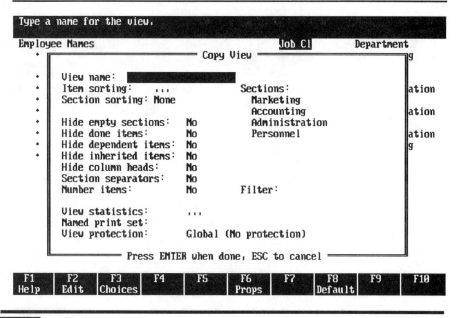

FIGURE 4-25.   The Copy View dialog box

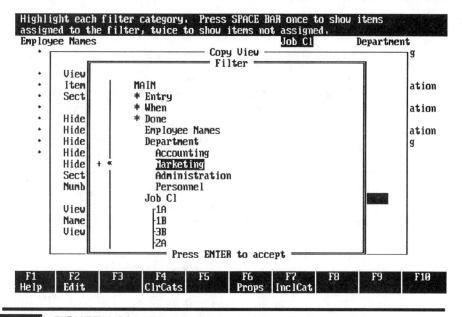

FIGURE 4-26.   The Filter dialog box for selecting filters for a view

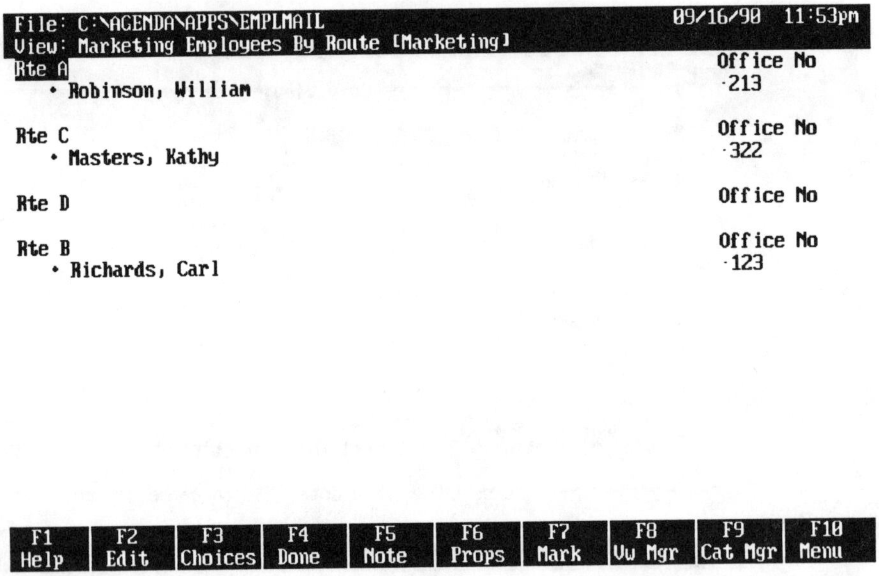

```
File: C:\AGENDA\APPS\EMPLMAIL                          09/16/90  11:53pm
View: Marketing Employees By Route [Marketing]
Rte A                                                 Office No
   • Robinson, William                                ·213

Rte C                                                 Office No
   • Masters, Kathy                                   ·322

Rte D                                                 Office No

Rte B                                                 Office No
   • Richards, Carl                                   ·123
```

F1	F2	F3	F4	F5	F6	F7	F8	F9	F10
Help	Edit	Choices	Done	Note	Props	Mark	Vw Mgr	Cat Mgr	Menu

FIGURE 4-27.   A view of employees using Marketing as a view filter

9. Press (**ENTER**) to accept the choices for filters.

10. Press (**ENTER**) again to accept the view definition.

The new view is displayed on the screen. Figure 4-27 shows that only three employees are assigned to the Marketing category. Notice on the second line of the screen that Marketing is listed with square brackets around it. The square brackets indicate that a filter is being used with this view and Marketing is the category being used as the filter. A minus symbol would have appeared before Marketing if the filter were filtering out all items that were assigned to Marketing.

When you filter multiple items through a mutually exclusive category group, the filter category selections are joined with an implied "or" because it is impossible to have more than one of the categories in a mutually exclusive group assigned to a single item.

A second example of filters uses a mutually exclusive group as a filter. In this example, assume that you want a listing of all supervisors by department. You know that a supervisor has to have a job classification of 1A or 1B. Therefore, you want to filter into the view all employees who are classified as 1A or 1B. To simplify the creation of the view, you will copy the Employee Roster By Department view.

1. Activate the View Manager by pressing (F8) (Vw Mgr).

2. Highlight the Employee Roster By Department view using the (ARROW) keys.

3. Press (ALT-F9) (Copy). The Copy View dialog box appears.

4. Type **Supervisors By Department** and press (ENTER).

5. Highlight the Filter setting using the (ARROW) keys.

6. Press (F3) (Choices) to display the Filter dialog box. Highlight the 1A category and press the (SPACEBAR). Highlight the 1B category and press the (SPACEBAR). Your screen should appear as in Figure 4-28.

Notice that the children of the Job Cl category have square brackets immediately to their left. These brackets indicate that these categories are mutually exclusive. An item cannot be assigned to more than one of these categories at a time. This means that the filter for these categories will look for a match of either one or the other.

7. Press (ENTER) twice to display the new view.

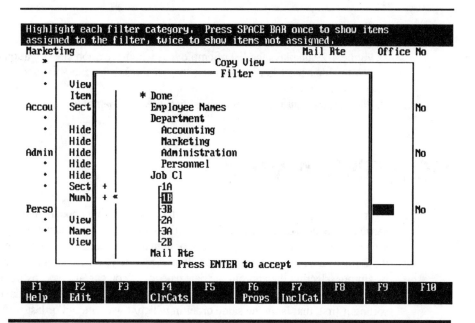

FIGURE 4-28.   Selecting categories 1A and 1B as mutually exclusive filters

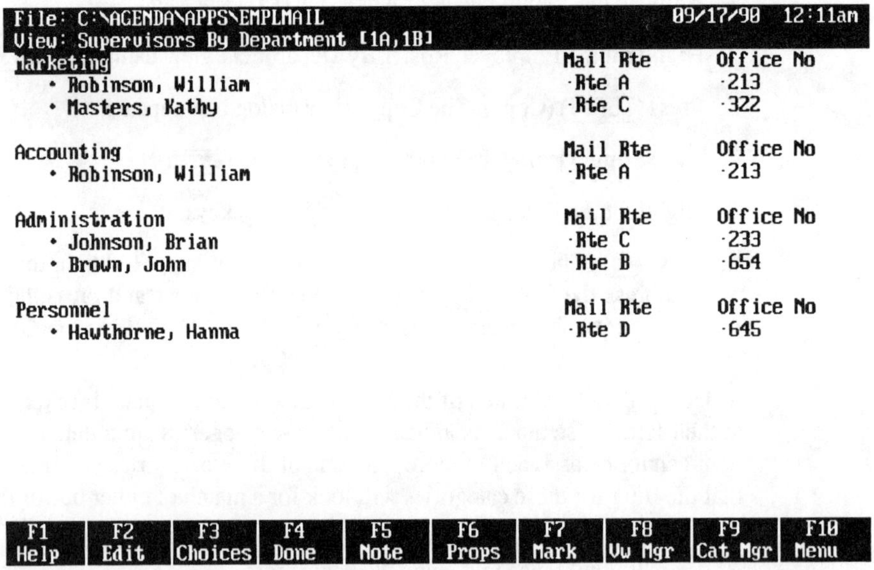

```
File: C:\AGENDA\APPS\EMPLMAIL                        09/17/90  12:11am
View: Supervisors By Department [1A,1B]
Marketing                                  Mail Rte    Office No
   • Robinson, William                      ·Rte A      ·213
   • Masters, Kathy                         ·Rte C      ·322

Accounting                                 Mail Rte    Office No
   • Robinson, William                      ·Rte A      ·213

Administration                             Mail Rte    Office No
   • Johnson, Brian                         ·Rte C      ·233
   • Brown, John                            ·Rte B      ·654

Personnel                                  Mail Rte    Office No
   • Hawthorne, Hanna                       ·Rte D      ·645
```

F1	F2	F3	F4	F5	F6	F7	F8	F9	F10
Help	Edit	Choices	Done	Note	Props	Mark	Vw Mgr	Cat Mgr	Menu

FIGURE 4-29. View of all items with job classifications of 1A or 1B

Figure 4-29 displays the list of employees who have a job classification of 1A or 1B. Notice that the filter works even though the Job Cl category is not displayed anywhere in the view.

Filtering through Date categories is discussed in Chapter 6.

SORTING A VIEW

Agenda's sort features can change the order in which data appears in a view or in a particular section of a view. Within sections of a view, you can display items in sequence by categories, category notes, or item text. Although you do not see Date on the Choices list for a sort, you can easily sort by Entry, When, Done, or custom date by simply selecting the appropriate date category. You can also sort by numbers in a date column by selecting the note column. You can also display the data without sorting it first, that is, in the same order in which it was entered or last sorted. Other sort options affect whether ascending or descending sequence is used and the collating sequence for the data. The complete flexibility of the sort features allows you to tailor a display to your needs; you may want to add database views simply to use the different sort options.

You will perform two sorts using views. For the first example of sorting, you will sort the section names of the Employee Listing By Route view. Currently, the sections are in the order they were entered when you created the database. To have Agenda sort the section heads, follow these steps:

1. Press (F8) (Vw Mgr) and highlight Employee Listing By Route. Do not press (ENTER) yet.

2. Press (F6) (Props). This takes you to the View Properties dialog box, which is similar to the View Add dialog box.

3. Press (DOWN ARROW) twice to highlight the Section sorting setting. This setting is currently set to None. Press (F3) (Choices) to obtain a listing of the choices for Section sorting, as shown in Figure 4-30.

4. The choices for sorting are Category order (which is the order the categories appear in the Category Manager), alphabetic order, and numeric order. Highlight Alphabetic and press (ENTER).

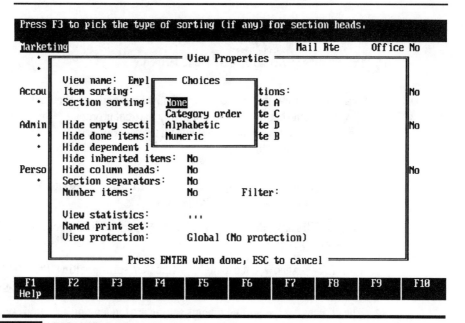

FIGURE 4-30.   The Choices dialog box listing the different section sorting options

```
File: C:\AGENDA\APPS\EMPLMAIL                    09/17/90  1:11am
View: Employee Listing By Route                          ᴼ
Rte A                                              Office No
   • Farley, Amanda                                 ·234
   • Robinson, William                              ·213

Rte B                                              Office No
   • Brown, John                                    ·654
   • Richards, Carl                                 ·123

Rte C                                              Office No
   • Hachman, Mabel                                 ·235
   • Johnson, Brian                                 ·233
   • Masters, Kathy                                 ·322

Rte D                                              Office No
   » Swift, Loretta                                 ·523
   • Hawthorne, Hanna                               ·645
```

```
F1     F2     F3     F4     F5     F6     F7     F8     F9     F10
Help   Edit  Choices Done   Note  Props  Mark  Vw Mgr Cat Mgr Menu
```

FIGURE 4-31.   The view with the Mail Route sections displayed
                    alphabetically

5. Press (ENTER) twice to display the redefined view.

Figure 4-31 shows that the sections are now arranged alphabetically. However, the items within each section are still not in any particular order.

The process for sorting the items beneath the sections is more complicated because there are more options involved.

1. Press (F8) (Vw Mgr) and highlight Employee Listing By Route. You can also press (F10) (Menu) and select View Properties.

2. Press (F6) (Props), displaying the View Properties dialog box, since this view is already displayed.

3. Press (DOWN ARROW) once to highlight the Item sorting setting. Press (F3) (Choices) to display the Item Sorting in All Sections dialog box, as shown in Figure 4-32.

4. The choices for the Sort new items setting are On leaving a section, When item is entered, and On demand. Use the default by pressing (DOWN ARROW) once to highlight the Primary sort key setting.

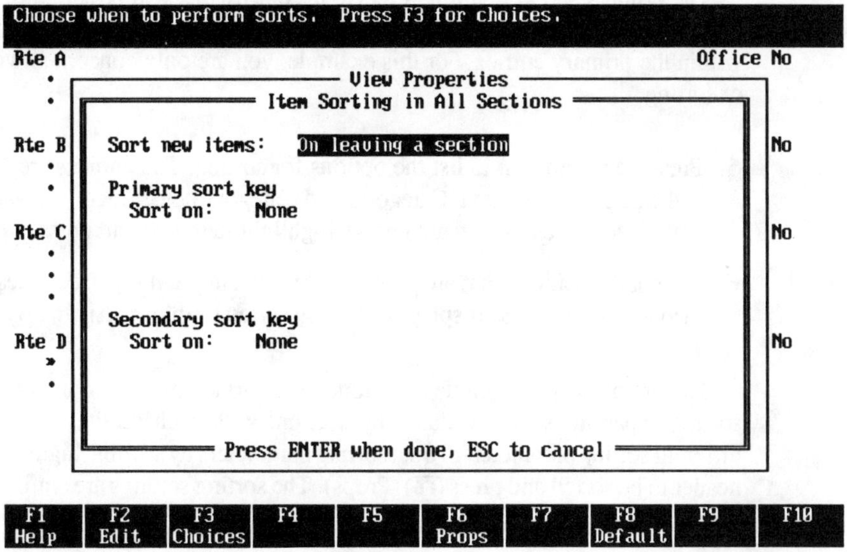

```
Choose when to perform sorts.  Press F3 for choices.
Rte A                                                          Office No
  •        ┌──────────────── View Properties ──────────────┐
  •        │────────── Item Sorting in All Sections ────────│
Rte B      │                                                │  No
  •        │  Sort new items:   On leaving a section        │
  •        │                                                │
Rte C      │  Primary sort key                              │  No
  •        │    Sort on:   None                             │
  •        │                                                │
  •        │                                                │
Rte D      │  Secondary sort key                            │  No
  »        │    Sort on:   None                             │
  •        │                                                │
           │                                                │
           │                                                │
           │──────── Press ENTER when done, ESC to cancel ──│
           └────────────────────────────────────────────────┘
```

F1	F2	F3	F4	F5	F6	F7	F8	F9	F10
Help	Edit	Choices			Props		Default		

FIGURE 4-32. The Item Sorting in All Sections dialog box displaying the default values

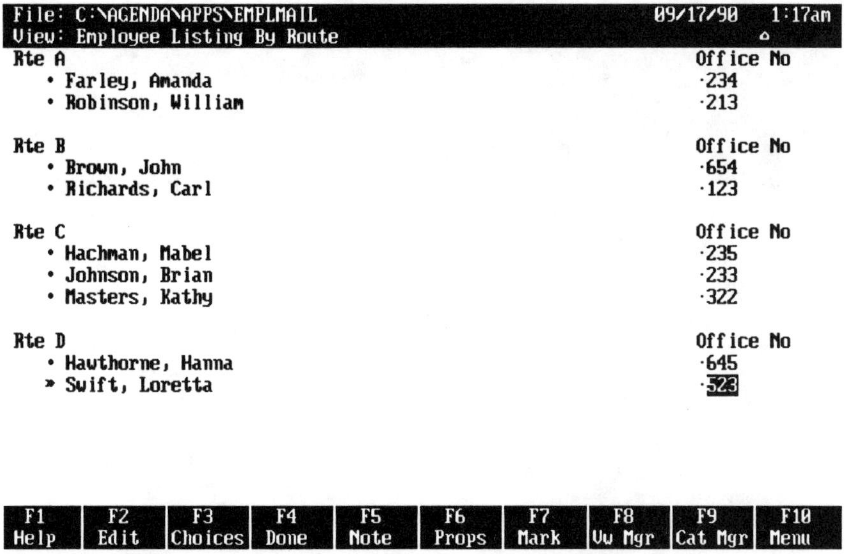

```
File: C:\AGENDA\APPS\EMPLMAIL                 09/17/90   1:17am
View: Employee Listing By Route                         ⌂
Rte A                                                   Office No
  • Farley, Amanda                                        ·234
  • Robinson, William                                     ·213

Rte B                                                   Office No
  • Brown, John                                           ·654
  • Richards, Carl                                        ·123

Rte C                                                   Office No
  • Hachman, Mabel                                        ·235
  • Johnson, Brian                                        ·233
  • Masters, Kathy                                        ·322

Rte D                                                   Office No
  • Hawthorne, Hanna                                      ·645
  » Swift, Loretta                                        ·523
```

F1	F2	F3	F4	F5	F6	F7	F8	F9	F10
Help	Edit	Choices	Done	Note	Props	Mark	Vw Mgr	Cat Mgr	Menu

FIGURE 4-33. Employee listing by route with items sorted under each section

The Primary sort key setting refers to the entries that will be sorted first within the view. The Secondary sort key setting refers to entries that would be alphabetized within the primary entries. For this example, you are only concerned with one level of sorting.

5. Press (F3) (Choices) to list the options for sorting. The choices are None (which is the default), Item text, Category, and Category note. Since you want to sort the employee names (which are items), highlight Item text and press (ENTER).

6. Accept the defaults that are presented by pressing (ENTER) three times to return to the view. Figure 4-33 displays the newly sorted Employee Listing By Route view.

The previous two examples just touch the surface of sorting in Agenda. Similar sorting capabilities are available by section, with each section being able to set different sorting parameters. To set sorting parameters by section, highlight the section header to be sorted and press (F6) (Props). The sorting settings are similar to those for the entire view.

ADDING OPTIONS
TO THE BASIC
BUILDING BLOCKS

5

MANAGING AND PRINTING YOUR AGENDA FILES

Managing Your Agenda Files
Printing

I n the first few chapters you learned how to use Agenda's basic building blocks to store your information. Now you will learn about other Agenda features that will help you use your information more effectively. In this chapter you will learn more about Agenda files and the commands that you can use to affect them. You will also learn about print features that allow you to produce reports from the information in your Agenda files.

Agenda's file features are a little different than those in most of the other programs you have used. Agenda automatically stores the data you enter in files on your hard disk. Most software packages require you to take a more active role in the save process. Since Agenda saves your data automatically, you must tell it the file name you plan to use before you can enter any data. In this chapter you will learn how to name and retrieve Agenda files, as well as how to create backup copies and abandon changes made to a file.

This chapter also covers all of Agenda's basic print options. You will learn how to select the information that you want to print. You will learn about Agenda's print defaults and how to select other options. Some of the formatting decisions you can control include the typeface, the type size, and the attributes of the characters, such as bold or italic. You can also add text to the bottom and top of each page to identify the output like the headers and footers supported with most word processing packages. With Agenda you have the same ability to control the format and contents of the output that you do when you are using a word processor.

MANAGING YOUR AGENDA FILES

Although data is stored in Agenda files automatically, you should learn how to use the commands in Agenda's File menu. You access this menu by pressing (F10) (Menu) and selecting File. The File menu options allow you to retrieve a file, save a file, and abandon the latest changes made to a file. You can make copies and erase the database using File Maintenance and set a description of the file and a password using File Properties. Some of these commands have an accelerator key that you can press in lieu of selecting the command from the menu. The other command you may need is the System command, which allows you to access DOS without leaving Agenda.

Naming Your Database Files

You must follow specific rules when naming files. The file name requirements are established by DOS, the operating system in your machine when you are running Agenda. If you are familiar with the file name requirements for another DOS program, you already know the rules for naming Agenda files. If not, read through this section to eliminate any potential problems with naming your files.

DOS has an eight-character limit on file names and a three-character limit on file name extensions. A period is used to separate the file name from the file name extension. Agenda automatically uses the extension .AG for Agenda databases and .BG for the backups of Agenda databases.

You can use any alphabetic or numeric characters when creating your file names in Agenda. Although DOS permits you to use some special symbols, you should restrict your use of the special symbols to the underscore character (_). This symbol is used as a separator in the file name since spaces are not allowed. You should avoid using other special symbols to guarantee compatibility between other versions of DOS and your file names.

If you enter a file name longer than eight characters, Agenda displays an error message and instructs you to reenter the name using eight characters or less. Agenda does not automatically truncate names to eight characters as DOS does when you name files with DOS commands.

Retrieving Agenda Databases

When you load Agenda, the name of the last database that you used is displayed. To open this file you only need to press (ENTER). To use a different Agenda file, press (F3) (Choices), highlight a different database, and press (ENTER). After Agenda is loaded and a file is opened, you can select a different database by using the File Retrieve command or its accelerator key, (ALT-G). This closes and saves the open database and opens another one. You can try creating and using a new database by following these steps:

1. Press (F10) (Menu) and select File Retrieve, or press (ALT-G).

    Agenda displays the Select File box,which lists the databases in the current directory, as shown in Figure 5-1. This is the same list that Agenda presents when you load Agenda and press (F3) (Choices) to list the files. From this dialog box you can select a different directory by selecting ..\ for the parent directory or selecting one of the subdirectories in the current one. You can use the function keys to change the information that Agenda lists in the dialog box.

2. Press (F7) (Dates).

    Agenda lists the dates and times that each of the databases was last saved.

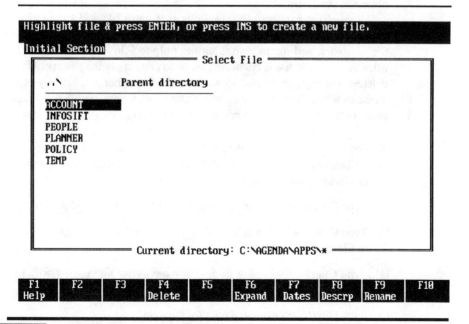

FIGURE 5-1.   Select File box

3. Press **F8** (Descrp).

   Agenda displays the file descriptions for each of the databases.

4. Press **INS** to create a new file.

   Agenda prompts for the new file name at the top of the screen.

5. Type **PREDICT** for the file name and press **ENTER**.

   Agenda displays this dialog box for you to enter a file description and a password:

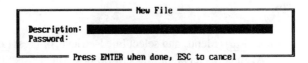

6. Type **Database for predicting sales** and press **ENTER**. File descriptions are limited to 40 characters. They are used when you open or print your database.

7. Press **DOWN ARROW**, type **files**, and press **ENTER** to add a password.

   A password allows you to restrict access to the file since it is not possible to open the file without the password. A password can consist of from 1 to 12 characters. Agenda displays dots in place of the characters that you type so that the password is not visible to others.

   Although the password feature limits access to a file, it does not provide security protection for the file. Anyone can delete the file from DOS without having to enter the password, and the password applies only to File Retrieve and does not restrict activities once the file is open. Anyone who can supply the password for the file can delete items, categories, and views from the file either accidentally or deliberately. You can add additional protection by protecting a view with View Properties View protection or by protecting a category with Category Properties Advanced settings.

8. Press **ENTER** to finalize the file description and password.

   This creates an empty database that has a description and password. Now the database needs some items.

9. Type **Check several economic predictions** and press **ENTER** for the first item.

10. Type **Check with the sales staff for what orders they expect their customers to place** and press **ENTER** for the second item.

11. Type **Check advertising budget for next year** and press **ENTER** for the third item.

12. Press **F5** (Note) to enter a note for the item.

13. Type **Statistical analysis indicates that advertising has a 50 percent effect on sales** and press (F5) (Return) to return to the Initial View.

  With the items added to the database, you are ready to try using the database to see how you can use the password features.

14. Press (ALT-G) to select the File Retrieve command.

15. Type **PREDICT** until the PREDICT database is highlighted and press (ENTER).
  As you type the file name, Agenda moves the highlight to the first database that matches your keystrokes. After you press (ENTER), Agenda displays this box prompting you for the password:

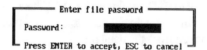

  As you type the password, your keystrokes appear as dots.

16. Type **files** and press (ENTER) to correctly enter the password.
  When you supply the correct password, the file is opened; if you do not supply the correct password, Agenda displays an error message. You can also change or remove the password protection.

17. Press (F10) (Menu) and select File Properties.
  Agenda displays a dialog box that controls several settings for the file. In the File Description field, you can edit or enter a new file description. The Set File Password field lets you change the password. The password will not appear on the screen when you type it.

18. Press (DOWN ARROW) to highlight ... and press (SPACEBAR) to alter the password.
  Agenda prompts for the existing file password. You must be able to enter the existing password before you can enter the new one. If you were adding a password to the database for the first time, you would not have to enter the existing password.

19. Type **files** and press (ENTER) to enter the existing password.

20. Type **safe**, press (ENTER), type **safe** again, and press (ENTER) to enter the new password.
  Entering a password twice ensures that you do not make any typing mistakes.

21. Press (ENTER) once more to leave the File Properties dialog box.

22. Press (ALT-G) to select the File Retrieve command.

23. Highlight the PREDICT database and press (ENTER).

24. Type **safe** and press (ENTER) to enter the password.

25. Press (F10) (Menu) and select File Properties.

26. Press (DOWN ARROW) and (SPACEBAR) to alter the password.

27. Type **safe** and press (ENTER) to enter the current password.

28. Press (ENTER) twice since you do not want a password.

29. Press (ENTER) again to leave the File Properties dialog box.

30. Press (ALT-G) to select the File Retrieve command.

31. Type **PREDICT** until the PREDICT database is highlighted and press (ENTER).
    This time you do not need to supply a password since the password protection is removed from the database.

OPENING THE LAST FILE USED   You can use the accelerator key sequence (ALT-F) to open the file you used previously. Pressing (ALT-F) first closes the file you are in and then opens the previously used file. This option allows you to toggle back and forth between two files easily; just continue to press (ALT-F) to switch between the files. Since Agenda permits only one file at a time to be open, the ease of toggling between files can save time when you need to move back and forth several times. If no file was opened between installing Agenda and creating PREDICT, the New File box is displayed when you press (ALT-F).

Backing Up Your Database

A backup copy of a database is a copy that you can use if something should happen to the original. The backup file has the same contents as the original at the time it is created and has the same file name as the database but with an extension of .BG. You can either create backups automatically or create them only when you want.

CREATING A BACKUP COPY WHEN YOU SAVE THE FILE   Create a backup of your database when you save the file by saving the file with the File Save command. You can see how to do this by following these steps:

1. Press (F10) (Menu) and select File Save.
    Agenda displays a dialog box with the fields Save to File and Also Save Backup. The Save to File field initially contains the drive, directory, and file name

of the current database. You can make a new entry to save the database with a different name or to a different location. To change this entry press (F2) (Edit), alter the entry, and press (ENTER). The Also Save Backup field selects whether Agenda makes a backup when it saves the database. Its default is Yes. You can change the setting by highlighting the field and pressing (SPACEBAR).

2. Make sure the Also Save Backup field is set to Yes and press (ENTER) to finalize your selections.

Agenda saves the current changes and makes a backup of the file. The backup copy of the database is called PREDICT.BG. Once you back up a database, Agenda displays a plus sign after the database name in the Select File box.

The File Save command also has an accelerator key, (ALT-W). Unlike the File Save command, pressing (ALT-W) does not display a dialog box. Instead, it saves the database using the same database name and does not create a backup. Note that (ALT-F) also does not create a backup when saving your file.

CREATING A BACKUP COPY AUTOMATICALLY   Another option for creating backups is to create them automatically whenever you open the database. An automatic backup copies the current database to the backup file when you open the database. To automatically back up the database, select the File Properties command. Press (DOWN ARROW) twice to move to the Make Backup on Open field, press (SPACEBAR) to change the No to Yes, and press (ENTER) to finalize your changes. Now every time you open the database, Agenda backs it up to the same file name with a .BG extension. If you do not want Agenda to make automatic backups, perform these same steps but change the Make Backups on Open field to No.

REVERTING TO THE BACKUP   If something happens to the original database, you will need to use the backup copy. To use the backup copy of the database, follow these steps:

1. Press (F10) (Menu) and select File Retrieve, or press (ALT-G).

2. Highlight PREDICT.
   Notice that Agenda displays a + after the database name to indicate that there is a backup copy of the database.

3. Press (F6) (Expand).
   This displays the backup below the original file name. To use the backup, select the backup file from the list.

4. Press (DOWN ARROW) and (ENTER) to select PREDICT.BG.
   Agenda displays a dialog box that asks if you want to replace the current database with the backup. If you select Yes, Agenda replaces the name PRE-

DICT.BG with PREDICT.AG. If you select No by pressing (SPACEBAR), Agenda prompts for a new name for the database. This database name becomes the name of the copy of the backed-up database you are using.

3. Press (ENTER) to finalize the settings.

Abandoning Changes

When you are working on your database, you may realize that you have made a mistake that you do not want to keep. If the mistake is simple, you probably can remove the effects of the mistake quickly. If the mistake is substantial, such as accidentally deleting several items, it may be easier to return the database to the state it was in when you first started working on it. This is called *abandoning your changes* and it works by retrieving the database saved on disk. You can see how it works by following these steps:

1. Type **Check current sales** and press (ENTER) to enter a new item.

2. Press (F10) (Menu) and select File Abandon.
   Agenda prompts you to confirm that you want to revert to the last saved version of the database.

3. Type **Y** or press (SPACEBAR) and (ENTER) to revert to the last saved version of the database.

Agenda restores the previously saved version. You can see the difference since the database is now missing the new item you added in step 1.

Renaming a Database

You can change the name of any of the databases in Agenda as long as it is not the open database. You might want to rename a database when the database name is misspelled, when you want an existing database to have a new name so that a new database can take its name, or when you want the file name to be more descriptive of its contents. To rename a file, move the highlight to the file that you want to rename in the Select File box and press (F9) (Rename). The prompt for the new file name looks like this:

Type the new name for the file and press (ENTER). Agenda changes the name of the .AG file to the new name. Any backup files will still have the old file name and will appear in the Select File dialog box with an extension of .BG after the database name.

Copying the Current Database

You can create a copy of the current database with Agenda's File Maintenance MakeCopy command. You use this command to save the database using another file name or to save it in a different location.

When you press (F10) (Menu) and select File Maintenance MakeCopy, Agenda displays a list of the files in the current directory. You can edit an existing file name by pressing (F9) (Rename), or you can copy to a new file name by pressing (INS) and typing a new name. Highlighting the name of an existing file will result in a loss of that file's data since it will be replaced with the contents of the current file. To make the copy of the database in another location, enter the drive and directory information before entering the file name.

Erasing a File

You can erase old files that you no longer need with Agenda's File Maintenance Erase command. This command removes the .AG and .BG files from your disk. When you press (F10) (Menu) and select File Maintenance Erase, Agenda displays a selection box with a list of the database files in the current directory. You can highlight your selection and press (ENTER). Since there is no way to restore the deleted file, Agenda asks for a confirmation. To delete the file, press (SPACEBAR) and press (ENTER) or type Y. Agenda permits you to delete files even if they are password-protected.

Agenda will not let you delete the file you are currently using. You must first close the file by opening another one. You can then erase the database.

Another method of deleting a database is to select the File Retrieve command, highlight the file to remove in the Select File dialog box, and then press (F4) (Delete) or (DEL).

Auto-Save Features

Most computer programs require you to take an active role in saving your data to disk. If you forget to save on a regular basis, you risk losing some of your data. Agenda automatically saves your file every time you switch to another database or you use certain commands like the System or Print commands from the menu. You can tell Agenda to automatically save the database at frequent intervals by pressing (F10) (Menu) and selecting Utilities Customize. In the Auto-Save Interval field, you can specify how frequently Agenda should automatically save changes. The default of 0 means that Agenda only saves the database when you switch to another database or use one of the commands that saves the database before it performs the command. You can enter any number between 1 and 60 to have Agenda also save the database in the number of minutes set by this field. Press (ENTER) when you are finished to leave the dialog box.

Executing DOS Commands From Inside Agenda

You can use DOS to perform many actions with Agenda files. Although you should use Agenda commands where possible, the tasks they perform are limited, so you may want to use DOS for some tasks. If you need to copy an Agenda file, use Agenda's features. If you need to list non-Agenda files or format a new floppy disk, you must use DOS. Agenda lets you perform DOS commands without leaving Agenda. Press (F10) (Menu) and select System, and a screen like the one in Figure 5-2 appears. From the DOS command prompt you can run many DOS commands like COPY, RENAME, DIR, and DELETE. When you are finished using the DOS commands, type **EXIT** to return to your database. You should avoid running TSRs (Terminate and Stay Resident programs) since these reside in memory even after you return to Agenda.

Making a Text File A Note for an Item

Another use of files is to use separate files to store notes for items. This is especially useful if you want to use other software, such as word processors, to modify the file as well as using the file for an Agenda database. For example, you might have a lengthy

```
Type EXIT to return to Agenda.


The IBM Personal Computer DOS
Version 3.30 (C)Copyright International Business Machines Corp 1981, 1987
              (C)Copyright Microsoft Corp 1981, 1986

C>
```

FIGURE 5-2.   Sample display when you use the System command

document typed on your word processor that you want to use as the note for one of your database's items. You can see how this works by following these steps:

1. Press (F10) (Menu) and select System to temporarily go to DOS.

2. Type **COPY CON NOTE.TMP** and press (ENTER).
    This DOS command will copy the text that you type to a file called NOTE.TMP.

3. Type **This note is stored in an external file** and press (CTRL-Z) and (ENTER).
    This creates an external file called NOTE.TMP that contains the text "This note is stored in an external file."

4. Type **EXIT** and press (ENTER) to return to Agenda.

5. Move to the item *Check several economic predictions*.

6. Press (F5) (Note) to display the note for the item.

7. Press (F10) (Menu) and select File Attach.
    Agenda prompts you for the name of the file that you want to attach to the note. If this item already had a note, Agenda would prompt you if you wanted to replace the contents of the note with the file. To do so, select Yes and the existing note will be erased.

8. Press (F3) (Choices) to see a list of files, start typing **NOTE.TMP** until Agenda highlights the file, and press (ENTER). Press (ENTER) to finalize the file name. The note looks like this:

```
Note for:   Check several economic predictions           Line 1 INS
Note file:  C:\AGENDA\NOTE.TMP      Font: Line Printer 8.5pt   Attr: Normal
This note is stored in an external file
```

The control panel indicates that this is an external file. Any changes made to the note from within Agenda are also made to the external file. You could use an external note for this item to store the predictions from several economic analyses. If the file is over 10K long (about seven double-spaced pages of data), Agenda will let you look at the lengthy note but will not let you edit it.

9. Press (F5) (Return) to return to the current view.

    Notice how Agenda displays a double note sign in place of the item marker.

10. Press (F5) (Note) to return to the note.

11. Press (F10) (Menu) and select File, Detach, and Yes.

    This detaches the external file from the note, but does not remove the file from the disk. The file remains on the disk until you remove it with Agenda's File Erase command or the DOS ERASE or DEL command.

12. Press (F5) (Return) to return to the current view.

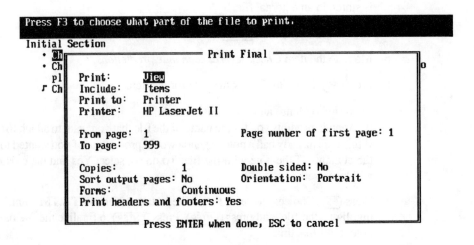

FIGURE 5-3.   Print Final dialog box

PRINTING

Agenda makes it very simple to print your database. You can tell Agenda what you want to print, and it will complete the print operation without your direction because it makes certain assumptions about how you want your print output to look. If you are not happy with these assumptions, you can change them in the Print Layout and Print Final dialog boxes. You can also see how the output will appear by using the Preview feature. This section of the chapter assumes that you installed a printer when you installed Agenda. If you did not, you should review Appendix A to see how you can tell Agenda which printers you plan to use.

Printing Your Database

Printing your database is as simple as selecting the Print Final command and pressing (ENTER). You can try printing the database by following these steps:

1. Press (F10) (Menu) and select Print Final to display the dialog box shown in Figure 5-3.

2. Press (ENTER) to use these default settings and Agenda will print the current view, as shown in Figure 5-4.

Since you used all of the default settings, Agenda printed the current view to the first printer you selected in the installation program. The printout includes the date, time, and view name at the top and the page number at the bottom. This information appears on every page when the database continues for several pages. The information at the top is called the *header* and the information at the bottom is called the *footer*. The header and footer are each separated from the database by a line. In the database area, Agenda underlines the section heads and prints section and column heads in boldface. Below each section head are the items and notes that belong to it. Agenda indicates note text by indenting it. These are the defaults, and you can change the appearance of the output using the print settings available through the Print Final and Print Layout dialog boxes.

CHANGING THE SETTINGS WITH PRINT FINAL You can change the default settings you use to print your database through the Print Final dialog box. Most of the settings can be changed by highlighting the field and then typing the first letter of the setting you want, pressing (SPACEBAR) to cycle through the options, or pressing (F3) to see a list of the available choices and then pressing (ENTER). Four of the settings

07/03/90 4:28pm   Initial View

Initial Section

- Check several economic predictions
- Check with sales staff for what orders they expect their customers to place
- Check advertising budget for next year

FIGURE 5-4.   Printed database

require that you type the number you want for the setting. You can change the following fields:

- **Print**   This field selects information Agenda prints. The default is View, which prints all of the information in the current view. You can also select Marked Items in View, Section, Current Item, and Assignment Profile (which prints the category hierarchy and marks the categories the current item belongs to).

- **Include**   This field selects whether Agenda prints items, notes, or both. Your choices are Items, Items and Notes, and Notes Only. This field is not available if you select Assignment Profile for the Print field.

- **Print to**   This field selects where the output is sent. Your choices are Printer, File with Printer Codes, Text File, Lotus Manuscript File, and DCA File. Printer prints the file to the printer; File with Printer Codes sends the information to a file on disk instead of the printer; Text File sends the information to a file that does not include the codes that tell the printer how to print the document; Lotus Manuscript File sends the information to a file that you can use with Lotus Manuscript; and DCA File sends the information to a file in the DCA format, which is a standard word processing format. If you select one of the choices besides Printer, Agenda adds a File field where you must enter the file name that Agenda is to print to. Since some of the subsequent settings do not apply to some of the possible destinations, changing the selection will change which settings appear in the dialog box.

- **Printer**   This field selects the printer that you are using to print. The choices are the ones you select during installation, as described in Appendix A.

- **File**   This field selects the file where the printed information is to be stored if you select a choice for the Print To field other than Printer. The default path is the current path. If you want to store this file to a different directory than the directory containing the database, you must enter this information before the file name. You can enter any valid file name. You do not have to enter an extension since Agenda adds a .PRN extension for print files that include the printer codes, a .PRT extension for print files that omit the printer codes, a .DOC extension for Manuscript files, and a .DCA extension for DCA format files. If the file already exists, Agenda asks you if you want to overwrite the file.

- **From page**   This field selects the first page you want printed and can be used with a printer or a file with codes.

- **To page**   This field selects the last page you want printed and can be used with a printer or file with codes.

- **Page number of first page**   This field selects the page number that Agenda uses for the first page when printing to a printer or a file with codes.

- **Copies**   This field selects the number of copies printed when using the printer only.

- **Double sided**   This field selects whether you want to print to both sides of the paper. Use this field only if your printer can print double-sided pages.

- **Sort output**   This field selects whether Agenda prints the pages in order. This only affects printers that stack their output and print in a reverse order.

- **Orientation**   This field selects whether to rotate the output on the page and whether to use the portrait or landscape fonts (described later). The two choices are Portrait, which prints top to bottom, and Landscape, which rotates the output so the database prints sideways on the page. You can use this with all print options except text files without printer codes. Some printers do not support Landscape.

- **Forms**   This field selects how the paper is fed to the printer. You can select Continuous if your printer uses continuous paper, Single Sheet (Auto feed) if the printer has a paper-feeding mechanism that continuously feeds the printer paper, or Single Sheet (Manual feed) if the printer must be fed one page at a time. If you select Single Sheet (Manual feed), Agenda will prompt you while it is printing when you need to insert the next sheet of paper.

- **Print headers and footers**   This field selects whether Agenda prints headers and footers. The default is Yes. If you change this to No, Agenda omits the headers and footers, providing more room for other printed information.

Previewing the Printed Output

Since you do not want to print out your database and then discover that it is not what you want, Agenda lets you preview on the screen how the printed output will appear. This requires that you correctly select your graphics adapter when you install Agenda with the instructions in Appendix A. You can preview your printouts to check the appearance and print the database only if it is what you want. To preview your database, follow these steps:

1. Press (F10) (Menu) and select Print Preview.
   Agenda displays the Print Preview dialog box. The fields in this box are identical to the ones in the Print Final dialog box, although some of the fields in the latter are not included in the Print Preview dialog box. If you make any changes in this dialog box, they will also appear in the Print Final dialog box when you select Print Final to print the database.

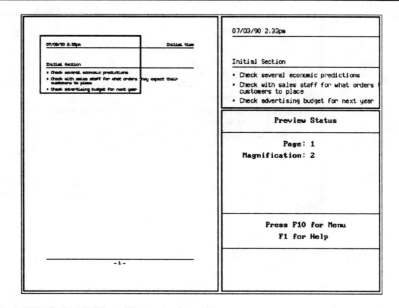

FIGURE 5-5.   Previewed database

2. Make any changes you want to the Print Preview dialog box.

3. Press (ENTER) to finalize the Print Preview dialog box.

    Agenda saves the database and displays on the screen how the printed output will look, as shown in Figure 5-5. The left half of the screen displays the full page of the printed output. The box around the text is called the *selector box*. The top of the right half of the screen shows a magnified version of the information in the selector box. This is called the *magnifier box*.

4. Press (DOWN ARROW) and (RIGHT ARROW) to move the selector box.

    The arrow keys move the selector box in the direction of the arrow. You can also use (HOME) or (END) to move the selector box to the upper-left or lower-right corner of the page.

5. Press the gray + and - keys to change the size of the selector box and the magnification of the text in the magnifier box.

    As the size of the selector box decreases, the magnification of the text in the magnifier box increases, so the text becomes larger. The magnifier box has nine different magnification levels, 2 through 10. The current level is shown in the Preview Status window below the magnifier box. This box also displays the page

```
┌──────────────────────────────────────────────────────────┐
│ ┌────────────────────────────────────────────────────────┐ │
│ │                                                        │ │
│ │ 07/03/90 2:33pm                           Initial View │ │
│ │ ──────────────────────────────────────────────────────│ │
│ │                                                        │ │
│ │                                                        │ │
│ │ Initial Section                                        │ │
│ │ ──────────────────────────────────────────────────────│ │
│ │ ᵒ Check several economic predictions                   │ │
│ │ ᵒ Check with sales staff for what orders they expect their │
│ │   customers to place                                   │ │
│ │ ᵒ Check advertising budget for next year               │ │
│ │                                                        │ │
│ │                                                        │ │
│ │                                                        │ │
│ │                                                        │ │
│ │                                                        │ │
│ │                                                        │ │
│ │                         Page: 1                        │ │
│ └────────────────────────────────────────────────────────┘ │
└──────────────────────────────────────────────────────────┘
```

FIGURE 5-6.   Displaying the contents of the preview

number of the page currently previewed and indicates that you can press (**F10**) (Menu) to display the menu and (**F1**) (Help) to display Help.

6. Press (**F10**) (Menu) and select Content to display the previewed document, as shown in Figure 5-6.

This changes the screen display to show an expanded view of the printed page. You can see a different portion of the page by pressing (**UP ARROW**) or (**DOWN ARROW**). You can also press (**PGUP**) or (**PGDN**) to move the display by a greater amount. If the printed output extends for several pages, you can change the page that is displayed by pressing (**ENTER**), (**CTRL-PGDN**), or (**ALT-N**), which is the accelerator key for the Page Next command. Pressing (**PGDN**) returns you to the view if there is only one page. To display a previous page, press (**CTRL-PGUP**) or (**ALT-P**), or use the Page Previous command. A third possibility is to select the Page Goto command or press its accelerator key, (**ALT-F5**) (GOTO). This displays the Goto Page box prompt. Type the number of the page you want to view and press (**ENTER**).

7. Press (**F10**) (Menu) and select Quit to leave the preview of the printed database.

You can also press the accelerator key (**ALT-Q**). Agenda returns you to the initial view. If the printed output is what you want, press (**F10**) (Menu), select Print Final, and press (**ENTER**) to use the settings. If the preview of the output is not what you want, you can change the print settings and then preview the output again.

Changing Print Settings
With the Print Layout Command

You can use the settings in the Print Layout dialog box to alter the appearance of the printed output. Select Print and Layout to display the dialog box, as shown in Figure 5-7. The selections you make in the Print Layout dialog box remain in effect for printing views until you make new selections. When you use Print Final, Agenda will use the settings you defined in Print Layout. The dialog box has the following settings:

- **Printer** This field selects the printer you are using to print your output. You can change the printer to one of the printers you installed with Agenda's installation program (covered in Appendix A). The selections available depend on the printers you selected during installation.

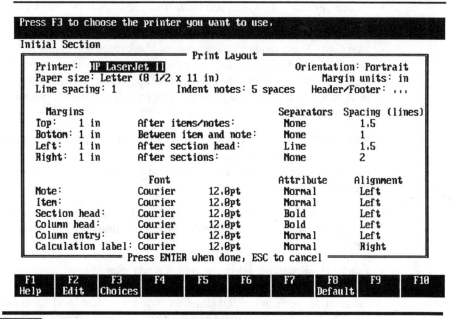

FIGURE 5-7. Print Layout dialog box

- **Paper size**   This field selects the size of the paper you are using. You can select one of the 16 predefined sizes or select Custom and enter the height and width of the paper.

- **Line spacing**   This field selects the spacing between lines in the printed output. The default is 1 for single-spacing. You can change this by entering any number between 0 and 150.

- **Orientation**   This field selects whether you will print in portrait or landscape mode. This is the same as the Orientation setting in the Print Final and Print Preview dialog boxes. This appears regardless of the printer, but some printers only support portrait mode. Note the Print Final Orientation setting overrides the Print Layout setting.

- **Margin units**   This field selects whether the margins and page sizes are measured in inches, centimeters, or millimeters. If you change this setting, Agenda adjusts the measurements for margins and page size to use the measurement system selected.

- **Indent notes**   This field sets the distance the notes are indented from the items or categories they belong to. Initially this is set to 5 to indent notes 5 characters to the right, but it can be changed to any number between -99 and 99. A negative number moves the note to the left.

- **Header/Footer**   This field sets the text that appears at the top or bottom of each page, as described previously.

- **Margins**   These fields set the amount of blank space that appears on each side of the pages. The default is 1 inch. You can enter a number between 0 and 10 inches, 0 and 26 centimeters, or 0 and 254 millimeters. Some printers require a minimum margin, so if you enter a margin that is too small, Agenda uses the minimum margin the printer needs.

- **Separators**   These fields select the separators that appear after items and notes, between items and notes, after section heads, and after sections. You can select None for no separators, Line to draw a line as a separator, or Page Break to break the page as the separator.

- **Spacing**   These settings select the line spacing after items and notes, between items and notes, after section heads, and after sections. You can enter any number between 0 and 150.

- **Font**   These settings select the font Agenda uses to print notes, items, section heads, column heads, column entries, and calculation labels. For each type of information, you can highlight the font currently selected and select one from the list. The fonts vary by printer and the fonts that you select with the Print Setup command.

- **Attribute** This setting selects the attribute of the text in the notes, items, section heads, column heads, column entries, and calculation labels. Your options include Normal, Bold, Italic, Underscore Words, Underscore All, Double Underscore Words, Double Underscore All, Subscript, Superscript, Strike Through, and Small Caps. The difference between the Words and All options for Underscore and Double Underscore is whether Agenda underlines the spaces between words. You can combine these selections by pressing (F3) (Choices) and then pressing (SPACEBAR) next to the attributes you want. The way your selections are printed depends on the printer since some printers cannot print all attributes.

- **Alignment** This setting selects the alignment of the text in the notes, items, section heads, column heads, column entries, and calculation labels. You can select between Left, Right, Center, and Even. Right creates flush right text with a jagged left edge, Center centers the text and creates a jagged right and left edge, and Even creates text that is both flush right and flush left, with extra spaces added between words to accomplish this. This setting has no effect on numeric columns. For items and column entries, the alignment is made within the columnar area that the item or column uses.

Adding Markers

You use the settings in the Print Layout dialog box to select the appearance of entire items or notes. You can also select attributes for portions of items or notes by adding *markers*. Markers indicate where the font or attribute should change. They also indicate where Agenda should substitute special information, including the date, file description, file name, page break, page number, path, printer code, time, and view name. The date, time, and view name that you see at the top of the page are actually date, time, and view markers that Agenda places automatically in the header of a new file. You can add a marker whenever Agenda displays Marker as the function for (F6). You can try using the different types of markers by following these steps:

1. Move to the *Check advertising budget for next year* item and press (F5) (Note).

2. Move the cursor to the *5* in *50 percent*.

3. Press (F6) (Marker) to display the Marker dialog box shown in Figure 5-8.

4. Press (F3) (Choices) to select an attribute.

5. Press (DOWN ARROW) until Underscore Words is highlighted, and press (SPACEBAR).

6. Press (ENTER) to finish selecting attributes.

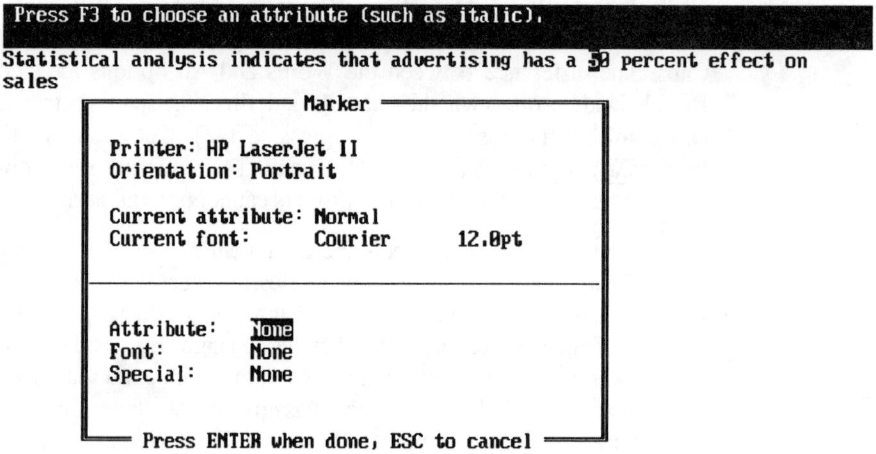

```
Press F3 to choose an attribute (such as italic).

Statistical analysis indicates that advertising has a 5⬛ percent effect on
sales
          ┌──────────────── Marker ────────────────┐
          │                                        │
          │  Printer: HP LaserJet II               │
          │  Orientation: Portrait                 │
          │                                        │
          │  Current attribute: Normal             │
          │  Current font:      Courier      12.0pt│
          │                                        │
          │                                        │
          │  ────────────────────────────────────  │
          │                                        │
          │  Attribute:  ▆None▆                     │
          │  Font:       None                      │
          │  Special:    None                      │
          │                                        │
          └────── Press ENTER when done, ESC to cancel ──────┘
```

─────────────────

FIGURE 5-8.   Dialog box to add a marker

7. Press (**DOWN ARROW**) and (**F3**) (Choices) to select a font.

8. Select a different font from the list and press (**ENTER**).

9. Press (**ENTER**) to complete the marker selections.

10. Move the cursor to the space after *percent*.

11. Press (**F6**) (Marker) to display the Marker dialog box.

12. Press (**F3**) (Choices), highlight Normal, and press (**SPACEBAR**) and (**ENTER**) to stop underlining.

13. Press (**DOWN ARROW**) and (**F3**) (Choices) to select a font.

14. Press (**HOME**) to select the first font and press (**ENTER**).

15. Press (**ENTER**) to finalize the marker.

16. Press (**CTRL-END**) and (**ENTER**) to move to the next line in the bottom of the file.

17. Type **This information is stored in the file** and a space.

18. Press (**F6**) (Marker) to add a marker.

19. Press (DOWN ARROW) two times to move to the Special setting.

20. Press (F3) (Choices), highlight File Name, and press (ENTER).

21. Press (ENTER) again to finalize the marker and type a period. The note looks like this:

```
Note for:   Check advertising budget for next year        Line 3 INS
                         Font: Courier 12.0pt  Attr: Normal
Statistical analysis indicates that advertising has a *50 percent* effect on
sales
This information is stored in the file *.█
```

22. Press (F5) (Return) to return to the current view.

23. Press (F10) (Menu) and select Print Preview.

24. Press (DOWN ARROW) to move to the Include setting.

25. Press (SPACEBAR) to change this setting to Items & Notes.

26. Press (ENTER) to preview the document.

27. Press (F10) (Menu), and select Contents to display the output shown in Figure 5-9.

28. Press (ALT-Q) to leave the preview.

```
07/03/90 2:58pm                                        Initial View


Initial Section
──────────────────────────────────────────────────────────────────
 o Check several economic predictions
 o Check with sales staff for what orders they expect their
   customers to place
 o Check advertising budget for next year
     Statistical analysis indicates that advertising has a 50
     percent effect on sales
     This information is stored in the file PREDICT.AG.




                          Page: 1
```

FIGURE 5-9.   Previewing a printout that uses markers

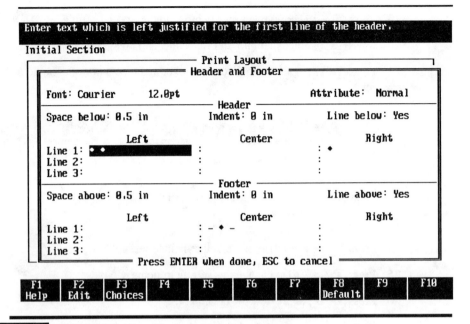

FIGURE 5-10.   Header and Footer dialog box

Adding Headers and Footers

One of the features Agenda automatically provides for your printouts is a header that displays the date, time, and view name and a footer that displays the page number. While these defaults are useful, you may want to change the information that appears at the top and bottom of each page. To change the header, press (F10) (Menu) and select Print Layout. In the Print Layout dialog box, highlight the dots after Header/Footer and press (SPACEBAR). This presents the Header and Footer dialog box shown in Figure 5-10. Use the top line of the dialog box to select the font size and attributes for your header and footer. Press (F3) (Choices) to select from a list of available choices. The format of the Header and Footer sections are identical. The Space Below and Space Above settings select, respectively, the space that Agenda leaves between the header or footer and the database. The Indent setting selects whether the header and footer align with the margin or are indented inward or outward. Line Below lets you select whether Agenda prints a line between the header and the database. Line Above lets you select whether to print a line between the footer and the database.

You use the last three lines of the Header and Footer sections to type the actual text that appears in the header or footer. Headers and footers can each contain up to three lines of text. Each line is divided into three sections. The first section is left-aligned, the second section is centered, and the third section is right-aligned. Each section can have up to 79 characters, with a total of 279 characters for the entire header or footer. The default entries display markers to indicate where the date, time, view name, and page number are placed.

To see how you can change the header and footer, follow these steps:

1. Press (F10) (Menu) and select Print Layout.

2. Press (DOWN ARROW) twice and (RIGHT ARROW) twice to move to the Header/Footer setting.

3. Press (SPACEBAR) to display the Header and Footer dialog box.
    Notice that markers appear in the location where Agenda displays the date, time, view name, and page number.

4. Press (RIGHT ARROW) to move to the centered section of Line 1.

5. Press (F2) (Edit) and then press (F6) (Marker) and (F3) (Choices) to change the attribute.

6. Highlight Bold, press (SPACEBAR) once, and press (ENTER) twice to add a marker to boldface the center section of the first line of the header.

7. Type **Plan for Predicting Next Year's Sales**.

8. Press (F6) (Marker) and (F3) (Choices). Highlight Normal and press (SPACEBAR) once and (ENTER) twice.

9. Press (ENTER) again to finalize this section of the header entry.

10. Press (DOWN ARROW) and (RIGHT ARROW) to move to the right-justified section of Line 2.

11. Type **Page:** and a space.

12. Press (F6) (Marker), (DOWN ARROW) twice, and (F3) (Choices) once to add a special marker.

13. Highlight Page Number and press (ENTER) twice.

14. Press (DOWN ARROW) three times and (LEFT ARROW) once to move to the centered section of Line 1 of the footer.

15. Press (DEL) three times.
    When you delete a marker, Agenda prompts for a confirmation.

16. Type **Y** and press (DEL) two more times to remove the footer.

17. Press (ENTER) three times to finalize the header, footer, and page layout.

18. Press (F10) (Menu) and select Print Preview.

19. Press (ENTER) to use the settings in the Print Preview dialog box. The top of your previewed output looks like this:

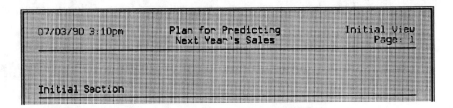

Notice that the centered text uses two lines since there was not enough room on the first line for all the text, and you did not specify anything for the second line.

20. Press (ALT-Q) to leave the preview.

Printing from the Category Manager

You can print from the Category Manager menu just as you can print views. The steps to follow are almost exactly the same, but most of the settings you used to print views do not apply to printing from the Category Manager. To print from the Category Manager, press (F9) (Cat Mgr) to activate the Category Manager, and then follow these steps:

1. Press (F10) (Menu) and select Print and Layout.
   Notice how many of the settings that you used for printing views do not appear for printing from the Category Manager.

2. Press (ESC) to leave the Print Layout dialog box, and select Final.
   The Print Final dialog box appears. Most of the settings are identical to printing a view. The only differences are the Print and Include fields. The selections for the Print field are Category Hierarchy and File Info. Category Hierarchy prints the category hierarchy primarily as it appears in the Category Manager. File Info prints the file name, its description, the files it uses (including the external files that are attached to notes and the file information that Agenda displays with the File Maintenance Info command). The Include field selects whether to print categories, notes, or both.

3. Press (**ENTER**) to start printing.

You can preview the printed output just as you preview printed output of views. The menu options for previewing a printed category hierarchy are the same as previewing a printed view.

Printing a Note

You can print from the view to print the current item or you can print a category note. The steps are similar to printing information from a view. Most of the settings you use to print a view do not apply to printing notes. To print a note, follow these steps:

1. Highlight an item or category with a note and press (**F5**) (Note).

2. Press (**F10**) (Menu) and select Print and Layout.
   Notice how many of the settings that you used for printing views do not appear for printing notes.

3. Press (**ESC**) to leave the Print Layout dialog box, and select Final.
   The Print Final dialog box appears. Most of the settings are identical to printing a view. The only difference is the Print field. The selections for the Print field are All Text in Note, which is the default, and Marked Text, which requires that you mark the text using (**F7**) before you press (**F10**) (Menu) to start printing.

4. Press (**ENTER**) to start printing.

You can preview the printed note just as you preview the printed output of views. The menu options for previewing a printed note are the same as those for previewing a printed view.

6

USING DATES
AND TIMES

Dates and times play an important part in most information management tasks. You may need to be aware of the date on which you receive an invoice, the date a loan payment is due, the projected completion date for a product, an employee's anniversary date, the date a lease expires, the time of a meeting, and many other date-related pieces of information. Date and time information can indicate when information was added to the file. Other dates that are sometimes recorded are a projected start date, a scheduled appointment date, a completion date for a construction project, a date for completing a proposal, or a date of receipt.

Most software packages allow you to record dates and times by defining and entering special fields with a date format. Agenda automatically assigns an entry date to an item you add to the file, a done date to a completed item, and a when date based on the contents of a note or item. Agenda understands typical date entries but can also interpret relative dates like "tomorrow" or "next Thursday."

Agenda's date features allow you to organize item information based on your priorities and the way you think. Any item in an Agenda file can have several types of dates attached to it. The date attached to an item can be the date the item needs to be completed, the date you first found out about the item, or the date you finished the item. Agenda allows you to incorporate these types of dates as part of the item or as a separate category. Agenda can also automatically assign these different dates to an item. Agenda can use times as well as dates.

You can think of Agenda's date features as additional categories to which items are assigned. You can show any of the date categories at the top of a column to see what date has been assigned for each item. You can also use Agenda's dates as categories in other ways since you can establish date filters and date conditions and actions.

This chapter examines Agenda's date features. In addition to establishing values for the different types of Agenda dates, you will learn how to use date filters to display items with specific date ranges and how to use dates for sequencing the items in your file. This chapter also covers the different settings you use for date categories and the new datebook view type, which lets you look at items and dates in a special way.

AGENDA'S THREE DATE TYPES

Agenda supports three different types of dates—entry, when, and done—which are automatically defined categories of every Agenda file you create. You can also create your own date categories, as described later in the chapter.

The first date type is the *entry date,* which is the date the item was entered or most recently edited. Agenda automatically gives each item an entry date whether or not it is subsequently used. If you use Agenda to record the date new employees are hired, the entry date can be the date of hire. A file that stores electronic mail information can use the entry date to store the date the message item was received. A project management system could use the entry date as the date the project was scheduled if project tasks are entered on the day that they are scheduled.

A *when date* can also be stored for each item. The when date represents the date that a project task should be completed, the date of a patient's next scheduled appointment, the date for a meeting relating to the item, the date the item should be purged from the file, and so on.

Every Agenda item can also be assigned a *done date* to represent the date an item is completed. Depending how you use it, the done date feature can also be used to purge items from the file.

You can create your own custom date categories for an Agenda file. For example, you might decide that you need a shipped or order date in addition to the automatic date categories created by Agenda.

You can create a new file to use as you try out the date features in this chapter. To create this file and add the three types of dates as columns, follow these steps:

1. Press (F10) (Menu) and select File Retrieve.

2. Press (INS) in the Select File box, type **DESIGN**, and press (ENTER) to create a new file.

3. Type **Stores project development information** as the file description and press (ENTER) twice.

4. Type **Develop general design for shopping mall** as the first item and press (ENTER).

5. Type **Acquire land** and press (ENTER).

6. Type **Create architectural blueprints** and press (ENTER).

7. Type **Call Shelley to develop 3-D model and drawing of proposed building** and press (ENTER).

8. Press (F10) (Menu) and select View Column Add.
   Agenda displays the Column Add dialog box.

9. Press (F3) (Choices), (DOWN ARROW), and (ENTER) to select the Entry category as the new column head. You can also start typing **Entry** and allow Agenda to auto-complete it and then press (ENTER).

Agenda automatically includes the Entry, When, and Done categories in the category hierarchy. The date categories have different settings in the dialog box that are appropriate for dates. You will learn later how you can change these settings.

10. Press (ENTER) to add this category as a column to the view.
    Agenda supplies an entry in the Entry column based on the time and date you added the item.

11. Press (ALT-R) to add a new column to the right of the Entry column.

12. Press (DOWN ARROW) three times to highlight Done in the category list and press (ENTER) once to use this category as the column heading.

13. Press (LEFT ARROW) and (ALT-L) to add a new column to the left of the Entry column.

14. Press (DOWN ARROW) twice to highlight When in the category list and press (ENTER) once to use this category as the column heading.

15. Press (DOWN ARROW), type **6/12/91** for the when date, and press (ENTER).
    Agenda knows that since this is a date column your entry must be a valid date. If you do not enter a date that Agenda can understand, Agenda will display a message and let you alter your entry.

16. Press (RIGHT ARROW) twice to move to the Done column.

17. Type **June 14, 1991** and press (ENTER). Now the dates for the first item look like this:

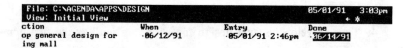

Your date in the Entry column will be different.

ENTERING DATES

You can enter and display dates in Agenda in several ways. Date formats like "31-Dec" or "12/31/90" are two acceptable date formats. A date entered in this type of format is called an *absolute date*.

Dates can also be described with words such as "tomorrow," "next Thursday," or "the end of this month." These are *relative dates*, since they are relative to the date in your computer system at the time they are entered. No absolute date is needed with this type of date entry because Agenda infers the actual date based on your entry and the current week, month, or year. When Agenda examines your entry, it searches the date entry for key words and then follows a set of rules for converting them to actual date entries. For example, "the end of the month" represents December 31 if it is entered in December, but it represents September 30 if it is entered in September.

Dates can also be described as *recurring* or *repetitive dates* to refer to an ongoing date commitment like "every Wednesday." This type of date entry is appropriate if you want to be reminded, for example, of a weekly sales meeting on Monday mornings or of the need to turn in weekly sales totals on Friday afternoons. You can try entering these types of dates by following these steps:

1. Press (CTRL-LEFT ARROW) to move to the Initial Section column.

2. Press (DOWN ARROW) to move to the *Acquire land* item.

3. Press (**ALT-F2**) (When) to enter a when date from this column.

4. Type **jun 12** and press (**ENTER**).

Agenda displays this entry as 06/12/91 (the year may vary) in the When date column. To speed up the entry of dates, Agenda allows several abbreviations, such as entering months using the first three letters and entering years with the last two digits for dates between 1900 and 1999. When you do not enter a year, Agenda uses the current year or the following year, depending on when you enter the date. In the example here, if the current date is on or before Jun 30, 1991, Agenda assumes that you want June 12, 1991. If the date is after June 30, 1991, Agenda assumes that you want June 12, 1992. Examples of allowable date formats are shown in Table 6-1. By using (**ALT-F2**) (When) to enter dates, you do not have to switch between the two columns as long as the highlight is on an item or the When column.

5. Press (**F4**) (Done).

This enters the current date in the Done date column (unlike the When key ((**ALT-F2**)) which requires you to enter the date manually). You can also enter done dates by moving the highlight to the Done column and typing a date following one of the acceptable formats.

6. Press (**RIGHT ARROW**) and (**DOWN ARROW**) to move to the When column for the third item, *Create Architectural Blueprints.*

7. Type **1st of July** for this item's when date and press (**ENTER**).

This entry displays as 07/01/91 (the year may vary). Ordinal numbers such as first, second, and so forth may be spelled out or abbreviated with the number and a suffix such as 1st or 2nd.

Syntax	Example
DD-MMM-YY	11-Sep-88
MM/DD/YY	9/11/88
DD MMM YY	11 Sep 88
DD MMM YYYY	11 Sep 1988
Ordinal numbers, spelled out	Second Sun in September
Ordinal numbers, abbreviated	11th of Sep

TABLE 6-1. Examples of Absolute Dates

8. Press (DEL).

   Agenda prompts if you want to remove this item's assignment to this category. This is how you can remove a when date or any date from a date column.

9. Type **Y** to select Yes or press (ENTER) since the default is Yes.

10. Type **Six weeks from today** for the item's when date and press (DOWN ARROW).

Relative dates are based on the current date when you enter the date information. Agenda processes this entry and displays a date that is 42 days after the date that appears in the control panel. For example, if the current date is May 30, 1991, Agenda returns July 11, 1991. As this entry shows, the date Agenda displays depends on whether you are entering this item on January 12, May 15, or October 1.

11. Type **End of July** and press (ENTER).

12. Type **Fourth fri of July** and press (ENTER).

Days of the week can be abbreviated to three letters. By typing a new entry over an old one, it replaces the previous entry.

The entries just covered are just a few of the possible words you can use to enter relative dates. A list of these words and examples of them are shown in Table 6-2. As you can see from the table, you do not need to learn new words to use the relative date options. If you give Agenda a date that it cannot figure out, it displays a message. To clear the message, press any key and edit the date entry or press (ESC) and try again.

With relative dates, Agenda remembers the entry as you made it. If you highlight the date and press (F2) (Edit), Agenda will display your entry in the control panel. If you press (ENTER), Agenda will re-evaluate the date. This means that if you enter **today** on June 3, 1991, Agenda will display 06/03/91. If you press (F2) (Edit) and (ENTER) on August 4, 1991, Agenda will change the displayed date to 08/04/91.

Using (F3) (Choices) To Enter Dates

Besides entering the dates using an absolute or relative date, you can also pick a date from a calendar that Agenda displays when you press (F3) (Choices). This is convenient when you are unsure of the exact date you want. To see how this works, follow these steps:

1. Press (LEFT ARROW) to move to the Initial Section column.

Word(s)	Example(s)	Interpretation (If System Date Is 6/15)
Today	Call Jennifer today	6/15
Tonight, tonite	Meeting tonight at 6	6/15
Tomorrow, tmorow	Stop by Jack's tomorrow	6/16
Yesterday, ystday	Will called yesterday	6/14
Day(s), week(s), month(s)	Two days ago	6/13
	In two weeks	6/29
	A month from today	7/15
From, after, before	Six months from today	12/15
	2 days after the first of June	6/3
	Day before yesterday	6/13
Of, in	First Monday of June	6/6
	Second Friday in July	7/8
Next (nxt), last	Next Friday	6/24
	Last Sunday	6/12
Each, every (for recurring dates)	Every Wed	6/15
	Each month	6/30
This	This Tuesday	6/14
Beginning (beg), end	Beginning of this month	6/1
	End of September	9/30

TABLE 6-2. Words Used in Relative Dates

2. Type **Open shopping mall** and press (ENTER).

3. Press (RIGHT ARROW) to move to the When column.

4. Press (F3) (Choices).

   Agenda displays the calendar for the current month like the one shown in Figure 6-1. To select a date from the calendar, highlight the date, and then press (ENTER) to remove the calendar from view (don't do this just yet).

5. Press (CTRL-RIGHT ARROW).

Pressing (CTRL-RIGHT ARROW) displays the month's calendar for the next year. Pressing (CTRL-LEFT ARROW) displays the month's calendar for the previous year.

6. Press (END).

```
Highlight the date and press ENTER. Use arrow keys, PgUp, PgDn,
CTRL (with arrows) to move to other months and years.
Initial Section                    When            Entry              Done
 • Develop general design for      ·06/12/91       ·05/01/91 2:46pm   ·06/14/
   shopping mall
 ‼ Acquire land                    ·06/12/91       ·05/01/91 2:46pm   ·05/01/
 • Create architectural            ·06/12/91       ·05/01/91 2:46pm
   blueprints
 • Call Shelley to develop 3-D     ·07/26/91       ·05/01/91 2:47pm
   model and drawing of proposed
   building
 » Open shopping mal┌══════ May 1991 ══════┐·05/01/91 5:01pm

                     Sun Mon Tue Wed Thu Fri Sat

                                   █1█  2   3   4
                      5   6   7    8   9   10  11
                     12  13  14   15  16  17  18
                     19  20  21   22  23  24  25
                     26  27  28   29  30  31
```

F1	F2	F3	F4	F5	F6	F7	F8	F9	F10
Help					SetTime				

FIGURE 6-1.   Displaying a calender with (F3) (Choices)

Pressing (END) highlights the last day of the month, and pressing (HOME) highlights the first day of the month. You can also use (RIGHT ARROW) or (LEFT ARROW) to move to the next or previous day, respectively, or (UP ARROW) or (DOWN ARROW) to move to the previous or next week, respectively.

7. Press (PGUP).

Pressing (PGUP) displays the calendar for the previous month and pressing (PGDN) displays the calendar for the next month.

8. Press (ENTER) to select this date.

Agenda removes the calendar from the screen and displays the selected date in the When column. You can use (F3) (Choices) to select a date any time by displaying the calendar with the highlight in a date column.

Placing the Date in Item Text

You can also enter a when date for an item by entering the date in the text of the item and letting Agenda use this date as the item's when date. For example, if the item is "Planning meeting next Friday," Agenda assigns Friday of next week's date for the when date. This automatic assignment feature for the when date also works with recurring dates. By including the when date as part of the item, you can enter both item text and when date with one effort. You can try this with the following steps:

1. Press (LEFT ARROW) to move to the Initial Section column.

2. Type **Planning meeting next Friday** and press (ENTER).

Notice how Agenda entered next Friday's date automatically in the When column based on the item's text.

3. Type **Call Pat today about Friday's planning meeting** and press (ENTER).

When an item mentions more than one date, Agenda uses the first one mentioned as the when date. For this reason phrases such as "Monday, Sept 10" should be avoided since Agenda will use the next occurrence of Monday, not 9/10.

Recurring Dates

Sales meetings, monthly status reports, weekly quotas, and quarterly budget updates all take place on a regular basis. Agenda helps you deal with these situations with recurring dates, which date items for multiple time periods.

The word "each" or "every" is used in recurring dates to differentiate them from relative dates. Recurring dates are treated differently from relative dates since Agenda reevaluates recurring dates that reference a day of the week or month that has passed. It re-evaluates the date with the previous reference and assigns it a new date for the first future occurrence of a matching date.

To try this feature, type **Submit department payroll vouchers at the end of every week** and press (ENTER). This sets the when date to the last date of the current week, starting with the following week. On the first day of the subsequent week, Agenda redates the item for the upcoming last day of the week. Even when recurring items are marked done, as described later, Agenda redates them for the next occurrence of the date regardless of any action that is taken on done items.

Creating Other Date Categories

You can create other date categories besides the three Agenda automatically provides. You can see how you might use an extra date category by following these steps:

1. Press (RIGHT ARROW) to move to the When column.

2. Press (F10) (Menu) and select View Column Add.
   You do not want to use the shortcuts (ALT-L) or (ALT-R) since they will not let you change all of the settings.

3. Type **Actual Completion Date** for the category name that you want to use for the column head and press (ENTER).
   Since this is a new category, it is added as a child category of the Main category.

4. Press (RIGHT ARROW) to move to the Category Type setting and type **D** for Date. Notice that all the settings associated with date categories now appear.

5. Press (LEFT ARROW) and (DOWN ARROW) to move to the Width setting, type **25**, and press (ENTER) twice to create this new column with the settings you have entered.

In the bottom of the dialog box, you can change the way dates and times display in this column, as described later.

6. Press (HOME) and (DOWN ARROW) to position the highlight where you will enter the first date for the category.

7. Type **06/15/91** and press (ENTER).

8. Press (DOWN ARROW), type **06/15/91**, and press (ENTER).

ENTERING TIMES

Agenda can handle times as well as dates. While Agenda does not automatically create several time categories in your file, you can enter times as part of a date category or as a separate category. You can enter times by typing the time you want in the date column or by including the time information as part of the item text. You can try using times by following these steps:

1. Press (DOWN ARROW) four times and (LEFT ARROW) twice to move to the *Planning meeting next Friday* item.

2. Press (F2) (Edit) and (END) to move to the end of the item's text.

3. Press (SPACEBAR), type **at noon,** and press (ENTER).

   Agenda automatically realizes that the When date should include the time 12:00 PM. Using the default settings, Agenda displays both dates and times in the same column.

4. Press (RIGHT ARROW) and (DOWN ARROW) to move to the When column for the next to last item, *Call Pat today....*

5. Press (F2) (Edit) to alter the date, press (END), type a space and **3 o'clock,** and press (ENTER).

Agenda accepts dates in several formats, but it displays all the dates and times that you enter in one format. Later you will learn how you can change how Agenda displays dates and times.

6. Press (DOWN ARROW) and (F3) (Choices).

   Agenda displays the calendar with the current when date highlighted.

7. Press (F6) (Settime).

   Agenda displays a dialog box prompting for a time entry. You can use the calendar and (F6) (Settime) to set both the time and date at the same time.

8. Type **6:00 pm** and press (ENTER).

   You can actually save a few keystrokes and not type **pm** since the default times for morning and evening in the Global date settings cause 6 to be treated as 6:00 PM.

9. Press (F2) and (END), press (BACKSPACE) six times, type **17:00,** and press (ENTER) three times.

Using a 24-hour clock is another way you can enter a time. A 24-hour clock uses 1 through 12 for the hours before 1:00 PM and 13 through 24 for the hours 1:00 PM through midnight.

10. Press (UP ARROW) and (RIGHT ARROW) to move to the Actual Completion Date column.

11. Type **now** and press (ENTER).

Agenda interprets "now" as a combination of the current time and date. This is different than "today," which Agenda only interprets as the current date. Phrases such as "in 3 hours" will also produce a date/time.

CHANGING THE SETTINGS OF DATES AND TIMES

Agenda has several options you can use to control dates and times. You have used some of these options before with the other categories you have created, but Agenda has additional options that only apply for date categories. The selections you make depend on whether you are changing the appearance of a column of dates, all dates, or all dates belonging to a particular category. You also have several options for using the Done date category to specially process the items that you mark done.

Changing the Appearance Of a Column of Dates and Times

You can select how each column of dates and times displays its information. The options control how the date and/or time appears, the column width, and whether changes you make to a date column in one section affect the date column in other sections. To try changing the date and time settings for the When date column, follow these steps:

1. Press (LEFT ARROW) to move to the When column.

2. Press (F10) (Menu) and select View Column Properties to display the dialog box shown in Figure 6-2.

You can also display this dialog box by highlighting the category name used as a column head and pressing (F6) (Prop). The first setting in the dialog box lets you change the category used for the column head.

3. Press (DOWN ARROW), type **20** for the column width, and press (ENTER).

This changes the column width to 20 so you can use the wider date and time formats. To the right of the Column Head and Width settings, the Category Type setting selects the category type of the category and the Line With Other Sections setting selects whether the changes made to the column in one section affect the column in other sections of the view.

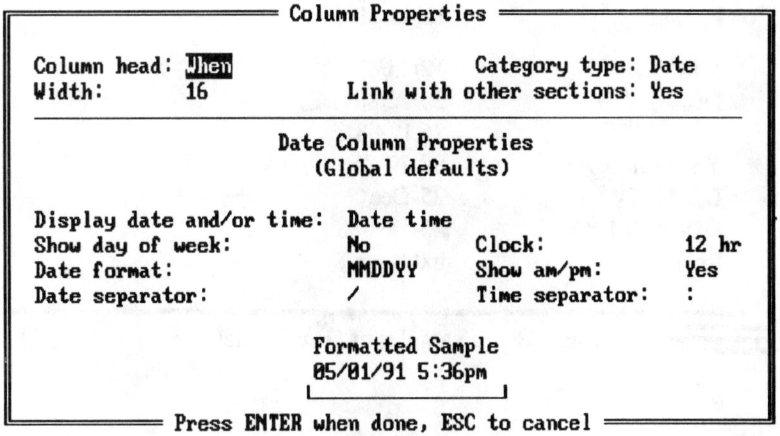

```
┌─────────────────────── Column Properties ───────────────────────┐
│                                                                  │
│   Column head: When                        Category type: Date   │
│   Width:        16              Link with other sections: Yes     │
│  ────────────────────────────────────────────────────────────    │
│                      Date Column Properties                       │
│                         (Global defaults)                         │
│                                                                   │
│   Display date and/or time:  Date time                            │
│   Show day of week:          No          Clock:          12 hr    │
│   Date format:               MMDDYY      Show am/pm:     Yes       │
│   Date separator:            /           Time separator:  :        │
│                                                                   │
│                       Formatted Sample                            │
│                       05/01/91 5:36pm                             │
│                       └─────────────┘                            │
│                                                                   │
└─────────────── Press ENTER when done, ESC to cancel ─────────────┘
```

FIGURE 6-2.   Dialog box for setting the properties of a column

4. Press (DOWN ARROW) and (F3) (Choices) to see the different choices for the Display Date and/or Time setting.

This setting lets you select whether the column displays dates, times, or both and the order that dates and times are displayed.

5. Press (ESC) to remove the selection box, press (DOWN ARROW) and (SPACEBAR) to change the Show Day of Week setting from No to Yes.

This setting selects whether Agenda displays the days of the week as part of the date. As you make changes to the lower half of the dialog box, Agenda displays the current date and time using the formatted sample.

6. Press (DOWN ARROW) and (F3) (Choices) to display the list of date formats.

Agenda has the 20 date and time formats shown in Table 6-3. You can select any one of them. DD indicates the day number, MM indicates the number of the month, MMM indicates the three letter abbreviation of the month, YY indicates the last two digits of the year, and YYYY indicates all four digits of the year. You can also use relative

Format	Example
MM/DD/YY	12/25/88
DD/MM/YY	25/12/88
DD.MM.YY	25.12.88
YY-MM-DD	88-12-25
DD-MMM	25-Dec
DD-MMM-YY	25-Dec-88
Relative	nxt Sun

TABLE 6-3.   Examples of Date Formats

format to display dates using relative terms such as "tomorrow" and "next Thursday." The # indicates the number of days or weeks in the current year that have gone by up to that date. Relative # also displays the number of days before the specified date.

7. Highlight MMMDDYYYY and press (ENTER).

8. Press (DOWN ARROW), (F3) (Choices) to look at date separator options, highlight the next to last selection (a space), and press (ENTER).

The Date Separator setting selects the character Agenda uses to separate the different parts of the date. You can select from a slash (the default), a hyphen, a period, a comma, a space, or a colon.

9. Press (UP ARROW) twice and (RIGHT ARROW) once to move to the Clock setting. Press (F3) (Choices).

The Clock setting selects whether the time is displayed using a 24- or 12-hour clock. The Show AM/PM setting below it selects whether Agenda displays AM or PM after a time to indicate whether it is before or after noon.

10. Press (ESC) once, (DOWN ARROW) twice, and (F3) (Choices) once to see the selections for the Time Separator setting.

The Time Separator setting selects the character Agenda uses to separate the different parts of the time. Your choices are a colon (the default) or hm, which displays an "h" after the hour and an "m" after the minutes.

```
File: C:\AGENDA\APPS\DESIGN                              05/02/91   4:08pm
View: Initial View                                             → *
Initial Section                      When              Actual Completion Dat
   ♪ Develop general design for      ·Wed Jun 12 1991  ·06/15/91
     shopping mall
   ‼ Acquire land                    ·Wed Jun 12 1991  ·06/15/91
   • Create architectual             ·Wed Jun 12 1991  ·05/12/92
     blueprints
   • Call Shelley to develop 3-D      ·Fri Jul 26 1991
     model and drawing of proposed
     building
   • Open shopping mall              ·Tue Apr 30 1991 5:00
   • Planning meeting next Friday    ·Fri May 10 1991 12:0
     at noon
   » Call Pat today about Friday's  [Thu May 02 1991 3:00] ·05/02/91 1:54pm
     planning meeting
   • Submit department payroll        ·Thu May 09 1991
     vouchers at the end of every
     week
```

```
┌────┬────┬───────┬────┬─────┬─────┬─────┬──────┬───────┬─────┐
│ F1 │ F2 │  F3   │ F4 │ F5  │ F6  │ F7  │  F8  │  F9   │ F10 │
│Help│Edit│Choices│Done│Note │Props│Mark │Vw Mgr│Cat Mgr│Menu │
└────┴────┴───────┴────┴─────┴─────┴─────┴──────┴───────┴─────┘
```

FIGURE 6-3.   DESIGN file after altering the When date column

11. Press (ENTER) twice to finalize these settings. Note that the Date Column Properties will override display formats made through Global Date Settings. Your view should look something like Figure 6-3 (the dates may vary slightly).

Making Property Settings
For a Date Category

Another group of settings you can change are the settings for a date category. These settings do not control how the dates appear, but they select how dates are assigned. The Done, Entry, and When date categories have default settings that you have already used. You can change these settings as well as the settings of the date categories that you create. To try changing the date and time settings for the When date column, follow these steps:

1. Press (RIGHT ARROW) twice and (HOME) once to highlight the Entry category used as a column head.

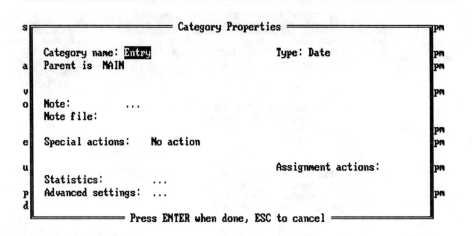

FIGURE 6-4.   Category Properties dialog box

2. Press (F10) (Menu) and select Category Properties to display the dialog shown box in Figure 6-4.

You can also display this dialog box by highlighting the category name when it is not used as a column head (such as in the Category Manager) and pressing (F6) (Prop). At the top of the dialog box, you can edit the category name and the category type. You cannot change Date, Numeric, or Unindexed Category types.

3. Press (DOWN ARROW), press (SPACEBAR) to display the note, type **This is the note for a date category**, and press (F5) (Return) to enter a note for this category.

This is the same as pressing (F5) (Note) when the category is highlighted. You can also attach a file as a note either using the File Attach command in the note or by typing a file name in the Note File setting.

4. Press (DOWN ARROW) twice and press (F3) (Choices) to see the possible choices you have for the Special Actions setting.

You can select between No Action, Discard Item, Designate Items as Done, and Export Item. For all date categories, the default is No Action. Later you will learn how you can use these different special actions.

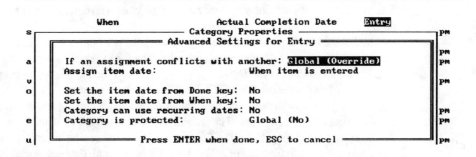

FIGURE 6-5.   Dialog box for setting advanced category properties

5. Press (**ESC**), (**DOWN ARROW**), and (**SPACEBAR**) to display the category statistics.
   Agenda displays a dialog box containing the number of items in the category, the number of child categories, and the number of times the category is used as a section head or included in a view filter, in conditions, or in actions.

6. Press (**ESC**) to return to the Category Properties dialog box.

7. Press (**DOWN ARROW**) and (**SPACEBAR**) to display the Advanced Settings dialog box shown in Figure 6-5.

This dialog box contains the settings Agenda uses to determine when it should enter dates for you. The first setting selects what Agenda should do if certain actions and conditions cause conflicting category assignments (you will learn about these actions and conditions in Chapters 8 and 9). The second setting, Assign Item Date, selects whether Agenda sets the date in the date column based on when you enter or edit the note and/or text, or whether Agenda searches through the item and/or note text for a date to use. The default setting for the When category is From the Item Text, the default setting for the Entry category is When Item is Entered, and the default setting for the Done category and other date categories is Never. You can also select Never for the Entry or When dates or your own date categories if you want Agenda to stop assigning dates to these categories. When you select From the Item Text, From the Note Text, or From the Item or Note Text, Agenda displays another setting, Which one, that selects which date in the item or note text Agenda should use for the date when the item and/or note contains more than one date. The default is 1, which explains why earlier in the chapter when you entered an item that contained two dates, Agenda used the first one.

8. Move the highlight to the Assign Item Date setting and press (**F3**) (Choices). Press (**END**) to highlight When Item or Note Text is Edited and press (**ENTER**).

This sets the date for the Entry category to the date when you edit the item or the item's note.

The Set the Item Date from Done Key setting selects whether Agenda sets the date for the date category to the current date when the (F4) (Done) key is pressed. This setting defaults to Yes in the Done date category. The When key lets you enter a date from any column after pressing (ALT-F2) (When). The Category Can Use Recurring Dates setting selects whether the date category accepts recurring dates and updates the recurring dates in columns. The default setting for the When date is Yes and for the other date categories is No. The Category is Protected setting selects whether you can makes changes to the category. The default setting for all date categories is Global (No), which uses the default category protection setting from the File Properties command.

9. Press (ENTER) twice to use the modified category properties for the Entry category.

10. Press (CTRL-LEFT ARROW) and (DOWN ARROW) to move to the first item.

11. Press (F5) (Note), type **This note is modifying the project**, and press (F5) (Return).

12. Press (RIGHT ARROW) three times to see the Entry column.

Notice how the date in the Entry column is the current time and date. This is because you changed the Assign Item Date for this category to When Item or Note Text is Edited.

Changing the Default Settings for Dates and Times

A third group of settings you can change are the global settings used by the entire file. These include settings for changing the appearance of the date and time and how Agenda interprets dates and times in item text. To try changing the date and time settings for the file, follow these steps:

1. Press (F10) (Menu) and select File Properties. This is the same dialog box you used in the previous chapter for changing the file description and password.

2. Press (END) once, (UP ARROW) twice, and (SPACEBAR) to display the Global Date Settings dialog box, as shown in Figure 6-6.

3. Press (SPACEBAR) to display the dialog box for Display format.

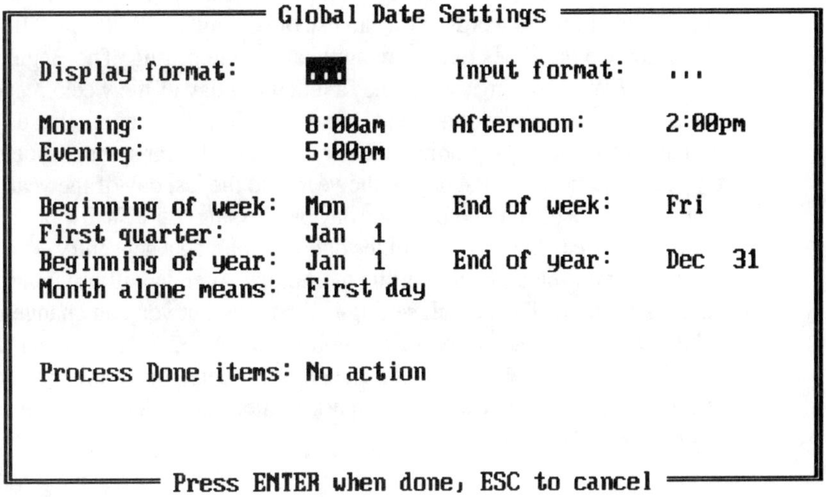

```
┌════════════════ Global Date Settings ════════════════┐
║                                                       ║
║   Display format:      ▪▪▪      Input format:   ...    ║
║                                                       ║
║   Morning:          8:00am      Afternoon:     2:00pm  ║
║   Evening:          5:00pm                             ║
║                                                       ║
║   Beginning of week: Mon        End of week:    Fri    ║
║   First quarter:     Jan  1                            ║
║   Beginning of year: Jan  1     End of year:    Dec  31║
║   Month alone means: First day                        ║
║                                                       ║
║                                                       ║
║   Process Done items: No action                       ║
║                                                       ║
║                                                       ║
└══════════ Press ENTER when done, ESC to cancel ═══════┘
```

FIGURE 6-6.   Global Date Settings dialog box

This dialog box selects how dates will appear when you do not select a different format with the View Column Properties command. The settings and the possible choices were described earlier in the chapter in the section "Changing the Appearance of a Column of Dates and Times."

4. Press (ESC), (RIGHT ARROW), and (SPACEBAR) to display the settings for the Input format.

This dialog box tells Agenda how you will enter dates and times. In the Number Order setting, you specify the order that you will enter the day, month, and year. Originally this setting is MDY, indicating that you will enter the month then day then year. You can change it to one of five other formats. The Input Date Separator setting selects whether you will use a slash, hyphen, period, comma, or colon to separate the different parts of the dates. The Input Clock setting selects whether you will use a 12-hour or 24-hour clock as the default type for entering times.

5. Press (ESC) to return to the Global Date Settings dialog box.

The remaining settings in this dialog box select how Agenda will interpret dates that you enter using words and how you want to treat items you mark as done. The

Morning, Afternoon, and Evening settings select the time Agenda uses when a date contains one of these words. You can use the defaults of 8:00 AM, 2:00 PM, and 5:00 PM, or change the times to a more applicable time setting. The Beginning of Week and End of Week settings select the first and last day of the week, respectively. You can use the defaults of Monday and Friday or change them to another day of the week. For the First Quarter, Beginning of Year, and End of Year settings, you select the first day of the quarter, the first day of the year, and the last day of the year, respectively. You can select a different month and day by pressing (LEFT ARROW) and (RIGHT ARROW) to switch between the two parts of the date and making a new entry. The Month Alone setting lets you select the day of the month that Agenda will use when the date only contains a month. The default setting is First Day but you can change it to Last Day or Nth Day. If you select Nth Day, you must enter the day number that you want Agenda to use. The Process Done Items setting lets you change the action Agenda performs on your items when you mark an item done. This is covered later in the section "Done Dates."

6. Press (ENTER) twice to finalize these settings.

SORTING BY DATE

You can use the date categories to change the order of the items in the view. To sort a view by a date category, follow these steps:

1. Press (F10) (Menu) and select View Properties.

2. Press (DOWN ARROW) and (SPACEBAR) to display the Item Sorting in All Sections dialog box, shown in Figure 6-7.

3. Press (F3) (Choices) to list the options for when you can have the sort performed, highlight On Demand, and press (ENTER).

Your other choices are On Leaving a Section and When Item Is Entered. If you select When Item Is Entered, Agenda will resequence all the items any time a date is changed. If you have to edit the dates in a column of entries, this constant reshuffling can make it difficult to keep track of which records have been changed.

4. Press (DOWN ARROW) to move the highlight to Sort On under the Primary Sort Key section. If Category is not the current choice for this setting, type **C**.

5. Press (DOWN ARROW) to move to the order setting under Primary Sort Key. If Ascending is not the current choice for this setting, type **A**.

```
┌─══════════ Item Sorting in All Sections ══════════┐
│                                                    │
│  Sort new items:    On demand                      │
│                                                    │
│  Primary sort key                                  │
│     Sort on:    Category                           │
│     Order:      Ascending        Sort n/a's: Bottom of section │
│     Category:   When                               │
│                                                    │
│                                                    │
│  Secondary sort key                                │
│     Sort on:    Category                           │
│     Order:      Ascending        Sort n/a's: Bottom of section │
│     Category:   ▓Actual Completion Date▓           │
│                                                    │
└─══════ Press ENTER when done, ESC to cancel ══════┘
```

FIGURE 6-7.   Dialog box to sort items in a view

6. Press (DOWN ARROW) to move to the Category setting. Press (F3) (Choices) to list the categories, highlight When, and press (ENTER). You can also type the category at the command prompt. You do not have to use a category that appears in the view as the category to sort the items by.

7. Press (DOWN ARROW) to move the highlight to Sort On in the Secondary Sort key section. If Category is not the current choice for this setting, type C.

8. Press (DOWN ARROW) to move to the Order setting.
   You can press (SPACEBAR) if you want to change the sequence of the sort to toggle between Ascending and Descending.

9. Press (DOWN ARROW) to move to the Category setting. Press (F3) (Choices) to list the categories, highlight Actual Completion Date, and press (ENTER).

10. Press (ENTER) twice to sort the view with these settings.

11. Press (CTRL-LEFT ARROW) once and (UP ARROW) once to highlight *Create architectural blueprints.*

12. Press (ALT-F2) (When), type **5/12/92,** and press (ENTER).
    Agenda does not sort the items since you told it that you wanted the sort performed on demand.

13. Press (ALT-S).

(ALT-S) resorts the items. Agenda will also resort the items when you load the view or print it.

Another option for sorting the items is to only sort the items within a section. To sort a section, press (F10) (Menu), select View Section Properties, and then perform steps 2 through 10 just as if you are sorting the view.

USING DATE FILTERS

Agenda allows you to filter items displayed in a view by their dates. This date filter option is useful if you want to isolate all the items entered on a day or to see all the items that are due to be completed today based on their current when date setting. You could also lay out a work plan for the next month if you changed the filter to look at all the when dates in the current month. You can create a filter, browse through it, change it, or delete it.

Creating a Filter

You can create a filter for the current month by following these steps:

1. Press (F10) (Menu) and select View Properties.

2. Press (END) once, (UP ARROW) twice, and (RIGHT ARROW) to move below Filter.

3. Press (F3) (Choices) to display the category hierarchy to select a category for the filter.

4. Highlight When and press (SPACEBAR).
   Agenda displays this dialog box:

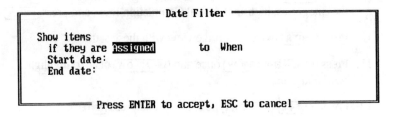

```
┌══════════════════ Date Filter ══════════════════┐
│                                                  │
│  Show items                                      │
│    if they are ▐assigned▌        to  When        │
│    Start date:                                   │
│    End date:                                     │
│                                                  │
└═════════ Press ENTER to accept, ESC to cancel ═══┘
```

5. Highlight Assigned and press (F3) (Choices).

You can also use a filter to display items that do not belong to a category, such as displaying all items that do not have a when date. The third option, Clear Filter, removes the filter from the view.

6. Press (ESC) and (DOWN ARROW) to move to the Start Date setting.
   This is the first date of the range.

7. Type **Beginning of month** and press (DOWN ARROW).

8. Type **End of month** for the End Date setting and press (ENTER).

Agenda assumes that the date you enter in the filter is a relative date. This means that if you use a start date of today and end date of today for the when date, Agenda will display the items that have a when date of today, making it a handy way to write today's to-do list. Tomorrow, Agenda will adjust the filter and display the items that have tomorrow as a when date. The only way you can make it an absolute date is to put a $ before the date, as in $July 12 1991. The last setting in this dialog box is Items Should Be. This setting is either Inside Range, which displays the items that have dates within the range, or Outside Range, which displays items that have dates before the start date or after the end date.

9. Press (ENTER) three times to use this filter and return to the view; then press (CTRL-LEFT ARROW). The view looks like Figure 6-8. Notice how the filter is partially described in the control panel. Since the dates may vary, the items that appear in the view will also vary. Notice also that all of the items have a date in the When column that is between the beginning and the end of the month.

You can also create filters that only use a start date or only use an end date. When you supply a start date without an ending one, the range of dates that the filter uses starts at the supplied date and continues to the last date possible. When you supply an end date without a starting one, the range of dates that the filter uses starts at the first date possible and continues to the supplied date. For example, using the When category as a filter with only an end date of today lists all items that have a when date before or up to today's date.

Another possibility is to create a filter that only applies to a section. To create a filter for a section, use the View Section Properties command and set the filter the same way you would for creating a filter for a view.

```
File: C:\AGENDA\APPS\DESIGN                           05/02/91    4:03pm
View: Initial View [When(Beg of this month*End of this month)]    →
Initial Section                        When                 Actual Completion Dat
   • Planning meeting next Friday      ·Fri May 10 1991 12:0
     at noon
   • Submit department payroll         ·Thu May 09 1991
     vouchers at the end of every
     week
   • Call Pat today about Friday's     ·Thu May 02 1991 3:00  ·05/02/91 1:54pm
     planning meeting
```

FIGURE 6-8.   View using a filter

Shifting Date Ranges

Once you create a filter, you may want to shift the dates included in the filter. For example, if the filter only shows the task you plan to complete today, you can change it to display the tasks you plan to complete tomorrow. You can change the dates used in the filter and browse from day to day by following these steps:

1. Press (F10) (Menu) and select View Browse.

    Agenda changes the control panel to look like this:

```
Use the cursor keys to display schedules for other dates.          BROWSE
Current filter:   [When(05/01/91*05/31/91)]
Initial Section                        When                 Actual Completion Dat
   • Call Pat today about Friday's    ▸Thu May 02 1991 3:00  ·05/02/91 1:54pm
     planning meeting  ·
```

2. Press (RIGHT ARROW).
       Notice how the control panel changes to display the dates for the second day of this month and the first day of the next month. Each time you press (RIGHT ARROW), Agenda shifts the dates used in the filter forward one day. Each time you press (LEFT ARROW), Agenda shifts the dates used in the filter back one day.

3. Press (CTRL-LEFT ARROW).
       Each time you press (CTRL-LEFT ARROW), Agenda shifts the dates used in the filter back one week. Each time you press (CTRL-RIGHT ARROW), Agenda shifts the dates used in the filter forward one week.

4. Press (ESC) to end Browse.

   This returns you to the view with the original filter. You can also use Browse by pressing the accelerator key, (ALT-B).

5. Press (ALT-B) to display the filter in the Browse mode.

6. Press (PGDN) twice.

   Each time you press (PGDN) Agenda shifts the dates used in the filter forward one month, and each time you press (PGUP) Agenda shifts the dates used in the filter back one month. You can also use (CTRL-PGUP) and (CTRL-PGDN) to shift the filter a year at a time.

7. Press (ENTER).

When you leave Browse by pressing (ENTER), Agenda leaves the shifted filter where you left it. This will cause a relative filter such as today to act as an absolute filter such as 8/9/91. Using (ESC) to leave Browse returns the filter to its original position.

Changing and Removing Filters

When you use filters, you will want to modify and remove them. Both of these are easy to do. You can try it with the filter you have added to the DESIGN file by following these steps:

1. Press (F10) (Menu) and select View Properties.

2. Press (END) once, (UP ARROW) twice, and (RIGHT ARROW) once to move to WHEN (Beg of this month ↔ En) representing the filter information.

3. Press (F4) (Values) to display the same dialog box that you used to create the filter.

4. Press (DOWN ARROW) twice to move to the End Date setting and press (CTRL-ENTER).

This removes the entry for the End Date setting. You can use the same process to remove the Start Date setting.

5. Press (ENTER) to finalize the changes.

6. Press (F3) (Choices) to select another category to use as a filter.

7. Highlight the Modified Last Date category and press (SPACEBAR).

8. Press (SPACEBAR) again to change Assigned to Not Assigned, and press (ENTER) three times to use the filter with these settings. Notice that by specifying Not Assigned, no date range is used.

This shows how you can create a filter that uses multiple categories. The view now only displays items that have a when date on or after the beginning of the month and do not have an entry in the Modified Last Date category. You can now remove these filters.

9. Press (F10) (Menu) and select View Properties.

10. Press (END) once, (UP ARROW) twice, and (RIGHT ARROW) once to move to the filter information.

11. Press (DEL) twice to delete the two filters and press (ENTER).

Since the filter is removed, Agenda displays all of the items in the view.

CREATING A DATEBOOK VIEW

Agenda has a special type of view that you can use with date categories called a *datebook view*. An example is shown in Figure 6-9. A datebook view separates items assigned to a date category by hour, day, week, or month. You can use a datebook view to list items that you need to complete. To create a datebook view, follow these steps:

1. Press (F10) (Menu) and select View Add.

2. Type **Datebook** or **My DateBook** for the View Name setting and press (ENTER).

3. Press (SPACEBAR) to change Standard in the Type setting to Datebook.

The Date category setting selects the date category used in the datebook view. The default is When but you can change it to any other date category by pressing (F3) (Choices) or (SPACEBAR). The End category setting is blank by default. The Section category selects the category entries that will divide the view into sections. Initially Agenda suggests the same category that is used in the Date category setting but you can change this to any category by typing the category name or using (F3) (Choices).

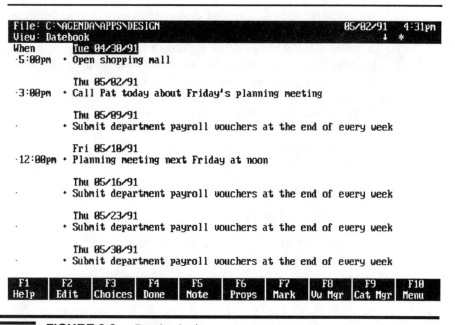

```
File: C:\AGENDA\APPS\DESIGN                          05/02/91    4:31pm
View: Datebook                                            ↓   *
When      Tue 04/30/91
-5:00pm  • Open shopping mall

          Thu 05/02/91
-3:00pm  • Call Pat today about Friday's planning meeting

          Thu 05/09/91
     .   • Submit department payroll vouchers at the end of every week

          Fri 05/10/91
-12:00pm • Planning meeting next Friday at noon

          Thu 05/16/91
     .   • Submit department payroll vouchers at the end of every week

          Thu 05/23/91
     .   • Submit department payroll vouchers at the end of every week

          Thu 05/30/91
     .   • Submit department payroll vouchers at the end of every week
```

F1	F2	F3	F4	F5	F6	F7	F8	F9	F10
Help	Edit	Choices	Done	Note	Props	Mark	Vw Mgr	Cat Mgr	Menu

FIGURE 6-9.   Datebook view

4. Press (**DOWN ARROW**) four times to move to the Period setting.

The Period setting determines the time period covered by the datebook view. The choices are Day, Week, Month, and Quarter.

5. Type **Q** to change the Period setting to Quarter.

The Interval setting selects how the period is broken into sections. The available choices depend on the Period setting. If Period is set to Day, the possible intervals are 15 minutes, 30 minutes, and one hour. If Period is set to Week, the Interval setting does not appear since the only choice is weekly. If Period is set to Month, the possible intervals are Daily and Weekly. If Period is set to Quarter, the possible intervals are Daily, Weekly, and Monthly.

6. Press (**DOWN ARROW**) and type **D** for Daily.

The two other settings you may see are Start At and End At. These settings appear when Period is Day or Week. They select the first and last time period or the first and last day of the week the datebook shows entries for. For these settings you can either type the time for the beginning or ending time interval or press (F3) (Choices) and select the day of the week the setting should use. The last setting that appears is Base Date On. This setting selects the date Agenda uses to determine the range of dates covered in the datebook. For example, if you want to display the items with a when date during next week, you can enter a date that occurs next week. The default of "today" means that Agenda sets up the day period to be for the current day, the week period to be for the current week, the month period to be for the current month, or the quarter period to be for the current quarter.

7. Press (ENTER) to display this view.

The new view has many dates with nothing below them. This view will be more useful if you only display a when date as a section head if an item appears below it.

8. Press (F10) (Menu) and select View Properties.
9. Press (DOWN ARROW) twice and (SPACEBAR) once to change the Hide Empty Sections setting from No to Yes. Press (ENTER) to display the view with this setting.

The view looks similar to the one in Figure 6-9, although since the when dates may vary, so will the items listed under each date. The small dot in the When column indicates that the item has an entry for the category. If you type anything where this dot appears it will replace the current entry.

You can use Browse to shift the dates covered by the datebook by using the View Browse command or by pressing (ALT-B).

DONE DATES

Done dates are used to mark the date an item is completed. They are useful because you can tell Agenda to perform a special action for items marked as done. For example, you can hide done items, discard them, or save them to a done file. To have Agenda take any of these actions, the item must be marked done and the setting must be set to perform the action you desire. As mentioned earlier, you can mark an item as done by highlighting the item and pressing (F4) (Done) or by entering a date in a Done date category column.

Follow these steps to change how Agenda handles items with a done date:

1. Press (ALT-F8) (Last Vw) and (CTRL-LEFT ARROW) to move to the first item in the Initial View section.

2. Press (F10) (Menu) and select View Properties.

3. Press (DOWN ARROW) four times to move to the Hide Done Items setting.

4. Press (SPACEBAR) to change No to Yes.

5. Press (ENTER) to leave the dialog box.

Notice how the items that are marked done disappear. They are still in the file but do not appear in this view.

6. Move the highlight to the *Call Pat today about Friday's meeting* item.

7. Press (F4) (Done).

This item disappears from the view but is still in the file.

8. Press (F10) (Menu) and select View Properties.

9. Press (DOWN ARROW) four times to move to the Hide Done Items setting.

10. Press (SPACEBAR) to change Yes to No and press (ENTER) to use this change.

Now the hidden items marked as done reappear. Another common operation performed on done items is deleting them. To try this with the DESIGN file, follow these steps:

1. Press (ALT-W) to save the file.

2. Press (F10) (Menu) and select File Properties.

3. Press (END) once, (UP ARROW) twice, and (SPACEBAR) to display the Global Date Settings dialog box.

4. Press (END) to move the highlight to Process Done Items.

5. Press (F3) (Choices) to display the options, highlight Discard, and press (ENTER).

The default of No Action leaves done items in your file. Export to Done file puts done items in an STF file that can be imported to another file, as described in Chapter 11. Discard eliminates done items from the file. Agenda adds a line below Process Done Items to ask you when you want the done items discarded.

6. Press (DOWN ARROW) to move to the When setting, press (F3) (Choices), and then press (ESC) to return to the dialog box.

The When setting determines when Agenda removes done items from the file. The default of Immediately removes the items as soon as you mark them.

7. Press (ENTER) twice to finalize these settings.

Now none of the done items appears since Agenda has removed them from the file. If you now used the Item Undisc command to retrieve them, the items would be retrieved but their category assignments would be lost.

8. Press (F10) (Menu) and select File Abandon. When Agenda prompts for a confirmation, type **Y** to return to the previously saved version of the file. This restores the file to its status before you deleted the done items.

7

USING MATH FEATURES

Many database applications can be made more useful by performing simple arithmetic operations on columns of numbers. Often all that is necessary to make a database more informative is to print out column totals. Lists of costs, prices, quantities in stock, and scores are all examples of values that can benefit by having a total at the bottom of a column.

Agenda provides a means for performing simple calculations within a column. It can produce totals and averages for columns of numbers within a section of a view. It can count the number of column entries within a section and display the minimum and maximum values for a column of numbers.

This chapter explains how to perform simple math functions by creating numeric columns in an Agenda database view. You will have Agenda compute totals and averages, display the number of items, and display the minimum or maximum entry for numeric columns. You will also determine the formatting for the numeric values.

In this chapter you will create a simplified inventory database to use as you try out Agenda's math features. Follow these steps to create the file:

1. Press (F10) (Menu) and select File Retrieve.

2. Press (INS) in the Select File dialog box, type **INVENTOR** and press (ENTER) to create a new file.

3. Type **Inventory of Equipment and Supplies** as the file description and press (ENTER) twice.

4. Press (F2) (Edit), press (CTRL-ENTER), type **Desks**, and press (ENTER) to change the name of the section category.

5. Type **Grey metal** as the first item and press (ENTER).

You can also press (INS) when you are entering successive items to start entering a new item.

6. Type **Black metal** and press (ENTER).

7. Type **Cherry** and press (ENTER).

8. Type **Walnut** and press (ENTER).

9. Press (F10) (Menu) and select View Section Add to create a new section for this view. You could also press the shortcut key, (ALT-D), for this activity.

10. Type **Credenzas** and press (ENTER) twice to return to the view.

11. Type **Grey metal** and press (ENTER).

12. Type **Black metal** and press (ENTER).

13. Type **Cherry** and press (ENTER).

14. Type **Walnut** and press (ENTER).

15. Press (ALT-D), or press (F10) (Menu) and select View Section Add to create a third section for this view.

16. Type **File Cabinets** and press (ENTER) twice to return to the view.

17. Type **Grey metal** and press (ENTER).

18. Type **Black metal - 2 drawer** and press (ENTER).

19. Type **Black metal - 4 drawer** and press (ENTER).

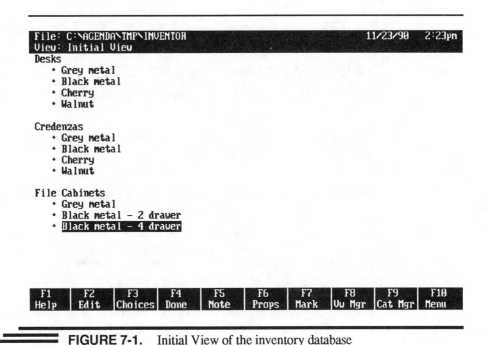

FIGURE 7-1.   Initial View of the inventory database

Figure 7-1 displays a view with the sections and items that your screen should currently contain.

CREATING NUMERIC COLUMNS

For Agenda to compute totals and do other arithmetic on a column, the column must first be defined as numeric. In previous chapters, you learned about three types of columns: standard columns, in which a column head is an Agenda category and whose column entries are its children, which are also categories; unindexed columns, in which the entries of the column are not categories and are not indexed; and date columns, which have their own special features and rules. Numeric columns are the fourth and last category type you will learn about.

The procedure for creating a numeric column and category is similar to that for the other three types of columns. To create a numeric column that lists the quantity of each item in the inventory list, perform the following steps:

1. Press (F10) (Menu) and select View Column Add. The Column Add dialog box shown in Figure 7-2 appears on the screen.

2. Type **Quantity** for the Column Head and press (ENTER).

3. Press (RIGHT ARROW) to highlight the Category Type setting. Press (F3) (Choices) to display the four types of categories.

4. Highlight Numeric and press (ENTER). The Column Add dialog box changes to include the Numeric Column Properties selections, as shown in Figure 7-3. You will learn about these properties later in this chapter.

5. Press (ENTER) to accept the settings for the column and return to the view.

A # symbol displays at the top of the screen whenever you highlight a column head or entry in the Quantity column. This symbol indicates the column is numeric. It will not appear when you highlight 0.00.

A Total heading also appears at the end of each section. This is a default setting for numeric columns, and you will learn later how to turn it off if desired. Notice also that the totals for each section are all zero. This is because no entries have been placed

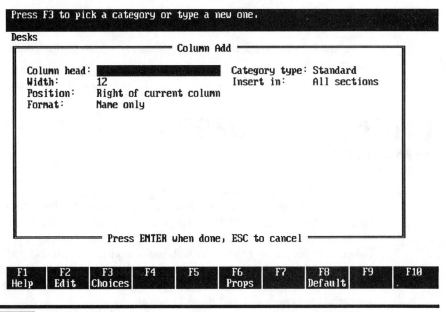

FIGURE 7-2.   Column Add dialog box used to create a numeric column

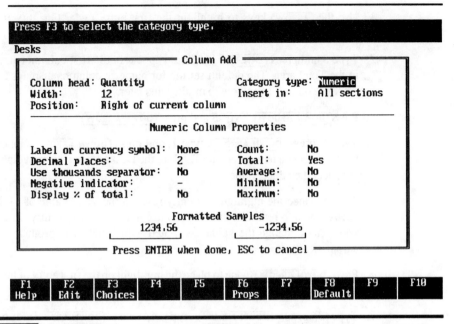

Press F3 to select the category type.

Desks
```
╔═══════════════════ Column Add ═══════════════════╗
║                                                   ║
║  Column head: Quantity          Category type: Numeric
║  Width:       12                Insert in:     All sections
║  Position:    Right of current column             ║
║ ─────────────────────────────────────────────────║
║                 Numeric Column Properties         ║
║                                                   ║
║  Label or currency symbol: None    Count:    No   ║
║  Decimal places:           2       Total:    Yes  ║
║  Use thousands separator:  No      Average:  No   ║
║  Negative indicator:       -       Minimum:  No   ║
║  Display % of total:       No      Maximum:  No   ║
║                                                   ║
║                   Formatted Samples               ║
║             1234.56              -1234.56          ║
║                                                   ║
╚════════════ Press ENTER when done, ESC to cancel ═╝
```

F1	F2	F3	F4	F5	F6	F7	F8	F9	F10
Help	Edit	Choices			Props		Default		

FIGURE 7-3.   Column Add Dialog Box after the Numeric category type is selected

in the Quantity column. The Total adds the entries contained in the column for the indicated section of the view.

ENTERING NUMBERS IN NUMERIC COLUMNS

The method used to enter numbers into numeric columns is very similar to the methods used for standard or unindexed columns. The biggest difference is that Agenda only allows you to enter numeric values. Also, Agenda does not recognize numbers in the item text as values to be used as numeric column entries. This avoids undesirable auto-completion. The digits 0 through 9 and the decimal point are always acceptable characters for your entries. The other possible character entries are discussed later. Complete the following steps to enter the numbers for the Quantity column:

1. Use the (ARROW) keys to highlight the first entry under Quantity in the Desks section.

2. Type **3** and press (ENTER). 3.00 should appear in the first column entry as well as in the Total area. The default setting for numeric columns displays two decimal places. You will learn how to modify this later.

3. Press (DOWN ARROW). Type **5** and press (DOWN ARROW).

4. Type **2**, press (DOWN ARROW), type **1**, and press (DOWN ARROW). Notice that each time you enter a new value, the Total for the Desks section is immediately updated to reflect the added values.

5. Type **6**. Since the highlight currently rests on the Total value of 11.00, Agenda beeps at you to remind you that you have made an invalid entry. This is because you cannot change the value associated with Total, it is produced by Agenda automatically.

6. Press (DOWN ARROW) twice to place the highlight on the first entry of the Credenzas section.

7. Type **3**, press (DOWN ARROW), type **4**, press (DOWN ARROW), type **2**, press (DOWN ARROW), type **1**, and press (DOWN ARROW).

8. Press (DOWN ARROW) twice to place the highlight on the first entry in the File Cabinets section.

9. Type **8**, press (DOWN ARROW), type **4**, press (DOWN ARROW), type **2**, and press (ENTER). Your screen should look like Figure 7-4.

Unlike standard columns, numeric columns can only have one entry per item. This usually does not create a problem, but it may mean that you occasionally have to rethink the design of your database or view.

Changing the numeric values that have been entered in numeric columns is easier than changing values in standard columns. In standard columns you must press (F2) (Edit) to change an entry's value. To replace a numeric entry, just highlight the entry, type the new number, and press (ENTER), although (F2) will still work if you continue to use it out of habit. For example:

10. If your cursor is not already there, use the (ARROW) keys to highlight the last entry of the last section.

11. Type **8** and press (ENTER). The original entry of 2.00 is replaced with 8.00. Notice also that the Total for the third section changed from 14.00 to 20.00.

```
File: C:\AGENDA\TMP\INVENTOR                              11/23/90   1:33pm
View: Initial View                                                   #
Desks                                                          Quantity
    • Grey metal                                                  3.00
    • Black metal                                                 5.00
    • Cherry                                                      2.00
    • Walnut                                                      1.00
        TOTAL                                                    11.00

Credenzas                                                     Quantity
    • Grey metal                                                  3.00
    • Black metal                                                 4.00
    • Cherry                                                      2.00
    • Walnut                                                      1.00
        TOTAL                                                    10.00

File Cabinets                                                 Quantity
    • Grey metal                                                  8.00
    • Black metal - 2 drawer                                      4.00
    » Black metal - 4 drawer                                      2.00
        TOTAL                                                    14.00
```

F1	F2	F3	F4	F5	F6	F7	F8	F9	F10
Help	Edit	Choices	Done	Note	Props	Mark	Vw Mgr	Cat Mgr	Menu

FIGURE 7-4.   Quantities added to the inventory database

You can use the (F2) (Edit) key whenever you wish to make a modification of a current entry. This will generally save you keystrokes when editing larger numbers.

12. Press (F2) (Edit). Type **1** to make the current entry of 8 into 18, and press (ENTER).

Another unique feature of numeric columns is that the entries are *right-justified* or aligned by the decimal point. This is a standard for most advanced software packages.

It was mentioned earlier that numeric columns accept only numeric characters. The digits 0 through 9 are always acceptable values. The other values that are allowed depend on the selections you have made for the numeric column properties. The defaults include a period (.) used as a decimal point and a hyphen (-) to indicate negative values. Unless you change these defaults, a period (.) and a hyphen (-) are allowed as valid entries.

To see what happens when you make an invalid entry, try the following:

13. Type **four** and press (ENTER). The following error message appears on the screen:

```
┌─────────────────────Error─────────────────────┐
│  The number you entered isn't valid.  Retype a number. │
│  ───────────────Press any key to continue───────────── │
└────────────────────────────────────────────────┘
```

14. Press (SPACEBAR) to erase the message.

15. Press (CTRL-ENTER) to delete the invalid entry, type **4**, and press (ENTER).

NUMERIC CATEGORIES AND THE CATEGORY MANAGER

Unlike standard columns, the entries of numeric columns are not child categories. The column head of a numeric column is a category, however. To create a numeric column, you can follow these steps:

1. Press (F9) (Cat Mgr) to display the Category Manager screen, as illustrated in Figure 7-5.

Notice that the Quantity category is listed with a # symbol to its left to indicate that the category is numeric. Also notice that none of the entries you entered for Quantity are listed below it. This is because those entries are numbers, not categories. If you choose to delete one of these values you will get the same confirmation box as when deleting a standard category.

2. Press (INS) to insert a new category.

3. Type **Value** and press (ENTER). The category Value has now been added to the database, although it does not now appear in any view.

4. To change this category to a numeric category, press (F6) (Props) to display the Category Properties box.

5. Use (RIGHT ARROW) to highlight the Category Type setting.

6. Type **n** to display Numeric and press (ENTER) to accept the current setting. If Value had child entries beneath it, you would get the confirmation box "Convert to numeric category?". Note that Value now has a # symbol next to it to indicate that it is a numeric category.

7. Press (ESC) to return to the view.

```
File: C:\AGENDA\APPS\INVENTOR
Category Manager
  MAIN
  * Entry
  * When
  * Done
    Desks
    Credenzas
    File Cabinets
  * Quantity
```

F1	F2	F3	F4	F5	F6	F7	F8	F9	F10
Help	Edit			Note	Props	Prn (←)	Dem (→)	To View	Menu

FIGURE 7-5. The Category Manager with the Quantity category
displayed

THE MATH FEATURES OF
NUMERIC COLUMNS

At the beginning of this chapter you were told that Agenda can compute averages,
count entries, and indicate the minimum and maximum entries as well as produce
totals. Although the INVENTOR database may not be the best example for using all
of these features, you can at least see how each works.

Follow these steps to modify the properties of the Quantity column for the entire
view, incorporating the math features of Agenda.

1. Use the (ARROW) keys to highlight an entry in the Quantity column if one is not
   currently highlighted.

2. Press (CTRL-HOME) to move the highlight to the first Quantity column head.

3. Press (F6) (Props) to display the Column Properties dialog box.

This box is similar to the Column Add box displayed earlier in Figure 7-3, but there is no Position setting as in the Column Add box. You can actually be on any section head in the column and press (F6) (Props) to display the Column Properties dialog box.

Notice the Formatted Samples at the bottom of the box. These provide a sample of how the entry 1234.56 would appear with the current settings for Numeric Column Properties. The left sample is a positive entry while the right is a negative entry value. The brackets underneath display the defined width of the column, which is currently set to 12.

4. Press (DOWN ARROW) three times to highlight the Decimal Places setting. Since the quantities assigned to inventory items are usually whole numbers, change the number of decimal places to zero by typing **0** and pressing (ENTER).

The Formatted Samples at the bottom now appear as 1235 and -1235. This is because 1234.56 and - 1234.56 round to these values.

5. Press (RIGHT ARROW) and (UP ARROW) once each. The highlight should now be on the Count setting. The current default value is No. For illustration purposes, you will turn on this setting and the other math settings.

6. Type **y** and press (DOWN ARROW) twice. (Total already is set to Yes.)

7. Type **y** to turn on the Average setting and press (DOWN ARROW).

8. Type **y** to turn on the Minimum setting and press (DOWN ARROW).

9. Type **y** to turn on the Maximum setting.

10. Press (ENTER) to accept the current settings and return to the view. Figure 7-6 shows the entries for Quantity with the current settings.

Notice that each of the five math settings only refers to the section to which it is assigned. There is no combined Total, Count, etc., for the entire view. If you want a math function to apply to all the items in a view, you need to define the view with only one section. This can often be done with a parent category or the Main category.

Look at the Average for the Desks section. Notice that the total quantity of desks is 11 with 4 kinds of desks listed. The average computes to 2.75, but Agenda displays the average as 3. This is because the setting for the number of decimal places was changed to zero. Agenda rounds 2.75 to 3 to fit the number of decimal places using

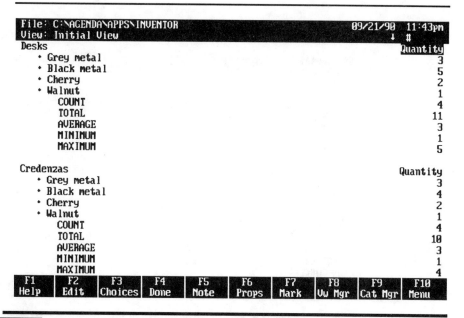

FIGURE 7-6.   Quantity column with zero defined decimal places and all
math functions turned on

standard rounding procedures. If the actual average had computed to 2.25, Agenda
would have displayed a 2.

11. With the Quantity header still highlighted, press (F6) (Props) to return to the
    Column Properties box. You are going to change the number of decimal places
    back to 2 for this section only.

12. Press (DOWN ARROW) and (RIGHT ARROW) once each to highlight the Link with Other
    Sections setting. Type **n** to change the setting to No. This means that the changes
    you make will affect only the current section of the view.

13. Press (DOWN ARROW) twice and (LEFT ARROW) once to highlight the Decimal Places
    setting.

14. Type **2** and press (ENTER). Press (ENTER) again to return to the view. The Average
    now displays as the correct value of 2.75.

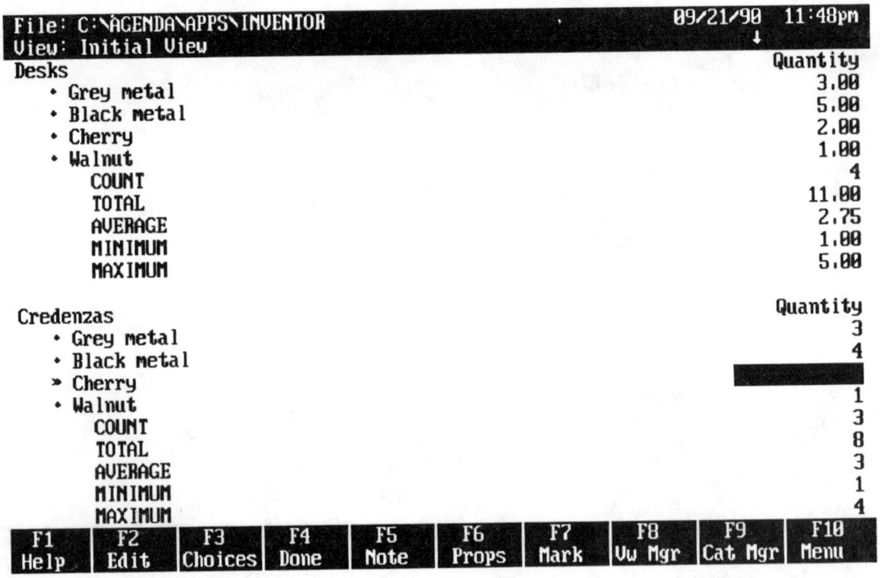

```
File: C:\AGENDA\APPS\INVENTOR                              09/21/90  11:48pm
View: Initial View                                             ↓
Desks                                                          Quantity
   • Grey metal                                                    3.00
   • Black metal                                                   5.00
   • Cherry                                                        2.00
   • Walnut                                                        1.00
        COUNT                                                         4
        TOTAL                                                     11.00
        AVERAGE                                                    2.75
        MINIMUM                                                    1.00
        MAXIMUM                                                    5.00

Credenzas                                                      Quantity
   • Grey metal                                                       3
   • Black metal                                                      4
   » Cherry                                               ████████████
   • Walnut                                                           1
        COUNT                                                         3
        TOTAL                                                         8
        AVERAGE                                                       3
        MINIMUM                                                       1
        MAXIMUM                                                       4
┌──────┬──────┬──────┬──────┬──────┬──────┬──────┬──────┬──────┬──────┐
│ F1   │ F2   │ F3   │ F4   │ F5   │ F6   │ F7   │ F8   │ F9   │ F10  │
│ Help │ Edit │Choices│ Done │ Note │ Props│ Mark │Vw Mgr│Cat Mgr│ Menu │
└──────┴──────┴──────┴──────┴──────┴──────┴──────┴──────┴──────┴──────┘
```

FIGURE 7-7.   Quantity column after defining the Desks section with two decimal places

As you create your own databases, you obviously will need to take into consideration the effect that decimal places may have on your displayed results. In this example, it makes sense to use whole numbers for the column entries because you are not working with fractions of furniture. However, if you use computed averages, you may decide to use decimal places to allow for fractional computations.

15. Move the highlight to the third Quantity entry of the Credenzas section (Cherry).

16. Press (DEL) to delete the entry. Press (ENTER) to confirm the deletion. Your screen should now look like Figure 7-7.

Notice that the Count for the Credenzas section changes from 4 to 3. This is because Count does not count the number of *items* in the section. It counts the number of *entries* in the Quantity column. You will need to keep this in mind when using Count in your databases. For the same reason, the Minimum function states that the minimum value for the section is 1 instead of zero. Since there is no entry for Cherry, it does not count as a value. If you wanted the quantity of Cherry Credenzas to be counted as zero, you would have to make sure that a zero entry was made.

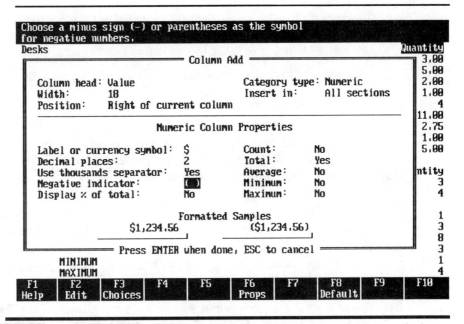

FIGURE 7-8.   Changing the Numeric Column Properties box to display a currency format

WORKING WITH CURRENCY

To show how Agenda can display currency values, you will now add another column to the view. This column will consist of the dollar values for the listed pieces of furniture. You will use the numeric category Value you created earlier for the column head.

1. Make sure the highlight is currently somewhere within the Quality column.

2. Press (F10) (Menu) and select View Column Add. Figure 7-8 displays the Column Add box with the numeric category Value as the column head.

3. Press (F3) (Choices) to select the Column head. Press (DOWN ARROW) until the Value category is highlighted. Press (ENTER) to select this as the column head.

4. Press (DOWN ARROW) once to highlight the Width setting. Type **18** and press (ENTER) to set the width.

5. Press (DOWN ARROW) twice to highlight the Label or Currency Symbol setting. Press (F3) (Choices) to display the choices, which are None (the default), % (percent), $ (dollar), ¢ (cent), £ (pound sterling), and ¥ (yen).

6. Press (DOWN ARROW) twice to highlight the dollar sign and press (ENTER).

7. Press (DOWN ARROW) twice to highlight the Use Thousands Separator setting. To indicate Yes type y.

8. Press (DOWN ARROW) once to change the Negative Indicator setting. Press (F3) (Choices) and (DOWN ARROW) once to change the indicator from the hyphen to parentheses. Press (ENTER) to accept your choice.

Notice the Formatted Samples display. Commas are used as a thousands separator, a dollar sign is displayed, and the negative value is surrounded with parentheses.

9. Press (ENTER) to return to the view. Press (CTRL-HOME) to move to the top of the Value column. The Value column is displayed.

10. To add the Value column entries for the Desks section, press (CTRL-HOME) and (DOWN ARROW) once. Type 125, press (DOWN ARROW), type 225, press (DOWN ARROW), type 500, press (DOWN ARROW), type 200, and press (DOWN ARROW) seven times. Agenda inserts two decimal places after every entry. Notice also that you did not type the dollar sign; however, if you did the results would have been the same.

11. To add the entries for the Credenzas section Values, type 100.50, press (DOWN ARROW), type 120.7, press (DOWN ARROW) twice, type 185.75, and press (DOWN ARROW) eight times.

12. To add the Value column entries for the File Cabinets section, type 200, press (DOWN ARROW), type −20, press (DOWN ARROW), type 750, and press (ENTER).

Assume the −20 value is the cost for carting the filing cabinets away. Notice that Agenda placed parentheses around the 20 even though you entered it with a minus sign. This is because you selected parentheses as the negative indicator. Figure 7-9 displays part of the view.

13. Press (UP ARROW) three times to highlight the Value column head.

14. Press (F6) (Props) to make one more setting change for this column.

15. Press (DOWN ARROW) six times to highlight the Display % of Total setting. Type y and press (ENTER) to return to the view.

```
File: C:\AGENDA\APPS\INVENTOR                          09/22/90    1:09am
View: Initial View                                               ↕  ↕
↑Desks                                          Quantity              Value
        AVERAGE                                    2.75
        MINIMUM                                    1.00
        MAXIMUM                                    5.00

Credenzas                                       Quantity              Value
   • Grey metal                                     3             $100.50
   • Black metal                                    4             $120.70
   • Cherry
   • Walnut                                         1             $185.75
        COUNT                                       3
        TOTAL                                       8             $406.95
        AVERAGE                                     3
        MINIMUM                                     1
        MAXIMUM                                     4

File Cabinets                                   Quantity              Value
   • Grey metal                                     8             $200.00
   • Black metal - 2 drawer                         4            ($20.00)
   ➤ Black metal - 4 drawer                        23            $750.00
        COUNT                                       3
┌──────┬──────┬──────┬──────┬──────┬──────┬──────┬──────┬──────┬──────┐
│  F1  │  F2  │  F3  │  F4  │  F5  │  F6  │  F7  │  F8  │  F9  │ F10  │
│ Help │ Edit │Choices│ Done │ Note │Props │ Mark │Vw Mgr│Cat Mgr│ Menu │
└──────┴──────┴──────┴──────┴──────┴──────┴──────┴──────┴──────┴──────┘
```

FIGURE 7-9.   Numeric entries defined with dollar signs and with parentheses used as the negative indicator

The following illustration shows part of the Value column entries:

```
Quantity        Value   %Tot Q
    8         $200.00     22%
    4         ($20.00)    -2%
   23         $750.00     81%
```

Notice that a second column has been added within the original Value column. This column displays the percent the current numeric value is of the total numeric value for this section. This percentage is created by Agenda and cannot be modified by you.

CHANGING THE NUMERIC FORMATS FOR THE FILE

There are two numeric formats you can select for the entire file. Some people have different conventions for representing numbers, and Agenda allows you to customize how it represents numbers to meet these conventions. These selections affect the entire file, not just one column.

1. Press (F10) (Menu) and select Utilities Customize. Agenda displays the Utilities Customize dialog box.

2. Press (DOWN ARROW) four times to highlight the Decimal Separator setting.

3. Press (F3) (Choices). The choices are a dot (the default) or a comma. Press (DOWN ARROW) to highlight Comma and press (ENTER).

4. Press (RIGHT ARROW) to highlight the Thousands Separator setting.

5. Press (F3) (Choices). The choices are a comma (the default), a dot, and a space. Press (DOWN ARROW) twice to highlight Space and press (ENTER).

6. Press (ENTER) to return to the view.

Notice that all the decimal places now contain a comma instead of a decimal point. The Total for the Desks section reads $1 050,00 instead of $1,050.00
To change the file settings back, follow these steps:

7. Press (F10) (Menu) and select Utilities Customize. Agenda displays the Utilities Customize dialog box.

8. Press (DOWN ARROW) four times to highlight the Decimal Separator setting.

9. Press (F3) (Choices). Highlight the Dot and press (ENTER).

10. Press (RIGHT ARROW) to highlight the Thousands Separator setting.

11. Press (F3) (Choices). Highlight the comma and press (ENTER).

12. Press (ENTER) to return to the view.

One word of warning: if you change the settings for the decimal and thousands separators, you must make sure they are different. You cannot select a dot or comma for both, or Agenda will display an error box.

CHANGING A STANDARD COLUMN INTO A NUMERIC COLUMN

Occasionally, you may need to change a standard column into a numeric one. This could happen if you had a standard column that contained numeric values and you later decided to use one or more of Agenda's math features with them. You might originally define a category as standard, but when you begin to use it as a column head discover that it would be more useful as a numeric column.

A major consideration to keep in mind is that you can never change a numeric column back to standard or any other column type. Once you change a standard column to numeric, there is no going back.

If the column does not have any entries (or the category has no defined children), changing it to numeric is easy. The steps to follow include these:

1. Highlight the category or column head.

2. Press (F6) (Props).

3. Press (RIGHT ARROW) to highlight the Category Type setting.

4. Type **n** for Numeric and press (ENTER).

If the column does have entries (or the category has children), a number of considerations come into play:

- A standard column (category) cannot be changed to numeric if it contains more than one level of children.

- If the standard column entry is in the form of a number, changing the column to numeric retains the number.

- If a standard column entry is not a number, changing the column to numeric changes the entry to zero.

- If a column head appears in more than one view, all occurrences of the column in all views will be changed to numeric.

- You can never change a numeric column (category) back to standard.

Once you decide to change a standard column with entries to numeric, you perform the following steps:

1. Highlight the column head.

2. Press (F6) (Props) to display the Column Properties dialog box.

3. Highlight Category Type and select Numeric. The following confirmation box appears on the screen:

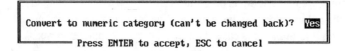

```
Convert to numeric category (can't be changed back)?  Yes
          ──── Press ENTER to accept, ESC to cancel ────
```

4. Press (ENTER) to accept the answer of Yes. If any of the entries in the column are not numbers, the following warning appears on the screen:

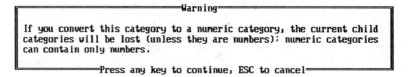

```
                      ═══Warning═══
If you convert this category to a numeric category, the current child
categories will be lost (unless they are numbers); numeric categories
can contain only numbers.
               ═══Press any key to continue, ESC to cancel═══
```

5. Press (ENTER) to accept and you are returned to the Column Properties box. Press (ENTER) to return to the view.

Figure 7-10 displays a view containing a Standard column defined as standard and a Numeric column that would result if the Standard column were changed to numeric. Notice that the word "four" was converted to 0.00. The fourth item was blank under the Standard column and remained blank when converted to numeric. Items that contained more than one entry (items 5, 6, and 7) transferred the value of the first entry and ignored the second.

```
File: C:\AGENDA\APPS\INVENTOR                        09/22/90   2:44am
View: Example of standard to numeric change
Type of Entry                                  Standard        Numeric
  • number                                      ·5               5.00
  • number - with decimal                       ·1234.56      1234.56
  • word                                        ·four            0.00
  • blank entry
  • more than one entry - numeric               ·35             35.00
                                                 23
  • more than one entry - words                 ·six             0.00
                                                 seven
  » one word and one numeric entry             »happy            0.00
                                               »13.4
       TOTAL                                                  1274.56
```

```
 F1  |  F2  |   F3   |  F4  |  F5  |  F6   |  F7  |  F8   |  F9    | F10
Help | Edit |Choices | Done | Note | Props | Mark | Vw Mgr|Cat Mgr| Menu
```

FIGURE 7-10.   Sample view displaying the results of changing a standard column into a numeric column

USING NUMERIC RANGES IN FILTERS

As discussed in previous chapters, filters are used to exclude items from appearing in a view or to determine which items are to appear in a view. You can use filters on numeric categories. If you choose a numeric category, Agenda displays a Numeric Filter dialog box that allows you to specify a numeric range of values to be included (or excluded) from the view.

Try now to add a filter to the Initial View that only includes those items in the view that have a Quantity of 3 or more by following these steps:

1. Press (F10) (Menu) and select View Properties.

2. Use the (ARROW) keys to highlight the Filter setting at the bottom right of the View Properties dialog box.

3. Press (F3) (Choices).

4. Highlight the Quantity category and select it by pressing (SPACEBAR). The Numeric Filter dialog box appears, as in Figure 7-11.

5. Since you want to include all items that are assigned to a particular range, accept the current setting by pressing (DOWN ARROW). This highlights the Minimum Value setting.

6. Type **3** and press (ENTER). This tells Agenda not to display any item that is less than 3.

7. Since there is no maximum number in this example (you want *all* numbers greater than 3), leave the Maximum Value setting blank.

8. Since you want the items within the defined range to be displayed, accept the last setting's default value. Press (ENTER) to accept the settings.

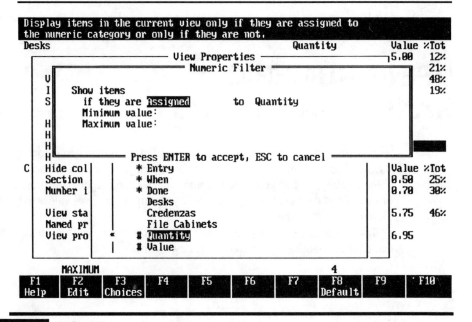

FIGURE 7-11. Defining a numeric filter

9. Press (ENTER) two more times to accept the filters and the View Properties settings and return to the view.

Notice in View Properties that the range of items of 3 or greater is depicted after Quantity below Filter as "Quantity (3 <->)". The only items included in the view are those for which a Quantity is 3 or greater.

If you would like some additional practice with math features, you can take a look at the Starter Applications provided with the Agenda package. The Account application (Expense view) and the People application (Employee Summary view) both contain numeric columns with which you can practice.

CONDITIONAL ASSIGNMENTS

Explicit Assignments Versus Conditional Assignments
Using Conditional Assignments
Text Conditions
Controlling Automatic Assignment Features
Profile Conditions

Given a choice between filing all office correspondence themselves and having a secretary file it, most professionals choose the latter alternative to save time. Agenda allows you to choose similar methods when assigning items to categories. Assigning the items yourself is called *explicit assignment*; when Agenda does it for you, it is called *conditional assignment*.

Explicit assignment is easy and is not without merit since it gives you complete control over the assignment of items. There are several methods for making explicit assignments of items to categories. You can insert new items in a section of a view, which assigns the item to the category used for the section head. From within a view you can assign items to a category by making an entry in a column. You can also use the Assignment Profile box to assign items to specific categories. Although each of these methods is simple, explicit assignment always takes some work on your part. Once you have made these assignments, they will not be affected by changes in the text or conditional criteria.

It takes a little time to feel confident about conditional (or automatic) assignments. It is really not any different from feeling confident about a secretary's ability to file items correctly. As you work with the secretary over time you become more comfortable with the relationship and are able to pinpoint instances where you need to specify the filing approach needed. This is also true with Agenda. As you learn the conditional assignment features and begin to use them, you will understand more about the way in which Agenda works and will realize that you can affect the accuracy of these assignments by the way you establish new categories and the wording of items. You will also know which areas may need additional attention in terms of assignment verification.

In this chapter you will learn how Agenda makes conditional assignments based on text entries in items or notes as well as assignments to other categories. You will also learn some of the customizing features that control the conditional assignment process and how you can leverage existing assignments to complete assignments to other categories.

EXPLICIT ASSIGNMENTS VERSUS CONDITIONAL ASSIGNMENTS

Explicitly assigned items are items that you assign to a category yourself. This assignment remains unbroken until you somehow break it. Conditionally assigned items are automatically assigned to a category based on predefined conditions. If the conditions are changed during the editing of your database, Agenda automatically breaks the assignment.

In Chapter 3 you looked at the simplest form of conditional assignment. You learned to type items and have them automatically assigned to a category when the words in the item text matched the words in the category entry. You also learned to use columns for explicit category entries and to display assignments as they were made. Perform the following steps to create a database named JOBLOG to review the difference between explicitly and conditionally assigned items:

1. With Agenda open, press (F10) (Menu) and select File Retrieve.

2. Press (INS) in the Select File box, type **JOBLOG**, and press (ENTER) to create a new file.

3. Type **Job assignments by staff and client** as the file description and press (ENTER) twice.

4. Type **Have Janet evaluate our performance regarding install at Acme, Inc.** as the first item and press (ENTER).

5. Create a Staff column for the view by pressing (F10) (Menu) and selecting View Column Add.

6. Type **Staff** and press (ENTER) twice.

7. *Explicitly* assign the first item to the category Janet by typing **Janet** under the Staff column and pressing (ENTER).

8. Press (LEFT ARROW) to move to the first column. Type **Meeting with Janet about Porter Co. proposal.** and press (ENTER). Notice that Agenda *automatically* assigns the second item to Janet under the Staff column by matching the word "Janet" within the text of the item to the category named Janet.

When you entered the first item, the Janet category did not exist, which is why Agenda did not assign the item automatically. You created the category when you assigned the first to Janet explicitly. When you typed the second item, Agenda matched the name "Janet" within the item's text to the Janet category and displayed the assignment by listing it in the Staff column. This second assignment was a conditional assignment.

9. Press (F3) (Choices) to display the Assignment Profile box shown in Figure 8-1. Notice the asterisk (*) to the left of the Initial Section category. This confirms that the current item was explicitly assigned to the Initial Section category by entering it within the Initial Section. The *c symbol to the left of Janet indicates that this item was assigned to the Janet category *conditionally* using conditional assignment. If the condition that made the assignment changes, Agenda will *unassign* the item.

10. Press (ESC) to return to the view.

11. Press (F2) (Edit), press (CTRL-RIGHT ARROW) twice to move to the "J" in "Janet," press (DEL) five times to delete "Janet," type **Floyd**, and press (ENTER). Notice that "Janet" is no longer listed under the Staff column for this item. This is because the condition of having the word "Janet" appear within the item is no longer met.

12. To make a similar change to the first item, press (UP ARROW) once, press (F2) (Edit), press (CTRL-RIGHT ARROW) once to move to the "J" in "Janet," press (DEL) five times to delete "Janet," type **Rachel**, and press (ENTER). Notice that this item is still assigned to the Janet category. This is because you explicitly assigned the item to this category by typing **Janet** in the column.

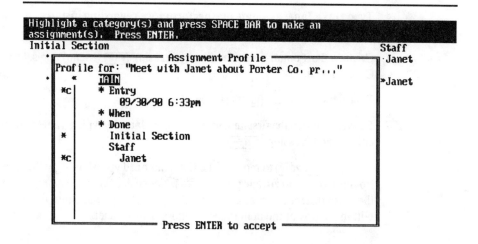

FIGURE 8-1.   Using the Assignment Profile box to display conditional assignments

13. You could break the assignment of this item to the Janet category by highlighting Janet, pressing (DEL), and confirming the deletion. However, to see how to use the Assignment Profile box to break assignments, press (F3) (Choices).

14. Press (DOWN ARROW) seven times to highlight Janet and press (SPACEBAR) to break the assignment, or use auto-completion by beginning to type the entry. Press (ENTER) to return to the view. The first item no longer lists Janet as a Staff assignment.

USING CONDITIONAL ASSIGNMENTS

Conditional assignments have more potential and versatility than the basic features just shown. In the following sections you will learn how you can use conditional assignments to assign items to many categories at once; how to extend category name entries to match items with text that is different than the category name; how to make

Agenda perform additional assignments based on an existing assignment once you have assigned items to a category; and how to have Agenda assign items to categories based on date or numeric values assigned to other categories.

These new conditional assignment features are divided into the following four types:

- Text conditions (shown in the example in the previous section)

- Assignment conditions

- Date conditions

- Number conditions

Text conditions are used to define or qualify categories in your category hierarchy to facilitate matching of items to categories. The other three condition types are used to assign items to categories based on their other category assignments. In later chapters you will look at actions, which provide other ways of controlling automatic assignments.

Text conditions are established differently than the other three types, so they are covered separately in this chapter. There is one major feature that these conditions have in common, however, and that is the timing Agenda uses to evaluate an item against the conditions of the database.

Whenever you edit or enter an item in your Agenda database, Agenda processes the item against all of the conditions established in the database. You can use the JOBLOG database to see how this works. Even though you are using very simple conditions, keep in mind that these same principles apply with more complex conditional assignments. You are going to add categories to the database using the Category Manager to see how text conditions affect the database. Follow these steps:

1. Press (F9) (Cat Mgr) to activate the Category Manager.

2. Use (DOWN ARROW) to highlight the Janet category.

3. To add a Floyd category, press (INS), type **Floyd**, and press (ENTER).

4. To add a Rachel category, press (INS), type **Rachel**, and press (ENTER).

5. Press (ESC) to return to the view. Notice that the first item is not automatically assigned to the Rachel category and the second item is not assigned to Floyd. Because the items existed before the conditions were defined, Agenda does not automatically go back and reevaluate all the previously entered items.

6. Press (DOWN ARROW) once, type **Have Janet monitor the development of the reports manual.**, and press (ENTER). Janet is automatically assigned to this newly entered item.

7. Edit the second item by pressing (UP ARROW) and (F2) (Edit). At this point you could make some changes in the text of the item, but it is not necessary to make this example work.

8. Press (ENTER) to end the editing. Because you edited the item, Agenda reevaluates the item against all conditions in the database. Because Floyd now exists as a category (and, therefore, as a text condition) the item is conditionally assigned to Floyd.

Whenever you modify the conditions of a database, you may want all or a group of pre-existing items to reflect the new conditions. Agenda provides a menu item as a shortcut for doing this.

9. To force Agenda to evaluate all the items of the database against all conditions, press (F10) (Menu) and select Utilities Execute. The Execute box displayed in Figure 8-2 appears on your screen. If your database is large, having Agenda compare all items to all conditions may take quite a while. This box allows you to limit the number of comparisons by limiting the conditions checked to a specific

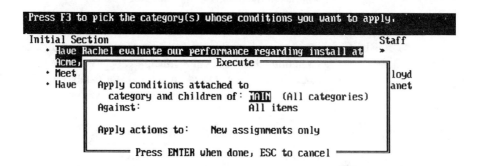

```
Press F3 to pick the category(s) whose conditions you want to apply.

Initial Section                                                    Staff
  • Have Rachel evaluate our performance regarding install at    »
    Acne,┌──────────────────── Execute ────────────────────
  • Meet │                                                        loyd
  • Have │  Apply conditions attached to                         anet
         │     category and children of: MAIN  (All categories)
         │  Against:               All items
         │
         │  Apply actions to:   New assignments only
         └──── Press ENTER when done, ESC to cancel ────
```

```
┌─────┬─────┬───────┬─────┬─────┬─────┬─────┬───────┬─────┬─────┐
│ F1  │ F2  │ F3    │ F4  │ F5  │ F6  │ F7  │ F8    │ F9  │ F10 │
│Help │Edit │Choices│     │     │     │     │Default│     │     │
└─────┴─────┴───────┴─────┴─────┴─────┴─────┴───────┴─────┴─────┘
```

FIGURE 8-2.   The Execute dialog box is used to determine how many conditions are to be evaluated

category and its children or by limiting the items to the current item, marked items, items in a section, the view, or all items.

10. Accept the default of comparing all conditions to all items by pressing (ENTER). The first item is now conditionally assigned to Rachel. As a shortcut you can press (ALT-X) to select All Items.

Agenda also checks the conditions against the items of the database whenever the system date changes.

TEXT CONDITIONS

The properties of category entries in your file hierarchy determine the text conditions used to assign items within the Agenda file. Depending on the settings you choose in the Auto-Assign Global Settings box in File Properties or the Advanced Settings box in Category Properties, Agenda matches on item text, on note text, or on both item and note text. The default setting is to use only the item text for assignments. Although the examples in this chapter focus on the use of item text, all the same rules apply if you choose one of the other settings.

The category entries made thus far have been simple, one word text entries. You can extend these entries to have additional words facilitate a match. You can also use special characters within the text condition to get more control of the assignment process. These features are covered in the "Controlling Automatic Assignment Features" section.

Expanding Text Conditions

If you expand your category definitions to include additional words, Agenda uses this additional text to match item entries and create text conditional assignments. These additions can be made when the category is created, or they can be edited in afterwards.

It is very likely that someone could make item entries in the JOBLOG database that reference staff members by something other than their first names, such as their nicknames or full names. You can make Agenda use text conditions to also match on these other names. Assume that Rachel's last name is Warner and that she is the only Rachel and Warner in the company. You can make Agenda match all references to Ms. Warner, R. W., and so on by performing the following steps:

1. Press (F9) (Cat Mgr) to activate the Category Manager.

2. Use the (ARROW) keys to highlight Rachel and press (F6) (Props) to activate the Category Properties box.

3. The Category name is listed as Rachel. Press (DOWN ARROW) to highlight the Short Name setting.

The short name that you enter here has two functions. First, Agenda uses it as a column or section head whenever the display width is smaller than the Category name. (If there is no short name, Agenda truncates the Category name to fit the display width.) Second, it is used as an alternative text condition.

4. Type **R. W.** as the short name and press (ENTER). Now whenever an item is entered Agenda will check its text for "Rachel" or "R. W." to conditionally assign the item to the Rachel category.

5. To add other phrases as text conditions, press (DOWN ARROW) to highlight the Also Match setting.

6. Type **Rachel W.;R. Warner;Rachel Warner;Warner** and press (ENTER). You can add additional words and phrases as long as the Category Name, Short Name, and Also Match entries are 69 characters or less and each entry is separated from the others with a semicolon (;) and no surrounding spaces, as shown in Figure 8-3.

The Match Category Name and Match Short Name settings in the right column of the Category Properties box allow you to turn off the text condition for the category name or the short name, respectively. This is useful whenever you have a category or short name that is a common word and that might appear in a context different than that meant by the category.

For example, you might have a staff member whose name is Bill. The word "bill" also might occur as a synonym for invoice. You probably do not want Agenda to make text conditional assignments based on the word "bill" because it might inappropriately assign the item to the person named Bill. In this case, you would change the Match Category Name setting to No or change the Match Short Name setting on the Invoice category to No.

7. Press (ENTER) to leave the Category Properties dialog box.

8. Press (ESC) to return to the view.

9. To see that the additional text conditions work, use the (ARROW) keys to highlight the last item in the view. Type **Have R. Warner meet with Porter Co. CEO re. proposed installation.** and press (ENTER). The item entry is automatically assigned to the Rachel category.

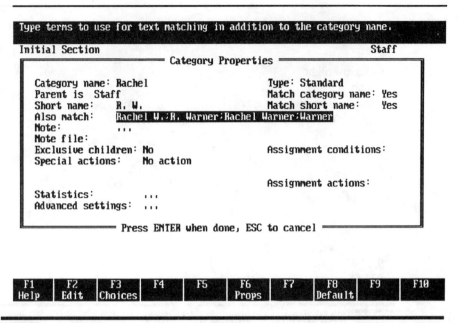

FIGURE 8-3.   The Category Properties dialog box for Rachel

How Agenda Matches Text

When Agenda performs text conditional assignments for an item, it looks for matches on a word-by-word basis. To Agenda a word is a group of characters separated by a space, period, comma, semicolon, exclamation point, or parenthesis. A word may include characters, numbers, apostrophes, dashes, or slashes. The caret (^), tilde (~), and underscore (_) can also be used to provide special ways to match item text. If the word begins with a number, Agenda treats any punctuation characters as part of the word. To process the words "stock split," for example, Agenda considers the words individually. On the other hand, Agenda considers "stock-split" to be one word because of the hyphen between the two words. Examples of how Agenda counts words are shown in Table 8-1. Agenda's basic rules pertain to exact matches with entries in the category hierarchy. A few exception conditions relate to proper names and suffixes on other entries.

SUFFIXES   When Agenda examines words in order to match item text to category text conditions, it ignores suffixes. This enables Agenda to be more flexible when

Text	Number of Words Counted
Pat's	1
tomorrow night	2
yes,no	2
Today;tomorrow	2
dog(Fido)	2
3d	1
in-between	1
and/or	1
MC^2	2
Wow!Amazing	2
If_Then	1
two~three	2
First.Second	2
9/27/87	1
$33.65	1

TABLE 8-1.   How Agenda Counts Words

deciding if a word in an item matches a category entry. A list of suffixes that Agenda ignores is shown in Table 8-2.

To see how Agenda ignores suffixes, you will add an Activity category to your JOBLOG database. You will add child categories of Meeting, Telephone, and Proposal. To do this, perform the following steps:

1. Press (F9) (Cat Mgr) to display the Category Manager box.

2. Highlight the Initial Section category using the (ARROW) keys.

3. Press (INS) to tell Agenda you want to insert a new category. This category will be at the same level as Initial Section.

4. Type **Activity** and press (ENTER).

5. Press (INS), type **Meeting**, and press (ENTER). Meeting appears as a category at the same level as Activity.

6. Demote the Meeting category by pressing (F8) (Dem), and press (ENTER) to confirm the demotion.

Suffix	Examples
able	workable, valuable
al	Educational, conditional
ally	Educationally, commercially
d	Executed, profiled
ed	Worked, crafted
es	Branches, boxes
er	Warmer, colder
est	Warmest, cleanest
ful	Careful, useful
ible	Edible, legible
ied	Qualified
ier	Qualifier
ies	Companies, copies
iful	Bountiful, plentiful
ily	Merrily, happily
ing	Billing, engineering
ly	Commercially, electrically
ment	Agreement, statement
s	Statements, employees
wise	Likewise, otherwise
y	Mousy, nosy

TABLE 8-2.   Suffixes Agenda Ignores

7. Press (INS), type **Telephone**, and press (ENTER). Telephone appears at the same level as Meeting.

8. Because there are synonyms for "telephone," you will add other text conditions for the Telephone category. Press (F6) (Props) to display the Category Properties screen.

9. Press (DOWN ARROW) once to highlight the Short Name setting, type **Call**, and press (ENTER).

10. Press (DOWN ARROW) once to highlight the Also Match setting, type **phone**, and press (ENTER).
    You can also add Phone to the short name list, separating it from the other entry with a semicolon.

```
File: C:\AGENDA\APPS\JOBLOG
Category Manager
  MAIN
  * Entry    Assign date when item is entered.
  * When     Assign date from the item text.
  * Done
    Initial Section
    Activity
      Meeting
      Telephone;Call;phone
      Proposal
    Staff
      Janet
      Floyd
      Rachel ;R. W.;Rachel W.;R. Warner;Rachel Warner;Warner
```

F1	F2	F3	F4	F5	F6	F7	F8	F9	F10
Help	Edit			Note	Props	Prm (←)	Dem (→)	To View	Menu

FIGURE 8-4.   The Category Manager after (ALT-F7) (ShowC/A) is
pressed to show the assigned conditions and actions

11. Press (ENTER) to return to the Category Manager.

12. Press (INS), type **Proposal**, and press (ENTER). Press (ALT-F7) (ShowC/A) to display
     the additional text conditions. At this point, your screen should be similar to Figure
     8-4. Notice that Telephone is now listed as Telephone;Call;phone. The category
     and short name entries are separated by semicolons just as the also match entries
     are separated. The category entry is first, the short name entry second, and the also
     match entries follow in order. Press (ALT-F7) (ShowC/A) again to return to the
     normal display.

13. Press (ESC) to return to the view.

14. Have Agenda make the text conditional assignments for the existing items by
     pressing (F10) (Menu) and selecting Utilities Execute. Press (ENTER) to accept the
     default values of the Execute box.

At this point, you could highlight each item and press (F3) (Choices) to see what
the conditional category assignments are. Instead, you will add an Activity column to
the view. Since you have not made any explicit assignments, you can assume that the
item assignments were made conditionally.

```
File: C:\AGENDA\APPS\JOBLOG                        09/30/98  11:50pm
View: Initial View
Initial Section                           Activity       Staff
   • Have Rachel evaluate our performance                ·Rachel
     regarding install at Acme, Inc.
   » Meeting with Floyd about Porter Co.   »Meeting       ·Floyd
     proposal.                            »Proposal
   • Have Janet monitor the development of the           ·Janet
     reports manual.
   • Have R. Warner meet with Porter Co. CEO re. ·Meeting ·Rachel
     proposed installation.                Proposal
```

```
 F1      F2      F3      F4      F5      F6      F7      F8      F9     F10
Help    Edit  Choices   Done    Note   Props    Mark  Vw Mgr Cat Mgr  Menu
```

FIGURE 8-5.   The Initial View displaying how Agenda ignores suffixes when making assignments using text conditions

16. Press (**F10**) (Menu) and select View Column Add.

17. Type **A** and press (**ENTER**) twice to accept the automatic selection of Activity. Press (**ENTER**) again to accept the Column Add box. Your screen should display the Activity column, as shown in Figure 8-5.

18. Press (**F10**) (Menu) and select Utilities Execute to force Agenda to make the necessary assignments.

Notice that the second item has been assigned to Meeting and Proposal, which are exact matches of the text within the item. The last item is assigned to the same two categories, but the text of this item contains the words "meet" instead of Meeting and "proposes" instead of Proposal. Agenda's ability to ignore suffixes saves you from having to enter each form of the word as an alternative text condition.

PROPER NAMES   Agenda can also identify proper names. To Agenda, any two or more words that are contiguous and start with capital letters constitute a proper name. This means that Agenda treats Bob Jones, Mary Smith, and Blue Ink as proper names. The ability to treat proper names in a different fashion from other entries enables Agenda to distinguish between people with the same last name but different first names. If you have categories established for more than one employee named

Brown, you needn't worry about all items being assigned to every Brown category since Agenda recognizes the name entries as proper names and assigns the item only to the proper Brown category. Agenda is also able to distinguish proper name entries that have the same first name but different last names, such as Mary Smith and Mary Peterson.

Agenda distinguishes proper names from other entries by the use of capital letters as the first character in two or more consecutive words and does not use its normal matching techniques. When the text entries in both the item and the category have these initial capital letters, the match will be for that specific combination of letters.

The item text plays a critical role in determining that the text refers to a proper name. If the words in the category are entirely lowercase but the item has the first letters of two or more consecutive words capitalized, the proper name matching features take effect. This means that a category entry of "jim miller" matches item text "Jim Miller." If two or more consecutive words in a category are capitalized and words in the item are lowercase, Agenda can make incorrect assignments. In this situation, Agenda cannot distinguish between same first names with different last names and same last names with different first names.

To see some examples of how proper names work, you will assume that Janet and Floyd both have last names of Brown. You will need to add text conditions to incorporate this fact. Instead of using the Category Manager display to enter the Category Properties box, this time you will enter it directly from the view.

1. Highlight the Floyd category at the second item by using the (ARROW) keys.

2. Press (F6) (Props) to turn on the Category Properties box.

3. Press (DOWN ARROW) twice to highlight the Also Match setting (there is no short name for the category). Type **F. Brown** and press (ENTER) twice.

4. Press (DOWN ARROW) to highlight Janet.

5. Press (F6) (Props) to turn on the Category Properties box.

6. Press (DOWN ARROW) once to highlight Short Name. Type **J. B.** and press (ENTER).

7. Press (DOWN ARROW) to highlight the Also Match setting. Type **J. Brown** and press (ENTER) twice.

8. Enter a new item by pressing (DOWN ARROW) and (LEFT ARROW) twice or by pressing (ALT-I). Type **Have Brown fix the coffee pot.** and press (ENTER). Notice that no conditional assignment was made. This is because you did not use a first initial. (If you had used Rachel Brown, the assignment would have been made due to the match with Rachel.)

9. Now type **Call f. brown re. planning committee meeting.** and press (ENTER). Both Janet and Floyd appear on the screen. This is because Agenda has trouble distinguishing matches of proper names when the names are entered in lowercase.

10. Edit the item by pressing (F2) (Edit), (CTRL-RIGHT ARROW), (DEL), and typing **F**. Press (ENTER). The item is now correctly assigned to Floyd.

TITLES   Agenda ignores certain titles for conditional assignment. All the titles shown in the following list are ignored whether they are used alone or as part of a proper name. This feature prevents item text that begins with "Mr." from being assigned to every "Mr." in the category hierarchy.

Dr.	Froker	Mademoiselle	Mme.
Fr.	Fru	Messrs.	Mmes.
Frau	Herr	Miss	Monsieur
Fraulein	Hr.	Mlle.	Mr.
Frk	M.	Mlles.	Mrs.
Frl.	Madame	MM.	Ms.

Determining Match Strength

When a category consists of a single word, it is clear whether a one-word item matches. As item entries become longer, it is still easy to scan an item to see if it contains the category name. As category names become longer, partial matches become possible. Agenda allows you to determine how strong the match must be between an item and a category for conditional assignment to occur. *Match strength* is measured by the number of words of a multiple-word category entry that an item contains.

The percentage of words from a category name found within the item is the item match strength. With a one-word description, the item either has 100 percent or 0 percent match strength. The match strength for a phrase is computed by determining the number of common words in both the item and the category phrase, divided by the number of words in the category phrase. The item *Meeting with Floyd about Porter Co. proposal* would have 100 percent match strength for the category Porter Co. Two words are common to both the item and the category, and there are two words in the category; 2/2 equals 1, or 100 percent.

To see how this works, you are going to create a Client category that lists the unique client number assigned to each client. Because items may not include the client number but may list the name of a company, you will include other text category entries that list the company names.

1. Press (F9) (Cat Mgr) to display the Category Manager. Use the (ARROW) keys to highlight the Initial Section.

2. Press (INS) to insert a new category, type **Client**, and press (ENTER).

3. Press (INS) to insert another category, type **P012** for the client number, and press (ENTER).

4. Press (F8) (Dem) to demote the category and (ENTER) to confirm the demotion.

5. Press (F6) (Props) to display the Category Properties box. Press (DOWN ARROW) twice to highlight the Also Match setting.

6. Type **Porter Co;Porter Company** and press (ENTER) twice. These category entries allow for the abbreviation or full spelling of the word "company."

7. Press (ESC) to return to the view.

8. Press (F10) (Menu), select Utilities Execute, and press (ENTER) to accept the default settings of the Execute box.

9. Press (UP ARROW) twice to highlight the Porter Co item and press (F3) (Choices) to display the Assignment Profile box for the item. A *c should appear next to the P012 entry to indicate that a conditional assignment was made.

If the Required Match Strength setting had been set to 50 percent, an item would only need to have the word "Porter" or "Company" for a conditional assignment to be made. In other words, any item with the word "Company" would be conditionally assigned to the Porter Company category if the Required Match Strength setting were set to Partial. Additional examples of match strengths are shown in Table 8-3.

Adjusting the Required Match Strength can increase the number of text conditional assignments.

10. Press (F9) (Cat Mgr) to display the Category Manager. Use the (ARROW) keys to highlight the P012 entry.

11. Press (INS) to insert another category, type **S456** for the client number, and press (ENTER).

Category	Item	Match Strength
Pay Bills	Did Bill call today	50%
Pay Bills	Pay all outstanding bills on Friday	100%
Pay Bills	Hire new person for accounts payable	50%
Pay Bills Today	We will start today	2%

TABLE 8-3.   How Agenda Computes Match Strength

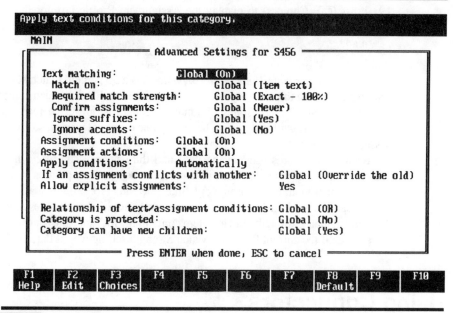

FIGURE 8-6. The Advanced Settings box for categories

12. Press (F6) (Props) to display the Category Properties box. Press (DOWN ARROW) twice to highlight the Also Match setting.

13. Type **Smith Roberts Jones;John Smith Ruth Jones** and press (ENTER). The name of the company is Smith, Roberts, & Jones, Incorporated. However, any item that contains most of the words within one of the two categories will probably refer to this company. When making its comparisons, Agenda will compare each category entry separately.

14. Press (DOWN ARROW) six times to highlight Advanced Settings and press (SPACEBAR). Your screen should appear similar to Figure 8-6. The top six entries refer to text conditions.

15. Press (DOWN ARROW) twice to highlight Required Match Strength. Type **p** to select the partial setting.

16. Press (ENTER) twice to return to the Category Manager box.

17. Press (ESC) to return to the view.

18. Press (PGDN) to quickly move to the bottom of the items. Type **Telephone John Smith re. photos.** and press (ENTER).

19. Press (F3) (Choices) to display the Assignment Profile box for the item. A *c should appear next to the S456 entry to indicate that a conditional assignment was made.

The item *Telephone John Smith re. photos* has a 50 percent match strength when compared against the category entry "John Smith Ruth Jones." When compared with the entry "Smith Roberts Jones," its match strength is only 33 percent. But the 50 percent match strength only has to be met by one of the categories, so the conditional assignment was made.

Each of the words used in the item and the category can affect how Agenda automatically assigns items. This is important when you use phrases in the category hierarchy that include common words like "the" and "for." Items that include these words can be erroneously assigned. The category Advice for the Investor would have 50 percent match strength with any item containing "for" and "the" and would qualify as a match if the current Required Match Strength setting was at Partial matches.

Using Connectors In Category Names

Text conditions can be modified by adding special symbols that represent connectors between text entries. These special symbols establish connections such as AND, OR, and NOT between the various entries in a text condition, and can manipulate which items are automatically assigned to a category. In the preceding examples, the category entries were separated by a semicolon. The semicolon acts as an OR connector:

Telephone;Call;phone

An item must include the word "telephone," "call," or "phone" to be assigned to this category. If the item *Call Gina* were entered, it would be assigned to the category because it matches "call." The item *Telephone John Smith re. photos* was assigned to the Telephone category because it contains the word "telephone."

The AND connector requires an item to match with two different category descriptions. It is represented by a comma rather than a semicolon. The following category name contains an AND connector:

Acme,Inc

To be included in this category, an item must include the words "Acme" and "Inc." An item with only one of these words would not be considered a match.

If a category has both an AND and an OR connector, Agenda evaluates the AND connections first to determine whether the specified combination matches the item text. It then evaluates the OR description and determines the match strength for that component. Follow these steps to see how this works:

1. Press (**F9**) (Cat Mgr) to display the Category Manager.

2. Highlight P012, press (**INS**), type **A134**, and press (**ENTER**) to add the Acme, Inc client number.

3. Press (**F6**) (Props), press (**DOWN ARROW**) twice, type **Acme,Inc;Acme,Incorporated**, and press (**ENTER**) twice.

4. Press (**ESC**) to return to the view.

5. Press (**F10**) (Menu), select Utilities Execute, and press (**ENTER**).

6. Highlight the first item by pressing (**HOME**) and (**DOWN ARROW**). Press (**F3**) (Choices) to display the Assignment Profile for the item.

The category A134 has a *c next to it to indicate that a conditional assignment was made for this item. Agenda then searches the text entry for "Acme" and "Inc" and determines whether both of these words are present in the item. Then it checks to see if "Acme" and "Incorporated" are both contained in the item. If either check proves to be true, the assignment is made because of the OR connection between the two pairs of words.

The NOT connector is represented by an exclamation point. For example, if you do not want items with the word "financial," placing an explanation point in front of the word in the category description prevents any item that has the word "financial" from being automatically assigned to the category. The NOT connector is evaluated before the AND or the OR connectors.

The NOT connector is frequently used in combination with the other connectors. To see an example of the joint use of connectors, follow these steps:

7. Press (**ESC**) to return to the view.

8. Press (**F9**) and highlight Proposal. Create a Reports Activity category by pressing (**INS**), typing **Reports**, and pressing (**ENTER**). This activity has to do with the writing of reports, and should not include anything involving the Reports Manual, as in the third item.

9. Press (**F6**) (Props) and press (**DOWN ARROW**) twice.

10. Type **Report,!manual** and press (**ENTER**). This category uses a NOT and an AND connector to mean that "report" must be contained within the item and "manual" must *not* be contained in the item. Both conditions must be met.

11. Press (UP ARROW), (RIGHT ARROW), and (UP ARROW) to highlight the Match Category Name setting. Type **n** to avoid matching the category name Reports because any item will match with this entry if it has the word "report" in it.

12. Press (ENTER) and (ESC) to return to the view.

13. Press (F10) (Menu), select Utilities Execute, and press (ENTER).

Notice that the item *Have Janet monitor the development of the reports manual* did not have the Reports activity assigned to it.

Special Characters
That Affect Matching

Agenda provides several special characters that can be used in category descriptions to modify how Agenda matches items to categories. These special characters tailor the text condition represented in the category to prevent it from being erroneously assigned to an item.

USING PARENTHESES TO TREAT WORDS AS PHRASE   Agenda will mistakenly assign items to a category when the phrase contains common words or words that can be used in several different contexts. In the Statements to the Press category, Agenda checks an item for the four words "statements," "to," "the," and "press" to determine whether to assign the item to the category automatically.

Since the words "to" and "the" are frequently used words, Agenda can assign many items incorrectly to this category, especially when partial match strength is used. This problem can be solved by placing parentheses around the phrase. Agenda assigns to the category (Statements to the Press) only items that have all four words in the exact order in which they are found in the category. The item cannot have any words interspersed with the matching words; the phrase must be exactly the same. If you want to allow words to be interspersed, you need to use one of the wild cards discussed in a moment.

USING QUOTES TO IGNORE WORDS IN A CATEGORY   In the previous example, an entire phrase was considered one unit because it was enclosed by parentheses. This prevented items with the words "to" and "the" from being assigned to the category automatically.

Another way to prevent erroneous assignment of items containing "to" and "the" is to enclose the two words in quotes within the category name. Words enclosed by quotes are ignored. If you enter the category name as **Statements "to the" Press**,

Agenda attempts to match items only on the words "statements" and "press." Quotes are the default text exclusion characters. You can assign others through the File Properties Global Assign settings, including:

```
< >
' '
( )
/ /
# #
[ ]
{ }
```

WILD CARDS   Wild card characters are probably the most important and powerful special characters that you can use in category names. Agenda provides two wild card characters: the question mark and the asterisk. Both characters operate like the same wild cards in DOS commands. The question mark is like a blank tile in Scrabble; that is, any one letter matches it. When a category name contains a question mark, Agenda automatically assigns to the category any item that has matching letters and accepts any character in the location of the question mark. Each question mark represents a single letter and must take the place of an actual letter in the category name. An item containing the word "Smith" or "Smyth" would both match with the category Sm?th. See Table 8-4 for more examples.

The asterisk is an even more powerful wild card character than the question mark. Any sequence of characters matches an asterisk. Agenda allows you to use the asterisk as the beginning, middle, or end of a word, or even a whole word or category. If you use A* as a word in a category name, Agenda matches any word that begins with an "a." For example, suppose you wanted to assign client prospects to sales representatives based on letters of the alphabet. You could handle the automatic assignment with entries in the category hierarchy under the representatives' names, like this:

A*;B*;C*;D*

Category	Matches	Does Not Match
1?3	123	1243
1?3	123	13
???able	curable	able
???able	potable	table

TABLE 8-4.   How the Question Mark Wild Card Character Works

The asterisk can represent more than one word when it is within a phrase enclosed by parentheses such as "(Statements * Press)." This is the correct way to enter the category name when you want to assign any item that has the word "statements" followed by the word "press" with one or more words between them. The wild card character appears in the category in View mode. In this example, you see "Statements * Press" when the category appears in a column or section head.

CONTROLLING AUTOMATIC ASSIGNMENT FEATURES

Agenda provides several options for modifying text conditions. You can tailor the automatic assignment features for one category using the Category Properties and Advanced Settings boxes. You can tailor the automatic assignment features for all categories in the database using the Auto-assign Global Settings box in File Properties.

Changing the Defaults For All Text Conditions

To view and change the default settings that affect all automatic assignments based on text conditions:

1. Press (F10) (Menu) and select File Properties.

2. Press (DOWN ARROW) eight times and (RIGHT ARROW) once to highlight Auto-assign Settings and press (SPACEBAR). This displays the Auto-assign Global Settings dialog box shown in Figure 8-7.

You can change any of these settings by moving to the setting, pressing (F3) (Choices) to view the choices in a selection box, and highlighting the desired choice. The selections you pick in the Auto-assign Global Settings dialog box affect all categories in the database. You can make settings similar to these for a single category with the Category Properties and Advanced Setting boxes, as discussed later in the chapter.

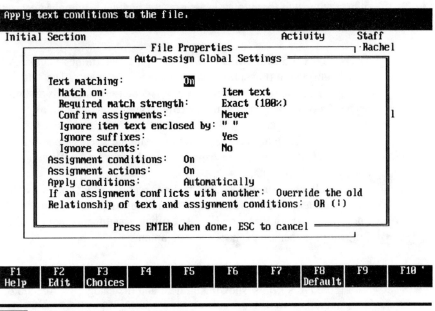

```
Apply text conditions to the file.

Initial Section                                    Activity    Staff
                    ┌─────── File Properties ──────────────┐ ·Rachel
                    ├═════ Auto-assign Global Settings ═════┤
                    │                                       │
                    │  Text matching:        On             │
                    │    Match on:                Item text │
                    │    Required match strength: Exact (100%)│
                    │    Confirm assignments:     Never      │  1
                    │    Ignore item text enclosed by: " "   │
                    │    Ignore suffixes:         Yes        │
                    │    Ignore accents:          No         │
                    │  Assignment conditions:  On            │
                    │  Assignment actions:     On            │
                    │  Apply conditions:       Automatically │
                    │  If an assignment conflicts with another:  Override the old │
                    │  Relationship of text and assignment conditions:  OR (!)│
                    │                                       │
                    └═════ Press ENTER when done, ESC to cancel ═════┘

  F1    F2     F3     F4    F5    F6    F7    F8     F9    F10 '
 Help  Edit  Choices                         Default
```

FIGURE 8-7.   The Auto-assign Global Settings box to determine the database defaults for condition assignments

TEXT MATCHING   This option determines whether Agenda tries to assign items to categories on the basis of the categories' text conditions. Your choices are On (the default) or Off to enable or disable automatic assignments on the basis of the text conditions. If this setting is On, several other settings relating to text conditions are displayed. If you choose Off, these additional settings disappear.

MATCH ON   This option determines what text Agenda uses for automatic assignment. The choices are Item Text, Note Text, and Both Item & Note. When you select an option that includes note text, Agenda examines all the text in the note regardless of its length.

REQUIRED MATCH STRENGTH   This option determines the minimum match strength Agenda uses to assign items automatically. Your choices are Exact Match, Partial Match, and Minimal Match. With Exact Match, the match must be 100 percent for an item to be assigned to a category. If a category contains a phrase, all of the words of the phrase must be in the item text. The Partial Match setting requires a

50 percent match for automatic assignment, and the Minimal Match setting requires a 2 percent match.

CONFIRM ASSIGNMENTS   This option determines whether Agenda asks for your confirmation on some or all automatic assignments. The settings are Always, Sometimes, or Never. If you select Never, Agenda automatically assigns items without asking for confirmation. If you select Sometimes, Agenda assigns items with a match strength of 100 percent without questioning them, and asks for confirmation of assignments for items with less than exact match strength but at least the required match strength. If you select Always, Agenda asks for confirmation on all possible automatic assignments.

A small question mark appears in the upper-right corner when Agenda has completed an automatic assignment and requires your confirmation. Assignments made using the confirmation box are explicit assignments, not conditional. You can follow this procedure to check the assignments:

1. Press (F10) (Menu) and select Utilities Questions. A dialog box like the one in Figure 8-8 appears, showing an item and the categories Agenda thinks the item should be assigned to.

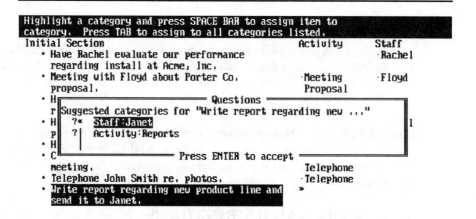

FIGURE 8-8.   Confirming condition assignments using the Questions dialog box

2. Press (**TAB**) if Agenda's category selections are correct. If they are not correct, press (**SPACEBAR**) to assign the item to the correct categories. When you complete the current item, press (**ENTER**). After you accept the choices for the item, Agenda prompts you with the next assignment question and continues to do so until all the assignments in question have been confirmed. The question mark in the upper-right corner disappears when there are no further assignment questions.

SKIP TEXT ENCLOSED BY   This option sets the character used to mark item and note text to be omitted when checking for automatic assignments. Agenda initially ignores characters enclosed in quotes. The other choices are double quotes ("), single quotes ('), parentheses (()), slashes (/ /), pound signs (##), brackets ([]), braces ({ }), and less-than and greater-than symbols (<>). Any portion of an item entry enclosed in the special character selected is ignored as Agenda searches items for automatic assignment.

IGNORE SUFFIXES   This setting determines whether Agenda ignores suffixes for determining assignments based on text conditions. As explained earlier in the chapter, Agenda's ability to match words even when the suffixes do not match extends the utility of its automatic assignment features. If ignoring suffixes is producing erroneous assignments, you may use this setting to disable that feature.

IGNORE ACCENTS ON CHARACTERS   Agenda lets you use special symbols for accenting characters. If you want Agenda to treat an accented character like an unaccented one for automatic assignment, you need to tell Agenda to ignore accents on characters. Your choices for this setting are Yes, to ignore accents, and No, to not ignore them.

Controlling Automatic Assignments for One Category

The automatic assignment features for text conditions can be modified for a single category. To make this type of change in View mode or the Catalog Manager, move the highlight to the category to be modified and press (**F6**) (Props), highlight Advanced Settings, and press (**SPACEBAR**). If the category is displayed as a section use the menu instead of (**F6**). A dialog box like the one in Figure 8-7 offers several options.

With the exception of the Ignore Item Text Enclosed By setting, the settings for a single category are the same as for the file. The only difference is that they affect only one category instead of all categories in the database. Settings made in the Advanced

Settings box override the settings made in the Auto- assign Global Settings box for the specified category.

PROFILE CONDITIONS

Text conditions are one method used to assign items to categories. Additional assignments can be made with *profile conditions.* A profile condition assigns an item to a category based on a profile of the other category assignments for the item. Any new or edited item that meets the assignment conditions in the profile that you establish for a category will be automatically assigned to the category.

The three types of profile conditions are assignment conditions, date conditions, and number conditions. Assignment conditions provide the ability to assign items to categories based on their other assigned categories. Date conditions assign items to categories based on the date value stored in a date category. Number conditions assign items to categories based on the numeric value stored within a numeric category.

Using an Assignment Condition

Assignment conditions are useful when you want items in one category to belong to a category in a different family. Assume that any item pertaining to the Porter Co. must also be assigned to Janet because she oversees all work done for this company. The assignment condition is that all items assigned to Client P012 (the Porter Co.'s client number) in the JOBLOG database must also be pulled into the category Janet. You can think of items as being pulled from categories in assignment conditions and pushed to categories in assignment actions. Perform the following steps:

1. Display the Category Manager by pressing (F9) (Cat Mgr). Use the (ARROW) keys to highlight the Janet category.

2. Press (F6) (Props) to display the Category Properties dialog box.

3. Press (DOWN ARROW) five times and (RIGHT ARROW) once to highlight the Assignment Conditions setting. This is where you list the category (or categories) from which you want Agenda to make an assignment.

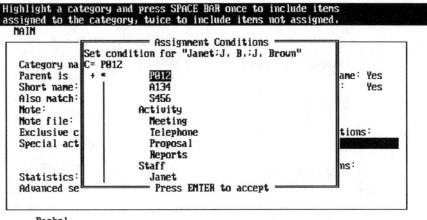

FIGURE 8-9.   Adding an assignment condition to the Janet category

4. Press (F3) (Choices) to display the Assignment Conditions dialog box. Use the (ARROW) keys to highlight P012.

5. Press (SPACEBAR) to place a plus symbol next to the P012 category, as shown in Figure 8-9. This plus sign means that any item that is assigned to P012 is also to be assigned to Janet.

6. Press (ENTER) to return to the Category Properties box shown in Figure 8-10. Press (ENTER) and (ESC) to return to the view.

7. Retroactively assign the current items based on the assignment conditions by pressing (F10) (Menu) and selecting Utilities Execute, or by pressing the accelerator key (ALT-X). Press (ENTER) to accept the default settings in the Execute box.

Notice that Janet is now assigned to the two items that contain references to the Porter Company.

Another type of assignment condition assigns items that are not assigned to a specified category. For this example, assume that any item that is not assigned to a staff member is to be assigned to a category called My Jobs. A view is created that

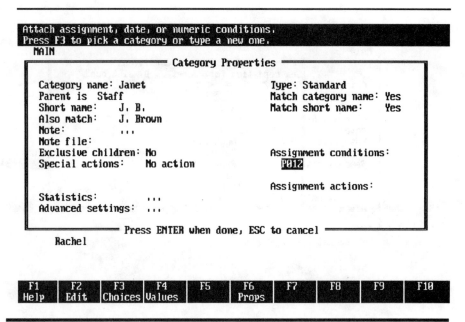

FIGURE 8-10. The Category Properties box with an assignment condition set to P012

lists all items belonging to My Jobs as a reminder to assign the items. Since the Staff category inherits all items belonging to its children, all that needs to be done is to check if there are any assignments to Staff. To do this, follow these steps:

8. Press (F9) (Cat Mgr) and highlight the Initial Section category in the Category Manager using the (ARROW) keys.

9. Press (INS) to add a category, type **My jobs**, and press (ENTER). Avoid the tendency to include the My Jobs category as a child of Staff. This could create a looping situation where Agenda assigns an item to My Jobs because it is not assigned to Staff, and then unassigns the same item because as an item of My Jobs it is now assigned to Staff, and so on.

10. Press (F6) (Props). Press (DOWN ARROW) six times and (RIGHT ARROW) once to highlight the Assignment Conditions setting.

11. Press (F3) (Choices) to display the Assignment Conditions box. Highlight Staff and press (SPACEBAR) twice. A minus symbol appears next to Staff. The minus sign indicates that an item not assigned to Staff will be assigned to My Jobs.

12. Press (ENTER) twice and (ESC) once to return to the view.

13. Press (F8) (Vw Mgr) and (INS) to create a new view. Type **Unassigned Jobs** and press (ENTER). Press (DOWN ARROW) and (RIGHT ARROW) once each. Type **my** and press (ENTER) to accept the automatic assignment of My Jobs, and press (ENTER) again to select the view.

14. No items are currently assigned. To retroactively assign the current items based on the current assignment conditions, press (F10) (Menu) and select Utilities Execute. Press (ENTER) to accept the default settings in the Execute box.

15. Press (DOWN ARROW) once to highlight the first item. You will now explicitly assign this item to Floyd. When done, the item will no longer appear in this view because it has been assigned to a Staff category.

16. Press (F3) (Choices), highlight Floyd, and press (SPACEBAR) and (ENTER). The item disappears from the view because it no longer belongs to the My Jobs category. You can also use (F10) (Item MakeAssign) or (ALT-M).

Using a Date Condition

A date condition assigns an item to a category based on the value in a date category. This can be useful for setting up views that represent specific time frames. The date condition can pertain to dates as well as times. For this example, you will first assign date values to the When category that Agenda sets up for all databases. These When values will represent the due dates for each item.

1. If you are not already there, return to the Initial View by pressing (F8) (Vw Mgr), highlighting Initial View, and pressing (ENTER), or by pressing (ALT-F8) if that was the last view opened.

2. Highlight the first item using the (ARROW) keys.

3. Press (ALT-F2) (When), type **tomorrow**, and press (ENTER).

4. Press (DOWN ARROW), press (ALT-F2) (When), type **end of next month**, and press (ENTER).

5. Press (DOWN ARROW), press (ALT-F2) (When), type **next Friday**, and press (ENTER).

6. Press (DOWN ARROW), press (ALT-F2) (When), type **this Monday**, and press (ENTER).

7. Press (DOWN ARROW), press (ALT-F2) (When), type **today**, and press (ENTER).

8. Press (DOWN ARROW), press (ALT-F2) (When), type **Wednesday**, and press (ENTER).

9. Press (DOWN ARROW), press (ALT-F2) (When), type **10/9/91**, and press (ENTER).

10. Press (DOWN ARROW), press (ALT-F2) (When), type **a week from today**, and press (ENTER). All items should now have a date assigned to their When category.

11. Press (F9) (Cat Mgr) and highlight the Initial Section using the (ARROW) keys.

12. Press (INS) to create a new category, type **Jobs due this week**, and press (ENTER).

13. Press (F6) (Props) to display the Category Properties box. Press (DOWN ARROW) six times and (RIGHT ARROW) once to highlight the Assignment Conditions setting.

14. Press (F3) (Choices) and use the (ARROW) keys to highlight the When category.

15. Press (SPACEBAR) to select the When category. Because When is a date category, the Date Condition box appears on the screen.

16. Press (DOWN ARROW), type **today** as the start date for the condition, and press (ENTER).

17. Press (DOWN ARROW), type **a week from today** as the end date, and press (ENTER). Your screen should be similar to Figure 8-11.

18. Press (ENTER) three times and (ESC) once to return to the view.

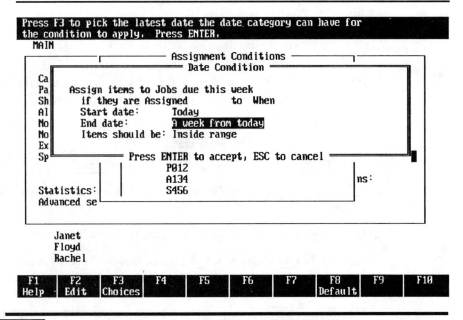

FIGURE 8-11.   The Date Condition box set to display this week's items

19. Create a new view using the Jobs Due This Week category by pressing (F8) (Cat Mgr), pressing (NS), typing **This week's jobs**, and pressing (ENTER). Press (DOWN ARROW) and (RIGHT ARROW) to highlight the Sections setting, type **jo** and press (ENTER) twice. The view contains no items.

20. To have Agenda assign the current items using the new conditions, press (F10) (Menu), select Utilities Execute, and press (ENTER), or press (ALT-X).

The This Week's Jobs view will display those items that have When dates assigned between today and a week from today. This condition is reevaluated whenever the system date changes. This means that tomorrow this view will display those items whose When category contains a date between tomorrow and a week from tomorrow.

Using a Numeric Condition

Numeric conditions assign items to categories based on the values assigned to numeric categories, in much the same way as date conditions make assignments based on date categories. A numeric condition could be used to flag high-cost items or pinpoint ranges of values. You could categorize items as being high, medium, or low.

The process for creating numeric conditions is identical to that of date conditions, except that you mark a numeric category in the Assignment Conditions setting instead of a date category and you designate a numeric range of values instead of a date range.

ACTIONS

You probably assign actions to members of your staff every day without thinking about it. For example, you might ask an employee to check the math on invoices being processed for payment. This is not very different from assigning actions to categories in an Agenda database. When you attach an action to a category, you are giving Agenda the responsibility for performing the action on items that are subsequently assigned to the category.

Just as your employee will not perform the task of checking invoices without your instructions, Agenda cannot perform an action until you establish it. Just as your employee cannot check an invoice before he or she receives it, the Agenda category cannot perform an action until it is assigned one or more items on which to do so. This chapter explores the various types of actions that can be applied to categories.

ACTIONS VERSUS CONDITIONS

In Chapter 8 you learned about conditions that could assign an item to a category based on the other categories to which it was already assigned. Although a condition is similar to an action, and in some cases can be constructed to perform similar tasks, there are substantial differences between the two. The effect of a condition is not as far-reaching as the effect of an action. The most that an individual condition can do is pull items from many categories into one category with a conditional assignment. An action is attached to a single category, but based on an item's assignment to the one category, Agenda can assign the item to many additional categories.

Conditions and actions differ in the category that is affected. In a condition the category with the condition attached is the category that is affected by the condition, since it is this category that might have items assigned to it. Thus, a category with a condition attached is passively involved in the changes that might take place because of the condition. In an action the category with the action is unaffected by the action regardless of the outcome except for special actions that discard or export items. With these special actions you see items assigned to the action category disappear. The action only affects other categories. Thus, a category with an action attached plays an active role in changing the database.

Conditions create conditional assignments that are removed when the underlying condition is no longer met. Actions create explicit assignments that are removed only by you or other actions.

Actions are also more versatile than conditions. Conditions can affect the assignment of items to a category. An action can affect the assignment of one or more items to one or more categories. An action can also remove an assignment from an item, discard an item, assign a date, mark an item as done, or export items to another file.

TYPES OF ACTIONS

Agenda categorizes actions as one of the following four types:

Assignment actions
Date actions
Numeric actions
Special actions

Each of these actions performs a specific function based on an item's assignment to a specified category. Assignment actions assign items to other categories; date actions assign items to a date category and are assigned a specific date; numeric actions assign items to numeric categories and are given a number value; and special actions discard items from the database, export items to structured files that can be used by other Agenda databases, or designate items as done. Assignment, date, and numeric actions can all also remove an item's assignment from a category.

CREATING ASSIGNMENT ACTIONS

Assignment actions are used whenever you want to assign an item to other categories based on its assignment to the current category. By attaching an assignment action to the current category, any new items that are assigned to this category, either explicitly or with conditional assignments, will be affected by the action. You can also prevent items assigned to the current category from being assigned to one or more other categories using assignment actions.

In this chapter you will work with an Agenda database named WORKINPR that tracks the work in progress for a company. Items are tracked based on the type of work and the managers responsible for its completion. The three stages for the work assignments are "Work requests," "Work in progress," and "Completed projects." Based on the stage an item is in, the item is assigned to different categories using actions.

To create the database, perform the following steps:

1. Assuming you are currently within an Agenda database, press (F10) (Menu) and select File Retrieve. Press (INS) to create a new file, type **workinpr**, and press (ENTER).

2. Type **Tracking of special projects** for the database description, and press (ENTER) twice to enter the database view.

3. You will now create the categories for this database using the Category Manager. Press (F9) (Cat Mgr).

4. Type **Work requests** and press (ENTER).

5. Type **Proposals** and press (ENTER). Demote this category to a child of Work requests by pressing (F8) (Dem), and press (ENTER) to confirm the demotion.

6. Type **Training** and press (ENTER).
   Notice that this category is now a sibling of Proposals.

7. Type **Prospecting** and press (ENTER).

8. Type **Work in progress** and press (ENTER). Promote this category by pressing (F7) (Prm), and press (ENTER) to confirm the promotion. Since this category name is fairly long and it is to be used as a column head, create a short name by pressing (F6) (Props) to display the Category Properties dialog box. Press (DOWN ARROW) once, type **in progress** as the short name, and press (ENTER) twice to return to the Category Manager.

≡ Note ≡   As a shortcut for adding short names, you can simply type **;In Progress** after the long name while creating it, but you must use (F6) to edit or delete short names.

9. Type **Completed projects** and press (ENTER). Create a short name for this category by pressing (F6) (Props) to display the Category Properties dialog box. Press (DOWN ARROW) once, type **Completed** as the short name, and press (ENTER) twice to return to the Category Manager.

10. Type **Management** and press (ENTER).

11. Type **Dorothy** and press (ENTER). Demote this category to a child of Management by pressing (F8) (Dem), and press (ENTER) to confirm the demotion.

≡ Note ≡   When you become comfortable with these and other tasks requiring confirmation, you can turn off Confirmation mode in Utilities Customize.

12. Type **John** and press (ENTER).

13. Type **Tom** and press (ENTER).

14. Type **Code number** and press (ENTER). Promote this category by pressing (F7) (Prm), and press (ENTER) to confirm the promotion. Make this category numeric by pressing (F6) (Props) and (RIGHT ARROW) to highlight the Type setting. Type **n** to select the numeric type and press (ENTER) to return to the Category Manager. Your screen should now look like the one displayed in Figure 9-1.

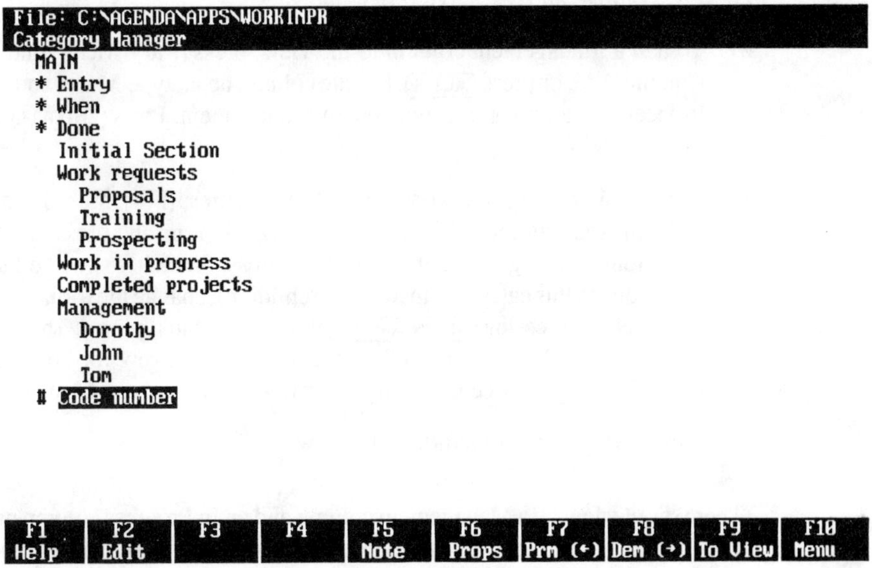

```
File: C:\AGENDA\APPS\WORKINPR
Category Manager
  MAIN
  * Entry
  * When
  * Done
    Initial Section
    Work requests
      Proposals
      Training
      Prospecting
    Work in progress
    Completed projects
    Management
      Dorothy
      John
      Tom
  # Code number
```

F1	F2	F3	F4	F5	F6	F7	F8	F9	F10
Help	Edit			Note	Props	Prm (←)	Dem (→)	To View	Menu

FIGURE 9-1.   Defined categories for WORKINPR

15. Press (ESC) to return to the view.

You will now create a view that will display its items within five sections. This view will emphasize how Agenda can reassign items using actions. You will be able to see items "jump" from one section to another as category assignments change.

16. To modify the current view, press (F8) (Vw Mgr). Edit the name of the view by pressing (F2) (Edit) and (CTRL-ENTER) to delete the current entry, typing **Tracking Of Work Requests**, and pressing (ENTER).

17. Press (F6) (Props) to display the View Properties box.

18. Press (RIGHT ARROW) to highlight the Sections setting. Press (DEL) to delete Initial Section.

19. Press (F3) (Choices) to display a list of categories to choose as section headings. Press (DOWN ARROW) once to highlight Work Requests. Press (F5) (Chldrn) to select the children of Work Requests. Press (DOWN ARROW) four times to highlight Work in Progress and press (SPACEBAR). Press (DOWN ARROW) once to highlight Completed Projects and press (SPACEBAR). Press (ENTER) to accept the current selections.

20. Press (ENTER) and (ESC) to return to the view.

21. To add a Management column to the view, press (F10) (Menu) and select View Column Add, or press (ALT-R). For the column head, type **Mana** and press (ENTER) to accept the automatic assignment of Management. Press (ENTER) again to return to the view.

22. To add a Work in Progress column to the view, press (F10) (Menu) and select View Column Add. For the column head, type **Work in pr** and press (ENTER) to accept the automatic assignment of Work in Progress. Since items will either belong or not belong to this category (there are no children), change the format of this column to Yes/No by pressing (DOWN ARROW) three times and typing **y**. This automatically changes the column width to 2. Since this is too narrow for your column head, press (UP ARROW) twice to highlight the Width setting, type **12**, and press (ENTER).

23. Press (ENTER) again to return to the view.

There should now be a Management column and an In Progress column on the screen. The In Progress heading was chosen by Agenda because you entered it as a short name when you defined the category, and the full category name of Work in Progress is too large for the 12-character width.

The In Progress column is appropriate for the first three sections of this view. You will now change the second column in the fourth and fifth sections as follows:

24. Press (DOWN ARROW) three times to highlight the In Progress column heading within the Work in Progress section. Press (DEL). A confirmation box appears asking you to confirm the deletion of the column from all sections. Press (SPACEBAR) to change the confirmation box so that it asks for confirmation to delete the column head from the current section only. The confirmation box should look like this:

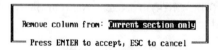

Press (ENTER) to confirm the deletion of the column from the fourth section.

25. To replace the deleted column head with a new one, press (F10) (Menu) and select View Column Add. Type **Completed p** and press (ENTER) to accept Completed Projects as the column head.

26. Press (RIGHT ARROW) and (DOWN ARROW) to highlight the Insert In setting. Press (SPACEBAR) to change the setting to Current Section. This means the column will only be added to the current section of the view.

27. Since items will either belong or not belong to this category, change the format of this column to Yes/No by pressing (LEFT ARROW) once, pressing (DOWN ARROW) two times, and typing **y**. This automatically changes the column width to 2. Since this is too narrow for your column head, press (UP ARROW) twice to highlight the Width setting, type **12**, and press (ENTER). Press (ENTER) again to return to the view.

28. To change the In Progress column for the fifth section, press (DOWN ARROW) once to highlight the In Progress column heading within the Completed Projects section. Press (DEL). A confirmation box appears asking you to confirm the deletion of the column from all sections. Press (SPACEBAR) to change the confirmation box and press (ENTER) to confirm the deletion of the column from the fifth section.

29. To replace the deleted column head with a new one, press (F10) (Menu) and select View Column Add. Type **Done** and press (ENTER). This Column Add dialog box is different than the one earlier, because Done is a date category. Done is defined by Agenda for all databases.

30. Press (DOWN ARROW) three times and (SPACEBAR) three times to change the Date format to Date only. By default, this changes the column width to 8 characters.

31. Press (UP ARROW) twice to highlight Width, type **12**, and press (ENTER).

32. Press (RIGHT ARROW) once to highlight the Insert In setting. Press (SPACEBAR) to change the setting to Current Section. This means the column will only be added to the current section of the view.

33. Press (ENTER) to return to the view. Your screen should now appear similar to Figure 9-2. Your database is now ready for you to learn about actions and how they work with Agenda databases.

Creating Assignment Actions to Assign Items To Other Categories

All actions can be created from the Category Manager or from View mode using (F6) (Props) to display the Category Properties dialog box. You will use the Category Manager to create your actions, but you could just as well define the actions from View mode.

In the example, Dorothy is responsible for monitoring the completion of all proposals, John for monitoring training, and Tom for prospecting for customers. Whenever an item is categorized as a Proposal, you want Agenda to also assign the

```
File: C:\AGENDA\APPS\WORKINPR                    10/08/90  12:52am
View: Tracking Of Work Requests                            *
Proposals                          Management    In progress

Training                           Management    In progress

Prospecting                        Management    In progress

Work in progress                   Management    Completed

Completed projects                 Management    Done
```

```
 F1      F2      F3     F4     F5     F6     F7     F8      F9     F10
Help    Edit  Choices  Done   Note  Props  Mark  Vw Mgr Cat Mgr  Menu
```

FIGURE 9-2.   Tracking Of Work Requests view

item to Dorothy. Similarly, you want all items assigned to Training to be assigned to John, and all items assigned to Prospecting assigned to Tom.

You might recall from Chapter 8 that assignment conditions can be used to assign an item to a category based on its assignment to another. Assignment conditions create conditional assignments. If an item is assigned to Dorothy based on its assignment to Proposals using an assignment condition, the item's assignment is conditional. If the item's assignment to Proposal is later broken, the condition would no longer be met and the item would no longer be conditionally assigned to Dorothy.

Actions create explicit assignments. In the database example for this chapter, items will be removed from their Work Requests category once they become assigned to Work in Progress. However, the items will still need to be tracked by their assigned managers. Therefore, you do not want the item assignments to the Management categories to be broken when the item is no longer assigned to the Work Requests of Proposals, Training, and Prospecting. For the required explicit assignments to be made, you will need to use assignment actions.

To create an assignment action that takes an item assigned to the Proposal category and also explicitly assigns it to the Dorothy category, follow these steps:

1. Activate the Category Manager by pressing (F9) (Cat Mgr).

2. Use (UP) and (DOWN ARROW) to highlight the Proposals category. Press (F6) (Props) to activate the Category Properties box.

3. Press (DOWN ARROW) seven times, or press (END) and (RIGHT ARROW) once, to highlight Assignment Actions.

4. Create the action assignment by typing **dor** and pressing (ENTER) to accept the automatic assignment of the Dorothy category. The following Assignment Action box appears on the screen:

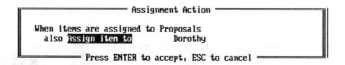

```
╔══════════════ Assignment Action ══════════════╗
║                                                ║
║ When items are assigned to Proposals           ║
║    also Assign item to        Dorothy          ║
║          ══ Press ENTER to accept, ESC to cancel ══          ║
╚════════════════════════════════════════════════╝
```

5. Accept the default selection of "Assign item to Dorothy" by pressing (ENTER). Your screen should now appear as displayed in Figure 9-3. Dorothy is listed under Assignment Actions as a category that an item will be assigned to if it is assigned to Proposals.

≡ Note ≡ More than one assignment action can be made for any one category. If necessary, you could add other categories as actions to Proposals just as you can have more than one condition assigned to a category.

6. Press (ENTER) to return to the Category Manager.

You will now make an assignment action for Training that assigns items to John because John is responsible for projects pertaining to training.

7. Press (DOWN ARROW) once to highlight Training and press (F6) (Props) to display the Category Properties box.

8. Press (END) and (RIGHT ARROW) once to highlight Assignment Actions.

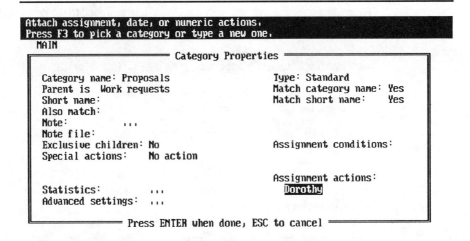

```
Attach assignment, date, or numeric actions.
Press F3 to pick a category or type a new one.
  MAIN
                         ═══ Category Properties ═══

   Category name: Proposals             Type: Standard
   Parent is  Work requests             Match category name: Yes
   Short name:                          Match short name:    Yes
   Also match:
   Note:            ...
   Note file:
   Exclusive children: No               Assignment conditions:
   Special actions:    No action

                                        Assignment actions:
   Statistics:          ...               Dorothy
   Advanced settings:   ...

            ══════ Press ENTER when done, ESC to cancel ══════
```

```
F1      F2      F3      F4      F5      F6      F7      F8      F9      F10
Help    Edit  Choices Values          Props
```

FIGURE 9-3.   Dorothy is defined as an assignment action for the
Proposals category

9. Instead of typing the category name for the assignment as you did previously, you will use another method for selecting the action category. Press (F3) (Choices) to display a list of the category choices available in the database.

10. Press (DOWN ARROW) six times to highlight the category John, and press (SPACEBAR) to select the category for the action. (At this point you could select other categories also to be included for the action by individually highlighting each category and pressing (SPACEBAR).) A plus sign (+) appears next to John to indicate that the item will be assigned to John by the action if it is assigned to Training.

11. Press (ENTER) to accept your selection and return to the Category Properties box. John is displayed under Assignment Actions. Press (ENTER) again to return to the Category Manager.

12. Similarly, use the Assignment Actions setting to assign items assigned to Prospecting to Tom by pressing (DOWN ARROW) to highlight Prospecting.

13. Press (F6) (Props) to display the Category Properties box.

14. Press (END) and (RIGHT ARROW) once to highlight Assignment Actions.

15. Press (F3) (Choices) to display a list of the category choices available in the database.

16. Press (DOWN ARROW) six times to highlight the category Tom, and press (SPACEBAR) to select the category for the action. A plus sign (+) appears next to Tom to indicate that the item will be assigned to it by the action if it is assigned to Prospecting.

17. Press (ENTER) to accept the selections and return to the Category Properties box. Tom is displayed under Assignment Actions. Press (ENTER) again to return to the Category Manager and (ESC) to return to the view.

Using Assignment Actions

Once the assignment actions have been defined for the database, you make item entries as normal. As an item is entered, Agenda checks the item against all conditions and then checks against all actions, making assignments accordingly. Perform the following steps to see how assignment actions are used by Agenda:

1. Press (CTRL-HOME) and then (CTRL-LEFT ARROW) to move the highlight to the Proposals section of the database.

2. Type **Write proposal for client 12 detailing costs associated with addition.**, and press (ENTER) to create the first item. Notice that Agenda immediately assigns it to Dorothy in the Management column as per the assignment action you defined in the Proposals category.

3. Press (DOWN ARROW) to move to the Training section. Type the item **Train 3 new sales personnel.** and press (ENTER). Notice that John is assigned to this item.

4. Press (DOWN ARROW) to move to the Prospecting section. Type **Use the new industry index to target previously unidentified prospects on the east side.** and press (ENTER). The item is immediately assigned to Tom. Except for the first item's assignment to John, which is explained in a moment, your screen should appear similar to Figure 9-4.

```
File: C:\AGENDA\APPS\WORKINPR                        10/08/90    9:01am
View: Tracking Of Work Requests
Proposals                                   Management    In progress
   • Write proposal for client 12 detailing costs   ·Dorothy       N
     associated with addition.                        John

Training                                    Management    In progress
   • Train 3 new sales personnel.            ·John              N

Prospecting                                 Management    In progress
   • Use the new industry index to target   »Tom              N
     previously unidentified prospects on the
     east side.

Work in progress                            Management    Completed

Completed projects                          Management    Done



 ┌────┬────┬───────┬────┬────┬─────┬────┬──────┬──────┬─────┐
 │ F1 │ F2 │  F3   │ F4 │ F5 │ F6  │ F7 │  F8  │  F9  │ F10 │
 │Help│Edit│Choices│Done│Note│Props│Mark│Vw Mgr│Cat Mgr│Menu│
 └────┴────┴───────┴────┴────┴─────┴────┴──────┴──────┴─────┘
```

FIGURE 9-4.   Database view showing the assignments made after three
items have been entered

Comparing Assignment Actions to Conditional Assignments

Conditions make conditional assignments. Actions make explicit assignments. The difference becomes apparent when you display an Assignment Profile for an item assigned by a condition and an action.

For this example, you will create an assignment condition that assigns any item assigned to the Proposals category to John. John shares responsibility with Dorothy for proposals when they are in the work request phase. Once the item's assignment is removed from the Proposals category, it no longer needs to be assigned to John (but still remains assigned to Dorothy). You can use an assignment condition to assign an item to John conditionally on its assignment to Proposals.

Perform the following:

1. Press (F9) (Cat Mgr) to activate the Category Manager. Highlight John using the (UP ARROW) and (DOWN ARROW) keys.

2. Press (F6) (Props) to display the Category Properties screen for John. Press (DOWN ARROW) five times and (RIGHT ARROW) once to highlight the Assignment Conditions setting.

3. Type **proposals** and press (ENTER) to define the Proposals category as the assignment condition. If an item is assigned to Proposals, it will be conditionally assigned to John.

4. The following Assignment Condition appears on the screen:

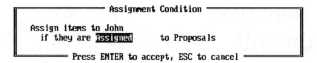

Press (ENTER) to accept the default condition that the item must be assigned to Proposals to be assigned to John.

5. Press (ENTER) to return to the Category Manager and press (F9) (To View) to return to the view.

6. Retroactively apply the condition to the database by pressing (F10) (Menu) and selecting Utilities Execute. Press (ENTER) to accept the default settings of the Execute dialog box. Figure 9-4 displays the resulting screen with John now assigned to the first item.

7. Press (UP ARROW) four times to highlight the item under the Proposals section.

8. Press (F3) (Choices) to activate the Assignment Profile for the item, and then press (CTRL-END) to move to the bottom of the category assignments.

Categories that have a *c next to them are conditionally assigned to the item. John is an example of a conditionally assigned category. Categories that are assigned through an action only have the asterisk, indicating an explicit assignment to the item. Dorothy is an example of an explicitly assigned category in which the assignment was made through an action.

9. Press (ESC) to return to the view.

 Note Agenda consistently evaluates item assignments based on conditions and actions. Items are first conditionally assigned to other categories based on the conditions that apply and then are explicitly assigned to categories based on the actions that apply. Therefore, a conditional assignment may trigger the application of an action. This means explicit assignments can be made by actions which are triggered by conditional assignments. For example, if you were to add a conditional assignment to this database that conditionally assigned an item to Proposals, the action you defined would then explicitly assign the item to Dorothy. If the condition that assigned the item to Proposals is removed, the item will no longer be assigned to Proposals, but will still be assigned to Dorothy.

Creating Assignment Actions to Remove Item Assignments

Another feature of assignment actions is that they can be defined to remove an item from a category. As with the previously discussed assignment actions, the removal of an item from a category assignment is based on its assignment to another category. Creating assignment actions that remove an item from a category is similar to creating assignment actions that assign items to categories. Regardless of the method chosen to define the assignment action, only one additional step is required to make the action remove the item from the specified category instead of adding the item.

In the WORKINPR database example, an item that is assigned to the Work in Progress category is to be removed from the Work Requests category. Items attached to Proposals, Training, and Prospecting are considered assigned to Work Requests because they are Work Requests' children. Items that are assigned to the Completed Projects category will be removed from the Work in Progress category. Assignment actions can perform this removal of assignments for you.

To remove an item's assignment to Work Requests when it is assigned to Work in Progress, perform the following steps:

1. Press (F9) (Cat Mgr) to activate the Category Manager dialog box. Use (UP ARROW) or (DOWN ARROW) to highlight Work in Progress.

2. Press (F6) (Props) to activate the Category Properties box. Press (END) and (RIGHT ARROW) once to highlight the Assignment Action setting.

3. Type **Work r** to accept Agenda's automatic assignment of Work Requests and press (ENTER). The Assignment Action box appears. Press (SPACEBAR) to change "Assign item to" to "Remove assignment from," as shown here:

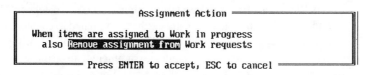

```
══════════════ Assignment Action ═══════════════
  When items are assigned to Work in progress
    also Remove assignment from Work requests

══════════ Press ENTER to accept, ESC to cancel ══════════
```

This Assignment Action box tells you that when an item is assigned to Work in Progress, the item will be removed from the Work Requests category. Recall that the items are probably not directly assigned to Work Requests, but to one of Work Requests' children. Whether the item belongs to Work Requests or one of its children, the assignment will be broken.

4. Press (ENTER) to accept the Assignment Action and return to the Category Properties box. The Work Requests category is listed under the Assignment Actions setting with a minus sign (-) in front of it. This indicates that an item's assignment (if any) to the Work Requests category is to be broken if the item is assigned to Work in Progress.

5. Press (ENTER) to return to the Category Manager.

6. To create an action that eliminates the assignment to Work in Progress whenever an item is assigned to the Completed Projects category, press (DOWN ARROW) to highlight Completed Projects.

7. Press (F6) (Props) to activate the Category Properties box. Press (END) and (RIGHT ARROW) once to highlight the Assignment Actions setting.

8. Use the alternative method for making assignment actions by pressing (F3) (Choices) to display the Assignment Action box.

9. Press (UP ARROW) to highlight Work in Progress. Press (SPACEBAR) twice to place a minus sign (-) in front of Work in Progress. (Pressing (SPACEBAR) a third time unselects the category.) The minus sign indicates that any assignment to Work in Progress will be removed.

10. Press (ENTER) to accept the selections. Press (ENTER) again to return to the Category Manager.

11. Press (ESC) or (F9) (To View) to return to the view.

12. Use the (ARROW) keys to highlight the "N" under the In Progress column of the *second* section. This is the item that reads *Train 3 new sales personnel.*

13. Assign this item to the Work in Progress category by typing **y**. The item is immediately listed in the Work in Progress section of the view and is no longer listed in the Training section. The assignment action removed the item's assignment to Training because Training is a child of Work Requests. Note that John remains assigned to the item, even though it has moved to the Work in Progress section.

Recall that John was assigned to the item in the Proposals section by an assignment condition. This means that John was conditionally assigned to the item because it was assigned to the Proposals category. If you assign the item to the Work in Progress

```
File: C:\AGENDA\APPS\WORKINPR                        10/08/90   2:25pm
View: Tracking Of Work Requests
Proposals                                    Management    In progress

Training                                     Management    In progress

Prospecting                                  Management    In progress
  • Use the new industry index to target     ·Tom               N
    previously unidentified prospects on the
    east side.

Work in progress                             Management    Completed
  • Train 3 new sales personnel.             ·John              N
  • Write proposal for client 12 detailing costs ·Dorothy       N
    associated with addition.

Completed projects                           Management    Done
```

```
  F1      F2      F3     F4     F5     F6     F7     F8     F9     F10
 Help    Edit  Choices  Done   Note  Props  Mark  Vw Mgr Cat Mgr Menu
```

FIGURE 9-5.   Database view showing the results of assignment actions that remove assignments to categories

category, the action assignment will remove the assignment to Proposals (remember, Proposals is a child of Work Requests). When this happens, the conditional assignment to John should also be broken.

14. Press (CTRL-RIGHT ARROW) and (CTRL-HOME) to move the highlight to the first In Progress column head. Press (DOWN ARROW) once to move to the "N" in the column.

15. Assign the item to Work in Progress by typing y. Figure 9-5 shows the resulting view. Note that the item is no longer listed in the Proposals section because the assignment action removed the assignment, but it does appear in the Work in Progress section. Note also that John no longer appears with the item under Management because John was a conditional assignment for the item.

USING THE UTILITIES EXECUTE MENU COMMAND

You have used the Utilities Execute menu command to apply new conditions to previously existing items. You can also use this command to apply new actions to these same items or to ignore assignments by the defined actions for these items. Use the WORKINPR database now to see how these features work.

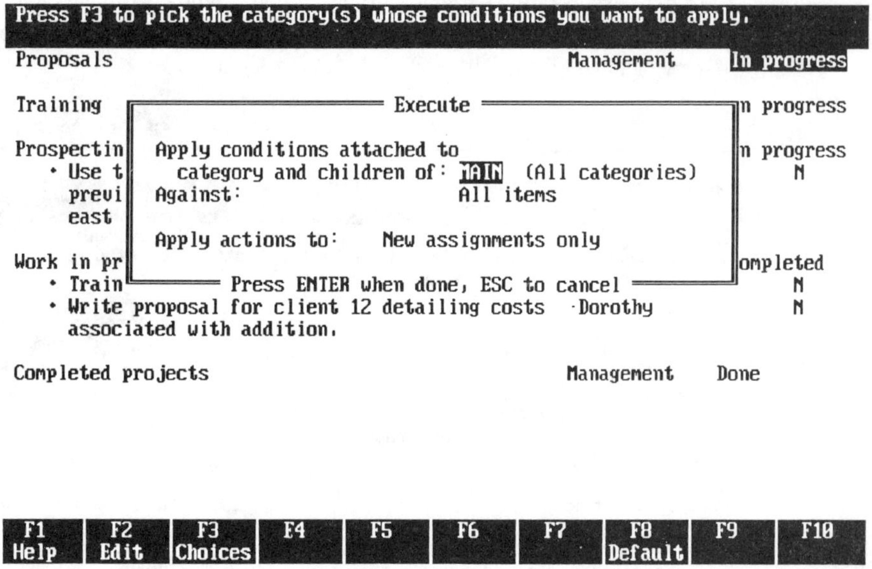

```
Press F3 to pick the category(s) whose conditions you want to apply.

Proposals                                    Management   In progress

Training                       ══════ Execute ══════        n progress

Prospectin    Apply conditions attached to                  n progress
 • Use t        category and children of: MAIN  (All categories)   N
   previ      Against:              All items
   east
              Apply actions to:   New assignments only
Work in pr                                                  ompleted
 • Train ═══════ Press ENTER when done, ESC to cancel ═══       N
 • Write proposal for client 12 detailing costs  ·Dorothy      N
   associated with addition.

Completed projects                           Management   Done
```

F1	F2	F3	F4	F5	F6	F7	F8	F9	F10
Help	Edit	Choices					Default		

FIGURE 9-6.   The Execute dialog box

1. Press (F10) (Menu) and select Utilities Execute to display the Execute box shown in Figure 9-6. The first two settings were described in Chapter 8. The last setting, Apply Actions To, determines whether the currently defined actions are to affect new assignments only or whether both old and new assignments are to be evaluated.

2. For this example, accept the default settings by pressing (ENTER). Figure 9-7 displays the view of the resulting database assignments. Notice that "Write proposal for client 12..." is again assigned to Proposals and is also assigned to Work in Progress. When Agenda evaluated the database, it did not use the actions against the current items. It is as if the actions did not exist.

3. To make Agenda evaluate all items in the database, including previously existing ones, press (F10) (Menu) and select Utilities Execute. Press (DOWN ARROW) twice to highlight the Apply Actions To setting.

4. Press (SPACEBAR) to change the setting to Old & New Assignments, and press (ENTER) to accept the Execute settings. When Agenda is finished, the view returns to the display shown earlier in Figure 9-5. Agenda evaluated *all* items, old and new, against all currently defined action assignments.

```
File: C:\AGENDA\APPS\WORKINPR                        10/08/90   2:32pm
View: Tracking Of Work Requests
Proposals                                    Management    In progress
  • Write proposal for client 12 detailing costs  ·Dorothy          Y
    associated with addition.                   John

Training                                     Management    In progress
  • Train 3 new sales personnel.              ·John              Y

Prospecting                                  Management    In progress
  • Use the new industry index to target     ·Tom               N
    previously unidentified prospects on the
    east side.

Work in progress                             Management    Completed
  • Train 3 new sales personnel.             ·John              N
  • Write proposal for client 12 detailing costs  ·Dorothy       N
    associated with addition.                   John

Completed projects                           Management    Done
```

```
  F1   |  F2   |  F3    |  F4   |  F5   |  F6   |  F7  |  F8    |  F9    |  F10
 Help  | Edit  | Choices| Done  | Note  | Props | Mark | Vw Mgr | Cat Mgr| Menu
```

FIGURE 9-7.   View after Utilities Execute is used with "Apply Actions To setting set to New Assignments Only

CREATING DATE ACTIONS

A date action assigns an item to a date category whenever the item is assigned to a specified category. A date and/or time can be specified. As with assignment actions, a date action can be used to either assign an item to a date category or remove an item from a date category.

By default, Agenda provides a when date category. Although you have not created one, a view for this database could be used to list the due dates for Proposals. Assume that a company policy states all proposals are to be completed by two weeks from this Friday. As items are assigned to the Proposals category, you could have Agenda automatically create a when date for the item.

To create the date action, perform the following steps:

1. Press (F9) (Cat Mgr) to activate the Category Manager. Use (UP ARROW) or (DOWN ARROW) to highlight the Proposals category.

2. Press (F6) (Props) to activate the Category Properties box for Proposals. Press (END) and (RIGHT ARROW) to highlight Assignment Actions.

3. Type **When** and press (ENTER) to tell Agenda that you want to make an action using When. Because When is a date category, the Date Action box displayed in Figure 9-8 appears on the screen.

4. Because this action is to assign a date to When, leave the default of Assign Item To as it is. Press (DOWN ARROW) to highlight the With Date setting.

5. Tell Agenda the date to be entered into the When category by typing **2 weeks from this fri** and pressing (ENTER). Press (ENTER) twice to return to the Category Manager.

6. Press (ESC) to return to the view.

7. To see how this date action works, press (CTRL-HOME) and (CTRL-LEFT ARROW) to move to the Proposals section.

8. Add an item to the Proposals section by typing **Smith, Smith, & Smith proposal for installing new equipment.** and pressing (ENTER).

9. To check if Agenda assigned the item to the When category, press (F3) (Choices) to display the Assignment Profile for the item. The Assignment Profile is shown in Figure 9-9. Note that the When category has an asterisk next to it, indicating an explicit assignment has been made to When and that a date has been entered. Dates will vary depending upon your system's date.

10. Press (ESC) to return to the view.

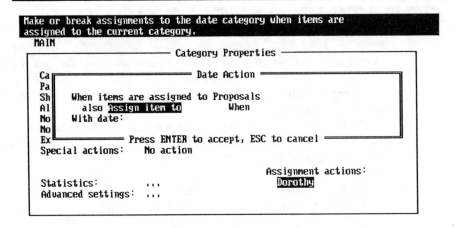

FIGURE 9-8.   The Date Action dialog box

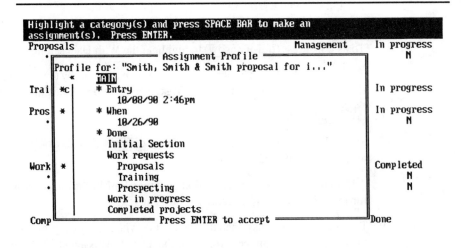

FIGURE 9-9.   The Assignment Profile of an item that has been assigned
a when date by a date action

11. Newly defined actions do not automatically affect previously created items. To see that this is true, move the highlight to the *Write proposal for client 12* item by pressing (DOWN ARROW) six times.

12. Press (F3) (Choices) to display the Assignment Profile for the item. Notice that no assignment has been made to the When category. This is because the item was assigned to Proposals prior to the creation of the date action.

13. Press (ESC) to return to the view.

14. To make Agenda evaluate all items in the database against all currently defined actions, press (F10) (Menu) and select Utilities Execute. Press (DOWN ARROW) twice to highlight the Apply Actions To setting.

15. Press (SPACEBAR) to change the setting to Old & New Assignments, and press (ENTER) to accept the Execute settings.

16. Press (F3) (Choices) to activate the Assignment Profile for the item. Note that the When category is now marked with an asterisk and a date has been assigned to the category.

17. Press (ESC) to return to the view.

CREATING NUMERIC ACTIONS

A numeric action assigns an item to a numeric category whenever the item is assigned to a specified category. A numeric value is assigned to the numeric category. As with assignment and date actions, a numeric action can be used to either assign an item to a numeric category or to remove an item from a numeric category. As an example of removing an item's numeric value from a category, you could use a numeric action to remove a dollar value from an Amount Due category when the item is marked as Paid.

The WORKINPR database has a defined numeric category called Code Number. Assume that all projects are assigned a numeric code based on whether they originated as a Proposals (code number 16), Training (code number 37), or Prospecting (code number 29) work request. As items are assigned to the Proposals category, you could use numeric actions to automatically assign numeric values to Code Number.

To create the numeric action to assign a code number of 16 to Proposals, perform the following steps:

1. Press (F9) (Cat Mgr) to activate the Category Manager. Use (UP ARROW) or (DOWN ARROW) to highlight the Proposals category.

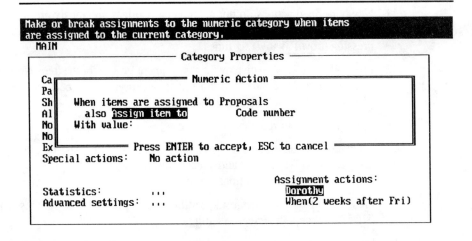

FIGURE 9-10.   The Numeric Action dialog box

2. Press **F6** (Props) to activate the Category Properties box for Proposals. Press **END** and **RIGHT ARROW** to highlight Assignment Actions.

3. Type **Cod** and press **ENTER** to tell Agenda that you want to make an action using Code Number. Because Code Number is a numeric category, the Numeric Action box displayed in Figure 9-10 appears on the screen.

4. Because this action is to assign a numeric value to Code Number, leave the default of Assign Item To as it is. Press **DOWN ARROW** to highlight the With Value setting.

5. Tell Agenda the numeric value to be entered into the Code number category by typing **16** and pressing **ENTER**. Press **ENTER** again to return to the Category Properties box.

Currently, the Proposals category has three actions assigned to it. They are the assignment action Dorothy, the date action When (2 weeks after Fri), and the numeric action Code Number (16). The 16 within the parentheses after Code Number represents the numeric value assigned to Code Number when the item is assigned to

Proposals. The Assignment Actions portion of Proposal's Category Properties box looks like this:

```
Assignment actions:
↑ When(2 weeks after Fri)
  Code number(16)
```

The small upward-pointing arrow indicates there is at least one more action assigned to this category that cannot fit in the display. To display it, you can press (UP ARROW), and the actions will scroll down the screen.

6. Press (ENTER) to return to the Category Manager.

7. To create a numeric assignment for Training that assigns the number 37 to Code Number, press (DOWN ARROW) to highlight Training.

8. Press (F6) (Props) to activate the Category Properties box for Training. Press (END) and (RIGHT ARROW) to highlight Assignment Actions.

9. This time, press (F3) (Choices) to list the choices of the Assignment Action box. Press (DOWN ARROW) eight times to highlight Code number and press (SPACEBAR). Because Code Number is a numeric category, the Numeric Action box appears on the screen.

10. Because this action is to assign a numeric value to Code number, leave the default of Assign Item To as it is. Press (DOWN ARROW) to highlight the With Value setting.

11. Tell Agenda the numeric value to be entered into the Code Number category by typing **37** and pressing (ENTER). Press (ENTER) three times to return to the Category Manager.

12. To create a numeric assignment for Prospecting that assigns the number 29 to Code Number, press (DOWN ARROW) to highlight Prospecting.

13. Press (F6) (Props) to activate the Category Properties box for Prospecting. Press (DOWN ARROW) seven times and (RIGHT ARROW) to highlight Assignment Actions.

14. Press (F3) (Choices) to list the choices of the Assignment Action box. Press (DOWN ARROW) seven times to highlight Code Number and press (SPACEBAR) or use Agenda's auto-complete feature as you begin typing. Because Code Number is a numeric category, the Numeric Action box appears on the screen.

15. Because this action is to assign a numeric value to Code Number, leave the default of Assign Item To as it is. Press (DOWN ARROW) to highlight the With Value setting.

16. Tell Agenda the numeric value to be entered into the Code Number category by typing **29** and pressing (ENTER). Press (ENTER) three times to return to the Category Manager.

17. Press (ESC) to return to the view.

18. Apply the newly defined actions to all previously entered items by pressing (F10) (Menu) and selecting Utilities Execute. Press (DOWN ARROW) twice to highlight the Apply Actions To setting, press (SPACEBAR) to evaluate both old and new assignments, and press (ENTER).

19. Create a new view by pressing (F8) (Vw Mgr) and (INS).

20. Type **Listing Using Code Numbers** as the name of the view and press (ENTER).

21. Press (RIGHT ARROW) and (DOWN ARROW) once each to highlight the Sections setting. Type **Main** as the section head and press (ENTER).

22. Press (ENTER) to display the new view. All items of the database will be displayed.

23. Create a column listing the code numbers by pressing (F10) (Menu) and selecting View Column Add. Type **cod** as the column heading and press (ENTER) to activate the auto completion feature and select Code Number.

24. Because Code Number is a numeric category, the Column Add box displays numeric settings. Since code numbers do not have decimal places, press (DOWN ARROW) four times to highlight the Decimal Places setting, type **0** for the number of decimal places, and press (ENTER).

25. Since there is no need to display totals of code numbers, press (RIGHT ARROW) to highlight the Total setting, and type **n** to set it to No.

26. Press (ENTER) to return to the view. The view should look similar to Figure 9-11. Notice that all of the items have code numbers assigned to them.

CREATING SPECIAL ACTIONS

There are three types of special actions. Special actions can discard items from the database, export items to be used by another database, and designate an item as being done. Agenda limits you to only one of these special actions per category.

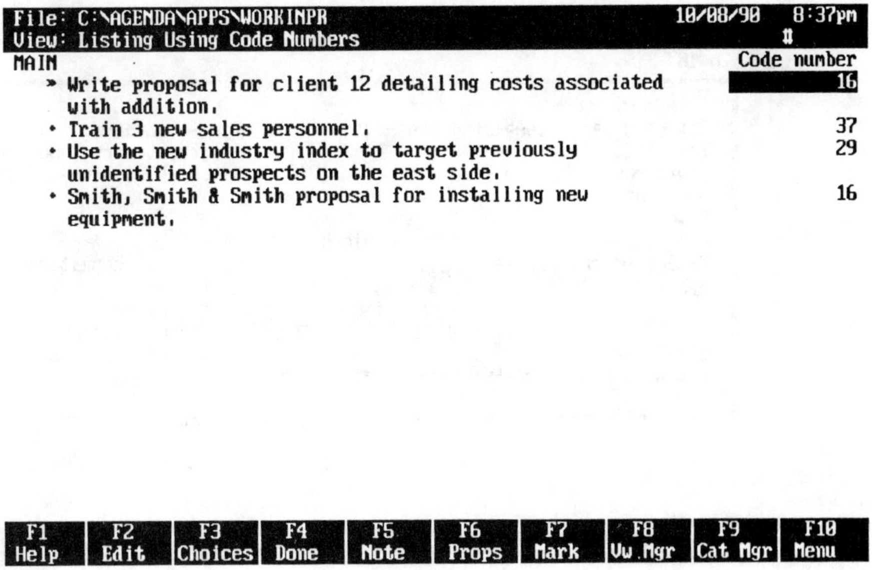

```
File: C:\AGENDA\APPS\WORK1NPR                    10/08/90   8:37pm
View: Listing Using Code Numbers                              ↕
MAIN                                                    Code number
  » Write proposal for client 12 detailing costs associated      16
    with addition.
  • Train 3 new sales personnel.                                 37
  • Use the new industry index to target previously              29
    unidentified prospects on the east side.
  • Smith, Smith & Smith proposal for installing new             16
    equipment.
```

```
 F1      F2      F3      F4      F5      F6      F7      F8      F9     F10
Help    Edit  Choices  Done    Note   Props   Mark  Vw.Mgr Cat Mgr  Menu
```

FIGURE 9-11.   New view that lists the items with their code numbers

Using a Special Action
To Designate Items As Done

For this example, you will create a special action for the Completed Projects category that designates the item as being done.

1. Return to the previous view by pressing (ALT-F8) (Last Vw).

2. Press (F9) (Cat Mgr) to activate the Category Manager. Use the (ARROW) keys to highlight the category Completed Projects.

3. Press (F6) (Props) to activate Completed Projects' Category Properties box. Press (DOWN ARROW) six times to highlight the Special Actions setting.

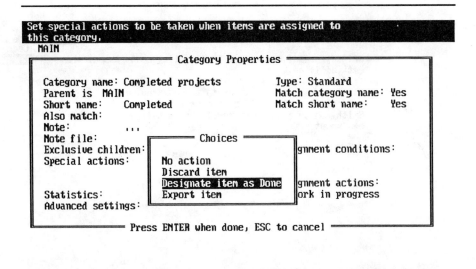

Set special actions to be taken when items are assigned to
this category.
   MAIN
┌──────────────────────── Category Properties ────────────────────────┐
│   │
│ Category name: Completed projects   Type: Standard   │
│ Parent is MAIN   Match category name: Yes   │
│ Short name: Completed   Match short name: Yes   │
│ Also match: │
│ Note: ...   │
│ Note file: ┌──────── Choices ────────┐   │
│ Exclusive children: │   │gnment conditions: │
│ Special actions: │ No action   │   │
│   │ Discard item   │   │
│   │ Designate item as Done │gnment actions: │
│ Statistics: │ Export item   │ork in progress   │
│ Advanced settings: └─────────────────────────┘   │
│   │
└════════════════ Press ENTER when done, ESC to cancel ════════════════┘

┌─────┬─────┬─────┬─────┬─────┬─────┬─────┬─────┬─────┬─────┐
│ F1 │ F2 │ F3 │ F4 │ F5 │ F6 │ F7 │ F8 │ F9 │ F10 │
│ Help│   │   │   │   │   │   │   │   │   │
└─────┴─────┴─────┴─────┴─────┴─────┴─────┴─────┴─────┴─────┘

FIGURE 9-12.   The Choices dialog box for the types of special actions

4. Press (F3) (Choices) to display the choices for the Special Actions setting. These choices are displayed in Figure 9-12. Press (DOWN ARROW) twice to highlight Designate Item as Done and press (ENTER) to select it.

5. Press (ENTER) to return to the Category Manager and (ESC) to return to the view.

6. Press (RIGHT ARROW) twice to highlight the second "N" in the Completed Projects column within the Work in Progress section.

7. Assign the item to the Completed Projects category by typing **y**.

Figure 9-13 displays the new view. Notice that the item is immediately removed from the Work in Progress section. This is because you previously created an assignment condition to remove an item assigned to the Completed Projects category from the Work in Progress category.

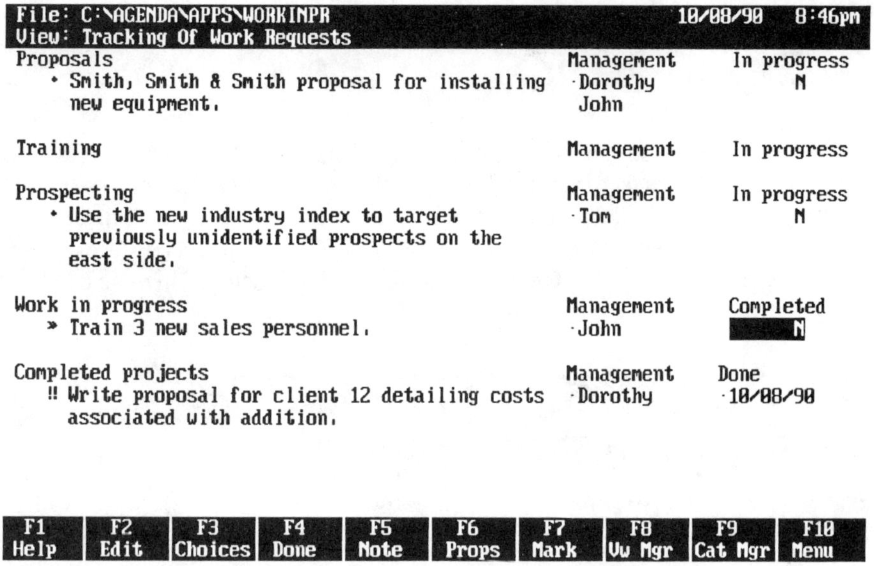

```
File: C:\AGENDA\APPS\WORKINPR                       10/08/90   8:46pm
View: Tracking Of Work Requests
Proposals                                    Management    In progress
   • Smith, Smith & Smith proposal for installing  ·Dorothy        N
     new equipment.                           John

Training                                     Management    In progress

Prospecting                                  Management    In progress
   • Use the new industry index to target    ·Tom              N
     previously unidentified prospects on the
     east side.

Work in progress                             Management    Completed
   ⇒ Train 3 new sales personnel.            ·John         ███ N

Completed projects                           Management    Done
   ‼ Write proposal for client 12 detailing costs  ·Dorothy  ·10/08/90
     associated with addition.
```

```
  F1  │  F2  │  F3   │  F4  │  F5  │  F6   │  F7  │  F8   │  F9   │  F10
 Help │ Edit │Choices│ Done │ Note │ Props │ Mark │Vw Mgr │Cat Mgr│ Menu
```

FIGURE 9-13.   Database view after a special action has assigned an item as being done

The item appears under the Completed Projects section. The double exclamation marks (‼) that appear to the left of the item identify the item as being done.

Using a Special Action To Discard Items

Another special action you can use discards items from the database. All occurrences of the items disappear from the database as if you had pressed (ALT-F4) (Discard).

To create a special action that discards items, you would follow the same steps you used in the previous section to create the special action for designating an item as done. The one difference is that in step 4 you highlight Discard Item instead of Designate Item as Done.

Using a Special Action To Export Items

The third special action allows you to export items to files that can be accessed by other Agenda databases. For example, you could have Agenda export to other files data not needed for the current database. This would permit individuals working with various types of data to have their own files. Chapter 11 focuses on importing and exporting files, and this special action will be discussed in more depth at that time.

DISPLAYING ACTIONS IN THE CATEGORY MANAGER

Occasionally you will find it useful to provide an overview of all the actions and conditions assigned to all categories in the database. Agenda provides this capability within the Category Manager.

1. Press (F9) (Cat Mgr) to display the Category Manager.

2. Press (ALT-F7) (ShowC/A) to display the condition and action assignments defined for each category, as shown in Figure 9-14.

Descriptions starting with A= are the actions defined for the category. For example, after the Prospecting category, the codes "A= Tom,Code number(29)" indicate that two actions have been defined for Prospecting. One action assigns an item to Tom and the other assigns the numeric value 29 to Code Number.

The John category has a C= following it, which represents conditions. If an item is assigned to Proposals, it is conditionally assigned to John.

The Completed Projects category has an action which removes an assignment to Work in Progress. The minus sign (-) in front of Work in Progress indicates the assignment is removed. The S= Done represents the special action that designates an item as done.

3. To return the screen to its less cluttered state, press (ALT-F7) (ShowC/A).

4. Press (ESC) to return to the view.

```
File: C:\AGENDA\APPS\WORKINPR
Category Manager
 MAIN
 * Entry    Assign date when item is entered.
 * When     Assign date from the item text.
 * Done
   Initial Section
   Work requests
     Proposals       A= Dorothy,When(2 weeks after Fri*),Code number(16)
     Training        A= John,Code number(37)
     Prospecting     A= Tom,Code number(29)
   Work in progress;In progress      A= -Work requests
   Completed projects;Completed      A= -Work in progress   S= Done
   Management
     Dorothy
     John    C= Proposals
     Tom
 # Code number
```

F1	F2	F3	F4	F5	F6	F7	F8	F9	F10
Help	Edit			Note	Props	Prm (+)	Dem (+)	To View	Menu

FIGURE 9-14.   The Category Manager set to display the conditions and actions defined for each category

TURNING OFF ACTIONS FOR THE ENTIRE DATABASE

Occasionally you may wish to turn off the evaluation of items against all defined actions in the database. This may occur when you are importing items into the database or when you are manually adding many items. When files become large, the evaluation process can slow down the process of adding the items. Once all the items are added, you can use the Utilities Execute menu command to evaluate all items in the file against the defined actions.

To turn off all the defined actions within the database, follow these steps:

1. Press (F10) (Menu) and select File Properties to activate the File Properties box.

2. Press (UP ARROW) three times and (RIGHT ARROW) once to highlight the Auto-assign Settings ... setting and press (SPACEBAR) to activate the Auto-assign Global Settings box.

3. Press (DOWN ARROW) eight times to highlight Assignment Actions. The choices are to turn actions On, which is the default, or Off. Do not change the default On setting now. The purpose of this example is just to show you how this is done.

4. Return to the view by pressing (ESC) four times.

TURNING ON OR OFF ACTIONS FOR A CATEGORY

Just as you can turn off all actions for the file, you can turn off the actions for a specific category. The reasons for doing this can be similar to the reasons for globally turning off actions. However, there are other reasons for working with categories.

Suppose you are entering a large number of items and you want to postpone most of the assignments based on actions. However, there are specific categories where you do want the items to be immediately evaluated by the actions. You could globally turn off all actions for the database, but then turn on the actions for the critical categories. Thus, you have the advantage of limiting the number of actions that are evaluated, but still have available the required actions.

1. To turn off or turn on the actions for a category, press (F9) (Cat Mgr) to activate the Category Manager. Highlight Proposals using the (UP ARROW) or (DOWN ARROW) keys.

2. Press (F6) (Props) to activate Proposals' Category Properties box. Press (END) to highlight the Advanced Settings and press (SPACEBAR) to activate the Advanced Setting for Proposals box.

3. Press (DOWN ARROW) seven times to highlight Assignment Actions. The choices are Global (On), On, and Off. Global is the default value. At this point, you could make a selection, but for this example you will leave the selection as is.

4. Press (ENTER) twice and (ESC) once to return to the view.

EDITING AND DELETING ACTIONS

Sometimes you will want to either change a defined action or delete it. Both are simple processes. For this example, the date action that assigns a when date of two weeks after Friday needs to be changed. The new company policy allows only two weeks to complete proposals. Perform the following steps to edit the date action.

1. Press (F9) (Cat Mgr) to activate the Category Manager. Highlight Proposals using the (UP ARROW) or (DOWN ARROW) keys.

2. Press (F6) (Props) to display Proposals' Category Properties box. Press (DOWN ARROW) seven times and (RIGHT ARROW) once to highlight the Assignment Actions setting. Use (UP ARROW) or (DOWN ARROW) to highlight the When(2 weeks after Fri) action.

3. Press (F4) (Values) to display the Date Action box.

4. Press (DOWN ARROW) once to highlight the With Date setting.

5. Type **2 weeks from today** and press (ENTER).

6. Press (ENTER) to return to the Category Properties box. The action has been changed.

7. To delete the Code Number action from this category, press (DOWN ARROW) once to highlight it.

8. Press (DEL) to delete the action.

9. Press (ENTER) to return to the Category Manager and (ESC) to return to the view.

REMOVING ALL ACTIONS FROM A CATEGORY

The process for removing all actions from a category is the same one used to remove all conditions. When both conditions and actions are used in a category, a confirmation box appears asking if the conditions, actions, or both are to be cleared from the category.

In general, the process for removing actions from a category is as follows:

1. Press (F9) (Cat Mgr) to activate the Category Manager.

2. Highlight the category from which the actions are to be removed.

3. Press (ALT-F8) (Clr C/A) to clear all conditions and actions.

4. Respond to the confirmation box(es), if any.

5. Press (ESC) to return to the view.

10

MACROS

A macro is a set of instructions for a procedure that you can store and use whenever you need. Macro features are available for almost all of the popular business software packages. Knowledgeable users expect macro capabilities in spreadsheet, database, and word processing products because they realize that macros automate some of their work with these programs. Because macros automate tasks, they can boost your productivity considerably and add flexibility to program features. You may have already seen the many macros included with the four Starter applications discussed in Chapter 1.

Agenda has a full set of macro features that allow you to record macros as you use menu commands. Agenda's macro features also include a set of special macro commands that you can use to add further sophistication to your macros.

Macros are useful for procedures that you execute frequently. For example, if you frequently use special print settings for a particular view of your database, you can create a macro that prints that view for you with the special settings. Having a macro print your view prevents you from forgetting to change a setting before you print the view. Agenda can learn the keystrokes for the macro as you type them, or you can edit the macro and type each keystroke in the macro. Macros can save you a lot of time when you repeatedly enter the same keystrokes.

Despite the unique features that macros offer, many users are intimidated by them because their previous attempts to create and run them were unsuccessful. There is no need to be intimidated by Agenda's macros, because the Learn feature makes them easier to create than the macros of many other products. Once created, a macro can be used by simply making a selection from the Macro Manager or entering a simple keystroke sequence.

MACRO BASICS

Before you start creating and executing your own macros, you need to know some basic macro concepts. Once you understand the various procedures and components, it is easy to follow the rules for successful macro creation and use.

Simply defined, a macro is a sequence of activities (or in its simplest form, a series of keystrokes) that are recorded to be replayed whenever you want to repeat the sequence of activities. The activities (or keystrokes) must be repetitive for a macro to be used. A macro simply performs these activities as if you were doing them manually.

Macros are used for two main reasons: to save time and to make it easier to perform tasks in a database. If you repetitively do a task in Agenda that either requires many keystrokes or a complex set of keystrokes, you can use macros to save time, since macros can be invoked with just a few keystrokes.

Sometimes you may use Agenda if you do not know how to use specific features of the program but still need to perform activities that require some of these features. You can often create macros to perform these activities, thus eliminating your need to know how to do them. All you need to know is how to start the macro.

TYPES OF MACROS

You can think of Agenda as having two types of macros. The first type is a keyboard alternative macro. In this type of macro, keystrokes represent numbers, letters, menu selections, function keys, and any other keystrokes you use to work with a database. When you run the completed macro, Agenda processes the keystrokes in the macro just as if you were entering them directly from the keyboard.

The other type of macro supported by Agenda is a command language macro. This type of macro combines the keystroke alternative macro with instructions from Agenda's macro command language. These instructions allow you to add logic capabilities to your macro and process operator responses during macro execution.

This chapter focuses on the keyboard alternative macro for two reasons. First, this type of macro is the easiest to create and understand since it is just a recording of tasks that you are already familiar with. Second, you will find that keyboard alternative macros tend to be the most useful. You will later have an opportunity to create a command language macro to learn some of the interesting and useful features of that type of macro.

Before you create your first macro, you will create an Agenda database in which you will create the macros. Perform the following steps:

1. Assuming that you are already within an Agenda database, press (F10) (Menu) and select File Retrieve to display the Select File box.

2. Type **Macro** as the database name and press (ENTER).

3. Type the database description **A database used to learn about macros** and press (ENTER) twice to display the view of Macro.

4. Change the name of the Initial Section by pressing (F2) (Edit) and (CTRL-ENTER) to delete the current name, typing **Description**, and pressing (ENTER).

5. Add an Organization column by pressing (F10) (Menu) and selecting View Column Add. Type **Organization** and press (ENTER) twice.

6. To add two categories under Organization using the Category Manager, press (F9) (Cat Mgr) to display the Category Manager box. The highlight currently should be on Organization.

Note You can add child categories while skipping the demote step by using (ALT-R) and then pressing (INS) for the next child.

7. Type **Jameson, MacYntyre, & Goldberg, P.C.** and press (ENTER) for the first organization. Demote this category by pressing (F8) (Dem) and pressing (ENTER) to confirm the demotion.

8. Press (F6) (Props) to display the Category Properties box for this category. Press (DOWN ARROW) once to highlight the Short Name setting. Type **JMG** and press (ENTER).

Note Remember you can create short names when you create a category by adding ";*xxx*", where *xxx* is the short name, but you must use (F6) to edit or delete.

9. Press (ENTER) to return to the Category Manager screen.

10. Type **Miller, Browne and Smythe Corporation** and press (ENTER) for the second organization.

11. Press (F6) (Props) to display the Category Properties box. Press (DOWN ARROW) once to highlight the Short Name setting. Type **MBSC** and press (ENTER).

12. Press (ENTER) to return to the Category Manager screen. Your screen should be similar to the one displayed in Figure 10-1.

13. Press (ESC) to return to the view. Press (LEFT ARROW) to highlight Description.

14. Add the first item to the database by typing **Sponsor of the ball for The Organization to Benefit All Living Creatures**, and then press (TAB).

15. Type **Mil** for the organization name and press (SHIFT-TAB) to accept the automatic assignment and move the highlight back to the left column. Because the column is not wide enough to display the entire organization name, Agenda displays the short name of MBSC under Organization.

CREATING A MACRO USING LEARN MODE

There are two methods you can use to create macros. First, you can use the Learn mode, which records the keystrokes as you perform the activity of the macro. This is

```
File: C:\AGENDA\APPS\MACRO
Category Manager
  MAIN
  * Entry    Assign date when item is entered.
  * When     Assign date from the item text.
  * Done
    Description
    Organization
      Jameson, MacYntyre, & Goldberg, P.C.;JMG
      Miller, Browne and Smythe Corporation;MBSC
```

F1	F2	F3	F4	F5	F6	F7	F8	F9	F10
Help	Edit			Note	Props	Prn (←)	Dem (→)	To View	Menu

FIGURE 10-1.   The Category Manager of the Macro database displaying short names

the easier method, providing less opportunity for making mistakes. The second method allows you to type in the keystrokes and functions in an Edit Macro screen in much the same way a programmer types a program. You must use this method if you are creating a command language macro.

The first macro you will create using the Learn mode is very simple, but even so, the procedures for creating, using, and editing macros that you will learn also apply to more complex macros. Later on you will have the opportunity to create other macros that use more of Agenda's macro features.

Your first macro will be used to enter a long and cumbersome name that you otherwise would type yourself. It is a good example of a macro designed to save you time and keystrokes. The assumption is that this name will often appear throughout the database.

Creating a macro using the Learn mode is as easy as typing the keystrokes once. You can begin recording macro instructions from View mode, the Category Manager, or a note. To create this macro from a note, follow these steps:

1. Press (F5) (Note). Start a memo by typing **To:**, pressing (TAB) twice, typing **Members of**, and pressing (SPACEBAR).

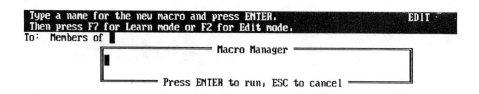

FIGURE 10-2.   The Macro Manager dialog box before any macros have been created

The name of an organization that appears often throughout this database is to be typed next. Instead of having to type this name over and over throughout the database, you will use this occurrence to create a macro that will type the name for you.

2. To start the process of creating the macro, press (ALT-F3) (Macro). A Macro Manager dialog box like the one shown in Figure 10-2 appears on the screen. Since there are no macros currently defined, Agenda assumes you want to enter the name of a new macro.

3. Type the name of the macro as **Text: Org. to Benefit Creatures** and press (ENTER). The Macro Manager box listing your new macro appears as follows:

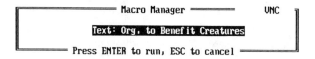

A macro name can contain up to 35 characters. Longer names can help you remember what the macro does and are especially useful when you are attempting to choose the correct macro from a macro selection box. Since a macro developed to execute in a view may not be effective in a note or some other area of Agenda, you might want to consider using a portion of the name to indicate the proper mode for each macro. Later you will learn how to disable various modes.

Even though the macro is currently listed in the Macro Manager, it cannot do anything. You must now tell Agenda what the macro is supposed to do.

4. Record the steps the macro is to execute by pressing (F7) (Learn). The dialog box disappears and you are returned to the note.

≡Note≡ Any key you now press will become part of the macro and will need to be removed in macro edit mode later if you do not want it to be a permanent part of the macro.

5. Type **The Organizatiom**, press (BACKSPACE), and type **n To Benefit All Living Creatures**.

Until you tell Agenda to stop, any keystroke you make (including your mistakes) is stored in the macro. You are intentionally making a mistake here for an example that will deal with it later in the chapter. If you make a mistake, press (BACKSPACE) and continue. You can fix mistakes later if they cause problems. As a key is pressed and stored, Agenda acknowledges it with a beep.

6. Press (ALT-F3) (Macro) to tell Agenda you have finished recording your macro. Agenda displays this message:

```
Learn mode has been turned off.
Press any key to continue
```

This indicates that you have finished defining the macro with Learn mode.

7. Press (ENTER) to continue.

8. Press (ENTER) twice to continue the memo.

9. Type **From:**, press (TAB), type your name, and press (ENTER) twice.

10. Press (F5) (Return) to return to the view.

When you create a macro using Learn mode, you are also executing the activity in your database. In this example, you were typing in the name of the organization as you were recording the macro.

EXECUTING A MACRO USING THE MACRO MANAGER

Macro instructions are designed to be played back later when you want to execute a task. It is important that you realize that macro instructions are executed in a mechanical fashion without regard to your current needs. You must assess the conditions necessary for a macro to execute correctly and either set up these conditions before executing the macro or add the commands necessary for the setup to the beginning of the macro. If your macro is designed to be flexible and work in many situations, the need for being in the right place or setting up the proper situation will be less critical.

To run the "Text: Org. to Benefit Creatures" macro perform the following steps:

1. Press (F5) (Note) to return to the note of this item. Your cursor should be positioned two lines below the From: line.

2. Type **The ball was a complete success.** and press (SPACEBAR) twice. You are now ready to start a sentence with the name of the organization.

3. Press (ALT-F3) (Macro) to activate the Macro Manager dialog box. Since you currently have only one macro defined for this database, the correct macro is already highlighted.

4. Press (ENTER) to run the "Text: Org. to Benefit Creatures" macro. The name of the organization immediately appears on the screen.

5. Finish the sentence by pressing (SPACEBAR) and then typing **received a check for $1,000.00.**

6. Press (F5) (Return) to return to the view.

7. To create another item that starts with the name of the organization, press (ALT-F3) (Macro) to display the Macro Manager. Press (ENTER) to run the macro. The name of the organization immediately appears on the screen.

8. Continue the item by pressing (SPACEBAR), typing **meeting location.**, and pressing (TAB).

9. Type **Jam** and press (SHIFT-TAB) to assign the item to the Jameson, MacYntyre Goldberg organization.

10. Create a note for this item by pressing (F5) (Note). Type **To:**, press (TAB) twice, type **Members of**, and press (SPACEBAR).

11. Use the macro to insert the name of the organization by pressing (ALT-F3) (Macro) and pressing (ENTER).

12. Press (ENTER) twice, type **From:**, press (TAB), type your name, and press (ENTER) twice.

13. Type **The meeting for**, press (SPACEBAR), (ALT-F3) (Macro), (ENTER), and (SPACEBAR), and then type **was held on June 6**.

14. Return to the view by pressing (F5) (Return).

In the preceding examples, you entered the organization's name into the database six times, but you only typed it twice. You typed the name of the organization in the first item as normal. The second time you typed the name of the organization, you used the Learn mode to also create the macro. For the rest of the entries, you ran the macro to produce the name of the organization instead of typing the name from the keyboard.

MODIFYING A MACRO

Agenda has a Macro Editor that displays the contents of a macro. You can use the Macro Editor to create a macro or to edit a macro that already exists. Once you have created a macro, you may need to change it to eliminate typing mistakes, to make it work more effectively, or to make it more versatile. One indication that you need to change a macro is if it beeps when you execute it. Normally these unexpected beeps indicate that the macro is trying to use keys and functions that are unavailable from the current mode.

For this example you are going to use the Macro Editor to change the name of your macro and eliminate any mistakes that were incorporated into the macro when it was created. Follow these steps:

1. Press (ALT-F3) (Macro) to activate the Macro Manager dialog box. The "Text: Org. to Benefit Creatures" macro is currently highlighted in this box.

2. Press (F2) (EditMac) to activate the Macro Editor. Figure 10-3 displays the Macro Editor for the "Text: Org. to Benefit Creatures" macro.

The first line of the macro in the Macro Editor is always the name of the macro. It is always enclosed in braces, as are any control keys or macro commands.

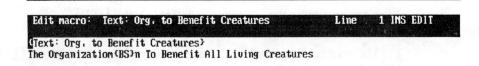

FIGURE 10-3.   The Macro Editor displaying the "Text: Org. to Benefit
Creatures" macro

3. To change the macro name to "Name: Org. to Benefit Creatures," press
   (RIGHT ARROW) once to highlight the first "T" in "Text." Press (DEL) four times to
   delete "Text" and type **Name**.

   The second line of the macro in the Macro Editor contains a {BS} code. This code
represents the pressing of the (BACKSPACE) key as you created the macro. This
"mistake" did not affect the proper execution of the macro, but whenever you ran the
macro you might have noticed that the macro typed an "m," backspaced over it, and
then typed "n." In some systems, this sequence might have been so fast that you did
not see it.
   Although this macro produces the desired results, the macro will run faster without
the extra steps. Of course, the difference in speed with the current example is probably
inconsequential, but other mistakes you make in more complex macros may make a
big difference in execution speed.

4. Highlight the mistake in the macro by pressing (DOWN ARROW) once and
   (RIGHT ARROW) ten times. This highlights the "m."

5. Press (DEL) five times to delete the "m" and the {BS} code.

6. Press (F5) (Return) to accept the changes you made in the Macro Editor and return to the Macro Manager. (If you had wanted to leave the Macro Editor without incorporating your changes, you would press (ESC) and answer Yes after the prompt "Discard changes?".) Notice that the macro listed in the Macro Manager now reflects the change you made to its name.

7. Press (ESC) to return to the view without running the macro.

CREATING A PRINT MACRO WITH LEARN MODE

You are now going to create a macro that prints the currently displayed view including the notes. This macro is an application that uses Agenda's menu and the function keys. However, the process for creating the macro is the same as it was for creating the previous macro.

To create the "Print View With Notes" macro, do the following:

1. Press (ALT-F3) (Macro) to activate the Macro Manager.

2. Press (INS) to tell Agenda you want to insert a new macro into the Macro Manager.

3. Type **View: Print View With Notes** as the macro name and press (ENTER).

When you name a macro, it is usually a good idea to indicate the mode that the user must be in for the macro to run properly. This macro is designed to be run only while the user is in View mode, which is why the name starts with the word "View". This naming convention is not required by Agenda, but you should use some method in naming macros that helps the user determine where the macro can be used.

4. Press (F7) (Learn) to have Agenda record your following keystrokes as part of a macro. From now until you press (ALT-F3) (Macro), all keystrokes will be incorporated into the macro.

5. Press (F10) (Menu) to activate the menu bar.

There are a couple of methods you can use to make your selections from the menu. You could use the (ARROW) keys to move to the menu function desired and then press (ENTER) to select the function. These keystrokes would be incorporated into your macro and would work fine. However, a better idea is to press the first letters of the functions you wish to select. There are two reasons why this is better than using the (ARROW) keys when working with the menu bar. First, it makes it much easier to read your macros in the Macro Editor. Second, your macros are much more likely to work with new releases of Agenda, since the letters for selecting major functions are more likely to remain the same than the order or position of the functions in the menu bar.

6. Type **p** for Print and **f** for Final. The Print Final box appears on the screen with the highlight on the Print setting.

Since you want to print the view with both items and notes, the only setting that seems to need changing is the Include setting. However, another consideration must be made as you create your macros. In many boxes, including the Print Final box, Agenda retains any changes that you make in the settings as the defaults for the next time you use the box. For example, if the last time you printed something you chose to print only the section, the Print setting would still be set to Section. As the Print Final box is currently set, Agenda would print the entire view. However, at some later time you may use the macro after printing a section, and the macro would only print a section instead of the expected entire view.

To get around this problem, always make sure that all settings are as they must be to obtain the required results. This requires some extra work on your part as you create the macro, but is well worth the time as you use the macro in your database.

Assume in this example that the only settings you ever change in the Print Final box are the first four. You need to make sure that these four settings are set properly for the macro to do what you expect it to. You want the Print, Print To, and Printer settings to be set to Agenda's default values. Fortunately, Agenda has a quick method for changing a setting to its original default value.

7. To set the Print setting to its default value, press (F8) (Default). Press (DOWN ARROW) once to highlight the Include setting.

8. Press (F3) (Choices) to display the Choices box for Include, which is displayed in Figure 10-4.

   You could use (DOWN ARROW) to highlight the selection Items & Notes. However, if the Include setting were already set to Items & Notes, pressing (DOWN ARROW) would highlight Notes Only. To avoid this problem, you should let Agenda's auto-selection feature work for you. Using auto-selection avoids the problem of not knowing what the current Include setting is.

9. Use Agenda's auto-selection feature by typing **Items & notes** and pressing (ENTER).

10. Continue by pressing (DOWN ARROW) and (F8) (Default) to make sure Print To is set at its default setting.

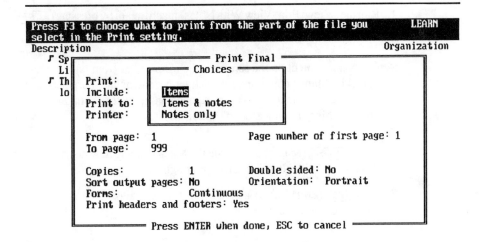

FIGURE 10-4.   The Choices box for the Include setting in the Print Final box

11. Press (DOWN ARROW) and (F8) (Default) again to make sure the Printer setting is also set at its default setting.

12. Press (ENTER) to start the printing.

13. When the printing is completed, press (ALT-F3) (Macro) to end the Learn mode. Press (ENTER) to return to the view.

CREATING A COMMAND LANGUAGE MACRO

You can create an entire macro from start to finish in the Macro Editor, but this can be an arduous process since you have to type in all of the commands yourself. Often you will find it easier to create as much of the macro as possible using the Learn mode and then incorporate the necessary macro commands using the Macro Editor. The following example takes the macro you just created and adds a macro command to it.

1. Run the "View: Print View With Notes" macro again by pressing (ALT-F3) (Macro), highlighting its name, and pressing (ENTER).

Notice the movement on the screen as the macro goes from one selection to another very quickly. Many people find this distracting, and an inexperienced user might feel that he or she did something wrong. Agenda has a macro command that you can use to eliminate this "jumping around" effect.

2. Press (ALT-F3) (Macro) to activate the Macro Manager. Make sure that the "View: Print View With Notes" macro is highlighted.

3. Press (F2) (EditMac) to activate the Macro Editor. The screen should appear similar to Figure 10-5.

The first line of the macro within the braces is the name of the macro. The second line is the listing of the keystrokes that make up the macro in its current form. {F10} means the (F10) function key was pressed. The next keys pressed were **p** (for Print) and **f** (for Final). {DOWN} means that the (DOWN ARROW) key was pressed, and {ENTER} represents the (ENTER) key. Although not included in this example, you will

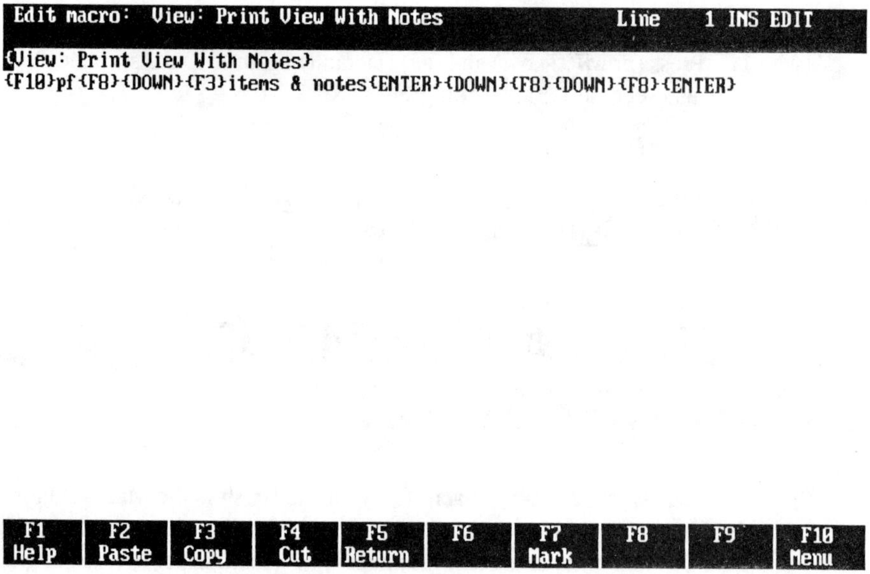

```
Edit macro:  View: Print View With Notes              Line    1 INS EDIT

{View: Print View With Notes}
{F10}pf{F8}{DOWN}{F3}items & notes{ENTER}{DOWN}{F8}{DOWN}{F8}{ENTER}
```

F1	F2	F3	F4	F5	F6	F7	F8	F9	F10
Help	Paste	Copy	Cut	Return		Mark			Menu

FIGURE 10-5.   The "View: Print View With Notes" macro displayed in the Macro Editor

occasionally see something like {DOWN;7}, in which the seven represents pressing the (DOWN ARROW) key seven times.

There are two methods for entering keys into a macro within the Macro Editor. To represent the names of function keys, accelerator keys, or special keys ((ENTER), (INS), (END)), type the name of the key surrounded by { }. For example, if you wanted to insert an (ENTER) key code into the macro, you would type {ENTER}. To enter characters into a macro, you simply type the character without any enclosing special symbol. If you wanted to insert a "t," you would type **t**. The second method is available to you for most character keystrokes. If you first press (ALT-=) (the (ALT) key plus the equal sign), Agenda will take the next keystroke you make and insert it into the macro. This is shown in the following step.

4. Press (DOWN ARROW) once to highlight the initial left brace in the second line. Press (ALT-=) and then press (ENTER). Agenda inserts {ENTER} into the text. Press (CTRL-BACKSPACE) to delete the code.

Agenda has a macro command named {WINDOWSOFF} that turns off the screen while the macro is running. This command's syntax is

{WINDOWSOFF[;*header,footer*]}.

The header and footer are optional.

5. Type **{WINDOWSOFF;PRINT VIEW WITH NOTES;}** to tell Agenda to display a box that has a "PRINT VIEW WITH NOTES" header at the top, a message inside the box asking the user to please wait, and a message at the bottom of the box saying that the macro is running. (Note that you can type the command in uppercase or lowercase letters.)

The macro should now appear as shown here:

```
{View: Print View With Notes}
{WINDOWSOFF;PRINT VIEW WITH NOTES;}{F10}pf {F8} {DOWN} {F3} items &
notes{ENTER} {DOWN} {F8} {DOWN} {F8} {ENTER}
```

Notice that the commands automatically wrapped from the second line to the third line.

6. Press (F5) (Return) to exit the Macro Editor and return to the Macro Manager.

7. Press (ENTER) to run the macro. The box you just created appears in the middle of the screen as the macro executes.

As you work with the Macro Editor, you should be especially wary of accidentally placing extra spaces in macros. Although an extra space in your macro may make your macro easier to read, it creates errors because Agenda responds as if you had pressed the (SPACEBAR) when it executes the recorded keystrokes during playback. Since the (SPACEBAR) is used to make choices for settings, you could unknowingly change a setting during the execution of the macro.

Another key to watch carefully is the (ENTER) key since it functions a little differently within a macro. If you press (ENTER) while editing your macro, the macro instructions move to the next line. However, when the macro is executed, the (ENTER) that you pressed is ignored. You use the {ENTER} command to tell the macro to function as though the (ENTER) key had been pressed. The ability to press (ENTER) while editing a macro allows you to structure the macro code in a readable format. That is, you can press (ENTER) after each macro command so that each command displays on a separate line. This will not affect how the macro runs.

CREATING A PAIR OF MACROS TO CHANGE THE WIDTH OF COLUMNS

It is not unusual to create macros in pairs or sets since there are often separate parts to a task you want to complete. You might create a macro for each task. For this example, you are going to create two macros. One macro will make a column of a view 40 characters wide, the other will make a column 12 characters wide. You will be able to use these macros to change the width of any columns within a view.

You will create the first macro using the Learn mode and the second using the Macro Editor. Since the macros are very similar, this will give you an opportunity to practice both methods of creating macros.

To create a macro that makes a column 40 characters wide using the Learn mode:

1. Place your cursor anywhere in the second column of the view.

2. Press (ALT-F3) (Macro) to activate the Macro Manager.

3. Press (INS) to tell Agenda that you want to add a macro to the Macro Manager.

4. Type the name of the new macro as **View: Make Wide Column (40)** and press (ENTER).

5. Press (F7) (Learn) to start Learn mode. From now until you press (ALT-F3) again, all of your keystrokes will be recorded as part of the macro.

6. Press (F10) (Menu), type **v** for View, **c** for Column, and **w** for width. Type **40** as the column width and press (ENTER). This returns you to View mode with the column width now set at 40.

Because there is enough room, the short names of the categories have been replaced with their category names, making the column entries much more readable.

7. Turn off Learn mode by pressing (ALT-F3) (Macro). Press (ENTER) to remove the dialog box telling you that you are no longer in Learn mode.

8. To view the macro you just created, press (ALT-F3) (Macro) to activate the Macro Manager. Press (F2) (EditMac) to display the Macro Editor for the macro. The following macro codes should appear within the Macro Editor:

```
{View: Make Wide Column (40)}
{F10}vcw40{ENTER}
```

The second line of the "View: Make Narrow Column" macro will be the same as this one except that the 40 will be replaced with 12.

9. Press (ESC) to return to the Macro Manager.

10. Press (INS) to tell Agenda you want to insert a new macro into the Macro Manager.

11. Type **View: Make Narrow Column (12)** and press (ENTER).

12. Press (F2) (EditMac) to display the Macro Editor. The name of the macro already appears at the top of the Macro Editor screen.

13. Press (END) to move to the end of the first line. Press (ENTER) to move the cursor to the beginning of the second line.

14. Press (ALT-=) to specify that the next key you press should be entered as a code. Press (F10). Agenda inserts {F10} as the first code.

15. Type **vcw12{ENTER}** for the rest of the macro. Instead of typing {ENTER}, you could also press (ALT-=) and then press (ENTER).

16. Press (F5) (Return) to return to the Macro Manager.

17. Press (ENTER) to run the "View: Make Narrow Column" macro. The column returns to the narrow width.

THE MACRO PROPERTIES BOX

The Macro Properties dialog box provides you with a variety of options for working with macros. One option allows you to limit where macros can be used. This can help eliminate the unexpected results that can occur when a macro is run from a location where it was not intended to be used.

Another option you can use is to assign a macro to a keystroke. This gives you the ability to run a macro that you use often by simply typing a keystroke combination.

Other capabilities available include protecting macros so that they cannot be changed in the Macro Editor and allowing macro instructions to be imported from a file created outside of Agenda with a word processor.

Restricting Where a Macro Can Be Used

Earlier in the chapter you learned that macros should be named so that you could tell what mode the macro was designed to run in. Agenda provides a method for restricting the use of macros. You have created a macro to print a view with its notes attached. This macro was designed to run from View mode. You will now use the Macro Properties box to prevent the user from accessing this macro when in other Agenda modes.

1. Press (**ALT-F3**) (Macro) to activate the Macro Manager.

2. Highlight the "View: Print View With Notes" macro using the arrow keys.

3. Press (**F6**) (Props) to activate the Macro Properties dialog box shown in Figure 10-6. Note that if you pressed the (**SPACEBAR**) with the highlight currently on the Contents setting, you would activate the Macro Editor.

4. Press (**DOWN ARROW**) three times to highlight the Macro Can Be Run From View setting. You want this macro to run in View mode, so leave this setting as is. Note that the "V" next to the Yes indicates that the macro can be run from View mode.

5. Press (**DOWN ARROW**) one time to highlight the Macro Can Be Run From Note setting. You do not want this macro to run from within a note, so type **n**.

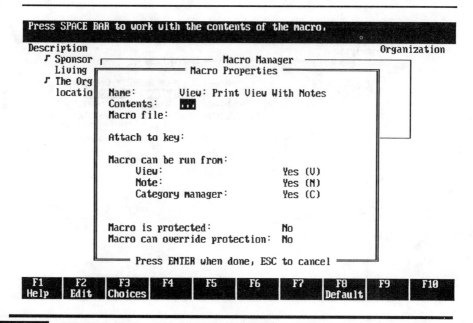

```
Press SPACE BAR to work with the contents of the macro.

Description                                                    Organization
    ♪ Sponsor  ┌─────────────── Macro Manager ───────────────┐
      Living   │ ┌───────────── Macro Properties ─────────────┐ │
    ♪ The Org  │ │                                            │ │
      locatio  │ │ Name:         View: Print View With Notes  │ │
             │ │ │ Contents:     ▪▪▪                           │ │
             │ │ │ Macro file:                                │ │
             │ │ │                                            │ │
             │ │ │ Attach to key:                             │ │
             │ │ │                                            │ │
             │ │ │ Macro can be run from:                     │ │
             │ │ │     View:                     Yes (V)      │ │
             │ │ │     Note:                     Yes (N)      │ │
             │ │ │     Category manager:         Yes (C)      │ │
             │ │ │                                            │ │
             │ │ │                                            │ │
             │ │ │ Macro is protected:           No           │ │
             │ │ │ Macro can override protection: No          │ │
             │ │ │                                            │ │
             │ └── Press ENTER when done, ESC to cancel ──────┘ │
             └────────────────────────────────────────────────┘
```

F1	F2	F3	F4	F5	F6	F7	F8	F9	F10
Help	Edit	Choices					Default		

FIGURE 10-6.   The Macro Properties box for the "View: Print View With Notes" macro

6. Press (**DOWN ARROW**) one time to highlight the Macro Can Be Run From Category Manager setting. You do not want this macro to run from the Category Manager, so type **n**.

7. Press (**ENTER**) to return to the Macro Manager. It should appear as shown in Figure 10-7. Notice the "V" in the upper-right corner of the Macro Manager box. This indicates that the highlighted macro can be run only from a view.

8. Press (**DOWN ARROW**) once to highlight the "View: Make Wide Column" macro. The upper-right corner now displays "VNC," indicating that this macro is currently set to run in View mode, in a note, and within the Category Manager.

9. Press (**ESC**) to leave the Macro Manager and return to the view. Highlight the second item by pressing (**LEFT ARROW**).

10. Press (**F5**) (Note) to display this item's note.

11. Press (**ALT-F3**) (Macro) to activate the Macro Manager. Notice that the Macro Manager does *not* contain the "View: Print View With Notes" macro. This is because you restricted the macro from use within a note.

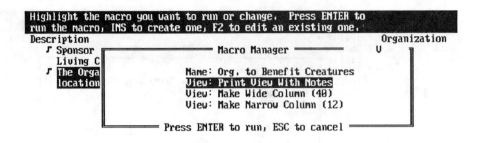

FIGURE 10-7.   The Macro Manager with a macro highlighted that can be run only from a view

12. Highlight the "View: Make Wide Column" macro and press (ENTER) to run it. Remember that this macro was designed to run from View mode and not from within a note. You have not restricted its use from within a note, however. The screen flashes and the computer beeps at you. When finished, the note disappears from the screen. This is an example of the unpredictable results that can occur when you run a macro from an area where it was not intended.

13. Press (ESC) to leave the note unchanged and type y to discard the changes made by the macro. You are returned to the view.

Assigning a Macro to a Key

As you work with macros, you will find that you use just a few of your defined macros most of the time. Oddly enough, these macros also tend to be the simpler ones designed to save keystrokes and time. Agenda provides a means for attaching a macro to a key or key combination so that you can run the macro by just pressing the key.

Another advantage of assigning a macro to a keystroke has to do with where macros can be run from. Usually macros are limited to a view, note, or the Category Manager. If you attach a key to the macro, you also have the opportunity to tell Agenda that the macro can be run from anywhere else in the database through the Macro Properties box settings.

The advantages of assigning a key to a macro may be obvious, but there are some disadvantages as well. First, using a simple keystroke to run a macro increases the chances of the macro being run by mistake. You might accidentally press a key that also happens to be a macro. Another difficulty arises when you forget which macro does what. For example, it would be hard to remember if (CTRL-X) moves marked text to the end of a note or takes you to a specific view. Running macros from the Macro Manager allows you to choose from descriptive names. Keeping in mind the disadvantages, a few chosen macros assigned to keystrokes can be a real time saver.

You can experiment with this feature using the first macro you created, the "Org. to Benefit Creatures" macro. Perform the following steps:

1. Press (ALT-F3) (Macro) to activate the Macro Manager. Use the (ARROW) keys to highlight the "Org. to Benefit Creatures" macro.

2. Press (F6) (Props) to activate the Macro Properties box. Press (DOWN ARROW) twice to highlight the Attach to Key setting.

3. Assign (CTRL-C) to the macro by typing {CtlC} and pressing (ENTER). In this example, "C" stands for "Creature." As you attach a key, notice that an Everywhere Else setting is added to the box.

4. Since this macro was not designed to be used in the Category Manager, press (DOWN ARROW) three times to highlight the Macro Can Be Run From Category Manager setting and type **n**.

5. Press (ENTER) to return to the Macro Manager and (ESC) to return to the view.

6. Use the (ARROW) keys to highlight the last item. Press (CTRL-C) to run the macro. The name of the organization appears as the beginning of an item.

7. Finish the item by pressing (SPACEBAR) and typing **contributor of $1,000,000**, and press (TAB).

8. Type **mil** and press (SHIFT-TAB).

So far you have used this macro only to begin an item. Agenda does not consider you to be in View mode after you have started making an item entry or are editing an item. To see how this works, continue with the following steps.

9. Type **Volunteers recognized for outstanding service to** and press (SPACEBAR) to start a new item.

10. Try to finish the item by pressing (CTRL-C). A heart appears in the place of the macro. This is because the macro cannot be run from within an item entry as it is currently configured. Press (BACKSPACE) to delete the heart and (ENTER) to temporarily end the entry of the item.

11. Press (ALT-F3) (Macro) to activate the Macro Manager. Press (F6) (Props) to turn on the macro's Category Properties box.

12. Press (DOWN ARROW) six times to highlight the Macro Can Be Run From Everywhere Else setting and type **y**.

13. Press (ENTER) and (ESC) to return to the view.

14. Press (F2) (Edit) to edit the last item. Press (END) to quickly move to the end of the current item, and then press (SPACEBAR) since the space inserted earlier was lost because no text followed it.

15. Press (CTRL-C). This time the macro works and adds the organization name to the end of the item.

16. Press (ENTER), press (RIGHT ARROW), type **ja**, and press (ENTER) to complete the entry.

You will now attach keystrokes to the "View: Make Wide Column" and "View: Make Narrow Column" macros so you can quickly make a column within a view either wide or narrow. You will use (CTRL-W) for wide columns and (CTRL-N) for narrow columns. It is a good idea whenever possible to use letters that somehow relate to the macro they run.

Note that you do not have to use the (CTRL) key plus a letter when making these key assignments. Any keystroke combination is allowed, including (SHIFT), (CTRL), and (ALT) combinations with letters, symbols, numbers, and function keys. You could also assign just one key to a macro. For example, you could assign the "View: Make Narrow Column" macro to the letter "n." Of course, this means that you couldn't use the letter "n" in View mode for anything other than making columns narrow, which limits quite a few words from your database entries. Therefore, it is prudent to decide on a key or key combination that cues you as to what the macro does but is not common enough to be pressed accidentally.

17. Press (ALT-F3) (Macro) to activate the Macro Manager.

18. Highlight the "View: Make Wide Column" macro and press (F6) (Props) to display the Macro Properties box.

19. Press (DOWN ARROW) twice, and then press (ALT-=) and (CTRL-W).

20. Since this macro should only be used in View mode, press (DOWN ARROW) twice, type **n**, press (DOWN ARROW), type **n**, and press (ENTER) to return to the Macro Manager.

21. Highlight the "View: Make Narrow Column" macro and press (F6) (Props).

22. Press (DOWN ARROW) twice, and then press (ALT-=) and (CTRL-N).

23. Since this macro should only be used in View mode, press (DOWN ARROW) twice, type **n**, press (DOWN ARROW), type **n**, and press (ENTER) to return to the Macro Manager.

24. Press (ESC) to return to the view without running a macro.

25. Move the highlight to anywhere in the Organization column. Press (CTRL-W). The view displays with the Organization column 40 characters wide.

26. Press (CTRL-N). The view again displays with the Organization column 12 characters wide.

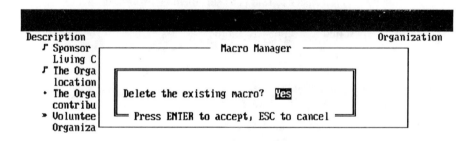

FIGURE 10-8.   The confirmation box for deleting a macro from the Macro Manager

REMOVING MACROS FROM THE MACRO MANAGER

Removing a macro from the Macro Manager is a simple process. Just activate the Macro Manager by pressing (ALT-F3) (Macro), highlight the macro to be deleted, and press (F4) (Delete). A confirmation box similar to the one in Figure 10-8 appears on the screen. Press (ENTER) to delete the highlighted macro.

SORTING MACROS IN THE MACRO MANAGER

Finding the macro you need in the Macro Manager can become cumbersome if you have defined a large number of macros for a database. One method you can use to make macros easier to find is to sort them. To sort your macros activate the Macro Manager by pressing (ALT-F3), and then press (ALT-F5) (Sort). The macros are immediately sorted into alphabetical order.

EXPORTING AND IMPORTING MACROS

The macros that you have created in this chapter are only accessible to the current database, MACRO. It is very possible that you will create a macro in one database that you would like to use in another. Macros are transferred to another database by exporting the macro from one database and importing it to the other. This topic is covered in greater depth in the next chapter.

11

IMPORTING AND EXPORTING DATA

Transferring Your Data from One Database to Another
Using Special Actions to Export Items to an STF File
Exporting Done Items
Importing Data Automatically
Exporting and Importing Macros
Using the TXT2STF Program
Importing Data Through Text Notes
Using the Metro Accessories

Any time you can bring data that is already recorded on disk or another source into an Agenda file, you eliminate typing and gain productivity. The process of bringing data into one program from another source is called *importing* data.

At times you may want to move some of the information in one Agenda database to another Agenda database or use some of it with another program. The process of taking data currently used for one purpose and transferring it to another database for another use is called *exporting* data. The flow of data in this process is opposite to the flow in the import process.

This chapter provides some of the basic information you need to import and export data while working with Agenda. You will learn how to export data from one Agenda database and import the data to another Agenda database. This data can consist of the structure, items, categories, and/or category assignments of the Agenda database.

Lotus includes a copy of the Metro program with several accessories to facilitate importing data from other programs, and these accessories are also covered here. You will learn how to use both the Clipboard and the Items Accessory to transfer data from other programs to Agenda.

The chapter also discusses how to use the TXT2STF conversion program to import an ASCII data file to a format that Agenda can import. Other methods for importing word processing files are also discussed.

TRANSFERRING YOUR DATA FROM ONE DATABASE TO ANOTHER

Agenda provides two commands for exporting information from one database to another. The first command, Template, transfers the settings and structure (that is, categories and views) for an existing database into another database. The Template command is useful when you want to split a large database into several smaller databases or establish a new database similar to yours for a business associate.

The second command, Export, takes part of your database and puts it into an STF or "structured" file. This is the file format to use when you want to import information into an Agenda database. The Export feature is also useful when you want to put the information from an Agenda file into more than one file.

Using the File Template Feature

Agenda's Template command allows you to take information from an existing database and create a new database from it. This operation uses your existing database as a pattern for the new database. Items and their assignments are not included in the transfer, but all the defined categories, views, macros, conditions, and actions do transfer.

For the following discussion, you will use the MACRO database created in Chapter 10 as the source database. If you did not create the MACRO database, use any database

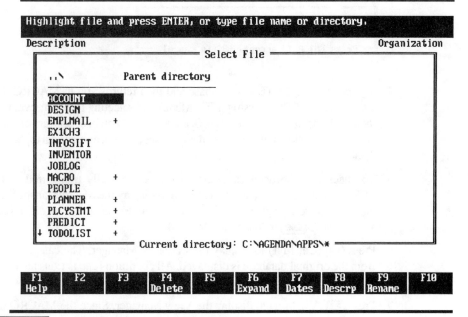

FIGURE 11-1. Template dialog box

that you currently have available by substituting the name of your database for
MACRO. Your source database will not be affected by the following procedures. To
transfer your database's pattern with Template, follow these steps:

1. Press (F10) (Menu) and select File Retrieve. Highlight the MACRO database (or
   the database you are using for this example) and press (ENTER). The MACRO
   database appears on the screen.

2. Press (F10) (Menu) and select File Transfer Template. Agenda displays the
   selection box shown in Figure 11-1.

3. Type **TEST1** as the file name that you wish to use for the target file and press
   (ENTER).
   If you pick an existing file name instead of typing a new one, you get the
   following confirmation box:

```
┌─────────────────────────────────────────┐
│ Replace the existing file?  No           │
│  └─ Press ENTER to accept, ESC to cancel ─┘
└─────────────────────────────────────────┘
```

4. Agenda creates the TEST1 database and then returns you to MACRO. Retrieve the new database by pressing (F10) (Menu) and selecting File Retrieve. Highlight the TEST1 database and press (ENTER). The TEST1 database appears on the screen. No items are listed, but otherwise the view should appear identical to the MACRO database.

5. To check that the database structure was successfully transferred to the new TEST1 database, press (ALT-F3) (Macro) to display the Macro Manager. The four macros that were originally defined in the MACRO database are displayed on the screen. Press (ESC) to leave the Macro Manager.

6. Press (F9) (Cat Mgr) to display the Category Manager. The category hierarchy from the original database is displayed. All conditions and actions have also been transferred from the original database. Press (ESC) to return to the view.

7. Press (F8) (Vw Mgr) to display the View Manager. Since the MACRO database had only one view, the box only displays the one view. If you used another database as your template, the box should list all views of the source database. Press (ESC) to return to the view.

Exporting Data to an STF File

When you use the Export command, Agenda puts the data into an STF file rather than placing it directly in a database. The STF file acts as an intermediate file between the *source* database and the *target* database. The source is the database from where the information is being exported, while the target is the database to where the information is to be imported. After completing the export operation, you can import the STF file to another database file.

The Export command allows you to transfer items, notes, categories, conditions, and/or actions to the STF file. It cannot export view definitions or macros.

To export one item of the MACRO database (or a database of your choosing), follow these steps:

1. Retrieve the MACRO database by pressing (F10) (Menu) and selecting File Retrieve. Highlight the MACRO database (or the database you are using for this example) and press (ENTER). The MACRO database appears on the screen. Use the (ARROW) keys to highlight the last item of the database view.

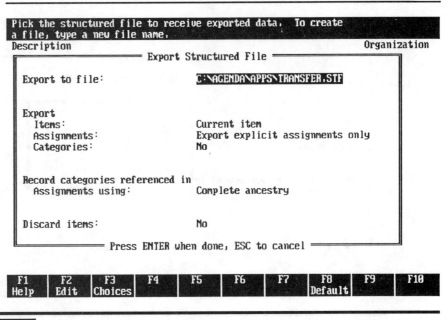

FIGURE 11-2.   Export Structured File dialog box

2. To perform the export, press (F10) (Menu) and select File Transfer Export. Agenda displays the Export Structured File dialog box shown in Figure 11-2.

3. The default name for the STF file is TRANSFER.STF. You could accept this as the STF name or, in this case, give it a name by typing **TEST1** and pressing (ENTER). Agenda adds the STF extension and assumes you want to store it in the same directory as your Agenda files. If you want the STF file to be saved to another directory, type in the full path name.

    If the STF file that you specify already exists, the following setting appears below the current one:

```
┌─────────────── Export Structured File ═══════════════┐
║                                                      ║
║  Export to file:          C:\AGENDA\APPS\TEST1.STF   ║
║  File already exists:      Append                    ║
║                                                      ║
└──────────────────────────────────────────────────────┘
```

Your choices are to append (or add) the current exported data to the end of the existing file, or to replace the current file with a new one.

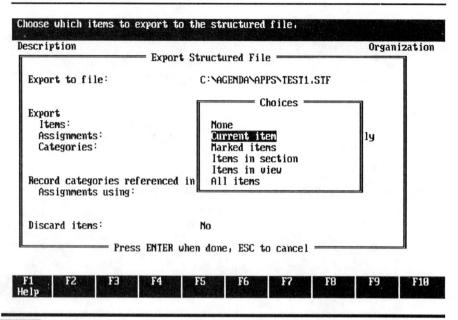

FIGURE 11-3.   The choices for Export Items

4. Press (**DOWN ARROW**) to highlight the Export Items setting. Press (**F3**) (Choices) to display the choices for this setting, as shown in Figure 11-3. See Table 11-1 for a description of each of these settings.

    The default choice for "Items" will depend on whether the highlight in the view is on an item or section head and whether there are marked items in the database.

5. Highlight Current Item if it is not already and press (**ENTER**) to export the item that was highlighted in the view when you displayed the dialog box.

6. Press (**DOWN ARROW**) to highlight the Export Assignments setting. Press (**F3**) (Choices) to display the choices for the setting, as shown in Figure 11-4.

The first choice is to not export any category assignments to the STF file. This is useful for transferring items from one database to another when the target database's structure is completely different from the source database. The second choice, which is the default setting, is to export explicit assignments only. This means that the only category assignments transferred are those that were explicitly made by someone or by an action. No conditional assignments will be transferred. The third choice is to export all assignments as explicit, including any conditional assignments.

If you choose:	Agenda exports:
None	The category hierarchy only
Current item	The highlighted item and its note
Marked items	The item(s) and their note(s) that were marked with the (F7) (Mark) key
Items in section	The item(s) and their note(s) that are contained in the current section of the current view
Items in view	The item(s) and their note(s) that are contained in the current view
All items	All the items and their notes in the database

TABLE 11-1.   Choices for Exporting Items to an STF File

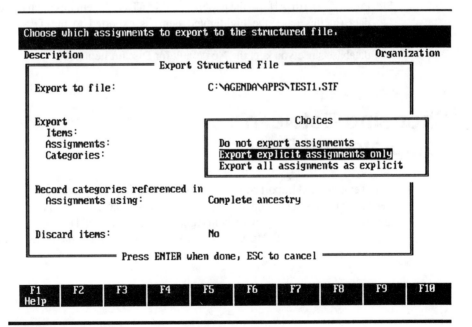

FIGURE 11-4.   The choices for Export Assignments

7. Highlight Export Explicit Assignments Only (if it isn't already) and press (ENTER).

8. Press (DOWN ARROW) to highlight the Export Categories setting. This setting allows you to export all categories, including those that were not assigned to any exported items. For this example, leave the default setting of No, meaning you do not want to include any categories that were not used by exported items.

    A good way to export only the category hierarchy from one database to another is to set Export Items to None and Export Categories to Yes.

9. Press (DOWN ARROW) to highlight the setting for determining how the category assignments are to be recorded. Your choices are Complete Ancestry or Category Name Only. If you choose the former, each item's category assignment will include its parent, grandparent, etc. If you choose the latter, only the lowest level category name is exported with the item. For this example, leave the default of Complete Ancestry.

10. Press (DOWN ARROW) to highlight the Discard Items setting. If the item(s) to be exported are no longer needed in the source database, you could change this setting to Yes. For this example, just accept the default setting of No.

11. Press (ENTER) to perform the export. The MACRO file remains unchanged, but the data (in this case, the highlighted item) is exported to the TEST1.STF file. Although the item is exported to an STF file, it is not deleted from your MACRO database since you kept the No default for Discard Items.

Choosing Between Template and Export

The Template and Export commands differ in that Export operates primarily on items while Template operates on the rest of the features of the database. Template produces a copy of the database with the items removed so you can add new items to it. Export extracts items without a database framework so you can add the items to a different database.

Importing an STF File
Into an Agenda Database

Once your information is stored in an STF file, you can incorporate it into one or more of your databases. To import the item stored in the TEST1.STF file into the TEST1 Agenda database, follow these steps:

1. Retrieve the TEST1 database by pressing (F10) (Menu) and selecting File Retrieve. Highlight the TEST1 database and press (ENTER). The TEST1 database appears on the screen.

2. Press (F10) (Menu) and select File Transfer Import. The Import Structured File dialog box shown in Figure 11-5 appears. If the TRANSFER.STF file does not exist, the second line of the dialog box reminds you of this.

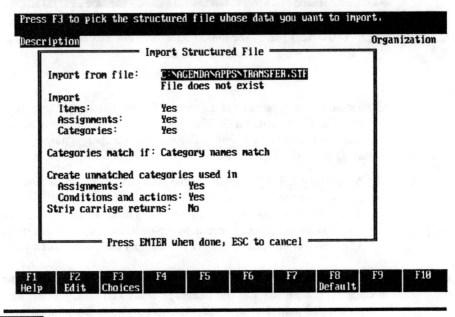

FIGURE 11-5.   Import Structured File dialog box

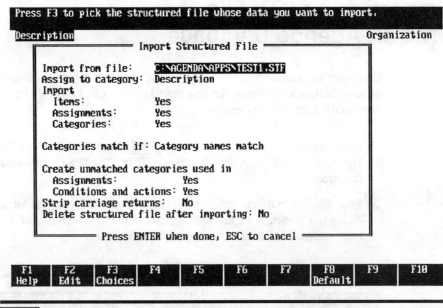

Press F3 to pick the structured file whose data you want to import.

Description   Organization

══════════════════ Import Structured File ══════════════════

Import from file: C:\AGENDA\APPS\TEST1.STF
Assign to category: Description
Import
  Items: Yes
  Assignments: Yes
  Categories: Yes

Categories match if: Category names match

Create unmatched categories used in
  Assignments: Yes
  Conditions and actions: Yes
Strip carriage returns: No
Delete structured file after importing: No

═══════════════ Press ENTER when done, ESC to cancel ═══════════════

| F1 | F2 | F3 | F4 | F5 | F6 | F7 | F8 | F9 | F10 |
| Help | Edit | Choices | | | | | Default | | |

FIGURE 11-6.   The Import Structured File box after an existing STF file has been selected

3. Instead of typing the name of the transfer file for this example, press (F3) (Choices) for a list of the current STF files. Select the data to import by highlighting the TEST1 file and pressing (ENTER). The Assign to Category setting appears, as shown in Figure 11-6.

4. Press (DOWN ARROW) to highlight the Assign to Category setting. This setting allows you to choose the category to which Agenda will assign the imported items. Agenda prompts you with the current section head, which in this case is Description. You can make your selection by typing in the category name or pressing (F3) (Choices). For this example, leave the category assignment as Description.

   If you want to import items into the database without explicitly assigning them to a category, choose Main as the category. You could choose or create a separate category if you wanted to segregate the imported items from the other items in the database.

   You use the next three settings to specify the types of information to be imported into the target database. Use Import Items to specify whether the items in the STF file are to be imported into the database. Use Import Assignments to specify whether each item's category assignments are to be imported into the database. Use Import Categories to specify whether the categories in the STF file that are not assigned to any of its items should be imported into the database. For this example, leave the settings with their default values of Yes.

5. Press (DOWN ARROW) four times to highlight the Categories Match If setting. Press F3 (Choices) to display the choices shown here:

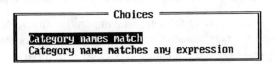

If you choose the Category Names Match option, any item category assignments from the STF file must exactly match the name of a category in the target database. If an exact match is found, Agenda assigns the item to the category. The Category Name Matches Any Expression option allows Agenda to check if a match is made with the target database's category name, short name, or other matches as defined in the Category Manager. If a match is found, the item is assigned to the category.

6. For this example, highlight Category Name Matches Any Expression and press (ENTER).

7. Press (DOWN ARROW) to highlight the Create Unmatched Categories Used in Assignments setting. If an item has a category assignment to a category that does not exist in the target database, you can have Agenda create the category. If you choose Yes, then Agenda creates the category; if you choose No, Agenda ignores the category assignment. For this example, keep the default setting of Yes.

8. Press (DOWN ARROW) to highlight the Create Unmatched Categories Used In Conditions And Actions setting. If an item has a category with a condition or action that refers to another category that does not exist in the target database, you can have Agenda create the category. For this example, keep the default setting of Yes.

9. Press (DOWN ARROW) to highlight the Strip Carriage Returns setting. This setting determines whether Agenda will strip single carriage returns from the text of items or notes. Keep the default setting of No.

If Agenda strips away the carriage returns that are part of note text, it reformats the note to fit within Agenda's margin settings. If Agenda does not strip the carriage returns from the text, it keeps the same carriage returns as in the original text. You might use the latter option for a database that imported poetry. Since most poetry has definite line breaks, you want to maintain them when they are imported. If the option is set to No and the text extends beyond Agenda's line length, Agenda wraps that line and keeps the carriage return at the end of the line.

10. Press (DOWN ARROW) to highlight the Delete Structured File After Importing setting. This setting determines whether Agenda will delete the STF file once the data is imported. If you will not need the STF file after the data is imported into the target database, you should set this option to Yes. To do so, type **y**.

11. Press (ENTER) to start importing the data. As it imports the file, Agenda displays a box showing you the percentage of completion. (When importing an STF file containing only one item, the percentage count may be too fast to see.)

When the import process is completed, the TEST1 database contains one item.

USING SPECIAL ACTIONS TO EXPORT ITEMS TO AN STF FILE

Agenda allows you to create STF files in a variety of ways. Earlier you created an STF file using the Export command. You can also set up special actions to automatically export any item assigned to a category to an STF file. For example, you could tell Agenda to export any item assigned to the Jerry category to the JERRY.STF file. Later, the items stored in the JERRY.STF file could be imported into Jerry's database.

To see how this works, you are going to create a Master Log category. Assume that any item assigned to this category should also be incorporated into a MASTERLOG database. You will create a special action that will export any item assigned to the Master Log category to a MASTER.STF file, which later will be imported into the MASTERLOG database.

1. Make sure you are in the TEST1 database by pressing (F10) (Menu) and selecting File Retrieve. Highlight TEST1 and press (ENTER). The TEST1 database appears on the screen.

2. Press (F9) (Cat Mgr) to activate the Category Manager.

3. Highlight the Done category using the (ARROW) keys.

4. Create the Master Log category by typing **Master Log** and pressing (ENTER).

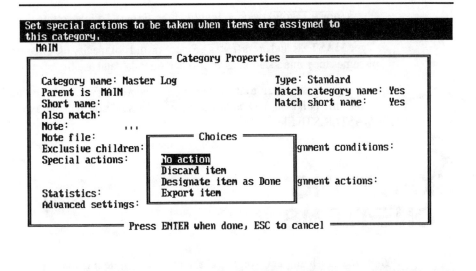

FIGURE 11-7. The choices for special actions in the Category Properties box

5. Press (F6) (Props) to activate the Category Properties box for Master Log. You are now ready to create the special action that will automatically export any item assigned to Master Log.

6. Press (DOWN ARROW) six times to highlight the Special Actions setting. Press (F3) (Choices) to display the choices for special actions, as shown in Figure 11-7.

7. Press (DOWN ARROW) three times or type E to select Export Item and press (ENTER). When you make this selection, the following two settings are added below the Special Actions setting:

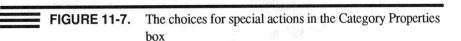

Discard Items is currently set to No. This means that the item will remain in the current database as it is exported to the STF file. If you change the setting to Yes, the item is removed from the current database as it is exported. For this example, keep the default value of No so that the items assigned to Master Log will remain in the TEST1 database.

8. Press (DOWN ARROW) twice to highlight the Export To File setting. This is where you tell Agenda the name of the STF file to which you want the items exported. Type **MASTER** and press (ENTER). Since you did not specify the directory, Agenda assumes the same location as your other Agenda database files.

9. Press (ENTER) to return to the Category Manager and (ESC) to return to the view. From this point on, any item assigned to Master Log will be exported to the MASTER.STF file.

EXPORTING DONE ITEMS

When you finish an item, you mark it done. Once an item is marked done, you can use the Process Done Items setting of the Global Date Settings box to determine what to do with the item. One possibility is to have Agenda export the done items to an STF file. You could then use the STF file in a database that presented monthly progress reports using the done items from other databases.

To have the done items in your TEST1 database exported to the file DONE.STF, follow these steps:

1. Make sure you are in the TEST1 database by pressing (F10) (Menu) and selecting File Retrieve. Highlight TEST1 and press (ENTER). The TEST1 database appears on the screen.

2. Press (F10) (Menu) and select File Properties to display the File Properties dialog box.

3. Press (UP ARROW) three times to highlight Global Date Settings. Press (SPACEBAR) to activate the Global Date Settings box.

4. Press (UP ARROW) once to highlight the Process Done Items setting. Press (F3) (Choices) to display the possible choices, as shown in Figure 11-8.

5. Press (DOWN ARROW) twice and press (ENTER) to choose the Export To Done File setting. The following settings are added to the Global Date Settings box:

```
Process Done items:  Export to Done file
    When:            Immediately
    Done file:       C:\AGENDA\APPS\TEST1!.STF
```

The When setting has three possible choices. You can select one immediately, when the file is closed, or when the system date changes at the end of the day. To

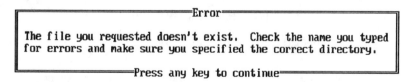

```
Choose what to do with items after you designate them as done.
Press F3 for choices.
Description                                                 Organization
                          ┌─── File Properties ────────────┐    ┐▶JMG
          ┌───────────── Global Date Settings ─────────────┐
     F    │                                                │
     S    │  Display format:     ...      Input format:  ...│
     M    │                                                │
     G    │  Morning:         8:00am   Afternoon:  2:00pm  │
     A    │  Evening:         5:00pm                        │
          │                                                │
     I    │  Beginning of week:  Mon      End of week:  Fri │
     E    │  First quarter:   Jan  1                        │
          │  Beginning of year:  Jan  1   End of year: Dec 31│
     T    │  Month alone means:  First day                 │
          │                       ┌──── Choices ───┐        │
     G    │                       │                │        │
     G    │  Process Done items:  │ No action      │        │
     U    │                       │ Discard        │        │
          │                       │ Export to Done file     │
          │                       └────────────────┘        │
          └───── Press ENTER when done, ESC to cancel ──────┘
┌─────┬─────┬─────┬─────┬─────┬─────┬─────┬─────┬─────┬─────┐
│ F1  │ F2  │ F3  │ F4  │ F5  │ F6  │ F7  │ F8  │ F9  │ F10 │
│ Help│     │     │     │     │     │     │     │     │     │
└─────┴─────┴─────┴─────┴─────┴─────┴─────┴─────┴─────┴─────┘
```

FIGURE 11-8.   The choices for Process Done Items

change the setting press either (**F3**) (Choices) or (**SPACEBAR**). For this example, leave the setting at the default of Immediately.

6. Press (**DOWN ARROW**) twice to highlight the Done File setting. Type the name of the file as **done** and press (**ENTER**). (You could also press (**F3**) (Choices) to see a list of the current STF files.) Agenda uses the file extension .STF by default. Since DONE.STF is not a current STF file, Agenda displays the following error message:

```
┌──────────────────Error──────────────────┐
│                                          │
│ The file you requested doesn't exist.  Check the name you typed │
│ for errors and make sure you specified the correct directory.   │
│                                          │
└───────────Press any key to continue──────┘
```

7. Press any key to remove the error message, and press (**ENTER**) twice to return to the view.

8. Insert an item into the view by typing **This is a sample item.** and pressing (**ENTER**).

9. Press (F4) (Done) to mark the item as done. As the done item is exported to the DONE.STF file, it is removed from the TEST1 database.

IMPORTING DATA AUTOMATICALLY

Besides manually importing an STF file into Agenda, you can have Agenda import an STF file automatically whenever you use your database. The steps you would follow to have Agenda import a file automatically are as follows:

1. Press (F10) (Menu).

2. Select File Properties to display the File Properties dialog box.

3. Press (DOWN ARROW) four times to highlight Auto-Import File.

4. Type the name of the file to be imported. If you press (F3) (Choices), you get a list of the STF files in the current directory and can move the highlight to the file that you want and press (ENTER). If you type a file name and do not provide an extension, the .STF extension is assumed. The file must be in STF format or Agenda will display an error message when it tries to import it. If the STF file does not currently exist, you will get the following error message:

```
┌─────────────────────Error─────────────────────┐
│                                                │
│ The file you requested doesn't exist.  Check the name you typed │
│ for errors and make sure you specified the correct directory.   │
│                                                │
└─────────────Press any key to continue─────────────┘
```

5. If the file name is correct, press any key to continue.

6. Press (ENTER) twice to return to the view.

When you open a database with an auto-import file, Agenda tries to import the specified file. If Agenda cannot find the file, the database is opened but data is not imported. If the import file is not in the proper format, you will see an error message. As items are imported, Agenda applies all category conditions and actions to them.

EXPORTING AND IMPORTING MACROS

You will often find that a macro created for one database could be used to great advantage in other databases. Agenda provides a means for importing and exporting macros, using an intermediate MAC file. Agenda automatically adds a .MAC extension to the name of the macro file.

Note that the Template command also transfers macros from one database to another, but since it transfers the complete database structure to a new file, it may not be very useful for only transferring a few macros.

To transfer a macro file from your TEST1 database to a database named TEST2, perform the following steps:

1. Make sure you are in the TEST1 database by pressing (F10) (Menu) and selecting File Retrieve. Highlight TEST1 and press (ENTER). The TEST1 database appears on the screen.

2. Press (ALT-F3) (Macro) to activate the Macro Manager. Use the (ARROW) keys to highlight the Print View macro (or any other macro you have defined).

3. Press (F2) (EditMac) to activate the Macro Editor. This lists the contents of the macro.

4. Press (F10) (Menu) and type **e** for Export. The File dialog box appears, as shown in Figure 11-9.

5. Type **printvw** as the macro file name and press (ENTER). Agenda automatically adds the .MAC extension to the end of the file name. Press (ENTER) to return to the Macro Editor screen.

6. Press (F5) (Return) to return to the Macro Manager. Press (ESC) to return to the view.

7. Create and enter a database named TEST2 by pressing (F10) (Menu) and selecting File Retrieve. Type **test2** and press (ENTER).

8. Type the description **Test File** and press (ENTER) twice. The new TEST2 database appears on the screen.

9. To import the macro, press (ALT-F3) (Macro) to activate the Macro Manager. Since there are no macros currently defined, you need to enter a temporary name for a macro.

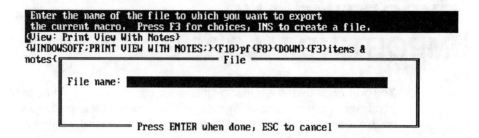

FIGURE 11-9.   The File dialog box for exporting a macro from the Macro Editor

10. Type **Print a View** and press (ENTER).

11. Press (F2) (EditMac) to activate the Macro Editor.

12. To import the macro, press (F10) (Menu) and type **i** for Import.

13. Type **printvw** as the file name. Press (ENTER) twice to return to the Macro Editor.

14. The contents of the PRINTVW.MAC file are inserted into the Macro Editor. The cursor is currently located at the end of the inserted macro and on the temporary name for the macro. Press (CTRL-ENTER) to delete the temporary name.

15. Press (F5) (Return) to return to the Macro Manager. To verify the macro exists for the database, you can run the macro by pressing (ENTER), or press (ESC) to return to the view.

USING THE TXT2STF PROGRAM

Agenda provides a special program that transfers a text file into an Agenda STF file. A text file contains regular characters and numbers that are not in a special format and do not use any special nonprintable (non-ASCII) characters. These text files are sometimes referred to as *ASCII files* or *DOS files*. The TXT2STF program processes a text file and changes the entries into items and notes.

Text (ASCII) files can be created by a variety of programs. If you are importing information from a word processor, remove from the text any special formatting characters added by your word processor. This is normally an option available from the word processor's menu, but in some cases you need to run a conversion program to strip away the special characters that represent print characteristics like boldface and underlining.

The TXT2STF program makes certain assumptions about how to convert the text into items and notes unless you override its defaults. The program assumes that two carriage returns separate items from one another. It makes the characters within an item the item text until it reaches the next item or the 350-character limit. If it reaches the 350-character limit before the end of the item, it moves backward to find the most recent ending punctuation mark (., ?, !, :, or ;) and uses that as the separator between the item and the note. If there are no punctuation marks, it ends the item text at the most recent space. Everything remaining in the item is put into the item's note. If the amount of information in the note exceeds 10K (approximately ten pages of information), the program goes back to the most recent punctuation mark or space and makes the rest of the information a new item, following the same rules. When TXT2STF follows these rules, it does not create any categories. By overriding the default rules with a definition file, you can have the program separate the data differently and can associate the items with categories.

TXT2STF Options

The TXT2STF program provides several options, discussed here briefly. You can use a wild card character to describe the file or files to be transformed. You can use any of six different parameters when you invoke the program. You can specify the output file, the separator character, and the definition file, and you can display conversion information on the screen as it converts your program. This last option is available if you write your own definition file.

Importing a WordPerfect File Using TXT2STF

The following example takes a WordPerfect 5.1 file and translates it to be incorporated into an Agenda database. You can use any word processing package that allows you to save the file in text (ASCII) format.

To create the file in WordPerfect:

1. Enter the WordPerfect program by typing **wp** at the system prompt.

2. Create the file by typing **This is the first paragraph of the text file. It will become the first imported item of the Agenda database.** and pressing (ENTER) twice.

3. Type **This is the second paragraph of the text file. It will become the second imported item of the Agenda database.** and press (ENTER) twice.

4. Type **This is the third paragraph of the text file. It will become the third imported item of the Agenda database.** and press (ENTER) twice.

If you are using a word processing package other than WordPerfect, skip steps 5 through 7, and take the appropriate steps to save the document as a text file with the name \AGENDA\APPS\WORD.TXT, and then exit the word processing program.

5. Save this as a text file by pressing (CTRL-F5) (Text In/Out). Type **t** for DOS Text and **s** for Save.

6. Type the file name **\agenda\apps\word.txt** and press (ENTER). (If your Agenda files are stored in another directory, use its path name instead.)

7. Exit WordPerfect by pressing (F7) (Exit), typing **n** to not save the document, and **y** to exit WordPerfect. You are now at the system prompt.

You have now created a text file consisting of three paragraphs, and you are ready to use the TXT2STF file to translate the text file into an STF file.

8. Move to the Agenda directory by typing **cd\agenda** and pressing (ENTER).

9. Type **txt2stf \agenda\apps\word.txt** and press (ENTER). Agenda translates the WORD.TXT file into an STF file named WORD.STF. You are returned to the DOS directory prompt when the process is complete.

10. Enter Agenda by typing **agenda** and pressing (ENTER).

11. Type **test1** as the name of the database and press (ENTER).

12. Press (F10) (Menu) and select File Transfer Import. The File Import dialog box appears on the screen.

13. Type **\agenda\apps\word** as the name of the import file and press (ENTER).

14. Press (DOWN ARROW) eight times to highlight the Strip Carriage Returns setting, and type **y** to strip the carriage returns from each item. (Standard text files will often add carriage returns at the end of each line.)

15. Press (ENTER) to activate the import and return to the view. The three items are added to the database.

You can use TXT2STF whenever you need to translate a text file into an STF file. Although you used the default settings in this example, TXT2STF can be used to translate almost any kind of text file using a definition file that tells it how to translate the files. This feature is beyond the scope of this book.

IMPORTING DATA THROUGH TEXT NOTES

You can also import data into an Agenda database as a note of an item. For example, you may want to add a Lotus 1-2-3 worksheet to one of your items as a note, or you may want to split a word processed file into a few items with sizable notes. This process may be simpler than converting the data into an STF file using TXT2STF. The note import option maintains the same format as the text before it was imported.

For this example, you will use the same text file that you created for the previous TXT2STF example. To avoid the confusion of having the same items entered twice into the same database, you will instead import this file into the TEST2 database. To import data through a text note, follow these steps:

1. While in your word processor, save the file that you are importing as text only.

   Some programs include special characters for formatting. If your word processor does not have a special option for creating a text file, print it to a file. If you want to create a text file from 1-2-3, print the section of your worksheet you wish to use as a note to a file. Set the right margin to 240, the left margin to 0, and the top and bottom margins to 0, and select Options Other Unformatted from the Print menu to create a text file without page breaks, headers, or footers.

2. Load Agenda by typing **agenda** at the system prompt and typing **test2** as the database to which you wish to add the text. Press (ENTER).

3. Create an item by typing **This is an example of an Agenda item** and pressing (ENTER). Activate the note for the item by pressing (F5) (Note).

4. Press (F10) (Menu) and select Import.
   A dialog box appears for you to enter the name of the text file to import, as shown in Figure 11-10.

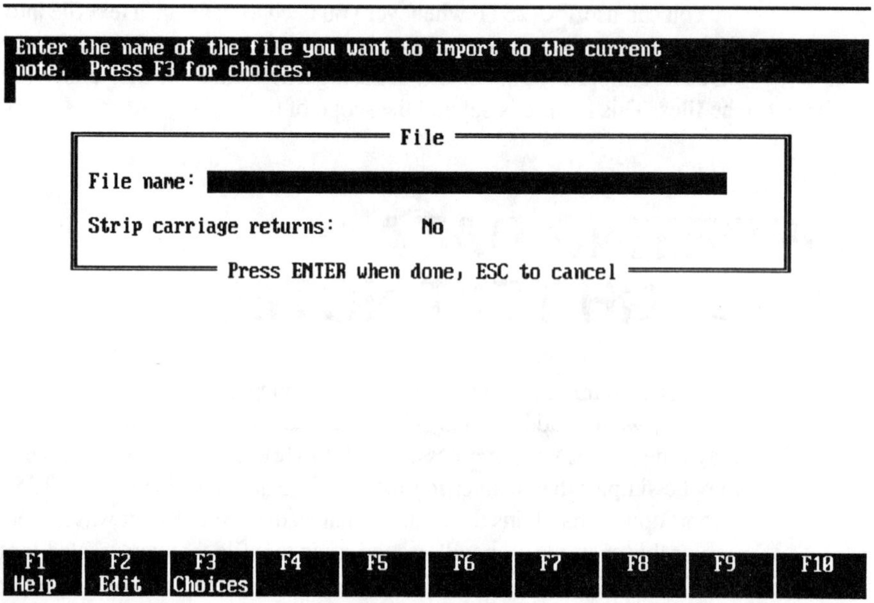

```
Enter the name of the file you want to import to the current
note,  Press F3 for choices,


                          ═══ File ═══
        ┌─────────────────────────────────────────────┐
        │ File name: ███████████████████████████████   │
        │                                              │
        │ Strip carriage returns:        No            │
        │        ═══ Press ENTER when done, ESC to cancel ═══
        └─────────────────────────────────────────────┘




  F1   │  F2  │  F3    │  F4  │  F5  │  F6  │  F7  │  F8  │  F9  │  F10
  Help │ Edit │Choices │      │      │      │      │      │      │
```

FIGURE 11-10. Importing a text file into a note

5. Type the name of your text file as **\agenda\apps\word.txt**, not word.stf, since you are working with a normal text file and not an Agenda STF file. Press (ENTER) twice.

6. If all you want is to import the text file into a note, you are done. However, for this example you will make the first paragraph into an item. Press (CTRL-HOME) to quickly move to the beginning of the note.

7. Press (F7) (Mark) and press (DOWN ARROW) twice to highlight the two lines of the note.

8. Press (ALT-F7) (MakeItm) to make the marked text into an item.

9. Press (F5) (Return) to return to the view. The first paragraph of the note is now displayed as an item in the view.

USING THE METRO ACCESSORIES

The Metro accessories provided with Agenda facilitate the transfer of information from other programs into Agenda items and notes. If you have not already installed Metro onto your computer, follow these steps now:

1. Insert the Agenda Installation disk into drive A.

2. Type **a:** and press (ENTER) to make drive A the current drive.
   Determine where you want the Metro program to be installed. For this example, assume the Metro program is to be stored on the C drive. If your system is different, substitute your drive letter for the C drive.

3. Type **minstall c:** and press (ENTER). This starts the installation process.

4. When prompted, replace the Installation disk with the prompted disk and press (ENTER). When finished, installation is complete.

Metro must be loaded into memory before your other programs if you wish to access Metro while using another program.

```
Items v1.00                        10-23-90 * 2:13a
Note File:                                  Item: 1
─────────────────────────────────────────────────
Unauthorized statements to the press are expressly
forbidden.  Authorizations for any and all
statements are to be processed through the public
relations department.
```

FIGURE 11-11.   The Items Accessory screen

Using the Items Accessory

The Items Accessory provides a convenient way to record new Agenda items while working in other programs. You can enter up to ten items in the Items Accessory before converting the items to a structured file and importing it into your Agenda file.

To see how this works, perform the following:

1. Type **metro** at the system prompt to activate the Metro program.

    For this example, you will work from the system prompt, although you could also load another program (such as WordPerfect, Lotus, or even Agenda) for the following example to work.

2. Press (**ALT-SHIFT-I**) to activate the Items Accessory box, shown in Figure 11-11.

3. Type the following for the first item: **Unauthorized statements to the press are expressly forbidden. Authorizations for any and all statements are to be processed through the public relations department.**

4. Press (**PGDN**) to move to item two. Type **Seven paid holidays are scheduled throughout the year.** You have now created two items in the Items Accessory box. (You can create up to ten.)

5. To transfer all of the items in the Items Accessory to an STF file, press (**F10**) (Menu) and select Transfer All.

6. Type **\agenda\apps\items** and press (**ENTER**). The program automatically attaches the STF extension for you.

7. Exit the program by pressing (**F10**) (Menu) and selecting Quit.

At this point you could enter a program and then type (ALT-SHIFT-I) to reenter the Items Accessory program again.

8. To incorporate the items from the Items Accessory, enter Agenda by typing **agenda** at the system prompt and pressing (ENTER).

9. Type **test2** as the name of the database and press (ENTER).

10. To import the STF file, press (F10) (Menu) and select File Transfer Import.

11. Type the name of the transfer file as **\agenda\apps\items** and press (ENTER).

12. Press (ENTER) again to activate the import. The two items are now listed as part of the TEST2 database.

If you find that you use the Items Accessory frequently, it is a good idea to define ITEMS.STF as your auto-import file in File Properties. Also, when you are ready to transfer your items in the Items Accessory to an STF file you can press (ALT-T) followed by (ENTER) to transfer items and then delete them from the Items Accessory.

Using the Clipboard Accessory

The Clipboard allows you to copy information between Metro accessories and other programs. It can be used to copy a screen, a block of text, or a rectangular area of text from another program, but it holds only one set of data at a time. You cannot edit on

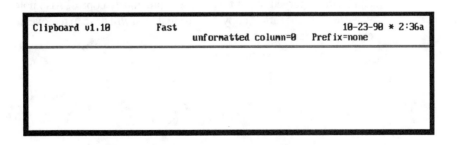

FIGURE 11-12.   The Clipboard Accessory screen

the Clipboard, and as soon as you use it to copy something else, the current contents are erased.

The Clipboard is a very versatile and useful accessory for transferring data from a word processor or a spreadsheet to an Agenda note. Its format settings provide the options you need to transfer any type of text or numeric data. You can activate the Clipboard by pressing (ALT-SHIFT-D) to produce the display shown in Figure 11-12.

The general instructions for using the Clipboard to transfer text to an Agenda note are as follows:

1. Activate the program from which the data is being transferred.

2. Move to the section of the text that you want to transfer, making sure you can see it on your screen.

3. Press (SHIFT-ALT-D) to activate the Clipboard.

4. Press (F10) (Menu) and select Copy Text. The cursor will start blinking in the upper-left corner of the screen. Use the (ARROW) keys to move the cursor to the point where you want to start copying.

5. Press (F7) to anchor the cursor to the point where you want to start copying and press the (ARROW) keys until all the text that you want to copy is highlighted.

6. Press (ENTER) to return to the Clipboard. The highlighted text is now on the Clipboard.

7. Leave the Clipboard by pressing (F10) (Menu) and selecting Quit.

8. Leave the program you are currently in.

9. Enter Agenda and activate the note that you want to put the text in.

10. Press (ALT-SHIFT-ENTER) to incorporate the Clipboard text into your note.

11. Press (F5) (Return) to return to the Agenda view. Each time you copy text, the Clipboard is purged of the text that was previously copied. Also note that when you use the Clipboard to copy Agenda text, you will have to remove item tags and extra spaces later.

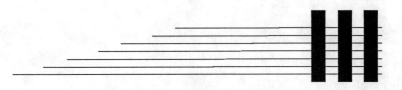

APPLICATIONS

12

BUSINESS AND FINANCIAL APPLICATIONS

Company Policy
Personnel Skills
Personnel Evaluations
Project Management
Sales
Electronic Mail
Lease Data
Real Estate Listings
Insurance Policies
Stock Portfolio Information

Since Agenda works with any type of text data, its applications in business are virtually unlimited. Agenda can manage a small base of information entered by a manager or professional, help organize large text bases entered with an optical scanning device, or import information from an electronic mail file or information service. It is also useful for extending the capabilities of some of the structured database systems that currently support company needs in areas like personnel management and company policy.

Agenda can be used to record financial data when the information to be stored is character based and does not seem to fit within the traditional database environment of predefined fields of a fixed length. With Agenda, the application of the data in your financial information system can evolve as your base of information grows larger.

This chapter introduces several general business applications in which Agenda is used productively. The general business areas examined are

- Company policy

- Personnel skills

- Personnel evaluations

- Project management

- Sales

- Electronic mail

The financial applications presented in this chapter are

- Lease data for a large real estate development firm

- Real estate property listings

- Insurance policy coverages

- Stock portfolio information

The presentations are not designed to provide a comprehensive look at the application, but they should make you think creatively about how Agenda can be employed productively in a variety of application areas.

COMPANY POLICY

You can use Agenda to create and maintain a company policy manual. Agenda's category features allow you to create a section within a view to look at the manual from any perspective desired. Agenda also provides a way to organize the information by subject matter and makes it easy for an item to appear in more than one section of the manual. The appearance of an item in multiple locations does not actually duplicate the item, since Agenda maintains only one copy of it and its associated note. Items can be assigned to many categories in the hierarchy and displayed when the category is shown in the current view. This means that updates made at one location are reflected everywhere the item appears. You never have to worry about whether you have updated the item information in multiple sections or views. This provides a significant advantage over manual methods of storing information.

Creating the Database

The initial hierarchy for the policy file example was created before any items were added to the file, since it was clear from the beginning what the different sections of the policy file should be. Figure 12-1 shows a section from this hierarchy that organizes policy topics by subject matter. If new categories are needed later, the expansion process is easy because new category entries can be added at any level in the hierarchy. In fact, as the file grows, additional subcategories are desirable to keep each section in a view display to a manageable size. The Hide Inherited Items setting

```
File: C:\AGENDA\APPS\POLICY3
Category Manager
  POLICY DATA
    Company policy
      Employer expenses paid by employee
      Publicity
        Statements to the press
        Written statements
      Reimbursements for educational expenses
        Company sponsored seminars
        Non-company sponsored seminars
        College courses
          Non-job related
            Degree
            Non-degree
          Job related
    Software
      Unauthorized copying
      Unauthorized use
    Travel
      Company car
      Lodging
      Meals
```

F1	F2	F3	F4	F5	F6	F7	F8	F9	F10
Help	Edit			Note	Props	Prm (←)	Dem (→)	To View	Menu

FIGURE 12-1.   A portion of the hierarchy from the policy file

in the View Properties box was set to Yes to keep the list from growing after subcategories are added.

Entries can be made into the appropriate section of the manual or added to the Initial Section and assigned to other categories either explicitly or implicitly. Text conditions are normally quite effective in assigning the item entries for policies into the multiple categories where a reference to a policy item may be appropriate. You can also use conditions and actions to push and pull items into categories based on their other assignments. For example, items assigned to a category for Company Car Expenses might also be assigned to a category for Travel Expenses—Transportation, with a condition on the latter category that would assign all items to it if they were already assigned to the Company Car Expenses category.

The details for any specific policy can be maintained with notes attached to each item, as shown in Figure 12-2. You can also attach a note to a category, as in a note attached to the Publicity category (and section head) stating the last revision date of Publicity Policy. This can be useful for general notes pertaining to section heads in a view. One drawback is that you cannot search on text in category notes. This allows an individual to browse through the information at any level. The category hierarchy can be used to browse through the major topical areas covered by the manual. The View mode can be used to browse through all the items of interest in any section of

```
Note for:   Credit Courses - Tuition Reimbursement      Line    1 INS EDIT
                          Font: Courier 12.0pt  Attr: Normal
To be reimbursed for courses taken, an employee must meet the following
qualifications:
1.   The course must be a college level course with an accredited institution.
2.   The employee must inform his/her supervisor before he/she enrolls in the
course.
3.   The employee must receive at least a "C" or better.
4.   The course must pertain to his/her profession.  The exception will be for
courses taken to fulfill the degree rquirements for a degree that pertains to
his/her profession.
5.   The annual limit an employee may receive for tuition reimbursement is
$2500.
6.   The employee will be reimbursed at the end of the term after reporting
his/her grade, for proof of requirement 3, to human resources.  The
reimbursement will be included in his/her next paycheck.
7.   Course work must not interfere with on-the-job performance.
8.   If the employee withdraws from the course, reimbursement will be denied.
9.   If the employee receives an incomplete, he/she will not be reimbursed
until the grade is finalized and the employee meets the other requirements.
10.  If the employee quits or is terminated, he/she will not be reimbursed.
```

```
F1      F2      F3      F4      F5      F6      F7      F8      F9      F10
Help    Paste   Copy    Cut     Return  Marker  Mark                    Menu
```

FIGURE 12-2.   Note containing information on a specific policy

the manual. As items of interest are identified within a section, press (F5) (Note) to bring the note text to the screen.

The note text for each item can be entered and maintained within Agenda. Note text can also be created with a word processing program as long as an ASCII data storage format is used. Some word processors support this format directly with a menu selection when the file is first created. With other word processors, you need to create a regular document file and convert it to ASCII format after it is complete. The ASCII note text can be imported into Agenda as described in Chapter 11, or it can continue to be maintained in the disk file.

Maintaining
The Policy Manual

The policy file can be maintained with a variety of Agenda's features. For example, you can use the entry date to track the date that the item was last updated if you allow the entry date to be updated when an item is modified (Category Properties for the Entry category). If policies are scheduled to be updated by a specific date, you can use the when date to track the deadline for completing the update or create your own deadline date category. You can add a column to show the individual responsible for the update process. You can show policy items that are not yet complete by adding a column with a date category that shows when a write-up of the newly established policy will be available. If members of the management team get copies of all newly written policies, you can establish a date condition to place new items in this category and produce copies with Agenda's print features.

Company policies that are no longer in effect can be retained for a specific period of time. This would allow you to check an expense report against the policy statements that controlled the reimbursements of expenses during a certain period of time.

PERSONNEL SKILLS

Traditional information management systems in the personnel area allow you to enter only well-defined fields of information. Some of these systems do not allow the flexibility needed to create a system with all the desired features when attempting to build a skills database.

To perform effectively as a skills database, the information base must be able to maintain a set of the skills possessed by each employee. The skills base must be extensive enough to meet present and future needs. It must be easy to update and yet allow you to enter descriptive information or job experiences that can clarify the skill level an employee possesses in each area. Although you must be able to enter and review the skills for an individual employee, you must also be able to search for employees with a composite set of needed skills. Agenda is especially suited to this application because it supports varying levels of detail and an extremely flexible structure and still allows you to focus on only the skill areas that are of interest at a particular time.

Creating the Database

The skills database consists of employee names as item entries and a category hierarchy that reflects all the skills that can be tracked for an employee. Although it is easy to expand this skill hierarchy over time, it makes sense to begin by entering all the skill categories you are aware of at the beginning. Figure 12-3 shows a section of one hierarchy.

You will find a number of categories with mutually exclusive children such as high, medium, and low. These prevent an individual from being assigned to more than one

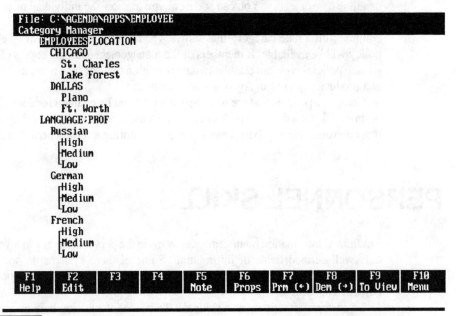

```
File: C:\AGENDA\APPS\EMPLOYEE
Category Manager
    EMPLOYEES:LOCATION
      CHICAGO
        St. Charles
        Lake Forest
      DALLAS
        Plano
        Ft. Worth
    LANGUAGE:PROF
      Russian
        ┌High
        ├Medium
        └Low
      German
        ┌High
        ├Medium
        └Low
      French
        ┌High
        ├Medium
        └Low
```

F1	F2	F3	F4	F5	F6	F7	F8	F9	F10
Help	Edit			Note	Props	Prm (←)	Dem (→)	To View	Menu

FIGURE 12-3.   A portion of the hierarchy from a personnel skills database

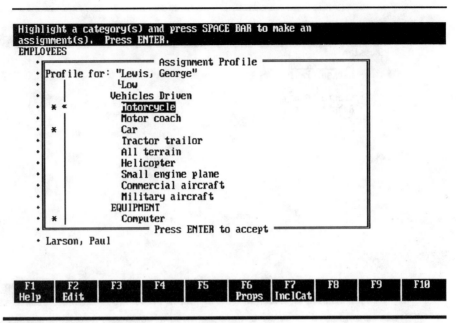

```
Highlight a category(s) and press SPACE BAR to make an
assignment(s).  Press ENTER.
EMPLOYEES
  •┌──────────────── Assignment Profile ──────────────┐
  •│Profile for: "Lewis, George"                       │
  •│              └Low                                 │
  •│       │      Vehicles Driven                      │
  •│  * «      Motorcycle                              │
  •│           Motor coach                             │
  •│  *        Car                                     │
  •│           Tractor trailer                         │
  •│           All terrain                             │
  •│           Helicopter                              │
  •│           Small engine plane                      │
  •│           Commercial aircraft                     │
  •│           Military aircraft                       │
  •│       EQUIPMENT                                   │
  •│  *    │   Computer                                │
  •└──────────────── Press ENTER to accept ───────────┘
 • Larson, Paul
```

F1	F2	F3	F4	F5	F6	F7	F8	F9	F10
Help	Edit				Props	InclCat			

FIGURE 12-4.   Adding skill indicators for an employee through the Assignment Profile

entry within a parent category. Mutually exclusive category entries for proficiency in an area are especially appropriate since they prevent an individual from being categorized as both having basic skills and being highly proficient; for example, they prevent an individual from being assigned both a high and low proficiency in German. The mutual exclusion property ensures that only one proficiency level is assigned. On the other hand, mutual exclusion is not appropriate at all levels in the hierarchy since it would be incorrect to block an individual's assignment to more than one language, for example.

Because each employee is entered as an item, the easiest way to add the skills profile to the database is through the Item Profile feature. After the employee name is entered, you can press (F3) (Choices) to bring up an Assignment Profile display like the one in Figure 12-4. You can use the (SPACEBAR) to mark items that you wish to assign to a specific category. You can mark as many categories as you need to represent the employee's skill set, as long as you do not mark more than one entry in a set of mutually exclusive entries. With one pass through the file hierarchy you can assign all the categories for an individual. You can also create new categories as you think of them while in Assignment Profile mode. All you need to do is press (INS), type a new category, press (ENTER), and then press the (SPACEBAR) to make the assignment.

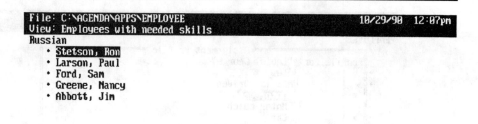

FIGURE 12-5.   Employees with proficiency in Russian

Selecting Employees
With a Specific Skill

Locating employees assigned to a specific skill is easy. You simply create a view with the name of the skill you are looking for as a section. It is easy to conduct a search for one skill level after another using this approach. The view in Figure 12-5 shows the employees that are categorized as knowledgeable in Russian. A quick change of category from Russian to computer skills in the section head produces a new list of employees, as shown in Figure 12-6. As an alternative, you can create a view filter to produce the skills you are looking for. You may want to hide empty sections (View Properties) if you use the view filter method.

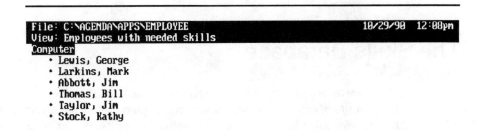

```
File: C:\AGENDA\APPS\EMPLOYEE                    10/29/90  12:00pm
View: Employees with needed skills
Computer
   • Lewis, George
   • Larkins, Mark
   • Abbott, Jim
   • Thomas, Bill
   • Taylor, Jim
   • Stock, Kathy
```

```
  F1      F2      F3      F4      F5      F6      F7      F8      F9     F10
 Help    Edit  Choices  Done    Note   Props   Mark   Vu Mgr Cat Mgr  Menu
```

FIGURE 12-6. Employees with computer skills

Finding a Particular Skill Set

To find employees with a composite set of skills, you can create a condition that places items with a specific profile into a category. The condition profile contains all the skills you are looking for. If you select multiple skills from a mutually exclusive category, the various categories are treated as if they are joined by an implied OR rather than AND, since an item cannot be assigned to more than one of the categories. For example, you might create a category called Positionx and specify German, Fortran, or Sword Swallowing in the assignment conditions of Positionx's Category Properties box.

Using Notes in
The Skills Database

There are two primary applications for notes in the skills database. Notes can be added to categories to describe the proficiency level required before a category is checked for an individual. A low proficiency level in Russian, for example, may be earned with 1 1/2 years of college-level Russian or a score of 500 or better on the AFLTA test for Russian proficiency. The level of proficiency and any self-study books that can help an individual reach this proficiency level are stored in the note attached to each skill category.

Notes can also be attached to items to describe an individual's unique set of skills. Although an Assignment Profile for an individual who is proficient in several languages provides meaningful information, recording in a note that the individual was of German heritage and had lived in Europe until the age of 18 would provide additional information not available through any category.

PERSONNEL
EVALUATIONS

Performance evaluation data is normally stored only in paper form since most personnel systems do not provide for storage of this free-form information. The data is normally typed on a word processor and then printed. Once printed, the electronic version is often discarded after a short time.

With Agenda you can retain the electronic version of the evaluation as a note for the database. This makes it available whenever you need to review it. Before the next evaluation you could review the previous evaluation to determine, for example, what objectives were discussed.

Creating the Database

Since evaluations are conducted periodically and an item can contain only one note, it is best to store each employee as a category. Figure 12-7 shows a list of the various evaluations for several employees. You can always use a date filter if the list becomes lengthy. You can create an item for the evaluation and store the evaluation itself in an

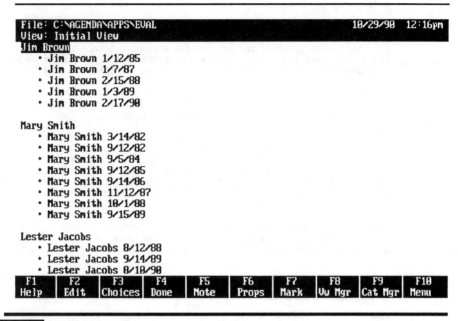

```
File: C:\AGENDA\APPS\EVAL                          10/29/90  12:16pm
View: Initial View
Jim Brown
    • Jim Brown 1/12/85
    • Jim Brown 1/7/87
    • Jim Brown 2/15/88
    • Jim Brown 1/3/89
    • Jim Brown 2/17/90

Mary Smith
    • Mary Smith 3/14/82
    • Mary Smith 9/12/82
    • Mary Smith 9/5/84
    • Mary Smith 9/12/85
    • Mary Smith 9/14/86
    • Mary Smith 11/12/87
    • Mary Smith 10/1/88
    • Mary Smith 9/15/89

Lester Jacobs
    • Lester Jacobs 8/12/88
    • Lester Jacobs 9/14/89
    • Lester Jacobs 8/10/90

  F1    F2     F3     F4    F5     F6    F7    F8    F9     F10
 Help  Edit  Choices Done  Note  Props Mark Vw Mgr Cat Mgr Menu
```

FIGURE 12-7.   Item entries showing evaluations for several employees

external note file. A portion of one of these evaluation files is shown in Figure 12-8. The fact that the evaluation is stored on disk does not affect your ability to review the evaluation comments.

If you prefer, the evaluation can be entered directly as a note for the item without using an external file. Agenda's print-customization features support this approach and still allow you to print the evaluation in a professional-looking format.

Using Dates

You can produce a list of employees who are due for evaluation if you assign a when date for the next evaluation at the time of the current evaluation. You can use a date filter to display only the entries having a when date within a specific time frame, such as the next two months. The items that appear list the names of the employees, and if the entry date is displayed you can also tell the exact date of the last performance evaluation. Since the evaluations themselves are in the attached notes, you can view

```
Note for:  Mary Smith 9/15/89                      Line   1 INS EDIT
Note file:  C:\....\MS091589      Font: Courier 12.0pt  Attr: Normal
     Mary Smith has held her current position as a team leader for the last
two years.  Over this time period the responsibilities of her group have grown
to departments for which her group has provided computer support.

     Mary's supervisory skills have continued to improve.  Her advice is
continually sought by members of her group as well as other team leaders
dealing with difficult customer or personnel problems.

     Mary's public speaking abilities have grown considerably over the last
year as she has made a concentrated effort to improve in this area since her
last review.  Although she does an excellent job when she has time to prepare
for these presentations, she is not inclined to offer her comments and ideas
at management meetings.  Mary should continue to try to overcome the shyness
she feels when speaking before a group.  Although her other skills would
qualify her for promotion to the position of manager, it is unlikely that she
will attain this promotion until she is more comfortable making a contribution
in general management meetings.  Mary should consider outside opportunities to
better her skills in this area and may want to join the Toast Master's Club or
some other social or volunteer group that will foster these opportunities.
```

F1	F2	F3	F4	F5	F6	F7	F8	F9	F10
Help	Paste	Copy	Cut	Return	Marker	Mark			Menu

FIGURE 12-8.   A section of an evaluation stored in an external file

the pertinent evaluations as you are preparing the evaluations for the individuals in this group. You might open and read the attached notes that are designated with the symbol (♪) and close and edit the current item note designated with a single note symbol. Or you can begin creating the new note within the attached note and cut and paste it into a new item note.

PROJECT MANAGEMENT

If you need a heavy-duty project management package capable of computing critical paths and producing Gantt charts, Agenda is not the solution. On the other hand, if you are looking for something a little less rigorous that can help you monitor various project tasks and track the dates they are scheduled to be completed, Agenda can provide a very flexible and satisfactory solution. Agenda's date categories not only help you track tasks that are due to be completed but also help you maintain historic information on the accomplishments of your department.

Creating the Database

Depending on your needs, Agenda can serve as either a personal to-do list or a vehicle for managing the tasks for several more formalized projects. To use Agenda as your personal to-do list manager, enter each of the items you need to track in a single section of the database. Enter a column to track the date when you need to complete each task. You can enter the date for each item as the item is entered, or you can move to the date column after the initial batch of items is entered.

The date entries for the date column can be either absolute dates like 3/10/89, relative dates like "next Wednesday," or recurring dates like "every Monday." If you use absolute dates, the date you enter is recorded and does not change. Relative dates also do not change and are evaluated at the time of entry. Recurring dates are normally evaluated based on the system date unless you disable the redating of recurring items through the Advanced Settings in the Category Properties box. Figure 12-9 shows an example of a to-do list managed by Agenda in which all three types of date entries were used in the When date column.

You can have Agenda automatically discard items as soon as you mark them done. If you want to retain them in another file, use the Process Done Items setting in the

```
File: C:\AGENDA\APPS\TO_DO                          10/29/90  12:37pm
View: Initial View
Tasks                                                          When
   • Call Bill Jones about contract                           ·03/23/90
   • Review education policy                                  ·03/19/90
   • Register for Business Law course                         ·03/29/90
   • Call Temp-Help about secretarial replacement during Doris'  ·04/16/90
     vacation
   • Review salary schedule                                   ·05/01/91
   • Call LP Magazine about placing a help-wanted ad for the June,  ·03/20/90
     July, and August issues
   • Write memo to sales staff about new promotion on the flexible  ·05/29/90
     widget product
   • Call Sherman & Associated and McGill and Lavers for a quote on  ·10/31/90
     their out placement services
   • Arrange for sales meeting for the end of June - check    ·06/28/91
     Headwell, Fortman, and Lakewood facilities
   • Cancel subscription to Trademark Magazine - two issues late  ·10/31/90
     and one never received in the last four months
   • Luncheon meeting with Dennis Walker at Lakewood          ·08/29/90
   • Meet Bill Scott to discuss expansion project             ·10/15/90
   • Finish RFP for new system untis, disk drives, printers, and  ·11/05/90
     accessories
┌──────┬──────┬───────┬──────┬──────┬──────┬──────┬────────┬───────┬──────┐
│  F1  │  F2  │  F3   │  F4  │  F5  │  F6  │  F7  │   F8   │  F9   │ F10  │
│ Help │ Edit │Choices│ Done │ Note │Props │ Mark │ Vw Mgr │Cat Mgr│ Menu │
└──────┴──────┴───────┴──────┴──────┴──────┴──────┴────────┴───────┴──────┘
```

FIGURE 12-9.   An example of a to-do list managed by Agenda

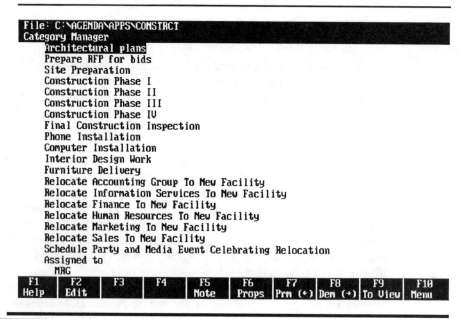

```
File: C:\AGENDA\APPS\CONSTRCT
Category Manager
    Architectural plans
    Prepare RFP for bids
    Site Preparation
    Construction Phase I
    Construction Phase II
    Construction Phase III
    Construction Phase IV
    Final Construction Inspection
    Phone Installation
    Computer Installation
    Interior Design Work
    Furniture Delivery
    Relocate Accounting Group To New Facility
    Relocate Information Services To New Facility
    Relocate Finance To New Facility
    Relocate Human Resources To New Facility
    Relocate Marketing To New Facility
    Relocate Sales To New Facility
    Schedule Party and Media Event Celebrating Relocation
    Assigned to
      MRG
 F1    F2    F3    F4    F5    F6    F7      F8      F9     F10
Help  Edit              Note  Props Prm (←) Dem (→) To View Menu
```

FIGURE 12-10. A category hierarchy for a construction project

Global Date Settings of the File Properties box. Unlike the when date entries, Agenda automatically supplies the current system date as the done date as soon as you mark the item done.

If you want to use Agenda to manage more formalized projects, add entries to the category hierarchy. You might add entries for each separate project and then add children to each project category to help structure the project tasks by major activities. Figure 12-10 shows a category hierarchy used to record some of the tasks connected with a construction project. You can use the promote/demote keys at any point to change the hierarchy.

When Agenda is used to monitor larger projects, the need for additional information increases. If, for example, your company is constructing an addition to its current office building, you may be working with a single contractor or with several subcontractors on different aspects of the project. Even with one contractor, you might have different internal personnel responsible for monitoring progress on the different phases. You might want to add columns to the report to record the internal personnel responsible for a given phase of the project as well as the individual contractors working on the various activities. Figure 12-11 shows the addition of three columns to the initial view that list some of the activities on the construction project. Initials are used for the internal personnel to conserve space in the display. A note attached to each category entry lists the individual's complete name, office extension, home

```
File: C:\AGENDA\APPS\CONSTRCT                      10/29/90  12:56pm
View: Initial View
Architectural plans                  Assigned to  Contractor   When
  ‼ Review potential sites            ·MRG         ·Albright     ·08/15/90
  ‼ Approve site selection            ·ARG         ·Albright     ·08/17/90
  ‼ Schedule meeting with Albright    ·LKT         ·Albright     ·08/20/90
    Inc.
  ‼ Review plans with management staff ·MRG        ·Albright     ·08/21/90
  ‼ Review changes with J. Brown of   ·WRE         ·Albright     ·08/24/90
    Albright, Inc.
  ‼ Review and approve final plans    ·STY         ·Albright     ·08/29/90

Prepare RFP for bids                 Assigned to  Contractor   When
  ‼ Determine optimal job breakout    ·MRG                       ·09/05/90
  ‼ Prepare RFPs                      ·TRW                       ·09/12/90
  ‼ Review bids and select contractor ·WRE                       ·10/01/90

Site Preparation                     Assigned to  Contractor   When
  ‼ Mark trees for removal            ·LKT         ·Quick Strip  ·10/15/90
  • Clear marked trees                ·ARG         ·Quick Strip  ·10/17/90
  • Excavate site                     ·MRG         ·Diggers Inc  ·10/29/90
  • Drive Pilings                     ·LKT         ·Elmo's Crew  ·11/05/90

┌──────┬──────┬───────┬──────┬──────┬──────┬──────┬───────┬───────┬──────┐
│ F1   │ F2   │ F3    │ F4   │ F5   │ F6   │ F7   │ F8    │ F9    │ F10  │
│ Help │ Edit │Choices│ Done │ Note │Props │ Mark │Vw Mgr │Cat Mgr│ Menu │
└──────┴──────┴───────┴──────┴──────┴──────┴──────┴───────┴───────┴──────┘
```

FIGURE 12-11.   Columns added to view to show additional category assignments

phone number, and address in case it is necessary to contact that person during the weekend. The note symbol does not precede these categories but does display in the control panel when one of these categories is highlighted.

Notes are also attached to the contractor categories listing the contractor's address and phone number. A contact person is listed, as well as workers who are authorized to be on the site, as shown in Figure 12-12. This listing is useful in the event of difficulties as well as for security purposes.

Using Date Filters

Agenda's filter features can be used with entry, done, and when dates. The when date is especially useful for an application like the one described here since you can focus on activities scheduled to be finished within a specific time frame. You can specify a range of dates and ask to see dated items that match that set of dates. If you select a range of dates that begins with the current date and ends two weeks from today, the current view shows only the items scheduled to be completed within the next two weeks.

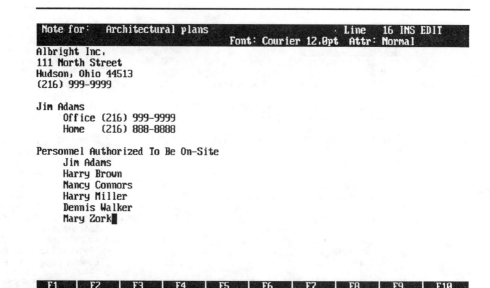

```
Note for:    Architectural plans                  . Line    16 INS EDIT
                             Font: Courier 12.0pt  Attr: Normal
Albright Inc.
111 North Street
Hudson, Ohio 44513
(216) 999-9999

Jim Adams
      Office (216) 999-9999
      Home   (216) 888-8888

Personnel Authorized To Be On-Site
      Jim Adams
      Harry Brown
      Nancy Connors
      Harry Miller
      Dennis Walker
      Mary Zork█
```

F1	F2	F3	F4	F5	F6	F7	F8	F9	F10
Help	Paste	Copy	Cut	Return	Marker	Mark			Menu

FIGURE 12-12.   Note for a category showing personnel for the project phase

Using Date Conditions

Date conditions allow you to assign items to categories based on their dates. This feature has a number of potential uses since you can assign items to a category based on a date range. If you want to look at the new tasks added to your Agenda file, you can establish a category for new entries and apply a condition to this category that assigns to it items with an entry date range of the last week. If you choose to have newly added items displayed, Agenda displays only the items that are inside the range.

You can also use the date condition feature to select items with dates outside a specific range. If a project is scheduled to begin on May 1, 1991, and end on August 4, 1991, creating a category to look at tasks that were misdated can help you correct errors easily. You can add a condition to this category that places items in the category that were assigned to the project but are outside the range for the project. This requires that both an assignment condition and a date condition be attached to the category.

Using Notes Creatively

Since each phase of a large project normally requires an approval and sign-off procedure, you can use item notes to record information from an inspection of the site. Information can be added to the notes, and the notes can be turned into a written report or memo. Agenda's ability to create an item from note text also allows you to record deficiencies and tasks needing additional items and turn them into items with the proper function key (MakeItem).

SALES

Effective sales personnel must have at their disposal a variety of information about client base, product line, and competition. Most traditional databases can only store information like product numbers and prices. Agenda can also store information like product descriptions, client needs and problems, and competitive strategies—information that is just as important but does not follow a predefined structure.

Creating the Sales Database

The text-processing features of Agenda are especially important for an application like sales since items can be entered at any time and organized through the text conditions of the package. Figure 12-13 shows some item entries that have no relationship to each other. Creating a view and defining as sections the categories you are interested in will allow you to focus on the items of interest for a particular sales proposal or product. You would need to assign items from Figure 12-13 to the new sections where they are not conditionally assigned using (ALT-U) or Assignment Profile.

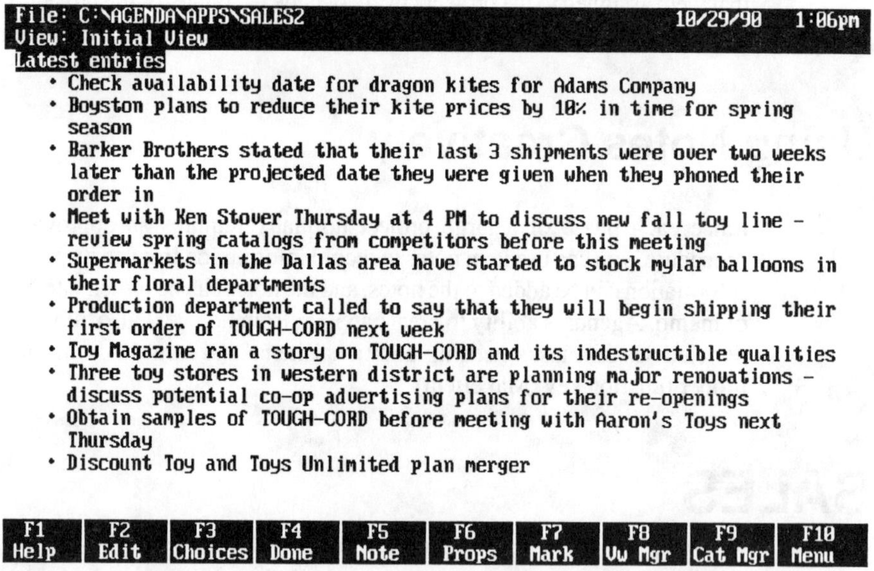

```
File: C:\AGENDA\APPS\SALES2                          10/29/90   1:06pm
View: Initial View
Latest entries
        • Check availability date for dragon kites for Adams Company
        • Boyston plans to reduce their kite prices by 10% in time for spring
          season
        • Barker Brothers stated that their last 3 shipments were over two weeks
          later than the projected date they were given when they phoned their
          order in
        • Meet with Ken Stover Thursday at 4 PM to discuss new fall toy line -
          review spring catalogs from competitors before this meeting
        • Supermarkets in the Dallas area have started to stock mylar balloons in
          their floral departments
        • Production department called to say that they will begin shipping their
          first order of TOUGH-CORD next week
        • Toy Magazine ran a story on TOUGH-CORD and its indestructible qualities
        • Three toy stores in western district are planning major renovations -
          discuss potential co-op advertising plans for their re-openings
        • Obtain samples of TOUGH-CORD before meeting with Aaron's Toys next
          Thursday
        • Discount Toy and Toys Unlimited plan merger




┌─────┬──────┬────────┬─────┬──────┬──────┬──────┬──────┬───────┬──────┐
│ F1  │ F2   │ F3     │ F4  │ F5   │ F6   │ F7   │ F8   │ F9    │ F10  │
│Help │ Edit │Choices │Done │Note  │Props │Mark  │Vw Mgr│Cat Mgr│Menu  │
└─────┴──────┴────────┴─────┴──────┴──────┴──────┴──────┴───────┴──────┘
```

FIGURE 12-13.   Screen showing random entries made by a salesperson

Making Follow-Up Calls

A salesperson makes hundreds of sales calls in a short period of time. It is difficult to remember information about previous calls unless this information is recorded. You can use Agenda to write up the information from each sales call and attach them as notes to sales call items. The notes could then be reviewed before subsequent sales calls to the same company. The notes from sales calls can also be used for other purposes. Often a salesperson obtains feedback on the quality of the company's products, competitors' products, a customer need that is not currently being met, and many other types of information. If both notes and item data are used when processing text conditions, the note data is assigned to the various categories representing all the topics discussed. It is possible to create separate items from some of this data, if certain topics require additional follow-up before the next sales call, by using MakeItem or cutting and pasting text into a different note or item.

ELECTRONIC MAIL

Information from an electronic mail system can be imported into Agenda after it is converted into a structured file or into a note if it is converted to ASCII. You use the TXT2STF program to convert the text data into a structured format. For text files that you routinely import, you can create a definition file to convert your text file into a customized structured file. Using the features of definition files, you need to define the exact structure of the electronic mail or voice message file, which is beyond the scope of this book. When you invoke TXT2STF with a definition file, the definition file definition can direct the TXT2STF program to find these patterns of characters and turn the information that follows them into items, notes, or categories.

Creating the Database

When you have figured out the pattern for your electronic mail data, the conversion and import process is easy. Your next major decision is the hierarchy you want to use to organize this information. One possibility is to have the definition file you create treat TO: and FROM: entries as categories. SUBJECT: might also be used as a category or an item. If SUBJECT: is treated as a category, you should use the text of the message as an item and associated note. If the subject of the message is entered as an item, the text can be entered as a note. The date of the message can be used as its entry date.

The hierarchy for the file depends on how many types of entries from the message are treated as categories. You might want to take all the messages addressed to all personnel and group them in one category. Items addressed directly to you may be categorized into more specific topics. You may want to discard all the entries that have a FROM: entry from anyone but your boss. The remaining category entries can be used to categorize the subject matter for the messages.

You can use special actions to discard items that are assigned to a category in which you have no interest. If the item is assigned to a specific category, it can be discarded from the database immediately, allowing you, for example, to discard notices relative to the Dallas location when you are working in Chicago.

Using Date Features
To Monitor Entries and
Purge Done Entries

If you go away for several days, a large number of electronic messages may be waiting for you when you return. You can use the entry date to screen items that are available for your review. You can look at the new items day by day by setting up a date condition to categorize everything received yesterday in a section named Yesterday, with appropriate names for the other date groups. Another option is to set up a condition to select all the new items in one category by using a date range for the conditions and electing to use only those items with an entry date inside the specified range.

LEASE DATA

Although the typical property lease has data elements like square footage, cost, term, and beginning date that are all fixed, commercial leases frequently contain a number of contract terms, improvement agreements, and other descriptive data that do not fit into the fields provided by a database package. Many firms store the variable portions of their leases in word processing files that permit free-form text entries of lease terms and any other information.

Although this solves one problem, it causes another. There is no index to the information included in a lease, and although you might recollect a lease with similar conditions to the one you are currently negotiating, it can be difficult to identify the correct lease to review when there are hundreds of possibilities. If you are offering a client multiple leases, it is advisable to review the terms of their existing leases before proposing new lease agreements.

Agenda can be a vehicle for storing all the text information connected with the lease. Even if the data is entered into a word processing program initially, it can be imported into Agenda and stored as a note, or the note can continue to be stored in a separate file. The item within Agenda can be the lease number or can include other information such as the tenant name and contact person.

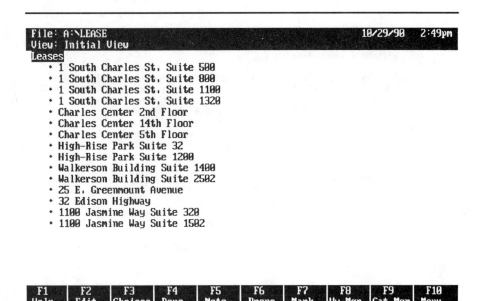

```
File: A:\LEASE                                    10/29/90   2:49pm
View: Initial View
Leases
   • 1 South Charles St. Suite 500
   • 1 South Charles St. Suite 800
   • 1 South Charles St. Suite 1100
   • 1 South Charles St. Suite 1320
   • Charles Center 2nd Floor
   • Charles Center 14th Floor
   • Charles Center 5th Floor
   • High-Rise Park Suite 32
   • High-Rise Park Suite 1200
   • Walkerson Building Suite 1400
   • Walkerson Building Suite 2502
   • 25 E. Greenmount Avenue
   • 32 Edison Highway
   • 1100 Jasmine Way Suite 320
   • 1100 Jasmine Way Suite 1502
```

F1	F2	F3	F4	F5	F6	F7	F8	F9	F10
Help	Edit	Choices	Done	Note	Props	Mark	Vw Mgr	Cat Mgr	Menu

FIGURE 12-14.   Lease entries

Entering Basic Data

Figure 12-14 shows a screen of item entries, each of which represents a lease. You can place specifics on the lease agreement and the contact person at the company leasing the property in a note for each property. The note can contain a complete copy of the lease agreement or only the amendments made to the standard lease contract. You can list specifics on leasehold improvements, the term of the lease, and any other exception conditions, as shown in Figure 12-15.

If the hierarchy for the lease file contains an entry for each of the properties managed by the real estate development firm, the Category Note feature will be useful. You can attach a note to each of these categories with specific information about any planned renovations, new tenants, promotional events, and other information that

```
Note for:   1 South Charles St. Suite 500              Line 10 INS
                                  Font: Courier 12.0pt  Attr: Normal
Leasehold Improvements

    Up to $10,000 of tenant designated improvements will be made to this
property under the terms of the three year lease. If notice is given to extend
the lease for an additional three years at the end of the first year, an
additional $10,000 of tenant designated improvements will be made.

    Changes requested cannot affect the structure of the facility and are
restricted to changes in the partitions between the rooms, wiring changes,
cosmetic changes, raised flooring, lighting, or coaxial cable.█
```

F1	F2	F3	F4	F5	F6	F7	F8	F9	F10
Help	Paste	Copy	Cut	Return	Marker	Mark			Menu

FIGURE 12-15.   Note with leasehold improvements

specifically relates to the property. Figure 12-16 is an example of such a note, where Charles Center is a category in a family of real estate development categories.

You can store the traditional smaller fields of information as part of the note, as part of the 350 characters of allowable item text, or perhaps more appropriately as entries in categories that are restricted to a limited number of entries. For example, if it is the rule rather than the exception to lease several properties to one client, you might want to establish a category for client entries. You can add a column to the view to track the tenant for the lease. After you enter the contact person, tenant address, and tenant phone number once as a note for the category, you can access the information for any lease with this client. Using a category to track the tenant also makes it easy to look at all the leases with one tenant and to ensure that terms are consistent among the leases. This information can also be stored in a note for an item and still be indexed as a category by including both item and note text for automatic assignment using text conditions.

```
Note for:   Charles Center                           Line 14 INS
                                Font: Courier 12.0pt  Attr: Normal
```
Major construction is planned for the general vicinity of the Charles Center
Building during the period from August 15, 1991 to December 1, 1991.
Arrangements have been made to increase the amount of on-street parking for
patrons of the building by limiting parking to 2 hours on the four streets
adjacent to the building. In addition a parking lot at 25 Green St. (1 block
south) of the facility has been leased for the period of the construction.

Additional security personnel have been added to the regular evening and
weekend staff. There have been no reported incidents of theft or vandalism
since this increase. As a precautionary measure all restroom facilities are
kept locked before 8 AM and after 5 PM. Employees without a key may request
one from any security officer.

F1	F2	F3	F4	F5	F6	F7	F8	F9	F10
Help	Paste	Copy	Cut	Return	Marker	Mark			Menu

FIGURE 12-16.   Note for one of the categories

Using Agenda's Date Features

You can use Agenda's date features in the lease application. For example, a recurring
date can cause the appropriate when date to be generated each year at the lease renewal
date. By using date filters you can display all the leases that are due for renewal in the
next month or all those where the lease contract has lapsed. You can use the done date
feature to mark the signing of a lease, although you want the Process Done Items
setting in the Global Date Settings of the File Properties box set to No Action so that
the lease does not disappear from the file after it is signed. You could also make a
category called Signed and specify assignment conditions as Leases and Done to make
it contain only signed leases.

```
File: C:\AGENDA\LEASE                              07/11/90    9:17am
View: Initial View                                              ＊
Leases                                      Sq. Ft.    Done
     ♪‼1 South Charles St. Suite 500         ·5000      ·01/15/92
     ‼ 1 South Charles St. Suite 800         ·3000      ·02/04/92
     ‼ 1 South Charles St. Suite 1100        ·2500      ·05/02/92
     • 1 South Charles St. Suite 1320        ·10000
     • Charles Center 2nd Floor              ·15000
     ‼ Charles Center 14th Floor             ·25000     ·01/12/92
     ‼ Charles Center 5th Floor              ·4500      ·02/03/92
     • High-Rise Park Suite 32               ·6500
     ‼ High-Rise Park Suite 1200             ·10000     ·01/27/92
     ‼ Walkerson Building Suite 1400         ·8000      ·02/02/92
     • Walkerson Building Suite 2502         ·12000
     • 25 E. Greenmount Avenue               ·8000
     ‼ 32 Edison Highway                     ·4500      ·01/15/92
     ‼ 1100 Jasmine Way Suite 320            ·7000      ·12/05/92
     ‼ 1100 Jasmine Way Suite 1502           ·8200      ·02/01/91
```

```
┌─────┬─────┬───────┬─────┬──────┬──────┬──────┬──────┬───────┬──────┐
│ F1  │ F2  │  F3   │ F4  │  F5  │  F6  │  F7  │  F8  │  F9   │ F10  │
│Help │Edit │Choices│Done │ Note │Props │ Mark │Vw Mgr│Cat Mgr│ Menu │
└─────┴─────┴───────┴─────┴──────┴──────┴──────┴──────┴───────┴──────┘
```

FIGURE 12-17.   Columns added to show additional lease data

Adding Columns to Show Additional Data

Figure 12-17 shows the addition of two columns to the lease display. The first column shows the square footage covered by the lease agreement. The column is unindexed because indexing the entries would not serve any useful purpose. (The special unindexed symbol is not displayed in the figure because the highlight is not in that column.) The second column displays a done date, which indicates that the lease renewal agreement has been signed. Notice that the items with a done date have a double exclamation point for their tag character.

You can construct different views of the lease database to meet various needs. You can use section names to group the items in the view by the various properties or list the items by the Tenant category. Since Agenda allows you to define many views, you can set up the various options and select the view that you need without having to perform any additional work.

REAL ESTATE LISTINGS

Most real estate firms have access to a multiple list file that contains listings on all the properties for sale in their metropolitan area. Unfortunately, this information is sketchy at best, and you must refer to the printed listing to obtain more detail. Even the printed listing may not contain sufficient information to describe the property adequately.

Additional detail is desirable for listings offered by your firm or those in the geographical area where the most properties are sold. After viewing the house during the initial agents' tour, you can use Agenda to capture many of these features with a minimal investment of time.

Creating an Item For Each Listing

You can enter the listing number or the property address as the item for each property. You may even be able to download this information from the brokerage system or enter it from the listing card when it is a property listed by your firm.

The category hierarchy for the listing file can contain an entry for each of the characteristics you are interested in recording on a property. Figure 12-18 shows a section of the category hierarchy. Features like the number of bedrooms, the number of baths, square footage, and house style are all listed. Some categories have numbers as entries, like the number of bedrooms category, which was established with mutually exclusive entries, or the category for square footage. The latter category is unindexed since each entry is likely to be unique.

Agents need to be able to provide both the specific price of a property and the properties generally within a given price range. You can use the Price category to assign listings to unindexed categories representing a specific listing price and the Price Group category to look at listings within a specific range. A note attached to the Price Group category might explain the different numbers used to group prices. For example, "1" might indicate properties less than $100,000 and "5" might indicate properties between $300,000 and $375,000.

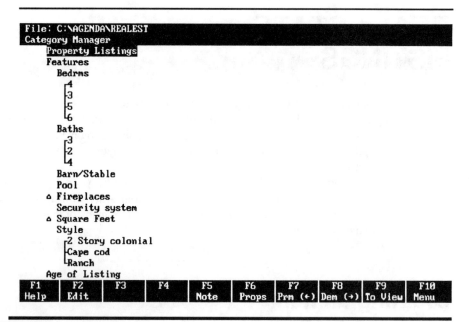

FIGURE 12-18.   Category hierarchy for a real estate file

Creating Categories For Property Locations

Another section of the category hierarchy for the real estate file might include property locations such as municipalities. The major locations would be mutually exclusive categories since you could not assign a property to more than one location. Although you can directly assign properties to one of the parent categories, you can also include the subdivision within each category. The larger parent categories could be subdivided into a number of subdivision entries. Each of these subdivision categories would also be defined as mutually exclusive categories.

You can construct a multi-category condition that includes exclusive categories such as Price groups. In this way you could view prospective properties that are new listings, have a fireplace, and are in price group 1 or 2. Without mutual exclusion you would have to construct separate conditions for 1 or 2.

You can add information on property taxes, the quality of the schools, proximity to recreational facilities, and other pertinent facts as notes to the location categories. You can supplement the information in any of the notes as you discover new facts

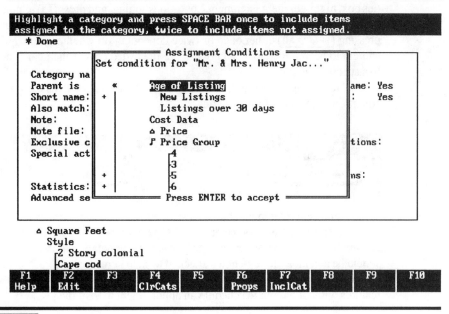

```
Highlight a category and press SPACE BAR once to include items
assigned to the category, twice to include items not assigned.
 * Done
                    ══════ Assignment Conditions ══════
                   Set condition for "Mr. & Mrs. Henry Jac..."
   Category na
   Parent is        «     Age of Listing            ame: Yes
   Short name:      +         New Listings           :   Yes
   Also match:                Listings over 30 days
   Note:                  Cost Data
   Note file:             ▵ Price
   Exclusive c           ♪ Price Group              tions:
   Special act          ┌4
                        │3
                  +     │5                           ns:
   Statistics:   +      └6
   Advanced se ═════════ Press ENTER to accept ═══════
```

```
    ▵ Square Feet
      Style
        ┌2 Story colonial
        └Cape cod
```

F1	F2	F3	F4	F5	F6	F7	F8	F9	F10
Help	Edit		ClrCats		Props	InclCat			

FIGURE 12-19. Conditions attached to a client category

about a community. You can also attach notes to each of the subcategories for specific information on the communities, such as zoning restrictions or minimum house size.

Selecting Listings
For Specific Clients

One of the uses of the Agenda real estate file is to select a group of homes that meet the profile established for each potential buyer. The buyers you work with can be listed as child categories to the Buyer category. You can use assignment conditions to assign listings to individual buyer categories. If a property meets all the conditions, it is assigned to the category for the prospective buyer.

Figure 12-19 shows the Assignment Conditions box for Mr. and Mrs. Henry Jacobs. This couple is interested in looking at all the new listings in the Lakewood subdivision that are in price groups 5, 6, or 7 and have 3, 4, or 5 bedrooms. To create this condition in the category hierarchy for Mr. and Mrs. Henry Jacobs, you would press (F9) (Cat Mgr), highlight the client category, press (F6) (Props) to display the Category Properties box, highlight the Assignment Conditions setting, and press (F3) (Choices). Select categories by moving to the categories to be included in the condition statement and pressing (SPACEBAR) either once or twice depending on whether you want to require an item to be assigned to a category or are interested only if the item is not assigned to a specific category.

The following illustration shows the properties selected based on the profile condition established for the Jacobses:

```
:\AGENDA\REALEST                                    07/11/90   9:49am
lient Listing
rs. Henry Jacobs                          Price        Bedrms
l Lake Drive Lakewood, OH                ·475500        ·5
l74 Beechwood Ave. Lakewood, OH          ·595000        ·3
i12 Pinecrest Lakewood, OH               ·615000        ·4
```

These items appear immediately in a separate view defined previously that consists of the category Mr. & Mrs. Henry Jacobs and includes columns that show the price and number of bedrooms for each property. A more detailed look at any of the items should be available through notes attached to each item. A note attached to properties can provide specific room sizes and decors to give buyers a better idea of the property features without having to schedule an appointment to visit the property.

INSURANCE POLICIES

Agenda can also be used effectively to track information on a large company's insurance policies. A number of fields of well-defined information must be recorded for this type of application, but there is an equally strong need to store descriptive information on each policy.

The fixed-length information that might be recorded includes policy number, insurance carrier, type of insurance policy, cost, and number of employees or square footage covered by the policy.

Descriptive text data might contain all the details of the insurance contract, riders added to specific policies, information on the carrier's service, rates within the insurance industry in general, and agent contact information. This descriptive information can be stored in items, category notes, or item notes.

Entering the Information
On an Insurance Contract

The following illustration shows item entries representing some of the insurance policies held by a company:

```
File: C:\AGENDA\INSURNCE                                    07/11/90   9:52am
View: Initial View
Policies          Carrier       Type         Cost        #Covered    When
  • KJ123/345     ·Aero         ·Life        ·75000       ·500       ·03/10/88
  • RT786-569     ·Markson      ·Auto        ·156000      ·350       ·04/01/88
  • KY145/321     ·Aero         ·Health      ·280000      ·1000      ·05/05/88
  ♪ HG66675-43    ·Cheap Care   ·Health      ·150000      ·1500      ·05/15/88
```

The items in this file contain nothing more than the policy number, with all the additional information entered as a category or a note. Additional columns include carrier, policy type, cost, number of square feet or employees covered by the policy, and a when date that represents the current policy's expiration date. The Cost and #Covered categories are unindexed because each category entry is unlikely to be repeated.

Agenda's automatic completion features facilitate the entry of the column data. After the first Aero policy is entered, typing A in the Carrier column causes Agenda to suggest the name Aero for the carrier. The same automatic completion capability exists for all the column entries as long as they have not been set to Unindexed.

Adding More Detail
With Notes

A note attached to a policy item can provide the complete text of a policy or information on the riders to the policy. The note data can be included in printed reports on policies if desired. If you include the complete text of the policy, comparing notes for similar policies allows for accurate comparisons of the details of two competing policies. Using the item notes to enter information on policy riders allows you to review policy extensions and include specific rider features and the date they took effect.

A completely different approach is to set up each policy number as a category with many items of text that pertain to it. Each item can be described more fully in item notes, and the policy text can be stored in a category note.

Agenda's category features make it easy to look at all the policies for a given carrier. You can attach a note to the category to provide additional detail about the carrier. This information might include the company contact. Another option is to use the notes for information on the payment performance of the carrier.

Organizing Seemingly Unrelated Items

One of the strong points of Agenda is its ability to organize facts entered over time into a related group. If you are responsible for negotiating insurance contracts in your company, you encounter many insurance-related facts throughout the year. If you enter these items into the database, you can bring them together under a related category and review this information when it seems appropriate. The data can help you monitor industry trends and new types of policies introduced by the various carriers.

Figure 12-20 presents a view of health insurance news. If you are ready to renegotiate some of your health insurance contracts, it might be useful to review this information. Facts like the savings for nonsmokers and nondrinkers remind you to find out whether the various companies offer this option. You can display an entry date for each item to help you determine the most recent entries, and you can use a date filter for screening purposes.

STOCK PORTFOLIO INFORMATION

Monitoring a stock portfolio requires integration of a significant amount of data. It is important to track the prices for issues of interest, but it is also important to retain other descriptive information about the company, its management team, the industry segment represented, and competing firms. All these factors can have a significant impact on the performance of the stock in the future.

```
File: C:\AGENDA\INSURNCE                         07/11/90  10:06am
View: Health Insurance News
Magazines articles
```
   • Coverall announces 15% discount for non-smokers on their health
     insurance contracts
   • Companies banning smoking save 20% on health insurance rates with
     Savemorinsur.
   • Health claims 25% lower for non-smokers
   • Insurance rates lower for non-drinkers - Health down 20% - Life down 35%
   • Fallston Insurance no longer offers individual health insurance plans to
     smokers

Newspaper
   • Health insurance companies meet in Akron to discuss rate reductions for
     non-smokers and non-drinkers
   • Local insurance firms set policies rates for non-smokers lower
   • Group insurance rates for smokers to rise
   • Letlive Insurance provides discounts to non-smokers

F1	F2	F3	F4	F5	F6	F7	F8	F9	F10
Help	Edit	Choices	Done	Note	Props	Mark	Vw Mgr	Cat Mgr	Menu

FIGURE 12-20.   Health insurance items

```
File: C:\AGENDA\STOCKS                           07/11/90  10:09am
View: PRICES
TXTR                     Open        High        Low        Close
```
   • TXTR 02/08/88   ·21 5/8   ·22   ·20 7/8   ·21 1/2
   • TXTR 02/09/88   ·21 1/2   ·22   ·21 1/2   ·21 5/8
   • TXTR 02/10/88   ·21 5/8   ·21 3/4   ·21 5/8   ·21 3/4
   • TXTR 02/11/88   ·21 3/4   ·22   ·21 5/8   ·21 3/4
   • TXTR 02/12/88   »21 3/4   ·21 5/8   ·21   ·21 1/4

FIGURE 12-21.   Price data for a stock listing

Agenda is the ideal vehicle for bringing together the various types of information required. Some of the data can be imported from other files and added as items or notes. Views of the data can focus on the industry group, a specific company, or information within a limited period of time.

Entering Descriptive Data

Information that relates to the stocks in an individual's portfolio can be found in business literature, newswire information, or discussions with one's broker or other investors. You can store items of information as items. Notes attached to these items supply as much detail as you need for any item in the file.

Depending on the category entries you establish, items can be assigned to individual categories, industry groups, or general market data. If the categories are not available for automatic assignment when the items are first entered, Utilities Execute will handle the assignments after the categories are added.

Adding Price Data

You can use unindexed categories to add price data to the file. Figure 12-21 shows some entries for a company. The categories Open, High, Low, and Close are added for the four price elements. This approach would be practical for keeping recent price data in the file but may not prove effective for historic data.

You can use a separate category with an entry date condition to purge the price data from the file after a specific period of time. You can also use a date filter to display recent items, including prices.

Adding Notes

You can add notes to individual categories or items. For example, you might add a note to a price data item to explain market movement for the date or give specific information that might explain a stock's price fluctuation. You could add general price trends, investment advice from a specific brokerage firm, and other details pertinent in a wider time range to such a note.

13

SPECIALIZED APPLICATIONS

Using Agenda to Keep Track of Medical Records
Using Agenda in the Legal Environment
Using Agenda to Analyze Large Legal or Technical Documents
Using Agenda for Specialized Writing Tasks

The applications in Chapter 12 were related by a common purpose or theme because they were all general business or financial applications. The applications discussed in this chapter are more specialized than the ones in the previous chapter. They may be of interest to users in a business environment, but they are oriented toward medicine, law, and writing.

The first application tracks patient history in a medical system. This system could also be used to help keep a physician abreast of new medical treatments in a particular specialty.

The second application records information for a law office. A law firm or corporate legal department could use the application to help analyze lengthy legal documents or to track filing dates. They could also use it to screen case data to prevent a large firm from accepting cases that represent a conflict of interest.

The third application uses Agenda to analyze a completed document. You could use an optical scanner to transfer printed data to a text file and then import the text file into Agenda. Agenda could be used to analyze a lengthy document of any type (for example, the bylaws of large municipal governments, contracts, technical manuals with part specifications, or any document in which it might be important to pinpoint occurrences of certain words or phrases) once it is stored as a text file and imported into Agenda.

The vertical market applications shown are just some of the tasks that Agenda can handle effectively. Other possibilities include databases for travel consultants or pharmacists. In a travel application, the database could include descriptive information on tours and scenic locations. Categories and automatic assignment could be used to pull information on any topic into a specialized view. A pharmacist could create a database for prescription drugs that could store a variety of information. The pharmacist could use it to obtain more information on a specific drug or to look at the records of patients whose prescriptions are filled at the pharmacy.

USING AGENDA TO KEEP TRACK OF MEDICAL RECORDS

Agenda can be used for keeping records in a medical office. Data can be organized in several ways. Each patient could be entered as a category, with each visit recorded as an item in the patient's category. The details of each visit would be recorded in an item note. Another approach would be to create an item for each patient, and store the patient's entire medical history as a note to the patient item. The final decision might be determined by the nature of the practice in terms of number of patients, number of repeat visits, time lapse between visits, and other factors.

Creating a Patient Database

Figure 13-1 shows one possibility for a database designed to store patient history information. In this database, each office visit by a patient is an item. The text of the item includes the date of the visit and a brief description of the problem. The detailed description of the medical visit and its results are kept in the note, as shown here:

```
Note for:    07/15/90 John Farrell returned.  The s         Line 1 INS
                            Font: Courier 12.0pt  Attr: Normal
```
Additional tests were run and it was determined that he has a slight allergic
reaction to caffine. He was advised to avoid all foods containing caffine,
and Emetherolyn was prescribed to relieve the itching due to the rash.

You need to be careful with this approach to ensure that the Assign Item Date
setting of the Category Properties Advanced Settings box is set to Never. You do not
want Agenda to create a when date from the item text. The dates are entered in the
item because the data on office visits is frequently not entered on the day of the visit.
If Agenda was set to create when dates, it would use the date that the item was entered
rather than the date of the actual visit. However, if the data for a given day were always
entered on that day, the date could be omitted from the item text and automatically
generated by Agenda as the entry date.

This approach offers a significant degree of flexibility since the attending physician
can access the data in many different ways by adding a few categories. The data can
be accessed by age if there is a date category for each patient that contains the patient's
birth date. It can also be accessed very easily by ailment by having Agenda scan the
note text for the description of a specific ailment and automatically assign it to the
appropriate category.

Figure 13-2 displays the office visits for John Farrell in a view. The doctor can look
for trends to determine the cause of the patient's problems. A complete patient history

---

```
File: C:\AGENDA\MEDICAL                           07/11/90  10:22am
View: Initial View                                          ⌐
Initial Section
    • 07/08/90 John Farrell came in complaning of a severe headache, stomach
      cramps, and a mild rash.
    • 07/08/90 Susan Parker came in for her yearly physical examination.
    ⌐ 07/08/90 Ray Parker made an emergency visit. He complained of back
      problems resulting from an automobile accident he was involved in late
      last week.
    ⌐ 07/09/90 David Smith came in with a severe sore throat and a slight
      fever.  He has had the sore throat sine last Tuesday but it did not
      become severe until Friday morning.
```

FIGURE 13-1.   Patient history database

```
File: C:\AGENDA\MEDICAL                                    07/11/90  10:42am
View: Initial View
John Farrell
     • 07/08/90 John Farrell came in complaning of a severe headache, stomach
       cramps, and a mild rash.
     ♪ 07/15/90 John Farrell returned.  The stomach cramps ceased but the
       headache remained and the rash worsened.
```

FIGURE 13-2.   Office visits for the patient John Farrell

can be printed by creating a view like this one and electing to print the notes along with the items.

Using the Date Features

In the sample application, the appointment date is part of the item text. The when date can be used for the date of the follow-up visit or the next checkup. Other date categories could be used to track lab test results or insurance filings.

Adding Medical Literature Data to the Database

Another way Agenda can be used in the medical office is to scan medical databases. For example, a doctor might want to include information in the database to aid in the diagnosis or treatment of a patient. This information can be added directly under items related to specific maladies, or it can be grouped under a category for the specific disease and accessed when a patient's diagnosis warrants looking at the latest advancements in treating the specific illness.

Many of the on-line database services have large databases of medical literature. Mead's BRS and DIALOG are two of the more prominent sources of this information. The databases can be searched on a weekly or monthly basis for new entries that pertain to specific diseases or treatments, and these can be extracted from the database and written to a disk file.

You would need to write a special data entry format (DEF) file to define the data format of the extract information. Once this is developed, you can use it month after month with TXT2STF to convert the data into a structured text file that can be imported into Agenda. You can assign the items of data to the category hierarchy entries that match specific fields in the on-line database records. Text matching also allows you to assign the items to a particular patient's category if you add category descriptors to a patient category. Actions and conditions further enhance Agenda's ability to place the information in the file without the intervention of the medical professional, who will be reviewing these additions as new information is needed. The entry date feature also allows the professional to browse quickly through the new items added to the database each week.

Supporting Insurance Filings

The data in the patient history items and notes will be useful when attempting to support insurance or Medicare claims. A patient's history may require him or her to stay overnight in the hospital for a procedure normally performed on an outpatient basis. A note can be printed to substantiate such a decision. It is also possible to print history data selectively if all of it is not needed. If the overnight stay is necessitated by previous problems with high blood pressure, the visits when abnormally high readings were obtained can be placed in a special category and printed separately. Another possibility is to mark the sections of a note that you want to print. You can remove the marking later when a more extensive history printout is needed.

The other important aspect of insurance filings is monitoring the receipt of payments. Since it is possible to estimate a normal length of time for processing the various types of claims, each filing can be assigned an appropriate date on the day that it is initially entered. These dates can be monitored, and filings that are not paid within a reasonable period of time after the estimate can be resubmitted.

Monitoring Referrals

It is common practice for physicians to refer patients to specialists for further treatment. Agenda makes it easy for referral information to be added to the file. The physician can examine this information by doctor, specialty, or any other category desired.

Such additional information would make it easy for a physician to contact colleagues on a patient's progress before the next regularly scheduled visit. The progress of patients who suffer from serious or chronic diseases can also be evaluated in terms of the referral source.

This same approach can be used to monitor laboratory tests that a physician has requested. A relative date can be entered that reflects the amount of time a test should take. The physician's staff can then check on test results if they are not received within the expected time frame.

Another approach would be to set up part of the database hierarchy as Referrals and have major categories of medicine as entries. Subcategories could be used for the more specialized medical areas under each major area. Items could represent the names of potential doctors to handle referrals for each specialty. Contact information for the physician and any other pertinent information about the physician's practice could be stored in a note attached to the item representing the physician's name.

USING AGENDA IN THE LEGAL ENVIRONMENT

Both large and small law offices have mountains of text data to be processed, filed, and copied. Some of this information can be handled adequately with boilerplate word processing forms that facilitate the completion of wills or other documents. Word processing programs and their associated merge packages are ideally suited to substantive specialties like probate, real estate, and collection activities because they allow the user to tailor documents with variable information in less time than a completely new document could be typed. In most cases, however, the word processing software cannot track filing dates, route information for the review of the partner in charge of the case, or examine the existing client list for conflicts of interest before accepting a new case.

Agenda provides some features that are not normally handled by word processing packages. Agenda can be used to examine a legal document, noting references to specific terms, individuals' names, or other words by using the automatic assignment features to assign to categories the text with the entries for which you are searching. All items and notes that contain the specific text references can be printed for further review.

The hierarchy established for an individual lawyer's data can have a number of major sections. Cases, clients, and important decisions in his or her area of law are three of the major categories shown in the hierarchy in Figure 13-3. The Cases category has child category entries representing each of the lawyer's active cases. The Client category might include additional categories for clients represented in cases, clients who paid a retainer, potential clients with whom preliminary meetings have been held, and clients for whom nonprobate services are being provided. If major cases currently include a case involving a merger and a copyright infringement case, the hierarchy would include subcategories for these two areas.

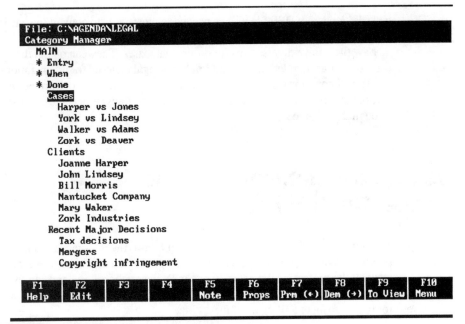

FIGURE 13-3. Hierarchy for legal data

Entering Items

The items assigned to the data in each of the major categories might be quite different. Data entered for a case might consist of all the individual filings needed for the case. A when date could then be assigned to the deadline for filing each individual item.

Appointments can also be entered as items under the particular case to which they pertain. The date and time for the appointment can be the when date. A to-do list of filings and appointments relating to an upcoming case would be easy both to use and to produce.

The client entries in the category hierarchy will have items attached for all the cases involving a particular client. Items pertaining to client discussions will also be grouped under the client category. This allows the professional to view all the data for a particular client by defining a special view.

Items relating to major new case rulings can be added to the database from one of the on-line databases, such as DIALOG, WESTLAW, and LEXIS. A search can be established for these databases that will put records matching defined criteria into a text file. A custom DEF file will be needed in most cases to convert the entries in this text file into a structured Agenda file that can be imported by the Agenda database.

Law firms have diverse uses for on-line databases. They can obtain the full text of court decisions, regulations, and international legal material for organizations like the European Economic Community. Other information, like the stock prices on a specific date or authors of articles in areas where an expert witness is needed, can also be found through these sources.

Using Case Items to Provide Docket Control Features

The items entered for clients and cases can be used with Agenda's date features to provide a docket control system for the legal professional. Although Agenda may not meet all the professional's needs, it can meet the major criteria and can immediately help minimize the chances that the law firm itself will become involved in litigation for failing to meet a filing deadline.

Deadline dates are easy to establish with date categories. Pre-deadline reminders can be produced using views that list items with a specific range of dates. Also, by assigning items to advance warning date categories in addition to the actual when date, you can set alarms to go off days or weeks in advance. In docket control systems it is important to retain the date that items are entered, and this can be captured with Agenda's entry date features. Other specifics concerning what is needed to meet the deadline, the location of the appearance, who must appear, and so on can be stored in the note on specific lines.

In addition to filings, Agenda can also retain client leases, statute of limitation expirations, trial appearances, review dates for wills, and closing dates for real estate transactions. Each of these can be accessed by client or type of legal work involved— such as case, lease, or real estate closing—if suitable categories are added to the file. Figure 13-4 shows an example of database entries used to help maintain a docket control system. You might create a datebook view for this week or next week. Also, a non-datebook view with categories such as pending, research, filing, post trial, continuance, or follow-up might be useful.

```
File: C:\AGENDA\LEGAL                          07/11/90  10:52am
View: Schedule for Harper Vs Jones
Harper vs Jones                                         When
     • Meeting with potential expert witness            ·05/20/88
     • Obtain deposition from B. Farley                 ·06/15/88
     • Obtain deposition from M. Greer                  ·06/18/88
     • File briefs                                      ·06/20/88
     • Pre-trial hearing                                ·07/01/88
```

FIGURE 13-4.   Item entries with dates providing docket control features

Transferring Client Data
To a Central File to Prevent
Conflict of Interest

One central source in a law firm must monitor existing client commitments to ensure that a conflict of interest does not arise. Although the obvious situation of representing both parties in a lawsuit can be eliminated easily, a search through the category hierarchy of a file that contains all client-related data will eliminate inconsistent representation before a new client is accepted. The data could be entered into a file as each new client is secured, or it can be transferred from the individual Agenda files used by the legal professionals on a periodic basis, such as once a week.

It is not sufficient to copy the items assigned to clients in each of the professional's files since the client names are stored as category entries. The File Transfer Export feature can be used to transfer data in the Client portion of the hierarchy to the central database. The Client category should be marked before invoking the File Transfer Export features to prevent the transfer of other categories and data in the file.

When the data are later imported by the central database, a selection of New Entries Only will cause only those entries that are not part of the central database file to be added.

A lawyer can check for other projects affecting a potential new client by looking for the client's name in the category hierarchy of the central database. The names for other cases the client has been involved in can serve as a double check.

USING AGENDA TO ANALYZE LARGE LEGAL OR TECHNICAL DOCUMENTS

Once a document is finally entered in its completed form, many people never consider dissecting it again. In specialized situations, however, the ability to dissect the text in a lengthy, complex document can be useful. References to particular words, technical terminology, bylaws, locations, or people can be used to assign an item of text to a category. You can then devise a view that contains sections for all the categories that interest you and print them out. This allows you to zero in on specific sections of the document.

If the document you want to examine in more detail is not available in a text file, you will need to have a scanner capable of reading the document into a text file so that it can be analyzed by Agenda. Although Agenda's ability to search for text patterns is useful, in most instances it does not warrant typing the entire document.

Figure 13-5 shows some of the text from a technical reference manual. The portion of the text shown in this figure contains a reference to part number EX-9876. Without reading through the remaining 50 pages of the manual, it is impossible to tell if there

---

```
     You will want to follow the assembly instructions for the high
performance apple picker carefully.  The first step should be
inspecting the parts provided.  Each apple picker should include
the following parts:  EX-9876, GY-8904, RT-5604, JU-5431, and YT-
8976.
     When setting up your new machine you will want to begin by
placing part JU-5431 on a flat surface.  The picker arm should be
attached to this part with the hairpin cotters that have been
provided.
```

FIGURE 13-5.   Technical reference text

are other references to this part number. However, the text in the document can be processed with TXT2STF to create a structured file, which is then imported by an Agenda database. References to the part number EX-9876 can be revealed by the automatic assignment features of Agenda. Figure 13-6 shows all the items that contain references to this part number in either the item or the attached note. Printing this data provides a quick look at all the references to the specific part number.

USING AGENDA
FOR SPECIALIZED
WRITING TASKS

Agenda is not designed to be a word processor, but it can be used effectively in many specialized writing tasks. For example, if the document you are preparing requires significant restructuring, you could enter the outline for the document as items or categories, and then attach notes to each entry for all the text on each topic. The text will automatically flow with the item or category to which it is attached, reorganizing the document instantaneously.

The organizational features of Agenda make it an ideal tool for the initial stages of speech writing or the creation of a report draft. Random thoughts, topics, and ideas can be recorded as categories in the file for the report or speech. Details can be added as child categories of the main topics. Notes can be added to categories at any level to store the text for the speech or the report. Categories can be moved anywhere in the

```
File: C:\AGENDA\TECHNICA                          07/11/90  10:48am
View: References to part number EX-9876
EX-9876
  • Part Number EX-9876 is available at local service centers due to the
    need for frequent replacement.
  ♪ The troubleshooting tips provided in this section can help  you achieve
    efficient performance from your new machine. Apples  which are bruised
    or mashed are caused by a tight spring in part  EX-9876. Loosening this
    spring should solve the problem. Sluggish performance of the equipment
```

FIGURE 13-6.   References to part number EX-9876

hierarchy as you begin to organize the various topics in the order that you want to present them. The notes attached to each category will print in the appropriate place when you print the category hierarchy with notes.

Agenda's sort features can assist you in reordering items, so that the items within a section are arranged alphabetically by item. The automatic search and replace features can be used in much the same way as in a word processor. To print the database in the double-spacing required for copyediting, special formatting commands can be used to print three lines to the inch to make the entire database look double-spaced. Another option is to print the Agenda data to a disk and then import the text file into your word processing package to handle the final editing and printing.

INSTALLING AGENDA

This appendix describes how to load Agenda into your computer and make it active under DOS. Since Agenda requires a hard disk, the directions assume that you will install your copy of Agenda on drive C, but you can use any available hard disk drive.

SYSTEM REQUIREMENTS

Agenda can run on a variety of computer systems, but there is a basic set of requirements that must be met, which are as follows:

- An IBM Personal Computer or IBM PS/2 computer, or one that is 100% compatible with these models

- DOS 2.1 or greater

- A hard disk with 3MB of disk space if you want to install two printers, 2.5MB without installing print and preview, or 3.8MB for installing all printers

- 640K of memory

- A CONFIG.SYS file with BUFFERS=20 and FILES=20

Note If your system has expanded memory, you should enable it to improve Agenda's performance. Refer to your hardware and DOS manuals.

REGISTERING YOUR COPY

Agenda comes will an install program that will guide you through the registration process for your copy of the product. You must enter your name and your company name to complete the registration. You cannot make backup copies of Agenda nor use the program until it is registered. To register your copy, follow these steps:

1. Boot your computer by turning on the computer and any attached peripheral devices such as monitors, printers, and disk drives. If DOS is installed on your hard disk, a C prompt that looks like

   C

   or

   C:\

   will appear on the screen.

2. Put the Agenda installation disk in drive A and make the drive active by typing **A:**. If you are using 3 1/2-inch floppy disks, this disk is called the Installation/Program disk; if you are using 5 1/4-inch floppy disks, this disk is called the Installation disk.

   If you have only one floppy disk drive, it is drive A. If you have two floppy disk drives, drive A is the one on the left when they are side by side, or the one on the top when one is above the other. The light for disk drive A comes on when you boot your system. If you encounter a problem with drive A and have a B drive, you can make the B drive active by typing **B:**, and then try again.

3. Type **INSTALL** and press (ENTER).

   The INSTALL.EXE program on the installation disk in drive A will execute, and a screen explaining installation will appear. After reading the screen you can press (ENTER) to begin, (F1) for more help text, or (CTRL-BREAK) to exit from installation.

4. Type your name when requested and then press (ENTER) to finalize the entry (you can type up to 30 characters).

    Use (BACKSPACE) to correct mistakes. You must enter something here since Agenda will reject a blank entry.

5. Type the name of your company (up to 30 characters) and press (ENTER).

    Again, you must enter something here.

6. Type **Y** and press (ENTER) to confirm your entries.

    Once you confirm your entries they can never be changed since you cannot repeat these steps. If you type **N**, Agenda will ask you to reenter your name and company name. The name and company name you enter will display on the initial screen each time you load Agenda, regardless of whether you reinstall from the floppy disks again.

Installing Agenda

After you complete the registration information, the installation program then transfers all of the Agenda files to your hard disk. Since Agenda will run on many different types of equipment, your task during installation is an easy one. Follow these steps to complete the installation process:

1. Press (ENTER) to confirm that you wish to install Agenda on drive C.

2. Press (ENTER) to accept AGENDA as the name of the directory where the program files will be placed.

3. Type **Y** to confirm the drive and directory and press (ENTER).

4. Respond to the prompt about installing the print and preview files. These files will require 700K of disk space if you select two printers. Additional printer selections will require more space. You can select the highlighted choice by pressing (ENTER), or you can type **N** to skip print and preview files. Press (ENTER) to confirm your selection.

5. If the detected drive is incorrect, Agenda will try to detect the display type your computer is using. This is important for Print Preview to work correctly. If correct, press (ENTER). If not, use the (ARROW) keys to highlight the correct drive, select it with the (SPACEBAR), and then press (ENTER) to confirm your selection.

6. Highlight the printer you plan to use and select it by pressing (SPACEBAR). You can select more than one printer (deselect by pressing (SPACEBAR) again). Press (ENTER) to accept your selection(s).

Note You can add or change print drivers at any point after installation by typing **Install** at your directory prompt and following the instructions in step 5. You can also do this from the system command, provided you have sufficient memory.

7. Read the informational messages that introduce you to Agenda's building blocks, and insert the remaining disks when requested.

8. To start Agenda after installation, press (ENTER), type **AGENDA**, and press (ENTER) again.

GLOSSARY

abandon   To discard the changes made to the current file and revert to the previous version of the file.

absolute date   A reference to a specific date (*e.g.*, 12/13/88). An absolute date reference will not change unless a new date is entered.

accelerator key   A shortcut to activating an Agenda command by pressing (ALT) and one of the letter keys.

accents   The foreign accents that appear above vowels in many foreign languages. You have the option of ignoring these accents in Agenda.

accessories   Utility programs supplied with Agenda that work with the Metro program and allow you to enter and access data without exiting from the current program.

action   A specification that is attached to a category that performs an explicit assignment function on its items. Two different types of actions are supported in Agenda: special actions and assignment actions. Special actions discard an item, mark an item done, or export the item to another file. Assignment actions remove and create item assignments by pushing them into or out of one or more additional categories. Creating item assignments can include setting entry when, done, or other dates.

ancestor   A category that is in the same family as the current category but at a higher level in the hierarchy.

ASCII   A set of codes representing each character that can be displayed or printed. ASCII characters from 0 to 127 are standard, but characters from 128 to 255 are nonstandard. A particular ASCII number may be represented on the screen as one character and printed on each of several printers as a different character. The translate feature of Agenda's print definition files (PD) is needed to alter the ASCII codes sent to many printers so that the higher-number ASCII codes print consistently with the display. You can import ASCII data into Agenda notes and export ASCII data from notes.

assign   To organize items under categories. Assignments can be performed explicitly with items in sections by typing a category name in a column. They are also performed automatically as the result of a matching text assignment, a date, or numeric condition or action.

assignment profile   A list of category assignments for an item.

auto-assignment   Automatic assignment of an item to a category by Agenda. This type of assignment is called an implicit assignment. You can control how Agenda makes this assignment through settings in the File Properties Auto-assign command.

automatic completion   The completion of your entry by Agenda. When you type a category name in a column, a file name from the open screen, or other data where automatic completion is in effect, Agenda attempts to match your entry to an existing entry and indicates when it has done so with a beep.

automatic save   The process whereby Agenda automatically saves the current database files. The default setting is 0 minutes or not to auto-save. You define the auto-save interval by typing a time interval value. The data is saved to the current AGA and AGB files.

back up   To create a copy of the database. The files created by this action have the extension .BG.

case sensitivity   Sensitivity to the differences in upper- and lowercase letters. Generally, Agenda is not case sensitive when it matches text.

category   An organizational unit within the file structure. Categories are arranged in a hierarchical structure with items assigned at any level within the hierarchy. Parent categories inherit the items assigned to their children, and actions belonging to the parent are also performed on the child category's items.

Category Manager   The feature in Agenda that allows you to change the organizational structure of the database.

child   A category that belongs to a higher-level category called the parent category. The categories within a column are the children of the parent category listed in the column heading. Items assigned to children are inherited by the parents to which the children belong. Parents and children together are called a family.

circular reference   A series of two or more actions or conditions that contradict each other's assignments. These contradicting assignments cannot be resolved regardless of the number of passes that Agenda makes through the category hierarchy.

Clipboard   A portion of Agenda's memory that stores text you have cut or copied.

collapse   To contract the display of child categories, displaying only section heads in a view or parent categories in the Category Manager. An ellipsis (...) is used to indicate that the display is contracted in the Category Manager, and a § is used in a view. You can contract one parent category or the entire display.

column   A vertical listing in a view that shows a category at the top of the column and below it the child categories that items are assigned to. Columns can be added locally to the current section within a view or globally to all sections within a view.

column head   A category or date entry at the top of a column.

command language   The special set of macro commands that allows you to automate Agenda applications.

Compose   A special keystroke sequence that allows you to create one of the special characters using two of the regular keyboard keys. In Agenda the Compose key sequence is (ALT-F1). This entry is followed by two characters, such as the letter "l" and a =, which create a British pound sign on the screen. The Compose key sequences control the characters displayed on your screen, but they do not always print out in the same manner that they display; depending on the model of printer, a different ASCII code may be used to represent the character.

compress   To remove free space from an Agenda file. Free space is created when items or notes are deleted and the trash is emptied. It can be removed from the file with the File Maintenance Compress command.

condition   A set of specifications that causes Agenda to assign an item to a category automatically. Agenda supports text, assignment date, and numeric conditions.

condition logic   Determines whether Agenda joins the various types of conditions with AND or OR.

confirmation box   A box that asks you to indicate your agreement with the action Agenda plans to take. If Agenda is about to delete a file or create a backup of the database, it may ask for your confirmation.

control codes   The special codes that must be sent to a printer to activate certain features or to print one of the symbols in its extended character set. The printer definition (PD) files are used to create these custom definitions for your files.

control panel   The area at the top of your Agenda screen where the menu displays when you press (F10) in a view.

cursor   The small flashing underline symbol that is used to mark your place in an item, note, or category name that you are editing.

customizing   The process of tailoring the system to meet your exact needs. You can customize the colors that Agenda uses, how it handles automatic assignments, and many other features.

database   Your pool of information. In Agenda this database includes the items, notes, and categories that you have entered. Every Agenda database has a file name extension of .AG.

DB2STF   Converts data from dBASE into an Agenda file.

demote   To lower the level of a category within the Category Manager. A demoted category is one level lower than the categories that were in its peer group before the demotion. If a demoted category is immediately beneath a category that was its sibling, the category is a child of the sibling after the demotion. The child categories of the demoted category are not demoted.

dependent   Items that require completion of other items for their own completion. Agenda permits you to mark the items that a task depends on and to establish the dependency. Once the dependency is established, you can hide dependent items or define a special display view that includes only dependent items.

dialog box   A box that is superimposed on the work area of your screen when certain menu commands are selected. Dialog boxes enable you to exchange information with Agenda. Agenda displays information for you in the dialog box and expects you to enter a response.

discard   To remove items from the database permanently. Discarded items can be restored with the Item Undiscard command if the trash has not been emptied.

done date   One of Agenda's three automatic date settings. This date is normally used to indicate that an item is completed. Preferences can be set to control what happens to items with a done date.

done items   Items with a done date indicating that they are completed.

edit   To alter an entry without completely retyping it.

entry date   A date that is initially assigned when an item is entered. This date can be retained permanently or updated when an item is edited or reassigned to a new category.

exclusive   A characteristic that can be established for the children of a category that will allow you to assign an item to only one of the categories. If you have priority categories of High, Medium, and Low, it would be logical to have the priority category mutually exclusive so that you could assign any task to only one priority.

expand   To display information in its expanded format by removing the collapse option.

expanded memory   Memory beyond the conventional 640K that DOS normally uses. Use Utilities Customize to activate this option.

explicit assignment   An assignment of an item to a category that you make as opposed to an assignment that Agenda makes for you. These assignments do not change with changing text conditions; you must change an explicit assignment yourself.

export   To transfer data from one Agenda database to a file so that the data can be added to another Agenda database or to another application if exported from a note to an ASCII file.

family   A parent category and all its child categories.

file   Organized information on disk. Agenda file names must conform to the DOS operating system rules. File name extensions are .AG for the Agenda database and .BG for backup files.

filter   Setting used to restrict or screen the data that displays in specific sections or views.

format   To change the display of information in a column with a standard category as a column head. The options are Name Only, Parent:Category, Ancestor, Star (*), Yes/No, and Category Note. Also date format for date columns and date display and Input formed for File Properties.

function keys   Keys labeled (F1) through (F10) that perform specific tasks when you press them. Pressing the (ALT) key and a function key requests a different task, effectively extending the function key selections to 20.

function key map   The line at the bottom of the Agenda screen that lists the feature activated by each of the function keys. This line can be removed by pressing (ALT-K) to allow the display of a few extra lines in your work area.

global   Having a comprehensive effect. When columns are added globally, they are added to each section in a view.

hard carriage return   Used to indicate that the data that follows should be placed on the next line.

hiding   Removing information from a view without removing it from the database. Dependent items and done items are two types of items that can be hidden from view.

hierarchy   The relationship of categories that defines the structure of the database file. The various indentations within the hierarchy display allow you to determine parent categories and the children that belong to them.

highlight   The bold bar on the screen that marks the current item, category, or section.

implicit assignment   An assignment made by Agenda based on text matching or conditions you have established. These assignments will break when the text condition creating them changes.

import   To bring data from another source into Agenda. Sometimes it is necessary to process this data before it can be imported. You define your exact conversion requirements in DEF files in order to prepare a file that is to be imported by the current database.

indexed   Category entries that are part of the database hierarchy.

indicators   Words and symbols that provide information about your database, such as attached notes, dependent items, and mutually exclusive categories.

inheritance   The process by which parent categories become parents of the items assigned to their children. Children also inherit the properties of their parents, such as mutual exclusiveness.

initial section   The category into which items are entered in a new Agenda file.

initial view   The view that Agenda creates for you in a new database.

insert   To add a section, item, column, or view to the current database. "Insert" can also mean the Edit mode in which characters entered from the keyboard are added to the information displayed on the screen by being placed in front of the current cursor location. In this situation "insert" is considered the opposite of "overstrike."

item   A piece of information entered into the database. An item cannot exceed 350 characters. Items can be assigned to one or more categories to control the organization and display of information in your database.

last view   The view you were working with before the current view.

LM2STF   Converts data from the Metro List Manager to an Agenda file.

macro   A command that automates a series of Agenda tasks.

mark   To select one or more items by placing a special indicator in front of them. Marked items can be operated on as a group. They can be deleted, discarded, moved, assigned dates, or assigned to other categories. You can also mark text in a note for copying.

match strength   The proportion of words in an item that match the total number of words in the category's text condition.

menu   A list of Agenda commands at the top of the screen when you press (F10) from a view.

Metro   A RAM-resident program that contains several useful accessories. The program can be run simultaneously with other programs.

note   Up to 10K of text attached to an item or a category. There can be only one note for each category and item. These notes can be stored as part of the database or in separate files.

options   Selections for the various settings in Agenda's dialog boxes.

overstrike   The typing mode invoked by pressing the (INS) key in a note, after which each character typed replaces a character on the screen.

parent   A category with at least one level of categories beneath it. The categories that belong to the parent are called children.

PD   The abbreviation and file name extension for a print definition file. A PD customizes the code sequences transmitted to fit the features your printer supports.

prerequisite   An item that must precede a dependent item. After prerequisite items are marked, the highlight is moved to the dependent item and dependency on the marked items is established.

print definition file   A file that contains instructions to tailor Agenda's print capabilities to the features supported by a specific printer.

profile   A particular set of assignments for an item. You can also generate profiles for a group of marked items to assign and unassign the entire group to categories.

promote   To raise a category by one level in the hierarchy. A category that was one of several siblings would be on the same level as the siblings' parents after it is promoted. If the category is immediately above the siblings in the hierarchy, it becomes the parent category for the other siblings. All of the promoted category's child categories are also promoted.

properties   Characteristics that define the appearance and operation of categories, columns, files, items, macros, sections, and views.

question   A setting specifying how final you want Agenda's assignments to be. You can have it question all assignments, only those with a low match strength, or none.

rearrange   To restructure the database hierarchy or reorder the items based on a sort.

recurring   A type of date that occurs repeatedly (*e.g.,* "every Thursday," "every month"). Agenda continually generates a new date to satisfy a recurring date.

relative   A method of expressing a date so that it relates to the current date (*e.g.,* "this Monday," "next Thursday," and "one week from today").

remove   To remove a category assignment from an item.

reorder   To resequence. The sort feature resequences the items within a section or view by the sort order specified in Properties.

required match strength   The matching strength required for an item to be assigned or considered for assignment to a category.

section   A division in a view that shows items assigned to a particular category. Category names are used as section heads in a view.

selection box   A box that is superimposed on the screen to permit you to select one of the alternatives listed. From selection boxes you choose file names and many of the other options needed to complete Agenda's dialog boxes.

Show view   A special Agenda view that can show selective database information, such as Match, Prerequisite, Depends, Items Done, Circular, Schedule, Every.

sibling   A category on the same level as another category within the same family.

special action   An action that discards an action, sets a when date for the item, marks the item done, or exports the item to a file.

star   A type of column that shows asterisks to indicate assignment to the category shown in the column heading.

string   A set of characters.

strong assignment   An assignment of an item to a category that you make as opposed to an assignment that Agenda makes for you.

structured file   A file with a defined structure, as opposed to a text file with no specific structure.

suffix   The ending of a word, such as "ing," "ed," "s," and "tion." You can set Agenda to determine whether suffixes should be used when attempting to match categories automatically for assignment.

tag character   A character used at the beginning of each item that you enter. This character can be changed through the Utility Customize command.

text condition   A condition that assigns items to a category based on text matching between the category and the item.

text matching   The process in which Agenda attempts to match the text in an item or note with text in a category name.

toggle   To change an entry with two possible settings to its other setting.

trash   A special area used to store discarded items. Depending on your settings for File Properties, all items or only the most recent item trashed can be recovered.

TXT2STF   A special program that is included with Agenda that converts ASCII data from another program into a format that Agenda can import.

unassigning   Eliminating the assignment of an item to a category. This can be done from the Assignment Profile or by deleting an item from a section within a view.

unindexed   A category whose child categories are not added to the hierarchy. The child categories cannot be used as section names since an index is not maintained of all the items that are entered for the category. This type of category can be used to enter information such as salaries, in which the child categories tend to be unique entries.

unmark   To remove the marks from database items that are marked with a special symbol. You can press (**ALT-F7**) to unmark all items.

view   A window into the contents of the database. You can define multiple views of a database to use for different applications.

when date   One of the automatic date options in Agenda. It can be used to enter the date when an item is scheduled to be completed, or it can be redefined for another date purpose.

wild card   A special character used to extend the matching features of text conditions.

work area   The area on the screen beneath the control panel and above the display of the function key map. Agenda displays items, notes, and the category hierarchy in this area.

COMMAND
REFERENCE

VIEW COMMAND
REFERENCE

Category Add

Description
The Category Add command adds a new category to the database. The dialog box that it displays allows you to define all settings that pertain to the category.

Options
The Category Add dialog box has the following options:

Category Name　　The name of the category can be from 1 to 69 characters long. This is the only setting that must be filled in.

Type   Agenda has four types of categories. Depending on the type of category you choose, the remaining settings of the Category Add dialog box will change. The four category types are as follows:

- **Standard**   The standard category type is the default type and is used most often. It can have children, and its children can be defined as mutually exclusive.

- **Unindexed**   The unindexed category type is a category that does not contain children. All information entered under a column that is defined as unindexed is not indexed as categories. This type of category is useful for information that does not recur.

- **Numeric**   The numeric category type allows Agenda to do simple arithmetic on columns of numbers. The numbers entered under a numeric column are not indexed.

- **Date**   The date category type stores dates and times in the category. Agenda has three date categories that are automatically a part of every Agenda database: Entry, Done, and When. You can define others.

Make Child Of   Enter the name of the parent category here. If a parent category is not entered, the default category is Main.

Short Name   This setting is available only when the category type is set to Standard. The short name is a second name for the category. Whenever a column in a view is not wide enough to display the category name, Agenda uses the short name (if one has been defined). Agenda will also automatically assign items to the category based on the short name. If a short name is not specified, Agenda truncates the category name to fit the column width.

Also Match   This setting is available only when the category type is set to Standard. Words and phrases other than the category name and short name can be added here for additional text conditions. Agenda can make conditional assignments of items to this category based on whether these words or phrases match the contents of the item.

Note   A category note can be created, and the first few words of the note are displayed in the dialog box.

Note File   Use this setting to designate a text file as the source of the category's note. If the text file is located in a directory other than the database directory, list the entire path name of the file. If you edit the note, Agenda makes the changes in the file.

Exclusive Children   This setting is available only when the category type is set to Standard. If you want an item assignment limited to no more than one of this category's children, change this setting to Yes. If an item can be assigned to more than one child, leave it at the default setting of No.

Special Actions   Special actions create actions for categories that perform one of several tasks automatically every time an item is assigned to that category. When a category has a special action, it can save assigned items to a file, discard them, or mark them as done. The default setting is No Action.

The special actions that can be assigned to a category are as follows:

- **Discard Item**   This setting discards any item assigned to the current category and puts it in the trash.

- **Designate as Done**   This setting marks any item assigned to a category as being done by setting its done date to the current date.

- **Export Item**   This setting exports all the items assigned to a category to an STF file, which you must specify. You must also determine whether the item is to be discarded after it is exported. Agenda assumes that the export file is in the same directory unless you indicate another directory.

Statistics   This setting provides information about the current category. The dialog box that it creates displays the number of items assigned to the category, including items assigned to the child categories; the number of child categories it has; the number of times it is used as a section head in the database; and the number of times it is included in view filters, conditions, and actions.

Advanced Settings   This option displays a dialog box that sets the preferences used in making automatic assignments for this category. The default settings are those chosen for the entire database through the File Properties command and can be selected here using the Global option. These settings control the manner in which Agenda handles automatic assignments, specify when Agenda should make automatic assignments, and determine when these assignments should be questioned. The advanced settings that can be made for a category are as follows:

- **Text Matching**   This option determines whether items are automatically assigned to categories based on text conditions.

- **Match On**   This option appears only if the Text Matching option is set to On. It determines the text associated with each item that is to be searched for text matching. The options are the item text only, the note text only, both the item and note text, or the Global setting.

- **Required Match Strength**   This option appears only if the Text Matching option is On. This setting determines the minimum match strength an item must have to be assigned to a category. The choices are Exact Match (100 percent), Partial Match (50 percent), Minimal Match (2 percent), or the Global setting.

- **Confirm Assignments**   This option appears only if the Text Matching option is On. It determines whether Agenda checks with you when it makes a conditional assignment. The choices are Always, Sometimes, Never, and Global. If you select Sometimes, Agenda checks to see if the assignment should be made whenever the text condition match is less than 100 percent.

- **Ignore Suffixes**   This option appears only if the Text Matching option is On. It determines whether Agenda ignores the suffixes of words when it matches text. Agenda can ignore the following suffixes: able, al, ally, d, ed, er, es, est, ful, ible, ied, ier, ies, iful, ily, ing, ly, ment, s, wise, and y.

- **Ignore Accents**   This option appears only if the Text Matching option is On and determines whether Agenda ignores accent marks when it considers text matches.

- **Assignment Conditions**   This setting allows you to disable Agenda's use of a category's assignment conditions. The options are On, Off, or Global.

- **Assignment Actions**   This setting allows you to disable Agenda's use of the category's assignment actions. The options are On, Off, or Global.

- **Apply Conditions**   This setting allows you to specify when Agenda should evaluate the conditions for automatic assignment. The options are Automatically (whenever an item is created or edited), On Demand (whenever you use the Utilities Execute command or the (ALT-E) and (ALT-X) accelerator keys), or Never.

- **If an Assignment Conflicts with Another**   This option determines what Agenda should do about an assignment that is made that conflicts with another assignment. This could occur when an item is assigned to one mutually exclusive category and then is assigned to another. The options are Keep the Old, Override the Old, and Global.

- **Allow Explicit Assignments**   Use this option to prevent explicit assignments from being made to a category or to eliminate existing explicit assignments from the category. The options are Yes and No.

- **Relationship of Text/Assignment Conditions**   Sometimes an item can be conditionally assigned to the same category based on more than one condition. Depending on the application, you may want an item assigned to a category if any one condition is met or only if all of the conditions are met. This option allows you to make this determination. If you choose Or, an item must meet only one of the conditions to be assigned to the category. If you choose And, an item must meet all of the conditions to be assigned to the category.

- **Category Is Protected**   Use this option to protect a category from deletion. The options are Yes, No, or Global.

- **Category Can Have New Children**   Occasionally you will want to make sure a category cannot have other children added to it. Use this setting to determine whether children can be added to the category. The options are Yes, No, or Global.

- **Assign Item Date**   This option appears only in the Advanced Settings for date categories. It determines when Agenda assigns dates to items. The options are Never, When Item Is Entered, When Item Text Is Edited, When Note Text Is Edited, When Item or Note Text Is Edited, When Item Is Assigned, When Item Is Assigned or Edited, From the Item Text, From the Note Text, and From the Item or Note Text. Some options require you to select which date to use if the text contains more than one.

- **Set the Item Date from Done Key**   This option appears only for date categories. It allows you to assign the system date to this category using the (F4) (Done) key. The options are Yes or No.

- **Set the Item Date from When Key**   This option appears only for date categories. It allows you to assign a date to this category using the (ALT-F2) (When) key. The options are Yes or No. If you choose Yes, you are prompted to enter the date.

- **Category Can Use Recurring Dates**   This option appears only for date categories. It allows you to use recurring dates, such as "every Friday" or "each Monday." If this option is set to Yes, Agenda treats these dates as recurring dates. If this option is set to No, Agenda ignores the words "every" and "each" and treats the dates as normal dates.

Match Category Name   This setting appears only for standard category types. It determines whether Agenda uses the category name for text condition assignments.

Match Short Name   This setting appears only for standard category types. It determines whether Agenda uses the short name (if any) for text condition assignments.

Assignment Conditions   This setting appears only for standard category types. It creates a condition that assigns items to the current category based on the item's assignment to other categories. Press (F3) (Choices) to display a list of the categories. To create a condition, highlight the category from which the condition is to be made. Press (SPACEBAR) once to flag the category with a plus symbol, which means the item must be assigned to the category for the conditional assignment to be made. Press (SPACEBAR) twice to flag the category with a minus symbol, which means the condition is met when the item is *not* assigned to the category. Press (SPACEBAR) three times to remove the condition. Press (ENTER) to return to the Category Add dialog box.

Assignment Actions   This setting creates actions that assign items to other categories based on the item's assignment to the current category. Press (F3) (Choices) to display a list of the categories. To create an action, move the cursor to the categories that you want to assign items to when they are assigned to the current category. Press (SPACEBAR) once to display a plus symbol next to the category name. To make the action remove items conditionally assigned to the current category from another category, move the cursor to the category that you want them removed from, and press (SPACEBAR) twice to display a minus symbol. Press (SPACEBAR) three times to remove the action. Press (ENTER) to return to the Category Add dialog box.

Category Discard

Description
The Category Discard command removes categories from the database when you no longer need them. To discard a category, highlight it and invoke the Category Discard command. Once you discard a category, it is completely removed from the database. All item assignments are broken. If items exist, a confirmation box is displayed to confirm the removal of the items before the category is discarded.

Note
You can also discard a category by highlighting it and pressing (ALT-F4) (Discard).

Category Properties

Description
The Category Properties command allows you to change the settings of a category in the database. The dialog box that it displays allows you to define all settings that pertain to the category.

Options
The Category Properties dialog box has the following options:

Category Name   Use this setting to change the name of the category. The name can be from 1 to 69 characters long.

Type   Agenda has four types of categories. Depending on the type of category you choose, the remaining settings of the Category Properties dialog box will change. Often you cannot change a category's type once child categories or data have been entered. For example, you cannot change an unindexed category back to standard. The four category types are as follows:

- **Standard**   The Standard category type is the default type and is used most often. It can have children and its children can be defined as mutually exclusive.

- **Unindexed**   The Unindexed category type is a category that does not contain children. All information entered under a column that is defined as unindexed is not indexed as categories. This type of category is useful for information that does not recur.

- **Numeric**   The Numeric category type allows Agenda to do simple arithmetic on columns of numbers. The numbers entered under a numeric column are not indexed.

- **Date**   The Date category type stores dates and times in the category. Agenda has three date categories that are automatically a part of every Agenda database: Entry, Done, and When.

Short Name   The short name is a second name for the category. Whenever a column in a view is not wide enough to display the category name, Agenda uses the short name (if it exists). If a short name is not specified, Agenda truncates the category name to fit the column width. This setting is available only when the category type is set to Standard.

Also Match   Words and phrases other than the category name and short name can be added here for additional text conditions. Agenda can make conditional assignments of items to this category based on whether these words or phrases match the contents of the item. This setting is available only when the category type is set to Standard.

Note   A category note can be edited or created. The first few words of the note are diplayed in the dialog box.

Note File   A text file can be designated as the source of the category's note. If the text file is located in a directory other than the database directory, list the entire pathname of the file. If you edit the note, Agenda makes the changes in the file.

Exclusive Children   If you want an item assignment limited to no more than one of this category's children, change this setting to Yes. If an item can be assigned to more than one child, leave it at the default setting of No. This setting is available only when the category type is set to Standard.

Special Actions   Special Actions creates actions for categories that will perform one of several tasks automatically every time an item is assigned to that category. When a category has a special action, it can save assigned items to a file, discard them, or mark them as done. The default is No Action.

The special actions that can be assigned to a category are as follows:

- **Discard Item**   This setting discards any item assigned to the current category and puts it in the trash.

- **Designate as Done**   This setting marks any item assigned to the current category as being done and sets its done date to the current date.

- **Export Item**   This setting exports all the items assigned to the category to an STF file, which you must specify. You must also determine whether the item is to be discarded after it is exported. Agenda assumes that the export file is in the same directory unless you indicate another directory.

Statistics   This setting provides information about the current category. The dialog box that it creates displays the number of items assigned to the category, including items assigned to the child categories; the number of child categories it has; the number of times it is used as a section head in the database; and the number of times it is included in view filters, conditions, and actions.

Advanced Settings   This option displays a dialog box that you use to set the preferences Agenda uses when making automatic assignments for this category. The default settings are those chosen for the entire database through the File Properties command, and can be selected here with the Global option. These settings control the manner in which Agenda handles automatic assignments, specify when Agenda should make automatic assignments, and determine when these assignments should be questioned and the text that should be used.

The Advanced Settings options are as follows:

- **Text Matching**   This option determines whether items are automatically assigned to categories based on text conditions.

- **Match On**   This option appears only if the Text Matching option is set to On. It determines what text associated with each item is to be searched for text matching. The options are the item text only, the note text only, both the item and note text, or the Global setting.

- **Required Match Strength** This option appears only if the Text Matching option is On. It determines the minimum match strength an item must have to be assigned to a category. The choices are Exact Match (100 percent), Partial Match (50 percent), Minimal Match (2 percent), or the Global setting.

- **Confirm Assignment** This option appears only if the Text Matching option is On. It determines whether Agenda checks with you when it makes a conditional assignment. The choices are Always, Sometimes, Never, and Global. If you select Sometimes, Agenda checks with you to see if the assignment should be made whenever the text condition match is less than 100 percent.

- **Ignore Suffixes** This option appears only if the Text Matching option is On. It determines whether Agenda ignores the suffixes of words when it matches text. The options are Yes, No, or Global. The suffixes Agenda can ignore are as follows: able, al, ally, d, ed, er, es, est, ful, ible, ied, ier, ies, iful, ily, ing, ly, ment, s, wise, and y.

- **Ignore Accents** This option appears only if the Text matching option is On and determines whether Agenda ignores accent marks as it matches text.

- **Assignment Conditions** This setting allows you to disable Agenda's use of a category's assignment conditions. The options are On, Off, or Global.

- **Assignment Actions** This setting allows you to disable Agenda's use of the category's assignment actions. The options are On, Off, or Global.

- **Apply Conditions** This setting allows you to specify when Agenda should evaluate the conditions for automatic assignment. The options are Automatically (whenever an item is created or edited), On Demand (whenever you use the Utilities Execute command or the (ALT-E) and (ALT-X) accelerator keys), or Never.

- **If an Assignment Conflicts with Another** This option determines what Agenda should do about an assignment that is made that conflicts with another assignment. This could occur when an item is assigned to one mutually exclusive category and then is assigned to another. The options are Keep the Old, Override the Old, and Global.

- **Allow Explicit Assignments** Use this option to prevent explicit assignments from being made to a category or to eliminate existing explicit assignments from the category. The options are Yes and No.

- **Relationship of Text/Assignment Conditions** Sometimes an item can be conditionally assigned to the same category based on more than one condition. Depending on the application, you may want an item assigned to a category if any one condition is met or only if all of the conditions are met. This option allows you to make this determination. If you choose Or, an item must meet only one of the conditions to be assigned to the category. If you choose And, an item must meet all of the conditions to be assigned to the category.

- **Category Is Protected**   Use this option to protect a category from deletion. The options are Yes, No, or Global.

- **Category Can Have New Children**   Occasionally you will want to make sure a category cannot have other children added to it. Use this setting to determine whether children can be added to the category. The options are Yes, No, or Global.

- **Assign Item Date**   This option appears only for date categories. It determines when Agenda assigns dates to items. The options are Never, When Item Is Entered, When Item Text Is Edited, When Note Text Is Edited, When Item or Note Text Is Edited, When Item Is Assigned, When Item Is Assigned or Edited, From the Item Text, From the Note Text, and From the Item or Note Text. Some options require you to select which date to use if the text contains more than one date.

- **Set the Item Date from Done Key**   This option appears only for date categories. It allows you to assign the system date to this category using the (F4) (Done) key. The options are Yes or No.

- **Set the Item Date from When Key**   This option appears only for date categories. It allows you to assign a date to this category using the (ALT-F2) (When) key. The options are Yes or No. If you choose Yes, you are prompted to enter the date.

- **Category Can Use Recurring Dates**   This option appears only for date categories. Agenda allows you to use recurring dates, such as "every Friday" or "each Monday." If this option is set to Yes, Agenda treats these dates as recurring dates. If this option is set to No, Agenda ignores the "every" and "each" and treats them as normal dates.

Match Category Name   This setting appears only for standard category types. It determines whether Agenda uses the category name for text condition assignments.

Match Short Name   This setting appears only for standard category types. It determines whether Agenda uses the short name (if any) for text condition assignments.

Assignment Conditions   This setting appears only for standard category types. It creates a condition that assigns items to the current category based on the item's assignment to other categories. Press (F3) (Choices) to display a list of the categories. To create a condition, highlight the category from which the condition is to be made. Press (SPACEBAR) once to flag the category with a plus symbol, which means the item must be assigned to the category for the conditional assignment to be made. Press

(SPACEBAR) twice to flag the category with a minus symbol, which means the condition is met when the item is *not* assigned to the category. Press (SPACEBAR) three times to remove the condition. Press (ENTER) to return to the Category Properties dialog box.

Assignment Actions   This setting creates actions that assign items to other categories based on the item's assignment to the current category. Press (F3) (Choices) to display a list of the categories. To create an action, move the cursor to the categories that you want to assign items to when they are assigned to the current category. Press (SPACEBAR) once to display a plus symbol next to the category name. To make the action remove items conditionally assigned to the current category from another category, move the cursor to the category that you want them removed from, and press (SPACEBAR) twice to display a minus symbol. Press (SPACEBAR) three times to remove the action. Press (ENTER) to return to the Category Properties dialog box.

Note
You can press (F6) (Properties) while a category is highlighted in the Category Manager to display the Category Properties dialog box for that category. If you press (F6) from the View, the Category Properties will reflect only those in the current section.

File Abandon

Description
The File Abandon command returns the database to the exact form it was in when it was last saved. If you have not saved the file during this session, it returns to the state it was in when you entered the database. All additions, deletions, and changes are removed. Agenda displays a confirmation box when you invoke this command.

File Maintenance Compress

Description
The File Maintenance Compress command reduces the amount of space that the current database uses by compressing the files. Excess space is created whenever you delete items and categories from the database. Eliminating excessive areas of blank space makes Agenda run faster.

File Maintenance Erase

Description

The File Maintenance Erase command erases an Agenda database. When you execute this command, the Select File box displays the existing databases. Move the highlight to the file that you want to erase and press (ENTER). If the file is on a different directory, move the highlight to that directory and press (ENTER). You cannot delete files that are not Agenda databases. Once you have chosen the file that you want to delete, a confirmation box appears for you to verify the deletion. (Note: The terms discard, delete, and erase are synonomous when discussing files.)

Note

You cannot delete the current database since a file cannot be deleted while it is open. Another way to erase a file from the Select File box is to highlight it and press (F4) (Delete).

File Maintenance MakeCopy

Description

The File Maintenance MakeCopy command copies the current database and gives the copy a different file name. You might use this command when you want to give a copy of the file to someone else, make a backup under a different name or on a different disk, or make a duplicate file so that you can make major modifications to the copy while leaving the original intact.

Only the database files are copied; external files are not.

File Maintenance Reservation

Description

The File Maintenance Reservation command is used in a network environment where you want to ensure that no more than one person is working on a database at a time. If more than one person was allowed to work on a database at a time, it is possible that one person could overwrite another's work.

File Properties

Description

The File Properties command governs the overall structure and the default settings of the database. It determines how dates are to be interpreted and displayed, whether categories can be added or deleted, and how automatic assignments are made. It also displays statistical information about the file.

Options

The File Properties dialog box has the following options:

File Description   Use this setting to enter or edit a description of the file. The file description can be up to 40 characters.

Set File Password   Use this setting to enter or edit the database's password.

Make Backup on Open   This option can have Agenda create a backup file of the current database whenever the database is opened. The backup file is stored in the same directory as the database and uses the same file name with an extension of .BG.

Get Reservation   This option either has Agenda try to get a reservation for the current database automatically, or requires the user to obtain one using the Maintenance Reservation command. This command is used for Agenda on networks.

Auto-Import File   This option can have Agenda automatically import information from an STF file whenever the database is retrieved. If you choose this option, you must enter the name of the STF file to be imported.

Insert New Columns In   This option determines where columns are to be added within views. The default setting is that a new column is added in all sections of the view. The other choice is to insert a column in the current section only. In either instance, the setting can be overridden for a particular column using the View Column Add command.

Empty Trash   This option determines when Agenda should remove discarded items from the file. Once the trash has been emptied, discarded items can no longer be undiscarded. The choices are On Demand, When File Is Closed, End of Day, and When Item Is Discarded.

Tab Size   This option can be used to adjust the default number of spaces that the (TAB) key uses. Use the gray + or - keys to advance or decrease the tab size, or simply enter the desired number.

Global Date Settings   This option displays a dialog box that determines the defaults for the database's date and times. When you are finished with the dialog box, press (ENTER) to exit or (ESC) to abandon your changes. The options are as follows:

- **Display Format**   This option determines the default settings for how dates and times are displayed in the database.

- **Input Format**   This option determines the default settings for how dates and times are entered into the database.

- **Morning/Afternoon/Evening**   The Morning, Afternoon, and Evening options determine how Agenda interprets these three words. The default settings are Morning at 8:00 AM, Afternoon at 2:00 PM, and Evening at 5:00 PM.

- **Beginning of Week/End of Week**   The Beginning of Week and End of Week options determine how Agenda interprets these two phrases. The default settings are Beginning of Week as Monday and End of Week as Friday.

- **First Quarter**   This option determines the date of the first quarter. The default is January 1.

- **Beginning of Year**   This option determines the date of the beginning of the year. The default is January 1.

- **End of Year**   This option determines the date of the end of the year. The default is December 31.

- **Month Alone Means**   This option determines the date Agenda is to assume if only the month appears in the text. For example, "every January" needs to be assigned a specific day in January. The default is the first day of the month. The other choices are the last day or the *N*th day, where *N* is a number that you specify.

- **Process Done Items**   This option tells Agenda what to do with items that have been marked as done. The default is No Action. The two other choices are to discard the item or export the item to a done file.

Global Protection   This option displays a dialog box that can limit access to the features that affect the structure of the database. The following options are available:

- **Default View Protection**   This option determines whether and how views can be modified. The choices are No Protection (the default), Append Only, and Full Protection. Append Only allows sections or columns to be added to existing views. Full Protection allows no modification of views.

    The choice made for the database can be overridden for a particular view with the View Properties command.

- **User Can Add New Views**   This option determines whether views can be added to the database.

- **Default Category Protection**   This option determines whether Agenda will allow or prevent categories from being changed or deleted. The choice made for the database can be overridden for a particular category with the Category Properties command.

- **Default Category Can Have New Children**   This option determines whether new children can be added for a category. This option can be overridden for a particular category with the Category Properties command.

- **Seal the File**   This option prevents the user from changing any of the protection settings of the file. If the file is sealed, a password is needed to unseal the file.

Update Defaults   This option can change the default settings of all future databases to those of the current database.

Auto-Assign Settings   This option designates the default settings for how automatic assignments are made for the database categories. These settings can be overridden for a particular category using the Category Properties command. The settings are as follows:

- **Text Matching**   This option determines whether items are automatically assigned to categories based on text conditions.

- **Match On**   This option appears only if the Text Matching option is set to On. It determines what text associated with each item is to be searched for text matching. The options are the item text only, the note text only, or both the item and note text.

- **Required Match Strength**   This option appears only if the Text Matching option is On. It determines the minimum match strength an item must have to be assigned to a category. The choices are Exact (100 percent), Partial (50 percent), or Minimal (2 percent).

- **Confirm Assignments**   This option appears only if the Text Matching option is On. It determines whether Agenda checks with you when it makes a conditional assignment. The choices are Always, Sometimes, or Never. If you select Sometimes, Agenda checks to see if the assignment should be made whenever the text condition match is less than 100 percent.

- **Ignore Item Text Enclosed By** This option determines the characters used to specify text that Agenda should ignore when making text matches. The possible characters are "*x*" (the default), /*x*/, '*x*', (*x*), {*x*}, <*x*>, #*x*#, and [*x*], where *x* represents the text to be ignored for text matching.

- **Ignore Suffixes** This option appears only if the Text Matching option is On. It determines whether Agenda ignores the suffixes of words when it matches text. The suffixes Agenda can ignore are as follows: able, al, ally, d, ed, er, es, est, ful, ible, ied, ier, ies, iful, ily, ing, ly, ment, s, wise, and y.

- **Ignore Accents** This option appears only if the Text Matching option is On and determines whether Agenda ignores accent marks when making text matches.

- **Assignment Conditions** This setting allows you to disable Agenda's use of a category's assignment conditions. The options are On or Off.

- **Assignment Actions** This setting allows you to disable Agenda's use of the category's assignment actions. The options are On or Off.

- **Apply Conditions** The Apply conditions setting allows you to specify when Agenda should evaluate the conditions for automatic assignment. The options are Automatically (whenever an item is created or edited), On Demand (whenever you use the Utilities Execute command or the (ALT-E) and (ALT-X) accelerator keys), or Never.

- **If an Assignment Conflicts with Another** This option determines what Agenda should do about an assignment that is made that conflicts with another assignment. This could occur when an item is assigned to one mutually exclusive category and then is assigned to another. The options are Keep the Old or Override the Old.

- **Relationship of Text/Assignment Conditions** Sometimes an item can be conditionally assigned to the same category based on more than one condition. Depending on the application, you may want an item assigned to a category if any one condition is met or only if all of the conditions are met. This option allows you to make this determination. If you choose Or, an item must meet only one of the conditions to be assigned to the category. If you choose And, an item must meet all of the conditions to be assigned to the category.

File Statistics   This option displays a box that presents statistical information about the database. The information displayed includes the following:

- **Unused Space** This is the percentage of space allocated to the database but not currently being used by it. Agenda recommends you use the File Maintenance Compress command whenever this percentage reaches 25 percent.

- **Items** The number of items currently in the database.

- **Items in Trash** The number of items that have been discarded since the last time the trash was emptied.

- **Items with Notes** The number of items that have a note attached to them.

- **Categories** The number of categories currently defined in the database.

- **Average Items/Category** The average number of items assigned to a category in the database.

- **Average Categories/Item** The average number of categories for which an item is assigned in the database.

File Retrieve

Description
The File Retrieve command opens the database that you choose or creates a new one. When you perform a File Retrieve, Agenda presents a Select File box listing of all the database files in the current directory. The current directory is the directory that contains the current database. If you want a file in a different directory, highlight the appropriate subdirectory or parent directory, press (ENTER), and then choose the file that you want. When you open a database, Agenda saves any unsaved changes in the current database and closes that file before it opens the new one.

Note
You can use the (ALT-G) accelerator key instead of the File Retrieve command to retrieve a file.

File Save

Description
The File Save command saves all changes made to the database since the last save or since the database was retrieved.

Options

You can save the file using the same database name or a new one. When the File Save command is invoked, a dialog box appears with the current name of the database. You can use the same name, press (F2) (Edit) to edit the name, or press (F3) (Choices) to list the names of all current databases.

A backup of the last previously saved file can also be made during the save.

Note

You can use the (ALT-W) accelerator key instead of the File Save command in order to save a file.

File Transfer Export

Description

File Transfer Export transfers a specified portion of your database into an external STF file. Agenda displays a dialog box to allow you to specify the data to be exported and whether it should be discarded once exported.

Options

This command has the following options:

Export to File   This setting determines the file to which Agenda will export this information. Agenda assumes it will export the information to TRANSFER.STF unless you specify otherwise. Since Agenda also assumes that you want the exported information to be stored in the same directory as your database files, you must tell it otherwise if you want the information stored in a different directory.

File Already Exists   If the export file that you name already exists, this option appears for you to choose whether the exported information should be appended to the existing file or replace it.

Export Items   This setting determines what will be exported. Your choices are None, Current Item, Marked Items, Items in Section, Items in View, or All Items. If you choose not to export any items, Agenda will export the category hierarchy chosen in the Export Categories setting.

Export Assignments   This setting determines how Agenda keeps track of assignments in the export file. The options are Do Not Export Assignments, Export Explicit Assignments Only, or Export All Assignments as Explicit.

Export Categories   This setting determines how much of the category hierarchy Agenda should export. If you choose No, Agenda only exports categories that have exported items assigned to them. If you choose Yes, you determine the part of the database's category hierarchy that is exported. If you choose Main as the category parent to be exported, the entire category hierarchy is exported.

Record Categories Referenced in Assignments Using   This setting determines how the categories are to be transferred to the export file. The choices are to export only the name of the category or to export the category with its complete ancestry.

Record Categories Referenced in Conditions and Actions Using   This setting determines how the categories mentioned within conditions and actions are exported. The choices are to export only the name of the category or to export the category with its complete ancestry.

Discard Items   This setting determines whether Agenda should discard the items after it exports them.

File Transfer Import

Description
The File Transfer Import command adds the data in an existing STF file to the database. The command also provides some control over how the imported items are assigned to categories.

Options
The File Transfer Import command has the following settings for importing files into Agenda:

Import from File   This setting determines which file Agenda will try to import. You also need to specify the path if the file is not on the current directory. If Agenda cannot find the file, it displays a warning message.

Assign to Category   This setting is the category to which all imported items are assigned. Agenda prompts you with the category name of the current section head, but you can choose a different category by typing it in or by pressing (F3) (Choices) to get a list of the categories. You might assign imported items to a new or independent category when you want to segregate the imported items from the others, for example.

Import Items   This setting determines whether items should be imported into the database.

Import Assignments   This setting determines whether the category assignments of imported items should also be imported into the database. This option appears only when Import Items is set to Yes.

Import Categories   This setting determines whether all of the categories contained in the import file are to be imported into the database. These would include categories that do not have any items assigned to them.

New Data Only   This setting determines whether Agenda imports only the items that it does not already have in its current database.

Categories Match If   This setting determines how Agenda matches categories in the current database with the categories in the import file. The choices are to only match those categories with the same category name or to match categories that match either the name or text conditions of the database's category such as the short name or Also Match expression.

Create Unmatched Categories Used in Assignments   This setting determines whether Agenda will create categories contained in assignments that do not currently exist within the database.

Create Unmatched Categories Used in Conditions and Actions   This setting determines whether Agenda will create categories referenced within the conditions and actions of imported categories that do not currently exist within the database.

Strip Carriage Returns   This setting determines whether Agenda will strip single carriage returns from the text. If Agenda strips the single carriage returns that are part of an item or note text, it reformats the data according to its own margins. If Agenda does not strip the carriage returns from the text, it retains the original text's carriage returns. If the option is set to No and the text extends beyond Agenda's line length, Agenda wraps the line and keeps the carriage return at the end of the line. You might need this command in a database used to import poetry, for example, which has definite line breaks.

Delete Structured File After Importing   This setting determines whether the STF file used for importing the information should be deleted after the import is completed.

File Transfer Template

Description
The File Transfer Template command extracts the structured part of your database and puts it into a new database that you specify. Views, conditions, actions, and categories are transferred, but items are not.

Item Alarm

Description
Agenda allows you to set an alarm for an item in the database based on a Date category of the item. The alarm can be set to go off from 0 to 60 minutes before the time set in the Date category. When the alarm time matches the system time, the alarm goes off and displays the alarm symbol (@) in the upper-right corner of the view.

Options
When the Item Alarm command is invoked, a dialog box appears with the following two options:

Date Category   This option defines the category containing the date on which the alarm is set. The default category is When. You can change this to any date category.

Minutes Before   This option specifies the number of minutes before the time set in the date category that the alarm should go off. You may specify up to 60 minutes.

Note
(ALT-A) is the accelerator key for the Item Alarm command.

Item BrkAssign

Description
The Item BrkAssign command removes the current item or marked items from the current section and performs the same function as the (DEL) key. The difference

between Item BrkAssign and Item Discard is that the latter removes items from all categories and places them in the trash while the former removes the item only from the section where the command was executed. If you have marked items, a confirmation box appears for you to choose whether you want to remove the marked items or the current item from the current section.

Note

If you remove an item from its only category assignment, the item is discarded after a warning message is displayed. Using the (DEL) key also breaks the assignment of the highlighted item from the section head.

Item Discard

Description

The Item Discard command removes an item from the database and assigns it to the trash. If the trash is not emptied immediately, you can retrieve discarded items with the Item Undiscard command. If you mark several items, a selection box appears for you to choose between discarding all the marked items or the current item.

Note

You can also use the (ALT-F4) (Discard) accelerator key to discard items. If you mark several items, a confirmation box appears for you to confirm that you want the marked items discarded.

Item MakeAssign

Description

The Item MakeAssign command assigns an item to a category. You can type the category name or list the existing categories by pressing (F3) (Choices). If items are marked, a selection box asks whether you wish to assign all the items marked or just the current item. If the category that you choose does not already exist, Agenda adds the category to the hierarchy. Agenda puts the new category into the hierarchy just below Main, although you can move the category to another location.

Note

You can also use the (ALT-M) accelerator key to assign items to categories.

Item Properties

Description

The Item Properties command displays a dialog box that lists the item's text, note, note file, statistics, and category assignments.

Options

The Item Properties dialog box has the following options:

Item Text   The text of the item, which can be edited from this box.

Note   The contents of the note (if any), which can be entered or edited from this box.

Note File   The note file is an optional text file used to create the note. When the note is edited, the contents of the file also change.

Item Statistics   The number of categories assigned to the item, the number of items dependent on this item, and the number of items this item is dependent on are displayed.

Assigned To   This option lists all the category assignments for this item. You can break an assignment by highlighting the category and pressing (DEL). You can add an assignment by either typing the name of the category or by pressing (F3) (Choices).

Note

You can also display the Item Properties dialog box by highlighting an item and pressing (F6) (Props).

Item Reposition

Description

The Item Reposition command moves the item within a section. This command allows you to reorder items. It does not work if the section is being sorted, since sorting overrides the Item Position command. When you execute this command, you use the (UP ARROW) and (DOWN ARROW) keys to point to where you want the item placed.

Item Undisc

Description
The Item Undiscard command takes either the last item or all the items from the trash and assigns them to the current category. When you invoke this command, a selection box asks whether you want to undiscard everything that is in the trash or just the last item. The Item Undiscard command does not restore the previous category assignments. The items are assigned to the current section. If there is nothing to be undiscarded, a message is displayed to let you know that the trash is empty.

Note
The (ALT-Y) accelerator key undiscards the last discarded item.

Print Final

Description
The Print Final command is used to print all or some of the contents of an Agenda database using the settings made with the Print Layout and Print Setup commands. The Print Final dialog box is used to specify the text to be printed, which printer to use, and the general formatting of the page. Once you make your selections, press (ENTER) to print the database. Settings made in the Print Final dialog box are automatically incorporated in the Print Preview dialog box.

Options
The Print Final dialog box has the following options:

Print   This setting determines what part of the database is printed. The choices are Current Item, Marked Items In View, Section, View, and Assignment Profile. If you print the Assignment Profile, you get a printout of the category hierarchy with asterisks next to the categories to which the current item is assigned.

Include   This setting determines if the notes and/or items are printed. The choices are Items, Both Items & Notes, and Notes Only.

Print To   This setting determines whether the output is to go to a printer, a print file including the printer codes, a text file, a Lotus Manuscript file, or a DCA file.

Printer   This setting allows you to choose which printer the file is to print to. The choices are specified in the Print Setup dialog box.

File   This setting determines the name of the file that the output will be sent to if the Print To setting was to a file. Agenda assumes that the file will be on the current directory unless otherwise specified.

From Page   This setting specifies the first page to be printed out. Although you usually want it set to 1 to start printing from the beginning, you may sometimes want to start in the middle of the document.

To Page   This setting specifies the last page to be printed. It is usually set to 999 to ensure that all the information is printed, but you may sometimes want to set it to a different number. For example, if you want to print only the first page of your database to make sure that the formatting is correct, set the To Page setting to 1.

Page Number of First Page   This setting is used to number the pages differently than their natural order. For example, you could use the From Page and To Page settings to print pages 3 through 7. You could then set the Page Number of First Page setting to 1 so the first printed page prints as page 1. This setting is not needed if the format is set to Text or the page numbers are not being printed.

Copies   This setting allows you to print up to 99 copies of the database at a time.

Double Sided   Use this option to print on both sides of the paper if your printer is capable of doing so.

Sort Output Pages   You can specify if you want Agenda to print the first page first, second page second, and so on, or print the pages in reverse order. For some printers, it is more convenient to print the pages in reverse order because they then stack up in numerical order.

Orientation   This option determines whether the paper is to print in Portrait mode (standard) or Landscape mode (sideways on the page). Your printer must support Landscape printing for this option to display.

Forms   This option tells Agenda whether it needs to stop and wait for the user to insert paper for every page. The options are Continuous, Single Sheet (auto feed), and Single Sheet (manual feed). If you choose the latter, Agenda prompts you to insert each sheet of paper into the printer.

Print Headers and Footers   Use this option to have Agenda print identifying information at the top and bottom of each page. The information that is printed is designated with the Print Layout command.

Print Layout

Description
The Print Layout command determines how a printed Agenda page is to look. You use the dialog box options to determine the margins, spacing, typefaces, headers, and footers to be used for the printed database.

Options
The Print Layout dialog box has the following options:

Printer   Specify the name of the printer to use for printing.

Orientation   This setting refers to the direction of the printing on the paper. Portrait is the standard method for printing on 8 1/2-by-11-inch paper. Landscape prints across the length of the paper.

Paper Size   This choice determines the size of the paper to be used for printing. If it is something other than 8 1/2-by-11 inches, press (F3) (Choices) to display a list of other standard paper sizes. If it is not a standard paper size, select Custom and then specify the width and length of the paper.

Margin Units   This option sets the measurement used to specify length. The choices are inches, centimeters, and millimeters.

Line Spacing   Select 1 for single spacing, 2 for double spacing, and so on, for blocks of contiguous text. You may also enter fractions such as 1.5 for one-and-a-half line spacing.

Indent Notes   This option specifies how much notes are to be indented from the margins. Use zero to indicate that no indentation is to be made.

Header/Footer   This option displays a dialog box, in which you can specify what is to print at the top of each page (the header) and the bottom of each page (the footer). Headers and footers can both be three lines long, with information placed at the left edge, center, and right edge of each line. The options for headers and footers are as follows:

- **Font**   If your printer is capable of printing with more than one typeface, you can choose the font for both headers and footers.

- **Attribute**   If your printer is capable, you can select one of the following attributes for the header and footer: Normal, Bold, Italic, Underscore Words, Underscore All, Double Underscore Words, Double Underscore All, Subscript, Superscript, Strikethrough, and Small Caps.

- **Space below/Space above**   You can specify the amount of space between the header and footer and the main text.

- **Line below/Line above**   You can specify whether Agenda should print a line separating the header and footer from the main text.

- **Header/Footer sections**   Headers and footers can both be three lines long, with information placed at the left edge, center, and right edge of each line.

Margins   The top, bottom, left, and right margins are set using the units of measurement specified with the margin units setting. Margins are the area of white space between the edge of the paper and the text.

Separators   This option determines what will separate different types of text. The choices are no separator, a solid line, or a new page break. You can place a separator after items or notes, between items and notes, after a section head, and after sections.

Spacing   The line spacing between different textual material can be varied. For example, you could single space after most text, but double space after a section head. You can vary the line spacing after items or notes, between items and notes, after a section head, and after sections.

Font   If your printer is capable of printing in different fonts, you can select different fonts for notes, items, section heads, column heads, column entries, and calculation labels. The list of available fonts is defined in the Print Setup dialog box.

Attribute   If your printer is capable of printing with different attributes (typestyles), you can select different attributes for notes, items, section heads, column heads, column entries, and calculation labels. The attributes that Agenda supports are Normal, Bold, Italic, Underscore Words, Underscore All, Double Underscore Words, Double Underscore All, Subscript, Superscript, Strikethrough, and Small Caps.

Alignment   You can choose to have Agenda align notes, items, section heads, column heads, column entries, and calculation labels differently. The choices for alignment are Left Justified, Right Justified, Centered, and Even.

Print Named Attach

Description
The Print Named Attach command is used to import a Print Set file into a view of the database. A Print Set file is a file that contains the printer settings of the Print Final, Print Preview, and Print Layout commands. The printer settings of the other views are not affected by attaching a Print Set file to a view. A Print Set file can be used in more than one Agenda file with similar printing needs.

Print Named Detach

Description
The Print Named Detach command is used to remove a Print Set file from a view of the database. The view's printer settings return to that of the general database. A Print Set file is a file that contains the printer settings of the Print Final, Print Layout, and Print Setup commands.

Print Named Erase

Description
The Print Named Erase command is used to remove a Print Set file from the disk.

Options
You can choose the Print Set file to be erased by either typing in the name of the file or pressing (F3) (Choices) to make a selection.

Print Named Retrieve

Description

The Print Named Retrieve command is used to import a Print Set file into an entire database. A Print Set file is a file that contains the printer settings of the Print Final, Print Preview, and Print Layout commands. The printer settings of all views are affected by retrieving a Print Set file. A Print Set file can be used in more than one Agenda file with similar printing needs.

Print Named Save

Description

The Print Named Save command takes the current database settings of the Print Final, Print Preview, and Print Layout commands and saves them in a Print Set file. These settings can then be incorporated into other Agenda databases using the Print Named Attach and Print Named Retrieve commands.

Print Preview

Description

The Print Preview command displays on the screen how the printed page would look if it were printed with the current settings. When you invoke the command, a dialog box appears with choices for what is to be printed and where. Settings made in the Print Preview dialog box are automatically incorporated in the Print Final dialog box.

Options

The Print Preview dialog box has the following options:

Print   This setting determines what part of the database is to be previewed. The choices are Current Item, Marked Items In View, Section, View, and Assignment

Profile. If you preview the Assignment Profile, you get a display of the category hierarchy with asterisks next to the categories to which the current item is assigned.

Include   This setting determines if the notes and/or items are to be previewed. The choices are Items, Both Items & Notes, and Notes Only.

Printer   The name of the printer to be used for the preview is specified.

From Page   This setting specifies the first page to be previewed. Although usually you want it set to 1 to start previewing from the beginning, you may sometimes want to start in the middle of the document.

To Page   This setting specifies the last page to be previewed. It is usually set to 999 to ensure that all the information is previewed, but you may sometimes want to set it to a different number. For example, if you want to preview only the first page of your database to make sure that the formatting is correct, set this option to 1.

Page Number of First Page   This setting is used to number the pages differently than their natural order. For example, you could use the From Page and To Page settings to preview pages 3 through 7. You could set the Page Number of First Page setting to 1 so the first page previews as page 1.

Print Headers and Footers   This option determines whether the headers and footers defined in the Page Layout command are to be included in the preview.

Orientation   This setting refers to the direction of the printing on the paper. Portrait is the standard method for printing on 8 1/2-by-11-inch paper. Landscape prints across the length of the paper.

Print Setup

Description
The Print Setup command is used to specify the type of monitor used to preview the printed documents, to specify up to two printers, and to define the list of availiable fonts for printing. These settings are presented in a dialog box.

Options

The Print Setup dialog box has the following options:

Print Preview Display Driver This option specifies the graphics driver available for your printer. If you do not have a graphics driver, you cannot preview the printed text. If you select a graphics driver, you are then given the option of choosing the foreground and background colors of the Print Preview screen. The defaults are a white foreground and a black background.

Primary Printer This option designates the printer to be used most often to print out database information.

Secondary Printer This option designates a different printer from the primary printer to be used to print out database information. If there is not a second printer available, choose None.

Port These options specify the location of the printers on the computer system. The possible locations are PRN; COM1, COM2, and COM3; and LPT1, LPT2, and LPT3.

Portrait Font List This option allows you to specify which fonts (typefaces) are available for printing in Portrait mode.

Landscape Font List This option appears only when the printer supports landscape printing. Landscape printing prints text across the length of the paper.

Quit

Description

The Quit command takes you out of Agenda after saving your database file and returns you to the DOS prompt.

Note

(ALT-Q) is the accelerator key for the Quit command.

System

Description
This command exits to DOS temporarily. You can execute DOS commands and return to Agenda by typing **EXIT** and pressing (ENTER).

Note
The amount of memory you have available for the DOS commands will vary depending on the amount of memory you have in your system and the number of terminate-and-stay-resident programs (TSRs) residing in memory (such as Lotus Metro).

Utilities Customize

Description
The Utilities Customize command lets you choose settings that relate to your hardware, language, and numeric conventions, rather than to a particular database. It also indicates how your computer's memory is being used by Agenda.

Options
The Utilities Customize command has the following options:

Color   This setting chooses what colors your screen will use. You can choose Mono for a monochrome display, Color for Agenda's customized color display, Plasma for a plasma screen display, or Custom for your own color selections.

Display Key Map   This setting determines if the bottom two lines of your screen are used for displaying what each function key does. If it is set to No, the key map will not be displayed and Agenda will use the extra two rows to display more of your database. (ALT-K) is the accelerator key used to turn the key map on and off.

Display Carriage Returns   This option can have Agenda display a triangle to indicate the location of carriage returns.

Beep on Auto-Completion   This setting determines whether Agenda will make high- and low-pitched beeps during automatic completion. If you turn off the beeps, most of Agenda's functions that make sounds will be silent.

Decimal Separator   This setting determines the character used as a decimal point in decimal fractions. The options are a period (.) or comma (,).

Display Cond/Act Info   This option specifies whether conditions and actions are automatically displayed with their categories in the Category Manager. This information can also be displayed in the Category Manager by pressing (F7) (Show C/A).

Item Tag Character   This setting determines the character that Agenda puts to the left of an item without a note. Press (F3) (Choices) to display the possible tag characters.

Suppress Snow   This setting determines if Agenda needs to suppress the snow that is visible in some color monitors. If you choose to suppress snow, Agenda will be a little slower in updating the screen.

Thousands Separator   This setting determines the character used as the thousands separator in large numbers. The options are a comma (,), period (.), or space.

Text Marker Display   This option determines how Agenda displays the attribute, font, and special markers on the screen. The options are a diamond (♦), the name of the marker, or no marker. Whichever method you choose to display the markers on the screen, the printed output is not affected.

Character Set   This setting determines which character set Agenda will use to display special characters. The choices are Use Agenda Default (CP 850) and Translate (CP 850 to 437).

Auto-Save Interval (Mins)   This setting determines the number of minutes that Agenda waits after a keystroke to save the most recent changes. The default is 0 minutes and can be as high as 60 minutes.

Memory Usage   This option produces a box that displays how Agenda is using the system memory. It tells how much regular and expanded memory is being used to store the database's data and program. You can also specify the maximum amount of expanded memory that can be used for data and for printing.

Confirm Mode   This option can eliminate the use of confirmation boxes. Normally, whenever you perform a task that deletes information, Agenda displays a confirmation dialog box for you to affirm that the information is to be deleted. When this option is set to No, the confirmation boxes no longer appear.

Utilities Execute

Description

The Utilities Execute command applies conditions and actions to existing items in the database. You can apply conditions and actions selectively by choosing the items and categories that will be used with this command, or you can apply them to every item in the database.

Options

This command has the following settings:

Apply Conditions Attached to Category and Children Of   This setting is used to name the category whose items are to be evaluated for conditions. If the category has children, their items will also be evaluated. If you want all categories to be evaluated, choose the category Main.

Against   This setting determines which items will be tested for conditions. Your choices are Current Item, Marked Items, Items in Section, Items in View, and All Items.

Apply Actions To   This setting determines the items to which Agenda will apply actions. The choices are New Assignments Only and Old and New Assignments. By having it set to New Assignments Only, you prevent actions such as exporting items to a file from being repeated unnecessarily.

Note

The (ALT-X) accelerator key applies all conditions and actions to all items in a database. Since this can be a lengthy process with a large database, you may want to reduce the scope of the reassignment with the Utilities Execute command.

Utilities Launch

Description

The Utilities Launch command executes a program from Agenda and immediately returns to Agenda once the program is finished.

Utilities Questions

Description
The Utilities Questions command brings up the confirmation box for you to confirm automatic assignments. This command is used when you have set the Confirm Assignments options of the the Category Properties or File Properties command to Always or Sometimes. The assignments you make using this command are explicit.

Utilities Show Alarm

Description
The Utilities Show Alarm command creates the *Show View* view and displays all items that contain alarms and whose alarms have rung. When you execute this command, Agenda sends all items with alarms to the !Current Alarms! section and all items whose alarms have rung to the !Past Alarms! section.

Utilities Show Circular

Description
The Utilities Show Circular command creates or appends to the *Show View* view all items containing circular references. When you execute this command, Agenda sends all circular referenced items into the !Circular Reference! section of the *Show View* view.

Utilities Show Depends

Description
The Utilities Show Depends command creates or appends to the *Show View* view items that are dependent on the current item or any item. Agenda lists the dependent items under the *Show* section of the view.

Options

You can choose One Level to display the next level of items dependent on the current item, All Levels to display all items dependent on the current item, or Every Item to display any items that have other dependent items.

Utilities Show Every

Description

The Utilities Show Every command displays every item in the database by creating a view called *Show View* with a section headed by the root category Main. The new view does not have any columns. If a *Show View* view existed before the command was executed, it is replaced by the output from this command.

Utilities Show ItemsDone

Description

The Utilities Show ItemsDone command creates or appends to a view all items that have been marked done. When you execute this command, Agenda sends all done items into the *Show* section of the *Show View* view. If the view already exists, a confirmation box asks you if you wish to clear the existing display view. If you press **Y**, Agenda replaces whatever is in *Show View* with the output from the Utility Show ItemsDone command. If you press **N**, Agenda adds a *Show* section to the top of the *Show View* view or appends the output to the existing section.

Utilities Show Match

Description

The Utilities Show Match command creates a *Show View* view that contains items that match the string you specify. A dialog box is presented for entering the search string, text match, and whether the search will be case sensitive.

Options

This command has the following options:

Search For   This setting specifies the search string that you want to find. It can consist of 1 to 60 characters. Words do not have to be in any particular order. If a specific phrase match is needed, enclose the phrase in parentheses.

Match On   This setting determines whether Agenda searches Item Text, Note Text, or Both Item & Note for the matches.

Ignore Case   Use this option to match words even if they have a different case. For example, the word "pat" would match the name "Pat" if this option is set to Yes.

Utilities Show Prereqs

Description
The Utilities Show Prerequisites command creates or appends to the display view all items that are prerequisites of the current item. When you execute this command, Agenda puts all the items that the current item is dependent on into the *Show* section of the *Show View* view.

Options
You can choose to display one level of prerequisites for the current item, all levels of prerequisites, or all items with prerequisites.

Utilities Show Schedule

Description
The Utilities Show Schedule command creates a *Show View* view that lists items for a specific date. The items that are displayed can be limited to a specific section. A dialog box is used to specify which items are to be displayed.

Options
The Utilities Show Schedule command has the following options:

Date Category   This option specifies which date category is to be used for the Show Schedule command. The default category is the When date.

Section Head   This option determines the category used for the section head. This limits the displayed items to those assigned to the section head category.

Date   This is where you specify the date for the items to be listed. This date is compared to the date stored in the Date category specified earlier. You can enter dates manually or press (ALT-C) to bring up the calendar. Relative dates such as "Fri" or "tomorrow" are also allowed.

Filter   This setting is optional but allows you to include or exclude a more specific group of items. A filter can limit the items displayed to either those that are assigned or those that are not assigned to a specific category.

Utilities Trash

Description
The Utilities Trash command is used to permanently discard all deleted items from the database. Once the trash has been emptied, the items put there cannot be restored. The File Properties command has an Empty Trash option that determines when the trash is automatically discarded.

View Add

Description
The View Add command creates a new view. When you create a new view with this command, you give it a name and an initial section. You also specify whether it is a standard view or a datebook view. Other options determine which items are to be displayed in the view.

Options
The View Add command has the following options:

View Name   This setting specifies the name of the new view. It should be a unique view name.

Type   Agenda has two types of views, standard and datebook. Depending on the type of view, the View Add dialog box options will change. The standard view is the one that is used for most applications. The datebook view is used for scheduling applications.

Sections   This option appears for standard views. It lists the section headers for the view, and you are required to make at least one entry. Either type the name of the category or press (F3) (Choices) to choose an existing category.

Item Sorting   This option displays a box that determines the default methods for sorting the sections of the view. This box is used to tell Agenda when to sort new items entered into the view, what is to be sorted, and whether the sorting is done in ascending or descending order.

Section Sorting   This option is only available for standard views. It is used to determine how section heads are sorted within the view. The options are None, Category Order, Alphabetic, and Numeric.

Hide Empty Sections   This setting determines whether sections that contain no items are hidden from the view.

Hide Done Items   This setting determines whether items marked done are hidden.

Hide Dependent Items   This setting determines whether items dependent on other items are hidden.

Hide Inherited Items   This setting determines whether sections will contain items that belong to a child category. If it is set to Yes, a section will contain items that are assigned directly to the category but will not contain items assigned to one of the section's child categories.

Hide Column Heads   This setting determines whether column heads are displayed for each section or just in the first section on the screen.

Section Separators   This setting determines whether Agenda will put lines between sections.

Number Items   This setting determines whether Agenda will number the items within each section.

View Statistics   This option displays a box that shows how many items, sections, and marked items the view contains.

Named Print Set   This setting allows you to attach a Print Set file to the current view. A Print Set file is a file that contains the printer settings of the Print Final, Print Preview, and Print Layout commands. The other views are not affected by this setting.

View Protection   This setting determines how the view is protected from further modifications. The options are No Protection, Append Only, Full Protection, and Global.

Filter   This option determines which items are to be included in the view based upon specific criteria. This criteria can include whether the item is or is not assigned to one or more categories. Filters can be used to include or exclude items based upon category assignments, dates, times, and numbers.

Date Category   This option appears only for datebook views. The date category specified is used to filter items into the view.

End Category   This option appears only for datebook views and is not required. The end category specified is used to keep track of the ending time of an item.

Section   This option appears for datebook views. It lists the section header for the datebook view. Either type the name of the category or press (F3) (Choices) to choose an existing category.

Period   This option appears only for datebook views. It determines the time interval used for the items within the view. The options are Day, Week, Month, and Quarter. The items contained within the view fit within the time frame specified. Depending upon the time period selected, time interval, start date, and end date are specified. For example, if Month is chosen for the time period, then the items can be listed for the month in daily or weekly sections.

Base Date On   This option appears only for datebook views. It specifies the beginning time frame for the items in the datebook view. The date can be either a specific date or a relative date (such as "tomorrow").

Note
You can also invoke the View Add command from the View Manager by pressing (F8) (Vw Mgr) and (INS). The View Add dialog box appears on the screen.

View Browse

Description
The View Browse command allows you to take a view or a section that uses a date filter and advance it forward or backward by a period. Use the (**LEFT ARROW**) and (**RIGHT ARROW**) keys to move up or down a time frame. For example, if you are looking at a view with a "today" date filter, pressing (**RIGHT ARROW**) will adjust the view to incorporate tomorrow's items.

Note
(**ALT-B**) is the accelerator key for the View Browse command.

View Column Add

Description
The View Column Add command adds a column to the current view. Several options allow you to choose the type of column you are adding, the location of the column, the name of the column, the initial format, and whether the column will be added to only one section or all sections within the view.

Options
The View Column Add command has the following options:

Column Head   This setting specifies the category that will be used for the column heading. The category can be an existing one or a new one. If you type a new category name, it is added at the same level as initial items. If you prefer to use one of the existing categories, you can press (**F3**) (Choices), highlight the category, and press (**ENTER**).

Category Type   This option specifies whether the category is standard, numeric, date, or an unindexed category. If the category specified as the column head is new, you will need to assign it a category type. If the category is one that was previously created, the category type is filled in for you. The Column Add dialog box's options will vary depending upon the category type selected for the column head.

Width   The Width option specifies how many characters wide the column should be within the view. The width of the column affects how the information appears on the screen, but it does not affect the data. The default width changes depending upon the category type of the column head.

Insert In   This option determines whether the column is to be inserted into the entire view or just the current section of the view.

Position   This setting chooses whether the column will be added to the left or the right of the highlight's position when this command is executed.

Format   This option appears only for standard categories. It determines how the column's categories appear. The choices are Name Only, Parent: Category, Ancestor, Star (*), Yes/No, and Category Note. See the Format option of the View Column Properties section of this appendix for more information about these format choices.

Date Column Properties   These options are available only for date categories. They specify how the date and/or time should be formatted in the column.

Numeric Column Properties   These options are available only for numeric categories. They specify the formatting for the numbers and determine what arithmetic operations should be done for the column.

Note
Accelerator keys are available to quickly create columns to the right or left of the cursor location. If you want to insert a column to the left of the highlight, press (ALT-L). If you want to insert a column to the right of the highlight, press (ALT-R). A dialog box displaying the category hierarchy appears. Highlight the category for the column and press (ENTER). The system defaults are used to create the column. If column properties need to be changed, you can use the View Column Properties command to make your selections.

View Column Move

Description
The View Column Move command moves a column within a section to the left or right. This command rearranges the columns within a section. When you use the command, the control panel prompts you for the direction in which you want to move

the column. Press (LEFT ARROW) to move the column with the highlight to the left and (RIGHT ARROW) to move it to the right.

View Column Properties

Description

The View Column Properties command allows you to determine the appearance of a column of categories and the method used to enter data in the column. Changes made to a column's appearance do not change how Agenda stores information, since changes to properties only affect the way the data displays. If your column is not wide enough, Agenda truncates the display of the column information.

Options

The View Column Properties command has the following options:

Column Head   This setting specifies the category that is used for the column heading. The category can either be edited or replaced. If you type a new category name, it is added at the same level as initial items. If you prefer to use one of the existing categories, you can press (F3) (Choices), highlight the category, and press (ENTER).

Category Type   This option specifies whether the category is standard, numeric, date, or an unindexed category. If the category specified as the column head is new, you will need to assign it a category type. If the category is one that was previously created, the category type is filled in for you. The Column Properties dialog box's options will vary depending upon the category type selected for the column head.

Width   The Width option specifies how many characters wide the column should be within the view. The width of the column affects how the information appears on the screen, but it does not affect the data.

Link with Other Sections   Changes made to this section's Column Properties box can either affect all sections of the current view with this column head or just the current section.

Format   This option appears only for standard categories. It determines how the column's categories appear. The choices are Name Only, Parent:Category, Ancestor, Star (∗), Yes/No, and Category Note.

- **Name Only**   The actual category name appears in the column. If a short name for the category exists and the width of the column is not wide enough for the category name, the short name appears.

- **Parent:Category**   Both the parent category and the actual category appear in the column, separated by a colon.

- **Ancestor**   The child of the category header that the item belongs to appears in the column. This puts all items on the same hierarchical level for the column. The child that an item belongs to is the category that inherits all the items its children have. This means that if you assign an item to the grandchild of the category in the column heading, the child of the category used in the column heading appears, not the grandchild.

- **Star** (∗)   An asterisk (∗) in the column indicates that the item belongs to the category that is the column header. A blank space indicates that the item is not assigned to the column header category. Items are assigned and unassigned by moving the highlight to this column and pressing (SPACEBAR) to toggle the star on and off.

- **Yes/No**   A "Y" in the column indicates that the item belongs to the category that is the column header. An "N" indicates the opposite. When entries are placed in this column, pressing any key other than **N** causes a "Y" to be shown.

- **Category Note**   This category shows a specific line number of the category note that appears in that column. If you select the Note format, Agenda asks which line of the note you want to use for the column display. The column shows as much of the line number of the note as will fit in the column.

Date Column Properties   These options are available only for date categories. They specify how the date and/or time should be formatted in the column.

Numeric Column Properties   These options are available only for numeric categories. They specify the formatting for the numbers and determine what arithmetic operations should be done for the column.

Note
You can highlight a column header and press (F6) (Props) to display the Column Properties dialog box.

View Column Remove

Description
The View Column Remove command removes from the current view the column that the highlight is on. It does not remove any information from the database; it only removes the column from the view.

Options
If the column appears in more than one section, you will see a dialog box asking if you wish to remove the column from all sections in the view or just the current section.

Note
You can also delete a column by highlighting the column header and pressing (DEL).

View Column Width

Description
The View Column Width command sets the width of the current column. When you perform this command, you need to tell Agenda how wide it should make the column. You can do this by typing the number of spaces representing the column's width, using the (LEFT ARROW) and (RIGHT ARROW) keys to move the width in and out, or typing ? so that Agenda adjusts the column to fit the largest entry in the column.

View Discard

Description
The View Discard command discards the current view from the database. It does not discard the categories and items contained in the view.

Note
You can also discard views using the View Manager. Press (F8) (Vw Mgr), highlight the view to be discarded, and press (DEL). Agenda displays a confirmation box for the deletion.

View Properties

Description
The View Properties command can be used to modify the settings of a view. It sets filters, hides certain types of items, defines the view name, and creates section separators. This command affects the current view only.

Options
The View Properties command has the following options:

View Name   This setting specifies the view name of the current view. It can be changed but not deleted.

Sections   This option appears for standard views. It lists the section headers for the view and it requires at least one entry. You can add or delete section headers from this option.

Item Sorting   This option displays a box that determines the default methods for sorting the sections of the view. This box is used to tell Agenda when to sort new items entered into the view, what is to be sorted, and whether the sorting is to be done in ascending or descending order.

Section Sorting   This option is available only for standard views. It is used to determine how section heads are sorted within the view. The options are None, Category Order, Alphabetic, and Numeric.

Hide Empty Sections   This setting determines whether sections that contain no items are hidden from the view.

Hide Done Items   This setting determines whether items marked done are hidden.

Hide Dependent Items   This setting determines whether items dependent on other items are hidden.

Hide Inherited Items   This setting determines whether sections will contain items that belong to a child category. If it is set to Yes, a section will contain items that are assigned directly to the category but will not contain items assigned to one of the section's child categories.

Hide Column Heads   This setting determines whether column heads are displayed for each section or just in the first section on the screen.

Section Separators   This setting determines whether Agenda will put lines between sections.

Number Items   This setting determines whether Agenda will number the items within each section.

View Statistics   This option displays a box that shows how many items, sections, and marked items the view contains.

Named Print Set   This setting allows you to attach a Print Set file to the current view. A Print Set file is a file that contains the printer settings of the Print Final, Print Preview, and Print Layout commands. The other views are not affected by this setting.

View Protection   This setting determines whether the view is protected from further modifications. The options are No Protection, Append Only, Full Protection, and Global.

Filter   This option determines which items are to be included in the view based upon specific criteria. This criteria can include whether the item is or is not assigned to one or more categories. Filters can be used to include or exclude items based upon category assignments, dates, times, and numbers.

Date Category   This option appears only for datebook views. The date category specified is used to filter items into the view.

End Category   This option appears only for datebook views and is not required. The end category specified is used to keep track of the ending time of an item.

Section   This option appears for datebook views. It lists the section header for the datebook view. Either type the name of the category or press (F3) (Choices) to choose an existing category.

Period   This option appears only for datebook views. It determines the time interval used for the items within the view. The options are Day, Week, Month, and Quarter. The items contained within the view fit within the time frame specified. Depending upon the time period selected, time interval, start date, and end date are specified. For example, if Month is chosen for the time period, then the items can be listed for the month in daily or weekly sections.

Base Date On   This option appears only for datebook views. It specifies the beginning time frame for the items in the datebook view. The date can be either a specific date or a relative date (such as "tomorrow").

Note
You can also display the View Properties dialog box using the View Manager. Press (F8) (Vw Mgr), highlight the view, and press (F6) (Props).

View Section Add

Description
The View Section Add command inserts a new section into the view. A filter can be defined for the section.

Options
The View Section Add command has the following options:

Section Head   This setting specifies the name of the category that is the section head. You can select a category by typing it in or by pressing (F3) (Choices) to display the category hierarchy and choosing the category you want.

Insert   This setting determines whether the new section is inserted above or below the current section.

Item Sorting   This option specifies how and when items are to be sorted within the section. If nothing is specified, the view's defaults are used for the section. This box tells Agenda when to sort new items entered into the view, what is to be sorted, and whether the sorting is to be done in ascending or descending order.

Section Statistics   This option displays a dialog box that states the number of items in the section.

Select Numeric Functions   This setting only appears when there is a numeric column. It produces a dialog box that indicates the calculations that are to be performed by the numeric columns in the section.

Filter   This setting can be used to filter in or out the items that appear within the section. The filters can display items within the section that are either assigned or not assigned to specific categories. They can also use the values stored in date and numeric categories to determine whether items are to be displayed within the section.

Columns   This option specifies the categories used for column headers for this section of the view. You can either type in the name of new or existing categories or press (F3) (Choices) to select column headers. To remove a column header, highlight it and press (DEL). The order the columns appear in this setting is the order they will appear in the view.

Note
Agenda has accelerator keys to insert sections. Press (ALT-U) to insert a section above the current one. Press (ALT-D) to insert a section below the current one.

View Section Move

Description
The View Section Move command moves a section in a view above or below its current position. When you use the command, the current view condenses so that you see only the sections and their category headers. Press (UP ARROW) to move the section with the highlight up a section and (DOWN ARROW) to move it down a section.

View Section Properties

Description
The View Section Properties command displays information regarding the current section. Column headers, filters, and sorting options can all be added or modified.

Options
The View Section Properties command has the following options:

Section Head   This setting specifies the name of the category that is the section head. You can edit it or select a new category by typing it in or pressing (F3) (Choices) to display the category hierarchy and choosing the category you want.

Item Sorting   This option specifies how and when items are to be sorted within the section. If nothing is specified, the view's defaults are used for the section. This box tells Agenda when to sort new items entered into the view, what is to be sorted, and whether the sorting is to be done in ascending or descending order.

Section Statistics   This option displays a dialog box that states the number of items in the section.

Select Numeric Functions   This setting appears only when there is a numeric column. It produces a dialog box that indicates the calculations that are to be performed by the numeric columns in the section.

Filter   This setting can be used to filter in or out the items that appear within the section. The filters can display items within the section that are either assigned or not assigned to specific categories. They can also use the values stored in date and numeric categories to determine whether items are to be displayed within the section.

Columns   This option specifies the categories used for column headers for this section of the view. You can add or delete columns from the view. You can either type in the name of a new or existing category or press (F3) (Choices) to select a category for the column headers. To remove a column header, highlight it and press (DEL). The order the columns appear in this setting is the order they will appear in the view.

Note
You can also display the Section Properties dialog box by highlighting the section header and pressing (F6) (Props).

View Section Remove

Description
The View Section Remove command removes from the current view the section that the highlight is in. It does not remove any information from the database; it only removes the section from the view. When invoked, a confirmation box appears. Confirm that the section is to be deleted and press (ENTER).

Note

You can also remove a section by highlighting the section header to be deleted and pressing (DEL). A confirmation box will be displayed.

NOTE AND MACRO COMMAND REFERENCE

Clear

Description

The Clear command deletes the text of the entire note or macro. If the text is an external file, Agenda deletes the contents of the file.

Export

Description

The Export command exports the marked text of the note or macro, or the entire text if nothing is marked, to an ASCII file. The note is not changed by the command.

Options

The only option for the Export command is the file name. Agenda assumes that the export file is in the same directory as the database unless told otherwise.

File Attach

Description

The File Attach command is used to import the contents of an ASCII file as an Agenda note or macro. The contents of the file remain in the file, but are accessed through the note or macro. Changes made to the contents of the text within Agenda are saved to the external file.

File Detach

Description
The File Detach command is used to break the attachment of an ASCII file created by the File Attach command.

File Erase

Description
The File Erase command erases an external file from the disk.

Import

Description
The Import command imports an ASCII file into the note or macro at the position of the cursor. The text becomes part of the database, just as if it were entered manually.

Options
The file name is the first option for this command. Agenda assumes that the import file is in the same directory as the database unless you specify another directory. A second option allows you to determine whether or not to strip carriage returns from the imported data.

Print Final

Description
The Print Final command is used to print all or some of the contents of an Agenda note or macro using the settings made with the Print Layout and Print Setup commands. The Print Final dialog box is used to specify the text to be printed, which printer

to use, and the general formatting of the page. Once you have made selections, press (ENTER) to print the note or macro. Settings made in the Print Final dialog box are automatically incorporated in the Print Preview dialog box.

Options

The Print Final dialog box has the following options:

Print   This setting determines what part of the note or macro is printed. The choices are All Text in Note or Marked Text.

Print To   This setting determines whether the output is to go to a printer, a print file including the printer codes, a text file, a Lotus Manuscript file, or a DCA file.

Printer   This setting allows you to choose which printer the file is to print to. You can specify printers in the Print Setup dialog box.

File   This setting determines the name of the file that the output will be sent to if the Print To setting was to a file. Agenda assumes that the file will be on the current directory unless otherwise specified.

From Page   This setting specifies the first page to be printed out. Although you usually want it set to 1 to start printing from the beginning, you may sometimes want to start in the middle of the document.

To Page   This setting specifies the last page to be printed. It is usually set to 999 to ensure that all the information is printed, but you may sometimes want to set it to a different number. For example, if you want to print only the first page of your note or macro to make sure that the formatting is correct, set the To Page setting to 1.

Page Number of First Page   This setting is used to number the pages differently than their natural order. For example, you could use the From Page and To Page settings to print pages 3 through 7. You could then set the Page Number of First Page setting to 1 so the first printed page prints as page 1. This setting is not needed if the format is set to Text or the page numbers are not being printed.

Copies   This setting allows you to print up to 99 copies of the note or macro at a time.

Double Sided   If your printer is capable of printing on both sides of the paper, you can use the Double Sided option to do so.

Sort Output Pages   You can specify if you want Agenda to print the first page first, second page second, and so on, or print the pages in reverse order. For some printers, it is more convenient to print the pages in reverse order because they then stack up in numerical order.

Orientation   This option determines whether the paper is to print in Portrait mode (standard) or Landscape mode (sideways). Your printer must be capable of landscape printing for this option to appear here. (If you don't see it in Print Setup under the printer that you have selected, you will not see it in Print Final, Print Layout, or Print Preview).

Forms   This option tells Agenda whether it needs to stop and wait for the user to insert paper for every page. The options are Continuous, Single Sheet (auto feed), and Single Sheet (manual feed). If you choose the latter, Agenda prompts you to insert each sheet of paper into the printer.

Print Headers and Footers   This option has Agenda print identifying information at the top and bottom of each page. The information that is printed is designated with the Print Layout command.

Print Layout

Description
The Print Layout command determines how a printed Agenda page is to look. The dialog box it produces determines the margins, spacing, typefaces, and headers and footers to be used for printing notes and macros.

Options
The Print Layout command has the following options:

Printer   Specify the name of the printer to be used for printing.

Orientation   This setting refers to the direction of the printing on the paper. Portrait is the standard method for printing on 8 1/2-by-11-inch paper. Landscape prints across the length of the paper.

Paper Size   This option determines the size of the paper to be printed on. If it is a size other than 8 1/2-by-11 inches, press (F3) (Choices) to produce a list of other standard paper sizes. If it is not a standard paper size, select Custom and then specify the width and length of the paper.

Margin Units   This option sets the measurement used to specify length. The choices are inches, centimeters, and millimeters.

Line Spacing   Select 1 for single spacing, 2 for double spacing, and so on for blocks of contiguous text. Fractions are also valid (for example, 1.5").

Header/Footer   This option displays a dialog box in which you can specify what is to print at the top of each page (the header) and the bottom of each page (the footer). Headers and footers can both be three lines long, with information placed at the left edge, center, and right edge of each line. The dialog box for headers and footers has the following options:

- **Font**   If your printer is capable of printing with more than one typeface, you can choose the font for both headers and footers in Print Setup.

- **Attribute**   If your printer is capable, you can select one of the following attributes for the header and footer: Normal, Bold, Italic, Underscore Words, Underscore All, Double Underscore Words, Double Underscore All, Subscript, Superscript, Strikethrough, and Small Caps.

- **Space Below/Space Above**   You can specify the amount of space between the header and footer and the main text.

- **Line Below/Line Above**   You can specify whether Agenda should print a line separating the header and footer from the main text.

- **Header/Footer Sections**   Headers and footers can both be three lines long, with information placed at the left edge, center, and right edge of each line.

Margins   The top, bottom, left, and right margins are set using the units of measurement specified with the Margin Units setting. Margins are the area of white space between the edge of the paper and the text.

Font   If your printer is capable of printing in different fonts, you can select different fonts for the note or macro text from Print Setup.

Attribute   If your printer is capable of printing with different attributes (typestyles), you can select different attributes for the note or macro text. The attributes that Agenda supports are Normal, Bold, Italic, Underscore Words, Underscore All, Double Underscore Words, Double Underscore All, Subscript, Superscript, Strikethrough, and Small Caps.

Alignment   Use this option to tell Agenda how to align the text. The choices are Left Justified, Right Justified, Centered, and Even.

Print Named Erase

Description
The Print Named Erase command is used to remove a Print Set file from the disk.

Options
You can erase the Print Set file by either typing in the name of the file or pressing (F3) (Choices) to make a selection.

Print Named Retrieve

Description
The Print Named Retrieve command is used to import a Print Set file into Agenda. A Print Set file is a file that contains the printer settings of the Print Final, Print Preview, and Print Layout commands. The printer settings of all notes and macros are affected by retrieving a Print Set file. A Print Set file can be used in more than one Agenda file that have similar printing needs.

Print Named Save

Description
The Print Named Save command takes the current note or macro settings of the Print Final, Print Preview, and Print Layout commands and saves them in a Print Set file. These settings can then be incorporated into other Agenda databases using the Print Named Attach and Print Named Retrieve commands.

Print Preview

Description
The Print Preview command displays on the screen how the printed page would look if it were printed with the current settings. When you invoke this command, a dialog box appears with choices for what is to be printed and where. Settings made in the Print Preview dialog box are automatically incorporated in the Print Final dialog box.

Options
The Print Preview dialog box has the following options:

Print   This setting determines what part of the note or macro is to be previewed. The choices are all the text in the note or just the marked text.

Printer   Specify the name of the printer to be used for the preview.

From Page   This setting specifies the first page to be previewed. Although usually you want it set at 1 to start from the beginning, you sometimes may want to start in the middle of the document.

To Page   This setting specifies the last page to be previewed. It is usually set to 999 to ensure that all the information is printed, but you may want to set it to a different number. For example, if you want to preview only the first page of a note or macro to make sure that the formatting is correct, set the To Page setting to 1.

Page Number of First Page   This setting is used to number the pages differently than their natural order. For example, you could use the From Page and To Page settings to print pages 3 through 7. You could then set the Page Number of First Page setting to 1 so the first page previews as page 1.

Print Headers and Footers   This option determines whether the headers and footers defined in the Page Layout command are to be included in the preview.

Orientation   This setting refers to the direction of the printing on the paper. Portrait is the standard method for printing on 8 1/2-by-11-inch paper. Landscape prints across the length of the paper. The Landscape option will not display unless the selected printer is capable of printing it.

Print Setup

The Print Setup command is used to specify the type of monitor used to preview the printed documents, to specify up to two printers and their ports, and to select fonts for portrait and landscape printing. These settings are presented in a dialog box.

Options

The Print Setup dialog box has the following options:

Print Preview Display Driver   This option specifies the graphics driver available on your printer. If you do not have a graphics driver, you cannot preview the printed text. If you select a graphics driver, you are then given the option of choosing the foreground and background colors of the Print Preview screen. The defaults are a white foreground and a black background.

Primary Printer   This option designates the printer to be used most often to print note and macro text.

Secondary Printer   This option designates a different printer from the primary printer to be used to print note and macro text. If there is not a second printer available, choose None.

Port   These options specify the location of the printers on your computer system.

Portrait Font List   This option allows you to specify which fonts (typefaces) are available for printing in Portrait mode.

Landscape Font List   This option appears if the printer supports landscape printing. Landscape printing prints across the length of the paper. It is not available with all printers.

Quit

Description

The Quit command takes you out of Agenda after saving your database file and returns you to the DOS prompt.

Note

$(\overline{\text{ALT-Q}})$ is the accelerator key for the Quit command.

Return

Description

The Return command returns you to your previous activity. This is usually the View mode or Macro Manager.

Note

The $(\overline{\text{F5}})$ (Return) key performs the same function as the Return command.

PRINT PREVIEW COMMAND REFERENCE

Full-Page/Content

Description

The Full-Page/Content command determines whether the Print Preview screen displays a reduced facsimile of the full printed page or whether it prints a larger, more readable version. The Full-Page feature allows you to look at the overall appearance of the page, but relies on a magnifier window to read its contents. The Content feature displays one-third of the contents of the page on the screen at once. (Note: If you press $(\overline{\text{CTRL-PGDN}})$, $(\overline{\text{ALT-N}})$, $(\overline{\text{ENTER}})$, or $(\overline{\text{F10}})$ while on the last page, Agenda exits Preview mode.)

Options

The Full-Page setting has a magnifier window that displays the contents of the selector box. The selector box can be moved around the page using the $(\overline{\text{ARROW}})$ keys. The contents of the magnifier window are displayed in the upper-right corner of the display. The size and hence magnifying power of the selector box can be decreased and increased by pressing the gray - and gray + keys.

The Content setting displays the page using the entire screen, but only includes one-third of the page at once. Use the (ARROW) keys to adjust the part of the page that is displayed on the screen.

Page GoTo

Description
The Page GoTo command displays a specific page of the preview document. After invoking the command, you must enter the number of the page you want displayed.

Note
You can also press (ALT-F5) (GoTo) to display a specific page of the preview document.

Page Next

Description
The Page Next command displays the next page of the Print Preview screen.

Note
(ALT-N) is the accelerator key for the Page Next command. You can also press (ENTER) or (CTRL-PGDN) to advance to the next page. If you use this command on the last page, you will leave Preview mode.

Page Previous

Description
The Page Previous command displays the page previous to the one currently displayed within the Print Preview screen.

Note
(ALT-P) is the accelerator key for the Page Previous command. You can also use (CTRL-PGUP).

Quit

Description
The Quit command takes you out of Print Preview mode and returns you to where you were before Print Preview was invoked.

Note
(ALT-Q) is the accelerator key for the Quit command.

Reverse/Normal

Description
The Reverse command and Normal command switch the Print Preview screen between normal and reverse video. Reverse video displays the text in what is normally the background color and the background in what is normally the text color.

CATEGORY MANAGER COMMAND REFERENCE

Category Add

Description
The Category Add command is used to add a category to the Category Manager. For a description of its features and options, see Category Add in the View Command Reference earlier in this appendix.

Category Discard

Description

The Category Discard command is used to remove a category from the database when you no longer need it. To discard a category, highlight it and invoke the Category Discard command. Once you discard a category, it is completely removed from the database. All item assignments are broken. If items exist that are only assigned to the category to be discarded, a confirmation box is displayed before the category is discarded.

Note

You can also discard a category by highlighting it and pressing (ALT-F4) (Discard).

Category Properties

Description

The Category Properties command is used to display and modify the properties of a previously defined category. For a description of its features and options, see Category Properties in the View Command Reference earlier in this appendix.

Print Final

Description

The Print Final command prints the category hierarchy or database information. A dialog box asks you to specify what you want to print, where you want to print it, and how you want to print it. When you print out the database information, the file description and all files associated with the database are printed.

Options

The Print command has the following options:

Print   This setting determines what information is printed. The choices are Category Hierarchy and File Info. The file information includes a description of the database, its associated files, and other statistics.

Include   This option appears only when the category hierarchy is to be printed. It determines if the categories, category and notes, or just the notes will be printed.

Print To   This setting determines where the printed output will go. The options are to the printer, a print file with codes left intact, a text file, a Lotus Manuscript file, or a DCA file.

Printer   This setting specifies which printer the document is to be sent to.

File   This setting determines the name of the file that the output will be sent to if the Print To setting was to a file. Agenda assumes that the file will be on the current directory unless otherwise specified.

From Page   This setting specifies the first page to be printed out. Although usually you want it set to 1 to start printing from the beginning, you may sometimes want to start in the middle of the document.

To Page   This setting specifies the last page to be printed. It is usually set to 999 to ensure that all the information is printed, but you may want to set it to a different number. For example, if you want to print only the first page to make sure that the formatting is correct, set the To Page setting to 1.

Page Number of First Page   This setting is used to number the pages differently than their natural order. For example, you could use the From Page and To Page settings to print pages 3 through 7. You could then set the Page Number of First Page setting to 1 so the first printed page prints as page 1. This setting is not needed if Print To is set to Text file or the page numbers are not being printed.

Copies   This setting allows you to print up to 99 copies of the database at a time.

Double Sided   Use this option to print on both sides of the paper if your printer is capable of doing so.

Sort Output Pages   You can have Agenda print the first page first, second page second, and so on, or print the pages in reverse order. For some printers, it is more convenient to print the pages in reverse order because they then stack up in numerical order.

Orientation   This option determines whether the paper is to print in Portrait mode (standard) or Landscape mode (sideways). The Landscape option will not work with all printers.

Forms   This option tells Agenda whether it needs to stop and wait for the user to insert paper for every page. The options are Continuous, Single Sheet (auto feed), and Single Sheet (manual feed). If you choose the latter, Agenda prompts you to insert each sheet of paper into the printer.

Print Headers and Footers   You can have Agenda print identifying information at the top and bottom of each page. The information that is printed is designated with the Print Layout command.

Print Layout

Description

The Print Layout command determines how a printed Agenda page is to look. The dialog box it produces determines the margins, spacing, typefaces, and headers and footers to be used for the document. For a description of the options available for the Print Layout command, see Print Layout in the View Command Reference earlier in this appendix.

Print Named Erase

Description

The Print Named Erase command is used to remove a Print Set file from the disk.

Options

You can choose the Print Set file to be erased by either typing in the name of the file or pressing (F3) (Choices) to make a selection.

Print Named Retrieve

Description

The Print Named Retrieve command is used to import a Print Set file into the Category Manager. A Print Set file is a file that contains the printer settings of the Print Final, Print Preview, and Print Layout commands. A Print Set file can be used in more than one Agenda file that have similar printing needs.

Print Named Save

Description
The Print Named Save command takes the current settings of the Print Final, Print Preview, and Print Layout commands and saves them in a Print Set file. These settings can then be incorporated into other Agenda databases using the Print Named Attach and Print Named Retrieve commands.

Print Preview

Description
The Print Preview command displays on the screen how the printed page would look if it were printed with the current settings. When you invoke this command, a dialog box appears with choices for what is to be printed and where. Settings made in the Print Preview dialog box are automatically incorporated in the Print Final dialog box.

Options
The Print Preview dialog box has the following options:

Print   This setting determines what part of the database is to be previewed. The choices for the Category Manager are Category Hierarchy and File Info.

Include   This setting determines if the notes and/or items are to be previewed. The choices are Categories, Categories & Notes, and Category Notes.

Printer   Specify the name of the printer to be used for the preview.

From Page   This setting specifies the first page to be previewed. Although usually you want it set to 1 to start printing from the beginning, you sometimes may want to start in the middle of the document.

To Page   This setting specifies the last page to be previewed. It is usually set to 999 to ensure that all the information is printed, but sometimes you may want to set it to a different number. For example, if you want to preview only the first page of your database to make sure that the formatting is correct, set the To Page setting to 1.

Page Number of First Page   This setting is used to number the pages differently than their natural order. For example, you could use the From Page and To Page settings to print pages 3 through 7. You could then set the Page Number of First Page setting to 1 so the first page previews as page 1.

Print Headers and Footers   This option determines whether the headers and footers defined in the Page Layout command are to be included in the preview.

Orientation   This setting refers to the direction of the printing on the paper. Portrait is the standard method for printing on 8 1/2-by-11-inch paper. Landscape prints across the length of the paper.

Print Setup

Description
The Print Setup command is used to specify the type of monitor used to preview the printed documents and to specify up to two printers with their respective font lists. These settings are presented in a dialog box. For a description of the options available with the Print Setup command see Print Setup in the View Command Reference section of this appendix.

Quit

Description
The Quit command takes you out of Agenda after saving your database file and returns you to the DOS prompt.

Note
(ALT-Q) is the accelerator key for the Quit command.

Return

Description
The Return command returns you to your previous activity, usually View mode.

Note
The (F9) (Return) key performs the same function as the Return command.

INDEX